001·942

UFOs
1947-1997

FROM ARNOLD TO THE ABDUCTEES:
FIFTY YEARS OF FLYING SAUCERS

Edited by Hilary Evans and Dennis Stacy

First published in Great Britain in May 1997
by John Brown Publishing Ltd., The Boathouse, Crabtree Lane, London SW6 6LU
Tel 0171 470 2400 Fax 0171 381 3930

Photo credits: VJ Ballester Olmos 178; Fortean Picture Library 11, 54, 58, 60, 62,
68, 82, 94, 100, 104, 110, 114, 176, 205, 214, 220, 253; Raymond Fowler 132, 137;
Mary Evans Picture Library 10, 13, 14, 18, 28, 32, 36, 44, 57, 67, 86, 89, 98, 116,
125, 150, 154, 166, 188, 202; David Perkins 140; Popperfoto 41; Chris Rutkowski
120; Spanish Air Force 181; J Templeton 255

ISBN 1-870870-999

Printed and bound in Great Britain by Butler & Tanner, Frome, Somerset.

CONTENTS

EIGHT DAYS
THAT SHAPED UFOLOGY

by Dennis Stacy

The modern UFO era was ceremoniously ushered in on the afternoon of June 24, 1947, when private pilot Kenneth Arnold reported nine, silvery crescent-shaped objects travelling at high speed near Mt. Rainier, in the state of Washington. Unexplained flying objects had been seen in the world's skies before. During the closing days of WWII, to cite but one example, combatants on both sides had seen glowing balls of nocturnal lights that could not be readily accounted for by any known flying device or natural phenomenon. The Allies referred to them as 'Foo-Fighters,' foo being a corruption of the French word for fire. Shortly after the cessation of hostilities, the Scandinavian countries were rocked by hundreds of reports of so-called 'ghost rockets.'

But it was the Arnold sighting and its consequences that captured global attention and which, half a century later, show no sign of loosening their grip. If anything, that grip – or fascination – is tighter than ever before in the 50 years since 1947. On the eve of the 21st century and the so-called Millennium (at least in Western minds), UFOs are ubiquitous. Whether or not they have physically invaded our planetary air space, they have certainly inundated our theatres, television sets, magazines and books; in some cases, our daily conversation, in others, our otherwise undisturbed sleep. UFOs are also universally assumed to be synonymous with alien visitation, an individual and cultural concept that no student of history, freshly home from the European or Pacific Theatres at the end of the last great war, could have remotely conceived, let alone confidently predicted, in their vaguest, most malaria-induced or shell-shocked dreams.

But then there was Arnold. And 50 years later, here we are. The following eight days or incidents, selected from among many challenging candidates, demonstrate how we got from there to here.

DAY I: JUNE 24, 1947

Charles Fort said that 'one measures a circle beginning anywhere.' History, however, prefers specific times and places, and so it is that the modern UFO era is generally assumed to have begun on this day with Kenneth Arnold's sighting of nine crescent-shaped objects in the American Pacific Northwest.

In retrospect, and compared to what would follow, Arnold's sighting seems relatively modest, almost mundane, by today's standards. True, the objects he reported had some unusual qualities, including their high speed and lack of any visible vertical tail structure. It was the repercussions of Arnold's going public, though, that would reverberate down to today. A literal torrent of similar reports soon surfaced, more than a thousand in the second half of the year in America alone. In the process, the Arnold sighting gave birth to the phrase, 'flying saucers,' which connotes a physical object(s). Originally coined by an anonymous headline writer, 'flying saucers' has since found its way into current consciousness and been translated into virtually every living language imaginable. At the same time, the Arnold sighting and its aftermath also gave a peculiarly American cast to such reports, one

5

used by critics to cast doubt and aspersion alike. As recently as 1995, despite its global aspects, a sceptic like aviation historian Curtis Peebles could still attribute the birth and rise of the UFO phenomenon to a local case of 'nuclear nerves,' cultural paranoia, and other existential anxieties with relative impunity, as if UFO reports represented little more than a post-WWII American industrial export on a par with Coca Cola, Ford automobiles, Hollywood movies, and the electronic transistor. A year later, French folklorist Michel Meurger, speaking specifically of UFO abductions, would claim that 'the current belief in alien captors may be interpreted as a borrowing from science fiction, fitted to convey the growing estrangement of the American masses from their social surroundings. Through the symbolism of alien abduction and experimentation, citizens of a powerful country are acknowledging their own powerlessness. Unable to cope with a menacing future, they have created the ultimate embodiment of scientific mastery and control: the surgeon from outside...'

DAY II: JULY 8, 1947

The second most potentially important day in UFO history unfolded exactly two weeks to the day after the Arnold sighting. On Tuesday, July 8, 1947, 'the many rumours regarding the flying discs became a reality' began a front page article in the *Roswell Daily Record*. Based on an official press release the article noted that the intelligence office of the 509th Bomb Group, Roswell Army Air Field, had been 'fortunate enough to gain possession of a disc through the cooperation of one of the local ranchers and the Sheriff's office of Chaves County.

> 'The flying object landed on a ranch near Roswell sometime last week. Not having phone facilities, the rancher stored the disc until such time as he was able to contact the Sheriff's office, who in turn notified Major Jesse A. Marcel of the 509th Bomb Group Intelligence office.

> 'Action was immediately taken and the disc was picked up at the rancher's home. It was inspected at the Roswell Army Air Field and subsequently loaned by Major Marcel to higher headquarters.'

The article was assured national and international headlines if for no other reason than the fact that the 509th just happened to be the world's only atomic bomb wing, the same one that had pulverised Hiroshima and Nagasaki at the end of WWII. But just as quickly as it was born, the Roswell Incident, as it would come to be called, died a quiet death. That same afternoon, General Roger Ramey, head of the Eighth Air Force, called a press conference at his headquarters in Fort Worth, Texas. Ramey told a handful of reporters that the flying disc, in reality, was nothing more than an ordinary weather balloon.

And there the matter rested, ignored and forgotten, until January of 1978, when nuclear physicist and UFO researcher Stanton T. Friedman chanced across Major Marcel, retired and now living in Louisiana. The story Marcel told in subsequent interviews was literally earthshaking. On Monday, July 7, 1947, a rancher by the name of Mac Brazel arrived in Roswell with samples of some strange debris that had fallen on his ranch. (Rewards of up to $3,000 were now being offered for a flying disc.) The sheriff called the Army and, as the intelligence officer for the 509th, Marcel went over to investigate. He and Lt. Sheridan Cavitt, with the Counter-Intelligence Corps (CIC), accompanied Brazel back to his ranch. They arrived too late to do anything other than spend the night, but the next day Brazel led them to what Marcel described as a huge debris field. Filling a Buick staff car and a jeep carry-all with material, the two military men returned to Roswell, where base commander Colonel William Blanchard authorised the press release announcing the recovery of a flying disc.

Marcel was so excited by what he had found that he took some of it home with him to show to his wife, Viaud, and 11-year-old son, Jesse Junior. In subsequent interviews (he died in 1986), Marcel would speak of the miraculous nature of the debris: so light, yet so strong that it couldn't be dented with a sledgehammer or burnt with a cigarette lighter. He compared it to the lightweight foil that cigarettes came wrapped in in those days. Son Jesse, now a Flight Surgeon in the Army Air National Guard, would later recall, both consciously and under hypnosis, small I-beams embossed with strange, hieroglyphic-like symbols.

In 1980, the first full-length treatment of the story appeared in print, *The Roswell Incident*, by Charles Berlitz and William Moore, for which Friedman served as primary researcher. The incident has gone on to become the single most heavily investigated and discussed case in UFO history, generating its own cottage industry in the process. There are presently two museums devoted to the subject in Roswell (population 50,000), one of which is mounting a gala 50th anniversary celebration this summer, numerous Roswell-related books and videos, and at least one major movie, with more no doubt to come. (There are even different crash sites now competing for the visitor's dollar.) The incident has also been the focus of two recent Air Force studies, as well as the object of an inquiry by the Government Accounting Office. Neither of those agencies could confirm the recovery of an extraterrestrial flying disc or bodies. Still, if asked to name the Best UFO Case Ever, many ufologists would no doubt stake both their reputations and that of ufology in general on the Roswell Incident alone. It is the linchpin that seemingly holds the whole complicated machinery together, the proposed *raison d'être* for a government cover-up in the first place. Thus, when ufologist Kent Jeffrey began circulating his Roswell Declaration in early 1994, he was able to collect over 20,000 signatures worldwide calling on the President of the United States to issue 'an Executive Order declassifying any U. S. Government information regarding the existence of UFOs or extraterrestrial intelligence.'

But Roswell's claim to primacy in the UFO canon has also encountered some recent setbacks. One self-claimed witness, a former official with one of the local museums, entertained investigators with the story of a nurse friend of his who had participated in the autopsy of alien bodies. When investigators conclusively demonstrated that no such nurse was ever stationed at Roswell, he admitted that he had given them the wrong name, but refused to provide the 'real' one.

More damaging news surfaced in 1996, with the release under the Freedom of Information Act of UFO documents from the late 1940s. The most damning of these was an exchange of messages between Major General C. P. Cabell, U.S. Air Force Director of Intelligence, and Colonel H. M. McCoy, chief of intelligence for the Air Material Command at Wright-Patterson Air Force Base, Dayton, Ohio, where any anomalous debris recovered at Roswell would almost have surely been shipped.

In a TOP SECRET memorandum dated October 11, 1948, Cabell, concerned about the public policy issues raised by UFO reports, requested an 'exhaustive study of all information' pertinent to the UFO problem. McCoy responded with a 3-page SECRET memorandum on November 8, 1948, titled 'Flying Object

Incidents in the United States.' Excerpts follow:

6   Although explanations of many of the incidents can be obtained from the investigations described above, there remains a certain number of reports for which no reasonable everyday explanation is available. So far, no physical evidence of the existence of the unidentified sightings has been obtained...'

8   The possibility that the reported objects are vehicles from another planet has not been ignored. However, tangible evidence to support conclusions about such a possibility are completely lacking...

Interestingly, what is perhaps Charles Fort's first and maybe only appearance in a classified government document occurs in the same letter:

9   Reference is made to 'The Books of Charles Fort' with an introduction by Tiffany Thayer, published 1941, by Henry Holt & Co., New York, N.Y. It appears that similar phenomena have been noted and reported for the past century or more.

McCoy continues:

10b There is as yet no conclusive proof that unidentified flying objects, other than those which are known to be balloons, are real aircraft.

10c Although it is obvious that some types of flying objects have been sighted, the exact nature of those objects cannot be established until physical evidence, such as that which would result from a crash, has been obtained.

The memorandum echoes sentiments McCoy had expressed earlier, on March 17, 1948, while briefing the Air Force Scientific Advisory Board, the recently declassified minutes of which were also classified SECRET at the time. McCoy tells the assembly of 31 scientists and technicians:

We have a new project – Project SIGN – which may surprise you as a development from the so-called mass hysteria of the past summer when we had all the unidentified flying objects or discs. This can't be laughed off. We have over 300 reports which haven't been publicised in the papers from very competent personnel, in many instances – men as capable as Dr. K. D. Wood – and practically all Air Force, airline people with broad experience. We are running down every report. I can't even tell you how much we would give to have one of those crash in an area so that we could recover whatever they are.

The most devout proponents of Roswell as the UFO case of the century were able to shake off McCoy's statements with a shrug of the shoulders. Either he was out of the compartmentalised intelligence 'need to know' loop, prohibited from discussing TOP SECRET or above matters in documents classified SECRET, or, as one Roswell advocate suggested, simply lying.

DAY III: JULY 19, 1952

Late on Saturday evening, July 19, 1952, Edward Nugent, an air-traffic controller at the airport serving America's capitol city, Washington National Airport, noticed seven returns on his radar screen. Over the next several hours the targets would appear and disappear from at least three separate radar screens, eventually resulting in the scrambling of two jet interceptors from nearby Newcastle Air Force Base.

The pilots were unable to establish visual contact. During the same period of time, however, coloured balls of light were reported by numerous ground and civilian air-borne observers. The following night, a similar scenario ensued.

A week later, on the evening of July 26, the unidentified targets were back in force. The crew of a B-25 light bomber directed toward one target could detect only a cruise boat on the Potomac River below, which they concluded to be the source of the radar return. Later, however, two more F-94 jet fighters were sent up from Newcastle for a closer look. One of the pilots, Lt. William Patterson, report-ed four white 'glows' that closed in on his fighter and then moved away; the other pilot was never able to establish visual contact.

On July 29, the largest press conference since the end of WWII was held in the Pentagon. In essence, the director of Air Force intelligence, Major General John A. Samford, attributed the Washington National Airport sightings to temperature inversions which had generated false radar returns. Project Blue Book, the Air Force agency charged with investigating UFO reports, later attributed the simulta-neous visual sightings to 'meteors coupled with the normal excitement of witnesses.'

According to American ufologist Jerome Clark, 'the Washington sightings proved to be a pivotal event in UFO history. They sparked high-level fears that UFO reports – if not UFOs themselves – might constitute a threat to national secu-rity.' (Military communication channels during the two July weekends in question had been crowded with UFO 'noise.') As a consequence, the Central Intelligence Agency convened a panel of scientists to assess the UFO problem. Meeting in January of 1953, the panel concluded that 'national security agencies take immedi-ate steps to strip the Unidentified Flying Objects of the special status they have been given and the aura of mystery they have unfortunately required.' This would ultimately prove to be an exercise in futility, if the present popularity of the subject is any indication. Worse, once the existence of the panel and its recommendations became known, the CIA, in the eyes of many ufologists, was simply seen as one more link in a growing chain of global government conspiracy and cover up, what some proponents would refer to as a 'Cosmic Watergate.'

DAY IV: OCTOBER 15, 1957

Perhaps a UFO sexual episode was only a matter of time. Indeed, according to some of the early 1950s 'Contactees' – those who first claimed to have met the fly-ing saucers' occupants – that time had already come and gone. But the mostly male Contactee claims were easy to dismiss. For the most part, the UFO occupants looked like you and I, only better. This was especially true of alien women. Consider Aura Rhanes, who was supposed to be the captain of a 'scow' from the planet Clarion, unseen by terrestrial astronomers because it always remained behind the moon as it orbited our sun. According to Contactee Truman Bethurum, 'she was a gorgeous woman, shorter than any of the [eight] men, neatly attired, and also having a Latin appearance: coal black hair and olive complexion.'

More puzzling was what was reported to have taken place on the night of October 15-16, 1957, in the state of Minas Gerais in Brazil. Because of the oppres-sive heat, Antonio Villas Boas was still ploughing the family's field at 1 A.M in the morning, when he saw a 'red' star in the sky which promptly drew closer, flooding the area with light. The object passed low over his head and landed nearby, reveal-ing itself to be an elongated, egg-shaped object supported by three landing legs or struts.

The tractor motor died. Villas Boas tried to flee, but four small figures surrounded him and wrestled him up a ladder into the object. Inside, five more helmeted beings stripped him of his clothing, swabbed him with some sort of liquid, then led him into another room where a blood sample was taken from underneath his chin. He was left alone in the room which was subsequently flooded with a gray smoke that caused him to vomit.

A 'beautiful' naked women, not entirely of Earthly appearance, later entered. Villas Boas became 'uncontrollably sexually excited,' a reaction he attributed to the fluid that had been spread over his body earlier. They had intercourse twice, an experience not wholly to the farmer's liking. 'Some of the growls that came from her...gave me the disagreeable impression of lying with an animal,' Villa Boas told the Brazilian investigators, ufologists Joao Martins and Dr. Olavo T. Fontes, a professor of surgery at the National School of Medicine. According to Villas Boas, as the 'woman' turned to leave she first pointed to her belly and then, smiling, to the sky. Perhaps all they wanted, he said, was a 'good stallion to improve their stock.'

The Villas Boas story was of such a fantastic and sensational 'tabloid' nature that even the original investigators were reluctant to publish it. Indeed, it would not be widely disseminated until 1965, when Gordon Creighton wrote a series of articles about the case for England's *Flying Saucer Review,* then one of the world's most highly regarded UFO journals. In the same year, the September 1961 abduction of Betty and Barney Hill burst on the scene, made famous by journalist John G. Fuller's *The Interrupted Journey.* Still, the Villas Boas case would prefigure those abductions allegedly involving forced sexual contact which were yet to come. Rightly or wrongly, for a period of time it would also predispose many American and European ufologists to regard UFO reports coming out of South and Central America with some hesitation.

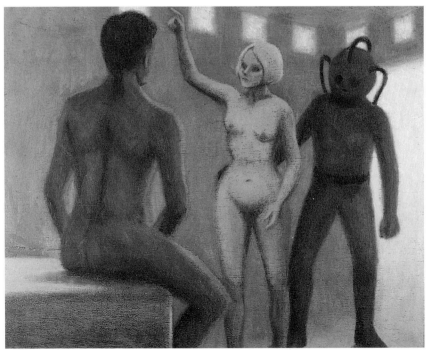

Antonio Villas Boas encounters a naked alien female

DAY V: MARCH 25, 1966

The sightings were inconsequential, it was the fallout that would matter. On the evening of March 20, 1966, the civil defence director for Hillsdale College, Hillsdale, Michigan, along with 87 female students, watched while a glowing object shaped like a football hovered over a nearby swampy area. It then abruptly approached the women's dormitory, stopped, and retreated. It dimmed in intensity when automobiles approached, then 'brightened when the cars left.' On the following day, 63 miles away in Dexter, two police officers and three other witnesses saw a large, glowing object, also above a swampy area.

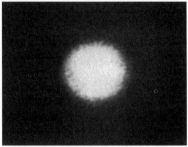

The Long Valley, New Jersey, spook light, photographed in 1976

As UFOs go, these were relatively mundane. It was the sheer number of witnesses involved – over 100 total – that apparently attracted national attention and had the media clamouring for answers. On March 25, Dr. J. Allen Hynek, astronomy consultant to Project Blue Book, addressed a crowded conference at the Detroit Press Club, the largest in the Club's history. Hynek suggested that the faint lights might be attributable to the spontaneous combustion of gases given off by rotting vegetation, popularly referred to as 'swamp gas.'

The public reaction was also spontaneous. Editorial writers and cartoonists immediately lampooned and ridiculed the idea that a UFO – whatever that was – could be so cavalierly dismissed as mere swamp gas. The public impression was that the Air Force would prefer to serve up any explanation that first came to mind rather than conduct a comprehensive scientific investigation of such reports. Hynek's reputation would suffer – he would later recant swamp gas and go on to found the Center for UFO Studies – but so would the military's, with public policy consequences.

Gerald R. Ford (then a Republican representative for the state of Michigan and national House of Representatives minority leader who would succeed Richard Nixon as president) complained that 'the American public deserves a better explanation than that thus far given by the Air Force.' As a result, on April 5, 1966, the House Armed Services Committee held the first Congressional hearings on the UFO subject. A second would follow under auspices of the House Science and Aeronautics Committee in July of 1968. The hearings set in motion a chain of circumstances that would ultimately allow the Air Force to 'retire' from active UFO investigation. Initially, the Air Force awarded a $500,000 contract to the University of Colorado, Boulder, to conduct a scientific investigation of the phenomenon. Noted physicist Edward U. Condon was in charge of the project. Despite internal contradictions, the Air Force used what became known as the Condon Report as the basis for their decision, on December 17, 1969, to permanently close the pages on Blue Book.

DAY VI: NOVEMBER 2, 1968

Writing in *High Strangeness*, the third volume of his UFO encyclopedia, Jerome Clark refers to the case of 'Dr. X' as 'among the most fantastic UFO stories ever recorded. Unlike most other bizarre UFO claims, however, this one is accompanied by physical evidence of an eerily compelling sort.' In late October of 1968, the anonymous French physician accidentally cut himself in the leg with an axe while chopping wood on his property in the south of France. For four days he was confined to bed.

In the early morning hours of November 2, he was awakened by his 14-month-old son. While refilling his bottle, X noticed intermittent flashes of light coming through the slats of the room's closed shutters. It was raining outside as a storm moved down the valley, but the flashes of light didn't seem to be accompanied by thunder. Eventually, he investigated by opening the double doors onto a terrace. To his amazement, X saw two luminous, cylinder-shaped objects moving down the valley from his right. Both appeared similar in that they were a silvery white colour on the top half and a deep red below.

Both cylinders had two antennae, one at the top and one at the bottom. And from each object a bright beam of light shined down. The flashes of light that first attracted his attention seemed to spark from an antenna on the left cylinder to a point behind the second one. The two objects moved closer together; their search-light beams crossed like an 'X' in the sky and then became one. And then, incredibly, according to Dr. X, the two objects themselves merged into one and approached the terrace on which he was standing. The united beam of light flooded the doctor, followed by a loud bang. Then object and light beam vanished, leaving only a white, fleecy shape like a cloud that soon dissipated. A white 'thread,' almost like liquid lightning, remained behind, shot up into the sky, turned into a dot and disappeared, also accompanied by the sound of an explosion.

Dr. X immediately wrote down what he had seen, made a few sketches of same, and woke his wife. It was she who noticed that he was now pacing about oblivious to the earlier axe wound – which appeared healed. More miraculously, wounds suffered a decade earlier, when the doctor stepped on a land mine in Algeria, also began to heal over the next few days. The case came to the attention of a family friend who just happened to be the French ufologist Aimé Michel, author of several classic books and articles in the field. Michel brought the case to the attention of Jacques Vallee and others, and eventually the medical records were documented.

By all logic – or violation of logic – the Dr. X case would already have earned itself a unique niche in the annals of ufology, but more was to follow. Soon after the event, a red rash in the form of an isosceles triangle formed around the doctor's navel. The phenomenon would appear roughly in intervals of three weeks, remain for two or three days, then fade in a matter of hours. Subsequently, it began showing up on the son's stomach, too!

Nor was this the end of the matter. Reported poltergeist phenomena would soon plague the family, Dr. X would claim a series of meetings with a certain stranger nonetheless familiar with what was going on in his household, and, eventually, the ability to levitate. Such claims would not only violate common sense and normal notions of reality, they would also rattle the cages of the 'nuts and bolts' school of ufologists who argued for a mainstream, scientific approach to the subject. If orthodox science was largely sceptical of the extraterrestrial explanation of UFOs by nature, how would it react to post-sighting claims of mysterious healings, triangular rashes, and unwitnessed levitations?

Michel himself noted the inherent absurdity of the situation. After an episode of levitation in which Dr. X supposedly attached a piece of flypaper to his high living room ceiling, he wondered: 'Will a reasonable man be more inclined to believe in the existence of a miracle, or more inclined to believe in the existence of a pole?'

Either way, there would be no turning back as far as the UFO reports themselves were concerned. As Arnold opened the way for reports of similar UFOs, so Dr. X paved the path for those reporting all sorts of paranormal occurrences in association with the sighting of a UFO or in its immediate aftermath. By 1996, the American ufologist Preston Dennett would be able to catalogue more than 100 cases of alleged UFO 'healing' incidents alone.

DAY VII: OCTOBER 21, 1978

Sex we've already seen in association with UFOs, alleged miraculous healings, too. Could that final arbiter of the human condition, death, be far behind? As with most aspects of the UFO phenomenon, a 'first' is almost impossible to point to. On January 7, 1948, for example, Captain Thomas Mantell, then a 25-year-old pilot with the Kentucky Air National Guard, died in a direct chase of a UFO. But was the metallic-appearing object Mantell was in pursuit of, when he lost consciousness from lack of oxygen, really a UFO? At first, it was attributed to the planet Venus; later it was believed to be a then-secret Skyhook balloon.

The Frederick Valentich case was altogether different. On the early evening of October 21, 1978, then 20-year-old Valentich took off from Moorabin Airport in Victoria, Australia, bound for what was supposed to be a 70-minute flight over the

Bass Strait to King Island. He would never arrive, nor would he be heard from again, except in voice recordings of his fateful flight later released by Melbourne air traffic controllers. Shortly after 7 p.m. Valentich asked Melbourne if there was 'any known traffic below five thousand [feet]' in his area. He was at 4,500 feet at the time. Melbourne replied that there was 'no known traffic,' but Valentich persisted, describing a large object

Artist's impression of Frederick Valentich's encounter

that was soon circling him. 'It seems to me that he's playing some sort of game,' Valentich said. 'He's flying over me two to three times...at speeds I [can't] identify.'

'Confirm that you cannot identify the aircraft,' said Melbourne, to which Valentich replied, 'Affirmative.' He then reported that the engine of his Cessna 182 had begun rough idling or sputtering.' Valentich next says 'that strange aircraft is hovering on top of me again...It is hovering, and it's not an aircraft.'

For the next 17 seconds Valentich's microphone remains open, transmitting a grating, metal sound before it lapses into silence. No wreckage of Valentich's plane was ever found, despite a search by local Australian authorities. While it would be ludicrous to suggest that such cases are commonplace, or automatically outside the bounds of rational, mundane explanation, Valentich's highly publicised and presently unsolved disappearance reiterates the fact that UFO reports are neither trivial nor exclusively 'American' in nature.

DAY VIII: NOVEMBER 30, 1989 BROOKLYN BRIDGE

The book by prime investigator Budd Hopkins, *Witnessed: The True Story of the Brooklyn Bridge UFO Abductions*, wouldn't be published until 1996, but the events it chronicles reportedly began early on the morning of November 30, 1989. The case would prove to be an extremely sensational one, even by 'usual' UFO abduction standards.

Sometime shortly before 4 a.m. Linda Napolitano would later declare, she had

Linda Napolitano is abducted from her Manhattan apartment

been transported through her 12th floor apartment window into a large UFO hovering nearby. Outside the building and still in her nightgown, she found herself in a beam of blue light with three small, spindly-limbed, large-eyed beings. All four were then 'beamed' aboard the UFO in a scene straight out of TV's *Star Trek*.

As the leading American researcher of abduction claims, Hopkins was fairly used to such cases, and there the matter might have lain but for some subsequent curious communications. The first of these arrived well over a year later, on February 1, 1991. It was signed by 'Police Officers Dan and Richard,' who claimed to have been parked underneath Franklin D. Roosevelt Drive on the night in question, and to have witnessed Linda's abduction through binoculars from a distance of no more than a couple of blocks (after which the UFO supposedly disappeared into the Hudson River). A surprising two years after the initial event, in November of 1991, Hopkins received yet another letter, this one from a Janet Kimball (a pseudonym), who claimed to have been crossing the Brooklyn Bridge at the same time. She said her car stalled, at which point she witnessed a scenario eerily similar to the one that Linda, Dan and Richard had already recounted.

As Hopkins delved deeper into the case, its implications exploded almost exponentially. Dan and Richard soon let it be known that they weren't simple city police officers, but were attached to an intelligence agency with international implications. There had also been a 'Third Man' involved they claimed. Hopkins never refers to him by name in the book, but it's common knowledge that he was supposed to be Javier Perez de Cuellar, then acting Secretary-General of the United Nations.

The anonymous Dan and Richard would later say there had been 15 other protective agents and political figures underneath FDR Drive, Linda would claim to have been kidnapped twice off New York City streets by the two, and de Cuellar himself would deny involvement altogether. According to Hopkins, ufologists had only two choices: either the case was a magnificently orchestrated hoax, or a powerful demonstration of alien prowess intended for the benefit of the political powers that be.

In either event, the Linda Case brings the abduction issue to a boil by raising the bar of believability. After all, once the Secretary-General of the United Nations has allegedly been abducted, who's left as victim or target? The President of the United States? It also illustrates a trend evident in Hollywood movies and blockbuster books at century's end: each one has to be more spectacular and sensational than its predecessor. Science is hardly immune to this phenomenon, either, the next Hubble Telescope picture of the universe being viewed as no better than the last, unless it reveals some new and totally unexpected discovery.

DAY NUMBER NINE

Of course the single most important day in UFO history has yet to happen. Presumably, that will be the day when the alien visitors step forth from the shadows that presently conceal them and make their presence publicly known – the so-called 'landing on the White House lawn' or equivalent scenario. It hasn't happened yet, however, and one can only wonder whether another fifty years will decrease or increase its likelihood. If it does happen, then any arguments about the nature of the UFO phenomenon will automatically be rendered moot.

But what happens in the absence of a defining ninth day? Without a reliable crystal ball, one person's guess is as good as another's. A conservative point of view would simply suggest more of the same – continually escalating claims and charges in spite of – but perhaps also because of – a lack of similarly escalating evidence. Nature abhors a vacuum and ufology is no exception. As long as the phenomenon remains essentially unknown and unresolved, individuals will be able to promote assertions, theories, and in some cases even 'evidence,' with relative impunity.

Part of the problem is that it's impossible to prove a negative – in this case, that UFOs don't exist. Even if science could convincingly demonstrate the absence of alien visitors, it wouldn't necessarily imply that we hadn't been visited in the remote past (the 'ancient astronaut' theory), or that we won't be contacted in the immediate future. All one can say with certainty is that the question of contact with another intelligent life form – and the ultimate uncertainty of its consequences – obviously has a profound resonance for *Homo sapiens* as a species. The mere hope (the flip-side of which is fear) of being contacted by a higher intelligence may well say more about us than it does about any alleged alien entities doing the contacting.

Claims of an ubiquitous UFO cover up – orchestrated by the United States, its agents and allies – can be seen in the same context. Any denial of same made by American government or military authorities is routinely greeted by conspiracy-minded ufologists with counter-claims of 'disinformation,' or 'what did you expect?' Denial, then, is routinely interpreted as confirmation.

The example usually used as evidence that a government can keep a secret when it wants to is the Manhattan Project, which resulted in the creation of the atomic bomb. Forgotten is the fact that, despite wartime circumstances and priorities, atomic secrets were leaked within years, if not months, of their creation, as a result of which the Soviets were soon exploding their own nuclear weapons shortly after war's end. That any single government or agency could somehow manage to keep the UFO phenomenon within a neatly compartmentalised closet for fifty years simply beggars belief.

What we presently have, then, is a situation in which ufology seeks the approval or sanction of mainstream science, without being able to bestow any equal blessings or benefits in return. The public, caught between the two extremes, so to speak, has already spoken. When asked for their opinion, a majority routinely report that they believe in the existence of extraterrestrial life and UFOs. Half of those polled in a 1996 survey conducted by Ohio University and Scripps-Howard News Service believed at least very likely or somewhat likely that 'flying saucers are real and the federal government is hiding the truth about them from us.' A survey taken at about the same time in Germany revealed that 25% of the populace thought that alien spacecraft had already landed among us.

An unconfirmed (and unconfirmable) rumour on the Internet has it that UFOs are now the second most popular subject on the World Wide Web after sex. I do know that while composing this article I did a Web search in late February for the Roswell UFO Museum which turned up 34,918 references. The Museum reported 129,000 visitors as of October 1996, 57,000 in the last ten months of that year alone, numbers which seem sure to increase with this year's 50th anniversary celebration.

In short, UFOs are an idea whose time has obviously come. In a brief fifty years they have gone from an insignificant player on the world stage to a significant somebody, from lowly Rosenkrantz to princely Hamlet. To be or not to be, that is the question. The answer is that the numbers, if not necessarily the evidence, are clearly on the side of the UFO.

THE 1940s

CHARLES FORT ONCE NOTED THAT 'ONE MEASURES A CIRCLE BEGINNING ANYWHERE.' STILL, ONE HAS TO BEGIN SOMEWHERE, AND SO, FOR ALL PRACTICAL PURPOSES, THE PRESENT STUDY OF THE UFO PHENOMENON STARTS IN THE UNITED STATES IN THE SUMMER OF 1947. WHILE IT'S NOT TRUE THAT THE UFO WAS EXCLUSIVELY AN AMERICAN 'HAPPENING' — AS SOME SCEPTICS HAVE ARGUED — IT'S ALSO ARGUABLE THAT THE MANY EARLY REPORTS EMANATING OUT OF THE US GREATLY INFLUENCED GLOBAL ATTITUDES AS A WHOLE, AS THE FOLLOWING SURVEY MAKES ABUNDANTLY CLEAR. JUST HOW MUCH ITS AMERICAN 'ORIGINS' SHAPED THE WORLD'S SUBSEQUENT PERCEPTION AND REPORTING OF THE PHENOMENON, HOWEVER, REMAINS A MATTER OF DISPUTE AMONG BOTH UFOLOGISTS AND HISTORIANS.

BECAUSE OF THE PIVOTAL ROLE OF THE YEAR 1947, AMERICAN RESEARCHER JAN ALDRICH RECENTLY ESTABLISHED PROJECT 1947 AS A CLEARING HOUSE FOR RELEVANT NEWSPAPER AND OTHER CLIPPINGS FROM THAT PERIOD. EXPANDED, THE PROJECT NOW ACTIVELY SOLICITS CLIPPINGS, PRE- AND POST-1947, FROM CORRESPONDENTS AROUND THE WORLD. IT ALSO WELCOMES HISTORICAL COLLECTIONS FOR ARCHIVING, ALONG WITH OFFERS OF RESEARCH AND ANALYSIS. INTERESTED PARTIES SHOULD CONTACT ALDRICH AT PROJECT 1947, P.O. BOX 391, CANTERBURY, CT 06331, TEL (860)-546-9135. E-MAIL: JAN@CYBERZONE.NET

1947: BEGINNING OF THE UFO ERA

by Jan L. Aldrich

Nineteen forty seven was a year of milestones. The Marshall Plan was proposed, India and Pakistan gained their independence, the Taft-Hartley labour bill became law, Indonesia rose up in revolt against the Netherlands, Chuck Yeager broke the sound barrier, the National Security Act created the Department of Defense, establishing the Air Force, the Central Intelligence Agency and National Security Council, the Dead Sea Scrolls were discovered, and Jackie Robinson became the first black baseball player to sign with a major league club.

In the summer of 1947 only two years had passed since the worldwide conflagration of World War II. The United States was in the midst of the transition to peace. Sugar rationing was just ending, there were still newspaper drives, housewives still saved fat to be reclaimed for industrial uses. With the returning troops quickly marrying and forming new families, housing was at a premium, and the archaic permitting procedures required to build new housing seemed destined to keep it that way. Looking back we cannot begin to understand the dread parents had of polio and what this devastating disease might do to their children. The countermeasures against this horror in 1947 included massive spraying of DDT to wipe out the fly population, a carrier of the disease. Health officials spoke of extinction for the pest, and every household was urged to help with its own anti-fly campaign. Europe too was slowly on the road to recovery, as evidenced by the 'New Look' in women's fashions from Paris.

It was what the press called 'the silly season,' the early summer when new fads commenced. Besides the lightheartedness of the season, a number of items were in place that would confuse the upcoming situation. Surplus military searchlights and weather balloons were plentiful and used everywhere for advertising. In the west seagulls were seen far inland away from their normal habitats. Many private pilots behaved recklessly, as if they were devil-may-care fighter pilots still at war. 'Flash Gordon' was featured in many newspaper comic strips flying his fantastic aerial machines.

On the 23 June 1947, a newspaper reported that Dr. Layman Spitzer, Jr., associate professor of astrophysics at Yale University, had speculated the night before on a Connecticut, radio station, that Martians might have already visited the earth. On the program 'Yale Interprets the News,' Spitzer reportedly said that if life on Mars 'developed a little earlier than on earth, it is possible that the Martians may have been civilized for millions of years as compared to our thousands. In such a case, their scientific knowledge, and their ability to control nature would, of course, be enormously greater than ours.'

Dr. Spitzer continued his talk, 'The Rocket: A Tool for Exploring the Universe,' by noting that 'if this is the case, unless they spent some time in a large city or landed sufficiently recently to be photographed, we would have no record of their having been here... any few men who had seen them would probably not be believed by anyone else.' Furthermore, 'the impact which our European civilization had on the African nations and on the South Sea islands might seem trivial indeed compared with the impact on Earth of a civilization millions of years older than ours.'

Two days after Dr. Spitzer's speculations an incident happened which would over the years make him sound like a prophet to some people. A businessman named Kenneth Arnold piloting a private plane he used to make business calls, decided to make a side trip to look for a C-46 Marine transport aircraft which had crashed on the ice-covered slopes of Mount Rainier in Washington state. After he had made a short search and climbed to 9,200 feet, his attention was attracted by a bright flash, 'as if a mirror were reflecting sunlight at me.' What he saw next was nine objects in 'a chain which looked to me like the tail of a Chinese kite, kind of weaving and going [at] a terrific speed across the face of Mount Rainier.' (For Arnold's firsthand account, see the following chapter.

At one point Arnold described the motion of the objects as that of a saucer thrown and skipping across water. The term 'flying saucer' was coined. Many headlines referred to mystery planes or missiles, but 'flying saucers' and then 'flying discs' quickly crowded the former names out. Both saucers and discs (the slang for phonograph records) lent themselves well to ridicule.

In the wake of Arnold's story, a number of people came forward to give similar accounts. But a search of official records and newspapers suggests that only a handful of 1947 UFO-like cases were actually reported prior to Arnold's. These came from Montana, Connecticut, Virginia, Wisconsin, England, France, Scandinavia, Hungary, Chile, and perhaps Belgium. The most prominent concerned 'ghost aeroplanes' which appeared over England, were tracked on radar and pursued by RAF aircraft. Project Blue Book files contain an official RAF account of a fighter pilot who chased a 'ghost aeroplane' for 30 minutes:

'During normal night-flying practice at 22.30 hours on 16 Jan, [a] British Mosquito was vectored on to an unidentified A/C [aircraft] at 22,000 ft. A long chase ensued commencing over the North Sea about 50 miles from the

Dutch Coast and ending at 23.00 hours over Norfolk. Two brief AI contacts were made but faded quickly. The unidentified aircraft appeared to take efficient controlled evasive action... No explanation on this incident has been forthcoming nor has it been repeated.'

Project Blue Book would later explain this case as a visual sighting of an aircraft combined with a radar contact attributable to atmospheric inversion effects. But if an aeroplane was responsible for the visual component of the sighting, why not for the radar returns as well? Alas, such contorted logic was typical of many Blue Book explanations.

The Associated Press picked up the story, datelined 30 April, 1947, and as late as July of the same year it was still running in many weekly newspapers all across North America. The AP article quoted the *Yorkshire Post* to the effect that 'Radar has plotted some strange things in its time, from children's kites and raindrops to formations of geese, but it surely never plotted a stranger thing than this.' The 'planes' always flew from east to west with no return trips indicated. One was so regular that it was even given its own designation, X362, X being the RAF symbol for an unidentified aircraft.

In mid-April, meteorologists of the US Weather Bureau at Richmond, Virginia, released a balloon and were tracking it with a theodolite when they spotted a silver, ellipsoid object just below. It appeared larger than the balloon when viewed through the theodolite and appeared to be flat on the bottom with a dome on top. The men tracked the object for 15 seconds before it sped away to the west on a level fight path. Project Blue Book carried this case as an unknown. Twenty years later, Walter A. Minczewski, one of the meteorologists, was contacted by Dr. James McDonald of the University of Arizona. Minczewski was surprised by McDonald's interest as he had only reported the sighting to his superiors. The unusual event was so vivid that Minczewski's recollection of the object was still distinct.

A recently released document from the US Army Intelligence Command (USAINSCOM), reveals the results of the investigation, this one conducted by the Air Officer at the US Delegation in Hungary:

17 May 1947
For G-2.
At approximately 20.30 hours on 14 May an airborne phenomenon was observed passing over BUDAPEST on a Southeast to Northwest course in an almost flat trajectory. Consensus of observers places altitude at about 3,000 feet and speed above 400mph and describes object as spherical in shape with diameter of approximately 3-4 feet. It appeared to be burning and left a thin trail of smoke uniform in shape and area except for periodic enlargements which seemed to suggest successive impulses. Object also apparently emanated tail of flame about 3m long but NO sound accompanied the passing.

Much controversy has begun in the press about it and [it] has been dismissed as 'in all probability a meteor.' Hungarian Meteorological Institute state they made NO official observation of the object and are awaiting further reports prior issuing any statement.

Comment by Air Officer: 'Although I did NOT observe the object, I am

NOT convinced by the reports to date that it was a meteor due almost 100 per cent agreement by observers on altitude and trajectory.'

A July 10, 1947, report from Hungary, classified SECRET at the time, noted: 'Rumors drifting in from rural areas of Hungary mention 'silver balls flashing across the sky in daytime'. No accurate description or confirmation of this phenomena has yet been obtained, but it does recall the flashing objects over the Scandinavian countries thru late 1946 and early 1947, and the current riddle of similar metallic objects seen over most [of] the United States since the 1st of July.'

On 19 May, 1947, personnel at the Del Salto Observatory in Chile saw and photographed a 'strange meteor' over Santiago. The object moved slowly, 'producing at intervals discharges of white smoke.' The report, not released to the public until after Arnold's sighting, indicated a change to high speed near the end of the object's flight.

Articles in the American press state that the Belgian newspapers carried reports reminiscent of flying saucer sightings during April or May, but local papers have been checked and neither features such stories.

What's clear is that these few scattered cases hardly alerted the press or officialdom that something unusual was about to occur. So it was, that with nearly no build-up, the 1947 UFO Wave burst upon the scene with Kenneth Arnold's landmark sighting of nine, shiny, crescent-shaped 'planes' or missiles flying in formation at unheard-of speeds. As the wave continued, however, more and more people came forward with old sighting reports, some of which dated back to the 19th century. In a few cases witnesses could point to previously published accounts that supported their claims.

A 1946 Iowa newspaper article told of a close approach by an unidentified something. 'Perhaps the Swedes aren't the only ones bothered by flying missiles, believed bombs, at least if reports by several Waterloo residents are reliable,' it read. 'Thursday night an object was seen buzzing around the trees in an east side neighbourhood, gradually ascending all the while, giving off, or surrounded by, a cloud of white, radiant vapour and eventually disappearing high in the sky... One person termed the object a great white bird, another a bomb.' Another witness, interviewed after the Arnold sighting, said 'If I'd been a religious woman, I'd have thought it was a vision.'

Veterans also came forward with stories of strange objects seen in the skies during the war. Their stories can be found in wire service dispatches, local newspaper stories, and in the files of letters sent to the Headquarters of Army Air Force. Other later letters in a Project Blue Book 'catch-all' file told of reports from 1913 to 1953. In some cases the writers cited newspaper reports, notices to observatories, wartime dairies, and entries in ship and aircraft logbooks to support their stories.

TED BLOECHER'S STUDY

During the year of 1947 the Air Force recorded 122 cases (about 60 of which were from June and July) in their files at Project Blue Book. Years later, Ted Bloecher, a tireless UFO researcher, started to research 1947 press accounts of UFOs. Apart from the Fortean Society and its journal, *Doubt*, there were few groups or publications that collected newspaper accounts of strange events at the time. Bloecher confirmed what reports he could by consulting contemporary newspapers and quickly realised that the 1947 wave was far larger than anyone had previously thought. He eventually consulted 142 newspapers from the United States and Canada, initially checking the period from 24 June to 10 July. Bloecher also consulted the files of the National Investigations Committee on Aerial Phenomena (NICAP), which included the records of several defunct organisations, the most prominent of which was Civilian Saucer Investigations of Los Angeles. He also checked the files of his own organisation, Civilian Saucer Intelligence (New York), other researchers' files and those of the US Air Force. Access to the Blue Book files was an unusual event for advocates of UFO reality in those days. Ultimately, Bloecher uncovered more than 850 UFO cases for the period 1 June to 31 July 1947, or an average of six reports per newspaper.

Bloecher found that, from a few cases per day in June of 1947, the total jumped to about 15-20 a day between 24 June and 30 June. After further increases during the first three days of July, the number of cases jumped wildly to 90 per day on 4 July, reaching a peak of more than 160 cases per day on 7 July. Following the Roswell debunking the number of cases per day rapidly fell off. The decline can be attributed, at least in part, to the fact that most of Bloecher's early searches ended at 10 July.

After his Report on the UFO Wave of 1947 was privately published in 1967, Bloecher and others continued researching this seminal year. In a letter to McDonald a couple of years later, he announced that the total number of newspapers now screened was over 200 and the number of cases over a thousand.

OTHER UFO STUDIES

Through the years there have been a number of other studies of 1947 UFO activity in Europe, South America, and the United States. The authors of some collection efforts and studies are unknown as their material was incorporated in other files with no credit. Some of the significant studies are:

1   Loren Gross's California study involving 101 California newspapers which contained 144 UFO reports.
2   Research on Kenneth Arnold and the early 1947 era by Pierre Lagrange.
3   Studies covering Kenneth Arnold by Gregory Long.
4   'Operations Origins' by Giuseppe Stilo, Edoardo Russo, and others in Centro Italiano Studi Ufologici (CISU). They collected about a hundred 1947 articles from the Italian press.
5   Barry Greenwood of Citizens Against UFO Secrecy (CAUS) consulted hundreds of newspaper from all around the world at various universities and archives.
6   The UFO Catalogue (UFOCAT) started by Dr. David Saunders as part of the University of Colorado study contains contributions from many investigators and also represents an extensive literature search. It is mostly in the form of a bibliography, with an entry for each time the case is found in the literature or in investigative files. Dr. Don Johnson is now the custodian. Nearly 1,600 cases from 1947 are catalogued.
7   Claude Gaudeau's recent study compares the 1947 US wave with the 1954 French wave.

Still other studies of the 1947 UFO wave were performed by individuals and organisations in Canada, Argentina, Bulgaria, Chile, Peru, Uruguay, Finland, and

Norway. There are probably other studies of which I am not aware. Collectively, they indicate that the 1947 UFO wave was not confined to North America.

Bloecher's Report still stands as the greatest single effort to date. Since its publication 30 years ago, however, things have changed drastically. Whereas Bloecher was able to spend only part of a day examining Project Blue Book files, for example, those records have now been released to the public, along with thousands of other government UFO documents. Space prohibits a complete listing of files that have subsequently surfaced, but among them are those of the US Air Force Directorate of Intelligence, the Federal Bureau of Investigation, the 1948 TOP SECRET 'Analysis of Flying Object Incidents in the United States,' the records of the Canadian Department of National Defense, Swedish Military Archives, and US Army Intelligence Command, among others, along with the files of Blue Book's predecessors, Projects Sign and Grudge.

PROJECT 1947

By 1993 Bloecher's work had been out of print for many years and had become a rarity. Most researchers felt that the 1947 wave had been exhaustively studied and no further effort was needed. Going through newspapers available at institutions near my home, though, I was able to locate many new 1947 cases. With short trips to libraries and state archives and help from other investigators, we were shortly able to bring the total of 1947 newspapers screened from 400 to 850. The time period for screening was increased, too, and was now 25 June to 15 July east of the Mississippi, and 25 June to 31 July west of the Mississippi and Canada. Some newspapers were checked for longer periods. I also visited the three major UFO organisations in the United States, the Mutual UFO Network (MUFON), the J. Allen Hynek Center for UFO Studies (CUFOS) and the Fund for UFO Research (FUFOR). I was able to check their files and extract copies of 1947 and other early and pre-1947 cases. When a patron became available, I requested a grant and secured a modest amount for travel, maintenance and copying from the newly formed coalition of CUFOS, FUFOR and MUFON. On 1 February, 1995, PROJECT 1947 began with the main goal of searching out 1947 cases, but as time allowed other tasks would be served, too, such as finding UFO-like reports before 1947, locating records of early scientific and official interest, finding reports from the early UFO era (1948 to 1965), and finally, finding anything new from later times.

Besides all the released government files, there were other advantages not available when Bloecher did his study. Large collections of clippings could now be easily assembled because there were active projects in most states to centralise and microfilm newspapers and make them available to the public with good copying equipment. No longer did you have to turn the pages in old volumes and hand copy each item. Dozens of weekly newspapers could be screened in a day. Daily newspapers took longer, but then the pay-off was greater. I visited well over 100 institutions in 45 states and Canadian provinces. After each trip, I had scores of letters and items from all over the world from people who wanted to help, copies of clippings and reports from private collections and organisations, and newspaper research from all over the world. Some people were only able to check one newspaper; others checked hundreds. Any assistance was welcome, as it stretched the dollars from the grant further.

Nearly 4,900 newspapers for 1947 worldwide have now been screened. This is far more than was ever expected, the original goal calling for a total of 2,000

North American newspapers to be reviewed by the end of the project. However, there were shortfalls. It was expected that over 400 newspapers outside North America would be sampled, and this has yet to be realised. Also, the Eastern Canadian provinces have not been thoroughly sampled, nor have Oregon and California. Despite these shortfalls, significant discoveries in other areas more that offset the disappointments.

New reports not in the literature came to light from several South and Central American countries, including Mexico, Guatemala, Panama, Peru, Chile, Argentina, Uruguay, Brazil, Venezuela, Surinam, and some of the Caribbean Islands. There were scattered reports in Australia, Asia, and Africa. In Europe there are less than 200 reports, but only a small sample of newspapers has been screened. It is possible to find references in the Argentine newspapers to reports from Switzerland and other places and in the Indian, Singapore and Hong Kong press to sightings in Great Britain. Unfortunately, little interest has been expressed in the British Isles for following up on old sightings in the local press archives.

Many forgotten aspects of the 1947 wave were rediscovered. UFO proponents reading the history of the early UFO era have said many time that they could not understand why UFOs were not immediately taken seriously. Unfortunately, most histories do not have the correct picture of the outright foolishness that was going on. Many advertisers thought that flying saucers were a godsend. Leaflets and paper plates with commercial messages were dropped from planes or the tops of building. Many newspapers recruited pretty young women to form 'flying saucer spotting clubs,' illustrating their reports with the appropriate 'cheesecake' photographs. Numerous people called the press to say they saw a flying saucer just to get their names in the newspaper. Some gave false names or, as a joke, the names of friends. Some editors and reporters immediately caught onto this ruse and carefully checked the supposed witnesses by telephoning back to confirm the story. Other newspapers did not have such careful staffs, and when the 'witnesses' called the newspaper to deny the story, the newspaper had to print a retraction.

A popular columnist, Hal Boyle, ran a two-part story about being kidnapped from an Oklahoma bar by a big hairy Martian. (I have seen these columns in well over 1,000 newspapers.) As a result, many subsequent witnesses, especially women, apparently felt compelled to end their UFO reports with a statement about their alcohol consumption habits. Besides the ample silly season stories, there were numerous hoaxes, both journalistic and individual.

A pilot claimed he knocked down a disc in Montana with a surplus P-38 fighter aircraft. He claimed that the wind stream from his engine caused the disc to break open like a clam shell, and it fell to the ground. This story was carried worldwide. Some foreign newspapers said the pilot shot down the disc. The next day the pilot admitted sheepishly that his story was just a yarn. As might be expected, not every newspaper which carried the first story informed its readers of the later confession. In Wisconsin a circular saw blade fell to the ground near a parish priest. Newspapers around the world showed the priest with the saw blade, noting a new wrinkle in the flying saucer mystery. Several other hoaxes caused many newspaper editors to tire of flying saucers altogether.

In addition to the hoaxes, instant explanations by experts and laypeople alike further contributed to the loss of media interest. The Associated Press's science editor wrote two negative articles on UFOs in which he cited a fictitious 'Law of Eyesight' which supposedly made distant objects appear round, adding that he had seen round objects flying near his own residence which, on closer inspection, turned out to be aircraft. This was not his first foray into the explanation, without study, of unusual aerial phenomena. When the 'foo-fighters' first appeared, he announced that they must be some type of electrical phenomenon. As the 'foo-fighters' explanation was printed in The *New York Times*, generally recognised as the national newspaper of record, it was enshrined for all time as a sceptical legend, and is constantly repeated in poorly researched books on the subject.

Scientists and aviation experts in Australia, Germany and at the University of Oklahoma all claimed that dust motes floating in the eyes were behind many reports of flying saucers. Against a bright sky these motes caused distant 'objects' to be perceived and with the movement of the eyes the objects appeared to move at great speed. The same explanation was used in World War II by intelligence officers to get rid on any unusual sightings of aerial objects by aircrews. Indeed, the mote explanation hung around until 1952, when an eye specialist submitted a long paper to the Air Technical Intelligence Center (supposedly with the approval of UFO arch-sceptic Dr. Donald Menzel) which catalogued a long list of eye ailments that could cause people to see flying saucers. Captain Edward Ruppelt, then head of Blue Book, took the paper and attached a short note to his superior which said, 'We have a large number of sightings involving multiple witnesses. This idea will not explain these reports.'

But the theory certainly gained wide acceptance in 1947. Once again the newspapers gathered up young women to stare into the camera while shading their eyes with their hands. Under the pictures of the smiling beauties was the caption 'Seeing Flying Saucers.' After almost all UFO accounts had disappeared from the press, the popular Ripley's 'Believe It or Not' feature that detailed fantastic stories and 'facts' told people they could see flying saucers by lying on their backs and staring into the sky. Soon they would see them – the motes floating in their eyes projected into the sky as 'flying saucers.' An accompanying drawing depicted an attractive young woman in a two-piece bathing suit reclining on the ground.

Following quickly on the heels of the P-38 hoax, headlines informed the public that a flying disc had finally been captured near Roswell Army Air Force Base, New Mexico. The military recanted the same day, however, maintaining that what had actually been recovered was a form of weather balloon.

Congressman Steven Schiff of New Mexico echoes one common query when he asks why the Army Air Force used the phrase 'flying disc' in the first place, if all that was found were the remains of a meteorological device. Part of the answer is that, while 'flying disc' is generally assumed to be synonymous with extraterrestrial UFOs and flying saucers nowadays, it wasn't always necessarily so. In the first Gallup poll taken in the same year, alien craft weren't even mentioned as a possible explanation. To say, in 1947, then, that you had a flying disc did not automatically imply an extraterrestrial spaceship. It merely meant that the personnel at Roswell had found what everyone thought they were seeing. In fact, dozens of 'crashed discs' were reported in the press at the time. For the most part they turned out to be weather instruments and, in some cases, hoax items no doubt constructed in hopes of winning the prize money several sources were now offering for a flying disc.

As events unfolded, the announcement that the Roswell flying disc was a weather balloon brought the 1947 wave to an end on about 10 July. Today, the Roswell crash continues to generate volumes of testimony. In 1947, however, it passed through the newspapers in a mere two days. With the announcement of the Roswell 'dud,' as it was called, a wire service story found in most newspapers all around the country reported, 'Army and Navy Work Hard to Still Flying Saucer Rumors.' Many newspapers carried stories with pictures of meteorological balloons being launched from Army, Navy or Weather Bureau sites. The presumption in many people's minds, but in those of newspaper staff in particular, by the middle of July, was that the whole furore was caused by mundane objects like balloons, with the result that the subject was soon deemed unworthy of discussion. Except for some foreign reports and humour items, UFO reports nearly disappear from the national and regional wire services, though they continue to appear in small local newspapers. The effect was felt worldwide. When an editor at the *Palestine Post* received stories of UFOs in Italy, his comment was that Roswell had already proved that only weather balloons were involved. Reports continued in Canada throughout July, although in declining numbers, and by September the subject had virtually disappeared there as well.

But as we all know, the UFOs would soon be back in force.

A sketch of one of the objects seen by Kenneth Arnold on 24 June 1947

THE TASK OF INVESTIGATING 'FLYING SAUCERS' – OR UNIDENTIFIED FLYING OBJECTS (UFOS) AS THEY WOULD SUBSEQUENTLY BECOME KNOWN – FELL INITIALLY ON THE SHOULDERS OF THE UNITED STATES AIR FORCE, FIRST IN THE FORM OF PROJECT SIGN (ESTABLISHED DECEMBER 30, 1947), FOLLOWED BY PROJECT GRUDGE (FEBRUARY 11, 1949), AND FINALLY PROJECT BLUE BOOK (MARCH, 1952). UNTIL ITS DEMISE ON DECEMBER 17, 1969, BLUE BOOK PERSONNEL RECEIVED OVER 13,000 REPORTS, APPROXIMATELY FIVE PER CENT OF WHICH, OR JUST OVER 700 CASES, WERE CLASSIFIED AS 'UNIDENTIFIED' AFTER INVESTIGATION. BLUE BOOK CASE NUMBER 12, A REPORT BY PILOT KENNETH ARNOLD NOT FILED UNTIL THREE WEEKS AFTER THE EVENT, WAS THE FIRST OF THE SO-CALLED UNKNOWNS.

WHAT FOLLOWS IS ARNOLD'S ORIGINAL WRITTEN REPORT AS SUBMITTED TO AMERICAN MILITARY AUTHORITIES ON JULY 12, 1947. IT IS REPRINTED VERBATIM, AS IT APPEARS IN THE HISTORICAL FILES OF PROJECT BLUE BOOK, WITH NO ATTEMPT ON THE PART OF THE EDITORS TO CORRECT OR EDIT SYNTAX OR PUNCTUATION.

THE CASE CAN BE MADE THAT IT IS THE SINGLE MOST IMPORTANT, OR AT LEAST INFLUENTIAL, DOCUMENT IN UFO HISTORY. WHILE OTHERS HAD REPORTED UNUSUAL FLYING OBJECTS BEFORE (VIZ., THE 'FOO-FIGHTERS' OF WWII), ARNOLD'S HIGHLY-PUBLICISED SIGHTING MADE NEWS IN MORE WAYS THAN ONE. IT NOT ONLY INADVERTENTLY INTRODUCED THE PHRASE 'FLYING SAUCERS' (COINED BY AN ANONYMOUS NEWSPAPER HEADLINE WRITER) INTO MODERN CONSCIOUSNESS, IT UNLEASHED, OR STIMULATED, DEPENDING ON ONE'S POINT OF VIEW, A LITERAL FLOOD OF SIMILAR REPORTS WHICH CONTINUES UNABATED TO THIS DAY. FOR BETTER OR WORSE, THE ARNOLD SIGHTING SET THE UFO ERA IN PERPETUAL MOTION.

WHAT HAPPENED ON JUNE 24, 1947

by Kenneth Arnold

PENDLETON ORG JULY 12 1233A
COMMANDING GENERAL

WRIGHT FIELD DAYTON OHIO

DEAR SIR: YOU HAVE MY PERMISSION TO QUOTE GIVE OUT OR REPRINT MY WRITTEN ACCOUNT AND REPORT OF NINE STRANGE AIRCRAFT I OBSERVED ON JUNE 24TH IN THE CASCADE MOUNTAINS IN THE STATE OF WASHINGTON. THIS REPORT WAS SENT TO YOU AT REQUEST SOME DAYS AGO. IT IS WITH CONSIDERABLE DISAPPOINTMENT YOU CANNOT GIVE THE EXPLANATION OF THESE AIRCRAFT AS I FELT CERTAIN THEY BELONGED TO OUR GOVERNMENT. THEY HAVE APPARENTLY MEANT NO HARM BUT USED AS AN INSTRUMENT OF DESTRUCTION IN COMBINATION WITH OUR ATOMIC BOMB THE EFFECTS COULD DESTROY LIFE ON OUR PLANET. CAPT. _____ CO-PILOT STEVENS OF UNITED AIR LINES AND MYSELF HAVE COMPARED OUR OBSERVATIONS IN AS MUCH DETAIL AS POSSIBLE AND AGREED WE HAD OBSERVED THE SAME TYPE OF AIRCRAFT AS TO SIZE SHAPE AND FORM. WE HAVE

NOT TAKEN THIS LIGHTLY. IT IS TO US VERY SERIOUS CONCERN AS WE ARE AS INTERESTED IN THE WELFARE OF OUR COUNTRY AS YOU ARE.

KENNETH ARNOLD

BOISE IDAHO PILOTS LICENSE_____

24 333487.

SOME LIFE DATA ON KENNETH ARNOLD

I was born 29 March, 1915 in Subeka, Minnesota. I was a resident of Minnesota until I was six years old when my family moved to Scobey, Montana, where they homesteaded. My grandfather also homesteaded in Scobey, Montana, and became quite prominent in political circles along with Burton K. Wheeler, the famous Montana senator.

I went to grade school and high school at Minot, North Dakota. I entered scouting at twelve years of age and achieved the rank of Eagle scout before I was fourteen. My former scout executive was H. H. Prescott, now a regional commissioner for the Boy Scouts in Kansas City, Kansas.

As a boy, I was interested in athletics and was selected as an all-state end in 1932 and 1933 in the state of North Dakota. I entered the U. S. Olympic trials in fancy diving in 1932; I was a Red Cross Life Saving Examiner during the years of 1932, '33 and '34. I taught swimming and diving at scout camp and the municipal pool in Minot, North Dakota. I went to the University of Minnesota, where I swam and did fancy diving under Neils Thorpe, and also played football, under Bernie Bierman, but upon entering college I was unable to continue my football career because of an injured knee. My high school football coach was Glenn L. Jarrett, who is now the head football coach of the University of North Dakota. I had little or no finances, and my ambition in furthering my education in college was through my athletics. As a boy in Minot, North Dakota, I did a good deal of dog sled racing, placed first with my dog in 1930 in the Lions Club Dog Derby.

In 1938 I went to work for Red Comet, Inc. of Littleton, Colorado, a manufacturer of automatic fire fighting apparatus. In 1939 I was made district manager for them over a part of the western states, and in 1940 I established my own fire control supply known as the Great Western Fire Control Supply. I have been working as an independent fire control engineer since, and I handle, distribute, sell and install all types of automatic and manual fire fighting equipment in the rural areas over five western states.

My flying experience started as a boy in Minot, North Dakota, where I took my first flying lesson from Earl T. Vance, who was originally from Great Falls, Montana. Due to the high cost at that time, I was unable to continue my flying and did not fly of any great consequence until 1943. I was given my pilot certificate by Ed Leach, a senior CAA inspector of Portland, Oregon, and for the last three years have owned my own airplane, covering my entire territory with same and flying from forty to one hundred hours per month since. Due to the fact that I use an airplane entirely in my work, in January of this year I purchased a new Callair airplane, which is an airplane designed for high altitude take-offs and short rough field use.

In the type of flying I do, it takes a great deal of practice and judgment to be able to land in most any cow pasture and get out without injuring your airplane;

the runways are very limited and the altitude is very high in some of the fields and places I have to go in my work. To date, I have landed in 823 cow pastures in mountain meadows, and in over a thousand hours a flat tire has been my greatest mishap.

The following story of what I observed over the Cascade mountains, as impossible as it may seem, is positively true. I never asked nor wanted any notoriety for just accidently being in the right spot at the right time to observe what I did. I reported something that I know any pilot would have reported. I don't think that in any way my observation was due to any sensitivity of eye sight or judgment than what is considered normal for any pilot.

On 24 June, Tuesday, 1947, I had finished my work for the Central Air Service at Chehalis, Washington, and at about two o'clock I took off from Chehalis, Washington, airport with the intention of going to Yakima, Wash. My trip was delayed for an hour to search for a large marine transport that supposedly went down near or around the southwest side of Mt. Rainier in the State of Washington and to date has never been found.

I flew directly toward Mt. Rainier after reaching an altitude of about 9,500 feet, which is the approximate elevation of the high plateau from which Mt. Rainier rises. I had made one sweep of this high plateau to the westward, searching all of the various ridges for this marine ship and flew to the west down and near the ridge side of the canyon where Ashford, Washington, is located.

Unable to see anything that looked like the lost ship, I made a 300 degree turn to the right and above the little city of Mineral, starting again toward Mt. Rainier. I climbed back up to an altitude of approximately 9,200 feet.

The air was so smooth that day that it was a real pleasure flying and, as most pilots do when the air is smooth and they are flying at a higher altitude, I trimmed out my airplane in the direction of Yakima, Washington, which was almost directly east of my position, and simply sat in my plane observing the sky and the terrain.

There was a DC-4 to the left and to the rear of me approximately fifteen miles distance, and I should judge, at 14,000 foot elevation.

The sky and air was as clear as crystal. I hadn't flown more than two or three minutes on my course when a bright flash reflected on my airplane. It startled me as I thought I was too close to some other aircraft. I looked every place in the sky and couldn't find where the reflection had come from until I looked to the left and the north of Mt. Rainier where I observed a chain of nine peculiar looking aircraft flying from north to south at approximately 9,500 foot elevation and going, seemingly, in a definite direction of about 170 degrees.

They were approaching Mt. Rainier very rapidly, and I merely assumed they were jet planes. Anyhow, I discovered that this was where the reflection had come from, as two or three of them every few seconds would dip or change their course slightly, just enough for the sun to strike them at an angle that reflected brightly on my plane.

These objects being quite far away, I was unable for a few seconds to make out their shape or their formation. Very shortly they approached Mt. Rainier, and I observed their outline against the snow quite plainly.

I thought it was very peculiar that I couldn't find their tails but assumed they were some type of jet planes. I was determined to clock their speed, as I had two definite points I could clock them by; the air was so clear that it was very easy to

31

The COMING of the SAUCERS

By Kenneth Arnold & Ray Palmer

Another version of Arnold's 'flying disks'

see objects and determine their approximate shape and size at almost fifty miles that day.

I remember distinctly that my sweep second hand on my eight day clock, which is located on my instrument panel, read one minute to 3p.m. as the first object of this formation passed the southern edge of Mt. Rainier. I watched these objects with great interest as I had never before observed airplanes flying so close to the mountain tops, flying directly south to the south-east down the hog's back of a mountain range. I would estimate their elevation could have varied a thousand feet one way or another up or down, but they were pretty much on the horizon to me which would indicate they were near the same elevation as I was.

They flew like many times I have observed geese to fly in a rather diagonal chain-like line as if they were linked together. They seemed to hold a definite direction but rather swerved in and out of the high mountain peaks. Their speed at the time did not impress me particularly, because I knew that our army and air forces had planes that went very fast.

What kept bothering me as I watched them flip and flash in the sun right along their path was the fact I couldn't make out any tail on them, and I am sure that any pilot would justify more than a second look at such a plane.

I observed them quite plainly, and I estimate my distance from them, which was almost at right angles, to be between twenty to twenty-five miles. I knew they must be very large to observe their shape at that distance, even on as clear a day as it was that Tuesday.

In fact I compared a zeus fastener or cowling tool I had in my pocket with them, holding it up on them and holding it up on the DC-4 that I could observe at quite a distance to my left, and they seemed smaller than the DC-4; but, I should judge their span would have been as wide as the furtherest engines on each side of the fuselage of the DC-4.

The more I observed these objects, the more upset I became, as I am accustomed and familiar with most all objects flying whether I am close to the ground or at higher altitudes. I observed the chain of these objects passing another high snow-covered ridge in between Mt. Rainier and Mt. Adams, and as the first one was passing the south crest of this ridge the last object was entering the northern crest of the ridge.

As I was flying in the direction of this particular ridge, I measured it and found it to be approximately five miles so I could safely assume that the chain of these saucer like objects at least five miles long. I could quite accurately determine their pathway due to the fact that there were several high peaks that were a little this side of them as well as higher peaks on the other side of their pathway.

As the last unit of this formation passed the southern most high snow-covered crest of Mt. Adams, I looked at my sweep second hand and it showed that they had travelled the distance in one minute and forty-two seconds. Even at the time this timing did not upset me as I felt confident after I would land there would be some explanation of what I saw.

A number of news men and experts suggested that I might have been seeing reflections or even a mirage. This I know to be absolutely false, as I observed these objects not only through the glass of my airplane but turned my airplanes sideways where I could open my window and observe them with a completely unobstructed view. (Without sun glasses)

Even though two minutes seems like a very short time to one on the ground, in the air in two minutes time a pilot can observe a great many things and anything within his sight of vision probably as many as fifty or sixty times.

I continued my search for the marine plane for another fifteen or twenty minutes and while searching for this marine plane, what I had just observed kept going through my mind. I became more disturbed, so after taking a last look at Tieton Reservoir I headed for Yakima.

I might add that my complete observation of these objects, which I could even follow by flashes as they passed Mt. Adams, was around two and one-half or three minutes, although, by the time they reached Mt. Adams, they were out of my range of vision as far as determining shape or form. Of course, when the sun reflected from one or two or three of those units, they appeared to be completely round; but, I am making a drawing to the best of my ability, which I am including, as to the shape I observed these objects to be as they passed the snow covered ridges as well as Mt. Rainier. When these objects were flying approximately straight and level, they were just a black thin line and when they flipped was the only time I could get a judgment as to their size.

These objects were holding an almost constant elevation; they did not seem to be going up or to be coming down, such as would be the case of rockets or artillery shells. I am convinced in my own mind that they were some type of airplane, even though they didn't conform with the many aspects of the conventional type of planes that I know.

Although these objects have been reported by many other observers throughout the United States, there have been six or seven other accounts written by some of these observers that I can truthfully say must have observed the same thing that I did; particularly, the descriptions of the three Western Air Lines (Cedar City, Utah) employees, the gentleman (pilot) from Oklahoma City and the locomotive engineer in Illinois, plus Capt. _____ and Co-Pilot _____ of United Air Lines.

Some descriptions could not be very accurate taken from the ground unless these saucer-like disks were at quite a great height and there is a possibility that all of the people who observed peculiar objects could have seen the same thing I did; but, it would have been very difficult from the ground to observe these for more than four or five seconds, and there is always the possibility of atmospheric moisture and dust near the ground which could distort one's vision.

I have in my possession letters from all over the United States and people who profess that these objects have been observed over other portions of the world, principally Sweden, Bermuda, and California.

I would have given almost anything that day to have had a movie camera with a telephoto lens and from now on I will never be without one, but, to continue further with my story, when I landed at the Yakima, Washington, airport I described what I had seen to my very good friend, Al Baxter, who listened patiently and was very courteous but in a joking way didn't believe me.

I did not accurately measure the distance between these two mountains until I landed at Pendleton, Oregon, that same day where I told a number of pilot friends of mine what I had observed and they did not scoff or laugh but suggested they might be guided missiles or something new. In fact several former Army pilots informed me that they had been briefed before going into combat overseas that they might see objects of similar shape and design as I described and assured me that I wasn't dreaming or going crazy.

I quote _____ , a former Army Air Force pilot who is now operating dusting operations at Pendleton, Oregon, 'What you observed, I am convinced, is some type of jet or rocket propelled ship that is in the process of being tested by our government or even it could possibly be by some foreign government.'

Anyhow, the news that I had observed these spread very rapidly and before the night was over I was receiving telephone calls from all parts of the world; and, to date I have not received one telephone call or one letter of scoffing or disbelief. The only disbelief that I know of was what was printed in the papers.

I look at this whole ordeal as not something funny as some people have made it out to be. To me it is mighty serious and since I evidently did observe something that at least Mr. John Doe on the street corner or Pete Andrews on the ranch has never heard about, is no reason that it does not exist. Even though I openly invited an investigation by the Army and the FBI as to the authenticity of my story or a mental or a physical examination as to my capabilities, I have received no interest from these two important protective forces of our country; I will go so far as to assume that any report I gave to the United and Associated Press and over the radio on two different occasions which apparently set the nation buzzing, if our Military Intelligence was not aware of what I observed, they would be the very first people that I could expect as visitors.

I have received lots of requests from people who told me to make a lot of wild guesses. I have based what I have written here in this article on positive facts and as far as guessing what it was I observed, it is just as much a mystery to me as it is to the rest of the world.

My pilot's license is _____ . I fly a Callair airplane; it is a three-place single engine land ship that is designed and manufactured at Afton, Wyoming as an extremely high performance, high altitude airplane that was made for mountain work. The national certificate of my plane is _____ .

[signed] Kenneth Arnold
Boise, Idaho

THE BIGGEST FISH ARE THE ONES THAT GET AWAY. THE BEST UFO STORIES ARE THE ONES THAT ELUDE INVESTIGATION, OFFERING US JUST ENOUGH EVIDENCE TO TANTALISE US, NOT ENOUGH TO CONVINCE US. THE CRASHED SAUCER OF SPITZBERGEN, THE LANDING AT VORONEZH, LT. GORMAN'S AERIAL DOGFIGHT – WE CAN'T QUITE BRING OURSELVES TO THROW THESE TALES AWAY ALTOGETHER, SO WE SET THEM ON ONE SIDE WITH A WARNING LABEL, NOT TO BE TAKEN TOO SERIOUSLY. THEY BECOME THE FOLKLORE OF UFOLOGY.

SCANDINAVIA, HOME OF SANTA CLAUS AND HAUNT OF TROLLS, HAS BEEN THE SCENE OF MANY OF THE FINEST STORIES, FROM THE NORWEGIAN GHOST PLANES OF THE 1930S TO THE PHANTOM SUBMARINES OF THE COLD WAR. THE STORY OF GENERAL DOOLITTLE AND THE GHOST ROCKETS IS ONE SUCH TALE. ANDERS LILJEGREN, WHO TELLS THE STORY, IS RESPONSIBLE FOR THE UFO-ARKIVET AT NORRKÖPING, ONE OF THE WORLD'S FINEST REPOSITORIES OF UFO DOCUMENTATION. LILJEGREN AND THE SCANDINAVIAN UFO INFORMATION (SUFOI) GROUP, WHICH INCLUDES COLLEAGUES FROM NORWAY AND DENMARK, HAVE MADE A SUBSTANTIAL CONTRIBUTION TO SERIOUS UFO RESEARCH. HE MAY BE CONTACTED AT POSTBOX 11027, S-600 11 NORRKÖPING, SWEDEN.

GENERAL DOOLITTLE AND THE GHOST ROCKETS

by Anders Liljegren

The visit to Sweden of the American General James H. Doolittle has, for fifty years, been the subject of surmise and speculation among ufologists. The summer of 1946 was marked by one of the most sensational episodes in UFO history, the reports of mysterious 'ghost rockets' streaking across the Scandinavian skies – and occasionally crashing in remote lakes. Remarkable enough simply as a phenomenon, the sightings acquired additional importance in the light of the 'Cold War' then prevailing between the communist Eastern Bloc and the West.

It goes without saying that the popular interest in the ghost rockets was more than shared by American intelligence, concerned as it was with the military and political implications. Was it simply coincidence that Doolittle should pay a visit to Sweden at the same time as this mysterious wave of sightings? Many ufologists have thought otherwise; indeed, Doolittle's supposed role in the 1946 drama has even promoted him to a candidate for membership of a top-secret, high-level UFO study group.

General Doolittle was one of the best-known military celebrities of WWII. It was he who had planned and commanded American/allied bombing raids over Africa, Italy, Germany and Japan. 'His expansive character and aggressiveness won the loyalty of his men, and concealed a shrewd tactician, skilled and persuasive', says one biographical dictionary. Even Swedes knew him as the American who initiated the famous 'Thirty Seconds over Tokyo' bomber strike in 1942. Inevitably, his visit to our country sparked front-page articles in our leading newspapers.

After demobilisation, the general had accepted a position as a vice president of the Shell Oil company which had employed him for ten years between the wars. At the time of his visit to Sweden he had held this position for some six months, and the official reason for his two-night stay was to confer with his colleagues of Swedish Shell, selling oil and gasoline and discussing mutual problems. That his trip had any connection with the ghost rockets which were currently creating such excitement was emphatically denied by Swedish Shell.

On the other hand – and it was this which encouraged conjecture – it is a fact that on the evening of Wednesday, August 21, Doolittle had a meeting with General Nordenskjöld, head of the Swedish Air Force, together with other Swedish military high brass. However, the topic of conversation over the meal at one of Stockholm's best known restaurants, was 'military oil problems', not ghost rockets.

DOUGLAS BADER

In Sweden, Doolittle was accompanied by his wife and by Douglas Bader, as much a legend in his own way as General Doolittle. Bader had lost both legs in a plane crash in 1931, and subsequently used artificial limbs. When war came, he was turned down by the Air Force, but after a spectacular display of flying before an audience of senior officers, he talked himself into a pilot's seat and became, despite his handicap, one of the most skillful and famous fighter fliers of the war. His life story is a legend in military and aviation circles, while books and a film made him a hero to the general public.

In July 1946, after six years of military service, Bader had gone back to work for the Shell group. He was officially head of Shell's Aviation Department in London. Shell provided him with a small low-wing Percival Proctor four-seater plane, in which his first assignment was to fly Doolittle on a European-African promotion tour. The trip was to take them to Scandinavia, down through France and Italy to North Africa, with high-level receptions at each whistle-stop.

Mystery surrounded the Swedish visit from the moment the visitors left Oslo for Stockholm. The evening newspaper *Expressen* surmised that Doolittle would arrive in Stockholm 'on the regular Oslo plane' at 13.45 hours. Another paper, *Stockholms-Tidningen*, stated that Doolittle and Bader had been delayed by their audience with King Haakon, 'and arrived on an extra flight this afternoon'.

The generally reliable *Svenska Dagbladet* published a lively account of the landing which, however, differs from both these sources as well as from Brickhill's biography of Bader:

'the two arrived at 16.20 hours at Bromma in 'Hellsapoppin', the private plane of the American military attaché in Oslo. As the Witchcraft landed, first an elegant, grey-haired lady jumped out. It was the general's wife. Then came an American officer.'

At this moment we stop to ask, Was something wrong with the Proctor plane? Could the officer that jumped out of the plane (Doolittle and Bader were both in civilian clothes), have been the American attaché in Oslo who, for some reason, had lent his plane to Bader/Doolittle?

Svenska Dagbladet continued their highly-coloured picture of the reception: 'The photographers' flashbulbs popped, but it isn't Doolittle. Only a while later does he come out, a middle-aged rather small but stocky man in a blue suit and a gray felt hat. When someone asks him to raise his hat and wave to the photographers… he says with a brilliant smile 'I m not a very good actor', and disappears in a waiting car.'

Expressen further speculated that a number of 'gold-laced dignitaries' would be present at the airport. So it may have been. One can read significance into the fact that a meeting of the 'ghost rocket committee', headed by Colonel Bengt Jacobsson, planned for 14.00 that afternoon, was postponed until the following Friday. Was this because some of the officers who made up the committee were present at Bromma airport? That can only be speculation.

The Shell Oil Company was reportedly represented at the airport by its Swedish director and the principal manager for Scandinavia, but also present were the American military attaché and a colleague from the Embassy – which some might take to imply that there was more to the occasion than a simple commercial visit.

GENERAL SARNOFF

Doolittle and Bader were not the only foreign VIPs to arrive at Stockholm that day. In the morning, independently from his fellow-countryman, another celebrity from WWII, General David Sarnoff, a one-time member of Eisenhower's war staff, arrived by regular plane from Oslo. While Doolittle was just starting his business tour, Sarnoff was near the end of his European tour, and would be returning via London to New York on the following Friday.

Sarnoff was a pioneer in the field of electronics, whose fame began when as a young telegrapher he picked up the S.O.S. from the sinking *Titanic* in 1912. He went on to found a giant electronic and media empire, and in 1946 it was in his capacity as president of RCA that he came to Stockholm.

The three military aces were portrayed as a group by several Stockholm newspapers on 21 August, so clearly they must have got together at some point in their overlapping visits – adding yet more fuel to the flames of speculation. The *New York Times* reported that Colonel Kempff, head of Sweden's Defence Staff, was 'extremely interested in asking the two generals' advice (on the ghost rockets) and, if possible, would place all available reports before them.' But Doolittle told *Stockholms-Tidningen*: 'We are not here for any military negotiations, only for our company. Of course we would like to stay in Sweden more than two days. Maybe I would be able to see one of the renowned ghost bombs. Naturally, I don't know anything about them, but I would be glad if I did.'

Sarnoff was less reticent, according to *Morgon-Tidningen*: 'I have read some about the ghost bombs in the press. It would be easy to confirm their origin, by radio-technical means, and if the Swedish state would use my services I wouldn't hesitate. But I suspect they have their own experts and will not divulge any of their results'. He explained that he was in Sweden to make contacts and to see which of his company's new developments might be of interest to Europeans.

Was it just coincidence that these high-level personalities should find themselves in Stockholm at the same time? Before we read too much into it, we should recognise that such visits were not exceptional events in the summer of 1946: industrial, trade and political delegations arrived almost daily. Sweden had managed – by delicate footwork – to remain neutral throughout WWII. Consequently, alone among western European nations, she found herself in the post-war era with an undamaged, fairly modern industry, that would eventually evolve into world-wide concerns such as Volvo, Electrolux, SAAB and Ericsson.

Sweden had also started to build a large air force, which by the 1950s was the fourth largest in the world. The planes were largely 'home-made' (by SAAB). Thus there was every reason for outsiders to have trade talks with Swedish men of power: industrialists, technicians, military men, and politicians.

THE KEMPFF LETTER

But did the visitors' interest extend to the ghost rockets? Researching the possibility at various Stockholm archives, Clas Svahn and I found two interesting documents that cast new light on the Doolittle and Sarnoff involvement. One was a letter written to the Swedish military attaché in Washington, just nine days after the Doolittle-Nordenskjöld dinner, by Colonel Curt Kempff, who headed the foreign section (attachés, espionage, etc) of the Defence Staff's Section II:

STOCKHOLM, 30 AUGUST, 1946.

DEAR _____ ,

ABOUT A WEEK AGO THERE WAS A STRANGE INCIDENT, ABOUT WHICH I FEEL I SHOULD INFORM YOU.

AS YOU HAVE DOUBTLESS SEEN IN THE NEWSPAPERS, THE AMERICAN GENERAL DOOLITTLE, AND ANOTHER HIGH-RANKING OFFICER, VISITED STOCKHOLM FOR COMMERCIAL REASONS A WHILE AGO. I WAS THEN ACTING AS CHIEF OF THE DEFENCE STAFF. ONE EVENING IMMEDIATELY AFTER THE ARRIVAL OF THESE GENTLEMEN I WAS CALLED ON THE TELEPHONE BY AN AMERICAN JOURNALIST IN STOCKHOLM (I DID NOT CATCH HIS NAME WITH CERTAINTY, BUT I BELIEVE IT WAS AXELSON OF THE WASHINGTON POST) WHO SAID THAT HE KNEW THAT GENERAL D. WOULD VERY MUCH LIKE TO PLACE HIS EXPERIENCE OF ROCKET MISSILES AT THE DISPOSAL OF SWEDISH AUTHORITIES, ESPECIALLY IN VIEW OF THE CURRENT GHOST BOMB AFFAIR. I ANSWERED THAT I WOULD INVESTIGATE THE POSSIBILITIES OF MAKING A CONTACT AND ASKED HIM TO CALL ME BACK THE NEXT DAY.

THE NEXT DAY I SPOKE TO AIR FORCE GENERAL NORDENSKJÖLD AND HE TOLD ME HE WOULD BE DINING WITH D. THAT SAME DAY, WHICH WOULD PROVIDE A SUITABLE OPPORTUNITY FOR D. TO EXPRESS HIS VIEWS.

A FEW DAYS LATER I LEARNED THAT N. HAD ASKED D. AT THE DINNER WHETHER HE HAD ANYTHING TO SAY, BUT, TO HIS SURPRISE, RECEIVED THE ANSWER THAT D. HAD NO VIEWPOINTS AT ALL TO GIVE US IN THIS MATTER. I THEREFORE TOOK THE INCIDENT TO BE A SIGN OF OVER-EAGERNESS ON THE PART OF AN ENTERPRISING AMERICAN JOURNALIST.

THAT WASN'T THE END OF THE MATTER, HOWEVER. THE OTHER DAY I HAD A VISIT FROM THE ACTING BRITISH MILITARY ATTACHÉ HERE, MAJOR DE SALIS, WHO SHOWED ME THE TRANSCRIPT OF A DESPATCH FROM HIS COLLEAGUE IN WASHINGTON. IN THIS I READ – WITH MY OWN EYES – THAT GENERAL D. HAD CONTACTED THE ACTING CHIEF OF THE DEFENCE STAFF (THAT'S ME!) AND HAD GIVEN US INFORMATION CONCERNING THE ROCKET MISSILE ISSUE. DE SALIS WONDERED WHAT THE TRUTH OF THE MATTER WAS AND WHETHER HE COULD SHARE THIS VALUABLE BRIEFING. I REPLIED BY TELLING HIM THE SEQUENCE OF EVENTS I HAVE DESCRIBED.

Another letter, in similar spirit, was written by Olof Rydbeck, ambassador at the Swedish legation in Washington (later he became prominent as the head of the Swedish Broadcasting Corporation), to the Counsellor Dahlman at the Swedish ministry of foreign affairs:

WASHINGTON, AUGUST 22, 1946.

DEAR _____,

GENERAL DOOLITTLE'S AND NOW ALSO GENERAL SARNOFF'S VISITS TO SWEDEN HAVE BEEN NOTED BY SEVERAL NEWSPAPERS AND CAUSED A NUMBER OF QUES-TIONS FROM NEWSPAPERS AND NEWS AGENCIES. WE HAVE DENIED THAT THE VISIT WAS INSPIRED FROM THE SWEDISH SIDE, DUE TO THE ROCKET BOMBS. ACCORDING TO SEVERAL OF THE QUESTIONERS, THE WAR DEPARTMENT (IN WASHINGTON) ALSO STATED THEY KNEW OF NO CONNECTION BETWEEN THE GENERAL'S TRAVELS AND THE MYSTERIOUS BOMBS.

Had there been any truth in the rumours about an active exchange of information between Swedish authorities and two semi-military American generals, both by this time supposedly out of active service, we would have expected to find some indication in the Confidential and Secret Swedish correspondence files we have inspected. We found none. Moreover, common sense suggests that to send two high-profile ex-generals on widely reported visits to Sweden would be complete-ly out of line with intelligence operating procedures.

Instead, what we found was indication of normal day-by-day exchanges of information at the military attaché level. Throughout the summer and autumn of 1946, questions about the rockets posed by American intelligence were duly answered by members of the Swedish 'space projectile' committee. On 20 June 1947, four days before the Kenneth Arnold sighting, the Swedish Defence Staff sent its attaché in Washington excerpts from the final secret ghost rocket report. Seemingly, this information did not reach American authorities, for in the wake of the summer 1947 wave of discs (and also many rocket-like objects) we find them asking the Swedish authorities for more complete information. A version of the report was delivered to the Americans in September 1947.

As for the Doolittle-Sarnoff connection, it can be seen in retrospect as no more than a media product, so far as the Swedish documents are concerned. However, Doolittle has continued to be a favourite of conspiracy buffs, and simi-lar suspicions have involved Sarnoff. Speaking at New York's Waldorf-Astoria Hotel on 30 September, Sarnoff said he was convinced that the ghost rockets were no myth but real missiles. Ufologist Stanton Friedman has speculated that either Doolittle or Sarnoff wrote a report on the ghost rockets for 'at least Eisenhower, then Chief of Staff'.

William L. Moore found some comments in the 9 January, 1947, issue of *Intelligence Review* which add a further dimension to the legend: 'The Scandinavian press, with the exception of the Communist papers, initially reported the incidents in some detail and openly attributed them to missiles fired by the U.S.S.R... The Communist press has continued to ridicule the matter... In fact, a charge was made that they came from the United States and that General Doolittle was sent over to observe the effects of the missiles!'

Further rumours proliferate. One of researcher Leonard Stringfield's anonymous sources named Doolittle, in 1947 back in military duty, as one of the 'top Air Force generals' to have flown in and out of New Mexico in July 1947, seemingly in connection with the Roswell crash. Another of his sources spoke of 'a special intelligence organisation' to investigate the WWII foo fighters, 'headed by Doolittle, maybe'.

Immediately after the Roswell crash, so William Moore states, high-level meetings were held on 9-10 July, 1947 in which generals Vandenburg and Doolittle met with Air Force Secretary Stewart Symington and President Truman. For what purpose?

UFO historian Loren Gross found a 1952 Blue Book document in which

Lieutenant General James Doolittle

Doolittle was suggested as a member of a small 'High Level Advisory Committee' to oversee and counsel UFO research at ATIC [Air Technical Intelligence Command], if Project Blue Book was to be expanded.

Friedman has made further attempts to involve Doolittle with high-level UFO research. In his Final Report on Operation Majestic 12, he links Doolittle to General Twining, Detlev Bronk, and other claimed members of the super-secret MJ-12 committee. Friedman reports that in 1948 Doolittle became a member of the board of NACA (the forerunner of NASA), and its chairman in 1956. In 1953 he headed Project Solarium, a top secret task force directed against the Soviet Union.

DENIALS

In an October 1981 interview with Moore, Doolittle stated that he was 'unable to recall the exact purpose of his visit to Stockholm'. Moore finds it suspicious that he could find no mention of the Doolittle-Sarnoff visit in the large file of official cables which passed between the American embassy at Stockholm and the State Department in Washington. 'If the general's visit was as 'routine' as some at the time tried to make it appear, then the absence of official diplomatic communications on the subject is most unusual'. Perhaps: but there is a much more plausible explanation for the silence: that Doolittle was on a purely civilian, commercial tour and had no active interest or connection to the ghost rocket investigations.

On 29 August, 1984 Doolittle wrote to Barry Greenwood: 'I have no firm knowledge of actual rockets or 'ghost rockets' in Sweden. Did know, of course, that various hypotheses were being bandied about – largely by the press'.

All the evidence suggests that Doolittle was telling the truth. But will the conspiracy theorists believe him?

THE 1950s

HOAXES MAKE UP A MINUSCULE PERCENTAGE OF ALL UFO REPORTS. ACCORDING TO ONE EARLY U.S. AIR FORCE STUDY OF 1021 CASES, FOR EXAMPLE, ONLY 1.66% WERE DISMISSED AS HOAXES, WHILE 20.1% WERE CLASSIFIED UNKNOWN. AT THE SAME TIME, SOME HOAXES UNDOUBTEDLY GO UNRECOGNISED AND THEIR POTENTIAL FOR CONFUSION CAN BE CONSIDERABLE. WHO KNOWS WHAT SORT OF 'EVIDENCE' HAS BEEN ENTERED INTO THE UFO LITERATURE AS THE RESULT OF A HOAX, INTENDED OR OTHERWISE?

KARL PFLOCK, AUTHOR OF ROSWELL IN PERSPECTIVE, HAS WRITTEN EXTENSIVELY ABOUT UFOS. HE IS CONVINCED OF THE REALITY OF THE PHENOMENON ITSELF AND STRONGLY SUSPECTS THAT AT LEAST SOME EARLY REPORTS REPRESENT PHYSICAL CRAFT FROM ANOTHER WORLD. HIS CURRENT RESEARCH IS BASED ON THE WORKING ASSUMPTION THAT THE ANSWERS TO THE UFO ENIGMA MAY WELL LIE IN THE DATA ACCUMULATED DURING THE 'GOLDEN AGE OF UFOS' FROM THE MID-1940S THROUGH THE MID-1960S. HE INVITES ANYONE WITH ADDITIONAL KNOWLEDGE OF THE DESVERGERS OR OTHER CLASSICAL UFO CASES TO CONTACT HIM BY MAIL, PHONE/FACSIMILE, OR E-MAIL: PO BOX 93338, ALBUQUERQUE, NM 87199-3338; (505) 867-0893; KTPEREHWON@AOL.COM

THE BEST HOAX IN UFO HISTORY?

by Karl T. Pflock

About 10 p.m. on the muggy, moonless night of Tuesday, August 19, 1952, Palm Beach County, Florida, Deputy Sheriff Mott N. Partin received an urgent call. The Florida Highway Patrol had just been contacted by a farmer who lived about 12 miles southwest of West Palm Beach on Military Trail, a rural highway running north-south roughly parallel to and about 10 miles inland from Florida's Atlantic coast. The highway patrol was handing the matter over to the sheriff.

It seemed the farmer and his wife had three frantic boy scouts in their living room. The boys' scoutmaster was in some sort of fix. Joined by Lake Worth Constable Louis Carroll, who followed in a separate vehicle, Partin hurried to the scene, arriving about 10:20. There they found the worried farm couple and the three scouts, Bobby Ruffing, 12, David Rowan, 11, and Charles 'Chuck' Stevens, 10. The boys said their scoutmaster, hardware clerk and ex-U.S. Marine D. S. (Dunham Sanborn) 'Sonny' Desvergers, 30, had gone into the scrub pine and palmetto just off Military Trail to investigate some odd lights. Moments later, the boys saw red, flare-like lights in the area where Desvergers had gone. Badly frightened, they ran to the farmhouse for help.

Taking the boys, the lawmen drove to Desvergers' car, parked about three-quarters of a mile south on the east shoulder of the road. Partin pulled over a few yards north of Desvergers' vehicle at about 10:30, Carroll drawing up behind. As the officers considered the situation, a man emerged from the palmettos about 75 feet from the road. He was waving a machete and shouting repeatedly, 'I'm coming, here I am!' He looked, said Partin, 'like a wild man' as he struggled up the highway embankment, babbling incoherently. It was Desvergers, white-faced and shaking. 'In all my 19 years of law enforcement work,' said Partin, 'I've never seen anyone as terrified as he was.'

With some reluctance, they followed the scoutmaster back through the woods. Desvergers's large, multi-cell flashlight was found resting lens-down in a small clearing, still on. Close by, the sparse grass was flattened as though someone had been lying on it. A search turned up nothing else unusual. Partin marked the locations of the flashlight and crushed grass with twigs and the three men trekked back to the road.

As Partin and Carroll drove Desvergers and the boys to the Palm Beach County Sheriff's office, Desvergers said the hair on his forearms was singed and the skin burned. At the sheriff's office, Desvergers and the boys were questioned again, and Partin examined Desvergers arms and found the hair singed and the skin of one arm reddened. He also noted three tiny holes burned in the scoutmaster's billed cap.

The burns were real, but of greater interest was their alleged cause: Desvergers claimed he had been attacked by a flying saucer.

Partin telephoned the U.S. Air Force Military Air Transport Service unit at West Palm Beach International Airport. He was put in touch with a Captain Carney, intelligence officer of the 1707th Air Base Wing. Carney talked with both Partin and Desvergers and, it appears from the record, followed up during the next two days with interviews of both men and the scouts.

Carney then filed a formal report in accordance with established Air Force procedure for 'unidentified aerial objects,' forwarding a teletype message to the Air Force Directorate of Intelligence in the Pentagon, Project Blue Book in the Air Technical Intelligence Center (ATIC) at Wright-Patterson Air Force Base, Dayton, Ohio, and to other required addressees. By the time Carney's unclassified message reached ATIC, Blue Book chief Captain Edward Ruppelt and his staff had left for the evening. Thus it was not until 8:40 a.m. the following morning, August 21, that Ruppelt learned of 'one of the weirdest UFO reports that I came up against.' By 3 p.m., he and Second Lieutenant Robert M. Olsson were winging their way to Florida aboard a B-25 bomber.

At almost the same time, Desvergers was being examined by an Air Force doctor, forty-six hours after the incident and the same day it first hit the press. He found Desvergers to be 'normal physically. The hair on the back of his forearms was singed, but not badly. The skin on his forearms showed no signs of blisters, burns, or redness. He stated that if the skin had been burned it was very minor as there was [sic] absolutely no after-effects.'

Desvergers told the doctor 'he had received an 'Other Than Honorable' discharge from the Marines in 1944' because of a stolen-car incident in which the charges against him eventually were dropped. He also claimed an automobile had fallen on him, resulting in three months' hospitalisation for diathermy treatment. The doctor found this 'highly unlikely' since such treatment does not require hospitalisation. Asked 'if he had ever had nightmares,' Desvergers answered the doctor with 'a flat "no", but said that once he did have a dream about a beautiful woman and was still looking for her.'

After the B-25 carrying Ruppelt and Olsson touched down in West Palm Beach, mechanical trouble delayed the plane's return to Dayton, so Ruppelt recruited the two pilots, Captains Bill Hoey and Douglas Davis, to help in his investigation. On Friday, August 22, the four officers met with Captain Carney who showed them the statements of Desvergers, the three scouts, and presumably those of Partin and Carroll. They then talked with the doctor who had examined Desvergers and, about noon, visited the scene of the incident, accompanied by Carney and an enlisted member of his staff, the doctor, Deputy Partin and Constable Carroll, and an airman staff-car driver.

There the lawmen gave their account of the incident, and the Air Force team searched '50 yards around the spot where the flashlight was found…There was no above normal radiation, no burned foliage or grass, no broken or trampled foliage or trees (other than that damaged by the sheriff and the search party), no sign of debris such as flares.' Also, grass specimens were collected, probably by Captain Carney or his staff assistant.

Ruppelt next interviewed the oldest boy scout, 12-year-old Bobby Ruffing, in the presence of his mother. Ruffing confirmed the basics of the account from his point of view. After a light was seen, Desvergers told them to wait ten minutes and then get help if he didn't return, which they did. According to Ruppelt, they could follow Desvergers' flashlight beam as it moved through the brush. The they saw 'a red light go toward him, saw him silhouetted in red light and saw him fall.'

At six o'clock that evening, Ruppelt interviewed the scoutmaster himself, who he described as 'very cooperative [and] normal,' if just a shade nervous. Sitting in with Ruppelt were Olsson, Hoey, Davis, Carney, and one of Carney's sergeants. Ruppelt asked each to note an insignificant detail in Desvergers account and then to ask him about it during follow-up questioning. If he were lying, he would forget the details or repeat them perfectly. He did neither.

Desvergers told them he was driving the boys around when he 'caught a flash of light out of the corner of my eye. I looked around and saw a series of fuzzy lights like the cabin windows of an airliner.' (All quotes, including any emphasis, are from Ruppelt's transcription of the interview.) The lights seemed to be headed into the woods at a 45-degree angle and his first thought was that an aeroplane might have crashed. Telling the boy scouts to seek help if he wasn't back in ten minutes, Desvergers went into the woods with a machete and two flashlights.

To his surprise, he came to a clearing where he noticed a peculiar smell, a sharp, sickening odour that made him feel 'woozy,' like being anaesthetised. 'I went two or three paces when I had the feeling somebody or something was watching me. I kept on going and began to feel heat, like walking close to an oven. It was hot and humid-like and it seemed to be coming from above. I hadn't thought of looking up, when I did I couldn't see the sky. I knew I had run into something rough. I stood frozen in my tracks, I wanted to throw something or hit it with my machete. I felt for my flash-light in my back pocket and thought of throwing it, but was too scared.'

The bottom of the object blocking Desvergers's view of the stars was 'dull black with no seams, joints or rivet lines. It had dirty streaks running straight across as if oil or dust had blown back.' He estimated its diameter as 30 feet and its thickness at 10 feet. As he backed slowly away, he looked up at the 'ship' and saw that it was 'round with a dome-shape top and with holes and fins running around the edge. The bottom edge seemed to glow with a sort of phosphorescent glow, like phosphorous in the sea at night. They seemed to be as scared of me as I was of them.' Asked how he knew that, Desvergers replied that the object appeared to move back as he approached it.

He then heard the sound of metal on metal, like a hatch opening. 'Next I saw a red flare which appeared slowly to move toward me. It came out of the side [of the ship]. I couldn't move or yell I was so scared.' Desvergers put his hands over his face as he was enveloped in a red mist, then passed out. When he first came to, he could-n't see and his eyes burned. Eventually, he saw lights on the road and ran toward them, thus encountering Partin and Carroll.

Desvergers next told the investigators he had already been approached by a scientist, university professors, print and broadcast reporters, and others, and had been offered money for his story. He said he refused to talk with any of them, and Ruppelt observed he seemed to be proud of this and 'how important he was.'

Desvergers asked what he should do about all these people, saying 'he would be very glad to cooperate with the Air Force and not talk to anyone if he was not supposed to.' Alas for Air Force conspiracy and cover-up theorists, Ruppelt told him he was perfectly free to talk to anyone he wished. Desvergers said he would go home and call the newspapers and give them the story just to 'get them off his neck, 'and again Ruppelt told him he was free to do so.

The next day, Saturday, August 23, the wire services quoted Desvergers as saying, 'It's better for me not to go any further for the public good because it might cause panic.' He was also quoted as saying, 'It's not foolish to say that it will determine the future of all of us someday,' and that 'The Army's [sic] theory and mine coincide,' adding, 'I'd like to get it all off my chest ...but I've told them I'd wait until they clear me from my security pledge.' The stories also revealed that Desvergers had hired a press agent and included a new claim by Deputy Sheriff Partin: he had found scorched grass at the encounter site.

The same day, Ruppelt and his team returned to Dayton, taking with them Desvergers's machete and burned cap for scientific examination. Somehow, they managed to leave the grass specimens behind, and these were forwarded five days later and sent to an agronomy laboratory for examination. Meanwhile, the situation back in Florida was getting rapidly out of hand. While conceding he was now 'free to talk...insofar as military authorities were concerned,' Desvergers also admitted that 'I feel I can make a little money out of this. That's why I want to keep quiet.' He told Carney that he had received several threatening telephone calls and had noticed 'a large black automobile cruising around near his house.'

In Ohio, Olsson had Desvergers' machete examined for radiation at the Wright Field Equipment Laboratory with negative results. He then took the cap to the Clothing Research Division of the Wright Field Aeromedical Laboratory, which confirmed that the three apparent burns were actual burns and that the bill and edges of the cap had been scorched, probably from exposure to high heat brief enough not to harm the wearer. Olsson then forwarded the cap to an FBI laboratory in Washington, D.C., which found no residue permitting identification of the cause of the burns. A 'minute burned area' was discovered, but considered 'too small to have been intentionally caused 'A more likely suspect was a small hot ember. The singing on the bill and edges of the cap was 'not uniform as would be expected if it had been caused by a single flash of flame.' Also noted was a lack of scorching under a fold which 'smooths out when the cap is placed on the head,' suggesting it was not being worn when damaged. However, as UFO historian Loren E. Gross has pointed out, Desvergers said he threw his hands up to protect his face from the flame, which could have pushed back and flattened the cap. Moreover, the cap was new and seen to be undamaged at the scout meeting just before the incident.

Olsson also considered the possibility of a parachute flare, but ultimately discarded it on the grounds that a burning flare would have set the dry grass on fire. 'No evidence of a fire was present down there as far as we could see,' he said, nor were any remnants of a flare ever found.

Ruppelt seems to have left Florida inclined to accept Desvergers' story, if bothered by the man's efforts to promote himself and turn a profit. Then a report on the ex-Marine's military record and brushes with the law revealed he had been discharged from the Marine Corps for being absent without leave (AWOL) and stealing an automobile, and had been imprisoned in the federal reformatory at Chillicothe, Ohio.

When Ruppelt and Olsson returned to Florida on September 8 for a follow-up investigation, Desvergers's reputation deteriorated even further. Although he had no official police record in the area, the scoutmaster wasn't squeaky clean, either. The officers were told he was 'a boy who never quite grew up, an exhibitionist' prone to wild exaggerations about himself and his background. He was known for showing off in his car and 'shady' dealings which included passing bad cheques. Two brothers who had known Desvergers for years said he 'seemed to always have a story that would top one told by anybody else. They said he was very clever and that he always had a very convincing answer for everything.' These men were very interested in flying saucers, but 'put absolutely no faith in anything' Desvergers said.

On the evening of September 9, Ruppelt and Carney attended a meeting of Desvergers's scout troop (Desvergers was not present) to interview the troop chairman and all three boys involved in the incident. The scouts, 'rather excited and nervous,' said Desvergers had agreed to drive them and another boy home after their August 19 troop meeting. On the way, they stopped for a drink. Then Desvergers drove toward a drive-in theatre, but 'something' happened, so instead they went to a stock-car speedway to 'see how much water was on the track from the recent rain.' Pressed about the reason for the change in plans, the boys 'were very vague' and seemed 'to be attempting to cover up' (A possibly relevant consideration: in an unpublished 1953 manuscript, James W. Moseley reports someone at the Air Force press desk in Washington told him Desvergers had been involved in homosexual activities).

Leaving the speedway, Desvergers dropped the fourth boy at home, then headed south on Military Trail. Nearing the site of the incident, Desvergers said he saw a light to the left, which none of the boys saw. Stopping the car, Desvergers 'got out… and removed two machetes… and two flashlights from the trunk…The boys asked him what he was going to do and he said he thought he had seen either an aircraft crack up or *a flying saucer.*' (Emphasis in the original. This was the first mention of Desvergers saying anything about flying saucers before the alleged attack.) Afraid, the boys persuaded Desvergers to drive on.

The oldest boy, Bobby Ruffing, 12, who 'seemed to be the leader of the group… anything he said was law', was 'not too cooperative' with Ruppelt and Carney. When pressed for an answer he would 'clam up'. He kept stating, 'Well that's what Sonny [Desvergers] said, so it must be the truth.' However he did say that, soon after the first stop when Desvergers made the comment about flying saucers, he 'saw a semi-circle of white lights about three inches in diameter' descending 'at an angle of 45 degrees into the trees.' Soon after Desvergers entered the woods, Ruffing said, he saw 'a series of red lights in the clearing' and he watched Sonny "stiffen up" and fall.'

When Ruffing finished his story, he was dismissed and, in the presence of the troop chairman, Ruppelt questioned David Rowan, 11, and Chuck Stevens, 10. Rowan 'was rather silly about the whole thing', but Stevens seemed a 'logical thinker and gave the straightest answers'. Up to the point of Desvergers's trek into the woods, the boys' stories closely matched what Ruffing said, although Stevens said he, too, had seen a white light as they drove on after the first stop, but it 'looked to him like it was a common, ordinary meteor.'

Stevens and Rowan said they could see Desvergers going through the woods, 'could see flashlights flashing on the trees and then he disappeared for a few seconds, at least the light disappeared. The next thing they saw was a series of red lights… a lot like flares… It… seemed to be… six or eight red lights going in all directions.' Then all three boys ran to the farmhouse to get help.

Clearly, there were important discrepancies in the scouts' recollections. And it is perhaps not insignificant that the oldest boy, who obviously had a strong – perhaps inordinate? – loyalty to Desvergers was the only one of the three who recalled anything supporting the scoutmaster's claims of seeing strange lights in the air and being knocked unconscious.

In their discussion with the troop chairman, a medical doctor, the officers learned he had not known Desvergers until the latter had volunteered to serve as scoutmaster. His first inkling that Desvergers might not be 'exactly normal' was about three months before the saucer incident. Desvergers had claimed his four-month-old son could walk and talk and had several teeth. As a physician, the troop chairman considered this 'rather absurd' and 'couldn't figure out why Desvergers would tell such a story.' Curious, he made a point of seeing the child, whom he found to be a 'strictly normal' four-month-old.

Leaving the meeting, Ruppelt and Carney were convinced they had a crackpot hoaxer on their hands, but they decided to visit the site of the incident that night, at about the same time and under lighting (no moon) and weather conditions similar to those on August 19. Joined by Lt. Olsson and Staff Sergeant Saeger of Carney's staff, they parked 'in approximately the same spot as Desvergers's car was parked.' Olsson and Saeger took a flashlight into the clearing where Desvergers said he was attacked. Ruppelt and Carney could see the light as the men moved through the woods (consistent with the scouts' accounts). However, when the men were in the clearing, their light could be seen only when Olsson held it 'about seven feet above the ground and shined it directly toward the road.' From this Ruppelt and Carney concluded 'a person in the clearing, holding a light at a normal level, could not be seen from the road.' Photographs in the Blue Book file seem to support this conclusion, although Pan American Airways pilot William Nash recently told the author his examination of the site two years later left no doubt a person in the clearing could be seen from the road.

Does this 're-enactment' also invalidate the scouts' claim to have seen red lights in the clearing? As Loren Gross has pointed out, not necessarily. According to Desvergers, the ball of red flame was launched at him from the saucer hovering just above the trees, more than 15 feet above ground.

While at the scene, the Air Force team 'noted that aircraft in the traffic pattern at the West Palm Beach Airport with landing lights on appeared to be white lights going down through the woods.' Does this mean that, if Desvergers and Bobby Ruffing saw any lights in the sky at all, they were merely aircraft landing lights? Not necessarily. Captain Carney's teletype of August 21 reveals he checked this possibility. He mentions only the landing of an SA-16 (Air Force air/sea rescue amphibian) at 5:23p.m., local time, more than four hours before the Desvergers incident.

Desvergers' story seemed to 'improve' with almost every new telling. In February 1953 he told sympathetic *American Weekly* reporter Marta Robinet he had seen a strange creature in the saucer. About the same time, Desvergers told Donald Howell of Jacksonville, Florida, he had climbed on the edge of the saucer and fought with three 'humanoids in greyish clothing' who had a 'sweaty odour.' The beings were weak, Desvergers said, so he was winning the battle when the saucer shifted and he lost his balance, falling to the ground. In an autumn 1953 interview with James Moseley, editor of *Saucer News*, Desvergers claimed he had never lost consciousness at all. Instead, there was a struggle and he was carried a short distance by the saucer.

But all this happened later. In mid-September 1952, Ruppelt was puzzling over how to write his report on the event, a report which is not in the Blue Book file. He was sure Desvergers's tale was a tall one. Still, though he and his associates had 'thought up dozens of ways' it could have been done, they hadn't made 'step one in proving the incident to be a hoax,' and they couldn't explain the burns in the scout-master's cap.

Then Ruppelt's telephone rang. It was the agronomy lab calling about the grass specimens. 'How did the roots get charred?' they asked. Ruppelt was stunned. Ruppelt's caller explained that when they had cleaned the soil from the roots they found them charred black. The above-ground portions of the plants were unharmed, except for the extreme tips of the longest blades. These seem to have been touching the ground and were charred, too. Only the specimens collected at the spot over which Desvergers said the saucer hovered were damaged. Those collected 50 and 75 yards distant were quite normal.

The lab had duplicated the charring by placing live grass clumps in a pan of sandy soil and heating it to about 300 degrees Fahrenheit. How this had been done in the Florida outback was anybody's guess.

So there you have it, the full story of the Florida saucer attack. Well, not quite. In fact, there were other sightings in the area at the time, at least one of them, accord-ing to press reports, known to the Air Force while the Desvergers investigation was under way,

This sighting took place about 7:30 p.m. on August 29. A Mr. and Mrs. Wendell Wells, their 15-year-old niece, June Tent, and two infants were on their way to a drive-in theatre when they noticed 'a bright glow' in the sky. According to Tent, it first appeared to be 'one big yellow-white light. It seemed to be drifting, slanting down. Then it got over the woods on the left side of the road and dropped straight down. When it got closer to the ground it looked like it had more lights. And right after it landed, we saw another light that seemed to hover over the spot.' The object seemed the size of a large transport airplane, but in appearance resembled 'the rim of a coin' with lights spaced around it. The family turned onto Military Trail, and a short drive brought them abreast of a spot in the woods illuminated by an eerie glow, and about eight miles south of the Desvergers site. They reported their sighting to the press on September 4. Queried by a reporter, the Air Force said it was 'investigating,' yet there is no record of the case in Blue Book files.

When Ruppelt came to write his classic Report on Unidentified Flying Objects, he was still puzzled by the charred grass roots. Admitting it was 'pure speculation,' he drew an analogy with the induction heating process used in foundries to melt metals. Solid rods or ingots of metal are subjected to an alternating magnetic current which sets up 'eddy currents' in the metal, raising its temperature.

Replace the solid metal with damp sand, 'an electrical conductor, and assume that a something [...] generating a powerful alternating magnetic field was hovering over the ground,' Ruppelt wrote, 'and you can explain how the grass roots were charred.' And to get an alternating magnetic field, some type of electrical equipment was needed, sparks from which could have conceivably burned the holes in Desvergers's cap.

Why didn't the flashlight and anything else metal the scoutmaster might have had with him get hot enough to burn him? Ruppelt felt the answer was that 'he was-n't under the UFO for more than a few seconds...He did feel some heat, possibly radiating from the ground.'

And what about the sharp, pungent odour? Ozone gas is sharp and pungent, Ruppelt said. Then, quoting from a chemistry book, he noted that 'Ozone is prepared by passing air between two plates which are charged at a high electrical potential,' adding that 'breathing too high a concentration of ozone gas will also cause you to lose consciousness.

Ruppelt said he ran his idea by a scientist with the RAND Corporation, 'who practically leaped at the idea.' When Ruppelt explained he thought his theory 'just happened to tie together the unanswered aspects' of the Desvergers case, the scientist replied in some exasperation, 'What do you want? Does a UFO have to come in and land on your desk?'

Finally, we are left with two choices. Either the Desvergers case was one of the best hoaxes in UFO history, or, as UFO historian Jerome Clark put it, 'the ufologist's worst nightmare: a real experience which happened to an unreliable individual.'

JAMES MOSELEY IS A LEGEND IN HIS OWN TIME, ONE WHICH JUST HAPPENS TO LARGELY COINCIDE WITH THAT OF THE MODERN UFO. NOT ONLY HE IS STILL ALIVE, UNLIKE MANY OF HIS CONTEMPORARIES AND EARLY PIONEERS IN THE FIELD, HE IS STILL ACTIVE – TO THE CONSTERNATION OF SOME, AND THE DELIGHT OF OTHERS. FOR MANY NEWCOMERS AND OLDSTERS ALIKE, MOSELEY'S IRREVERENT AND NOT INFRE-QUENTLY SCATOLOGICAL NEWSLETTER, SAUCER SMEAR, IS MUST READING, WHEREAS HIS MAIN DETRACTORS AND CRITICS CAN'T QUITE BE BOTHERED, CONSIDERING SAME AN EXERCISE IN JOURNALIS-TIC JUVENALIA AT BEST, AND ONE THAT LONG AGO RAN ITS COURSE AT THAT. TRADITIONALLY CIRCULATED ONLY IN A XEROX FORMAT MAILED FREE TO SELECT 'NON-SUBSCRIBERS' – ALTHOUGH DONATIONS ARE ALWAYS WELCOME – SAUCER SMEAR IS NOW AVAILABLE TO THE MASSES ON-LINE. POINT YOUR WEB BROWSER TO HTTP://WWW.MCS.COM/~KVG/SMEAR.HTM.

AMONG MOSELEY'S VARIOUS CAREERS AT ONE TIME OR ANOTHER WERE THOSE OF A DEALER IN SOUTH AMERICAN ANTIQUITIES (SPECIALISING IN PRE-COLUMBIAN PERUVIAN ARTIFACTS), ART GALLERY OWNER, AND KEY WEST, FLORIDA, LANDLORD. WE ACCEPT THE FOLLOWING ACCOUNT AS ENTIRELY ACCURATE – TO THE BEST OF ITS AUTHOR'S MEMORY AND NOTES, AND UNTIL ADVISED OTHERWISE. MOSELEY CAN BE REACHED IN WRITING AT PO BOX 1709, KEY WEST, FLORIDA, 33041.

UFOS OUT WEST

by James Moseley

Back in the autumn of 1953, after having dropped out of college in search of something more adventurous, I made a trip by car all around the country, interviewing people who were mentioned in the early flying saucer books written by Major Donald Keyhoe, Frank Scully, George Adamski, and others. I intended to write a book of my own, which never materialised. Fortunately, I made detailed typewritten notes of all these interviews, so in a sense they are still fresh in my mind after all these years. Little did I realise then that, instead of investigating a passing fad, I was getting in on the ground floor of a movement which, as we all know, persists more strongly than ever to this very day.

Many of my most interesting interviews were in the Los Angeles area, where a group of engineers led by a man named Ed Sullivan (no relation to the famous TV entertainer) had organised a semi-scientific group called Civilian Saucer Intelligence (CSI) as far back a 1951. An unrelated New York City group with the same name came along a couple of years later, as did APRO (Aerial Phenomena Research Organization) and finally NICAP (National Investigations Committee on Aerial Phenomena).

In late 1953 I had already missed the first and greatest of the many UFO conventions held at Giant Rock, in the California desert, hosted by contactee George Van Tassel; and I had also missed the first indoor UFO convention hosted by Max Miller at the old Hollywood Hotel, which has long since been torn down. Miller was a bright young photographer with an interest in the paranormal, whereas Van Tassel was a pilot of sorts with an obvious interest in outer space.

Through his contacts with extraterrestrials, George Van Tassel was given instructions on how to build a unique edifice called the Integretron, which was financed with donations from wealthy followers. The Integretron served as fountain of youth

because of the magnetic energy which supposedly flowed under its circular dome. People who went inside the empty dome didn't look younger when they came out, but they felt younger!

Perhaps my most amusing interview in Los Angeles was with an actor and movie producer named Michael Conrad, who was responsible for the 1950 B-film called *The Flying Saucer*. When I tracked Conrad down one afternoon at a seedy apartment building, he was apparently on the skids. He was drinking heavily with a fellow he introduced as his cameraman, and at first he refused to open the door as he thought I was a process server.

Once Conrad was assured that I 'only' wanted to talk about flying saucers, he let me in and became very talkative indeed. The producer weaved a yarn concerning 900 feet of authentic UFO film he had shot in Alaska, most of which had sadly been confiscated by the Government. They took all the good parts, which included footage of Conrad walking up to a landed saucer and conversing at some length with the pilot, who was 'frightening in appearance.' The less exciting unconfiscated UFO footage was used on the actual movie; but all I remember from having seen the movie is that the saucer scenes looked dreadfully fake and poorly done.

Then there is the long-forgotten story of the Two Men from Venus, who approached *Los Angeles Times* reporter Maurice Beam in late 1952 or early 1953. Beam would not talk to me, as he expected to make a lot of money from selling the story; but other informants gave me the outline:

> These two fairly ordinary looking men came up to Beam at his job one day and said they were from Venus and that they wanted to be hired by the newspaper. Beam asked them to prove their interplanetary origin, and at that point one of them leaned over Beam's desk and made a deep gouge in it with his thumb. The next day Beam presented the same Venusian with a metal bar he had made, and the fellow made a gouge in it that later analysis (supposedly) showed would take 1,700 pounds of pressure to produce!
>
> After the first day there was only one Venusian, who gave his name as Wheeler. Beam got him a job at the Bureau of Missing Persons, and it is said that he had phenomenal success in locating people during the week or so he worked there. Wheeler supposedly quit and disappeared forever when it looked as though he could not avoid getting publicity, even though one would think his reason for coming to the *Times* in the first place was to get publicity.
>
> A later check of records at the Bureau of Missing Persons did not confirm that anyone named Wheeler had worked there during that period. Furthermore, Beam is known to have confessed to a few close friends that the whole story was – not surprisingly – a hoax.

My next story is a bit more unnerving. In November of 1953, very shortly before I arrived in Los Angeles, two young men really did disappear mysteriously. They were electricians, Karl Hunrath and Wilbur J. Wilkinson, who were married men who had left their families for personal reasons and moved into a small apartment together. There they apparently channelled messages from spacemen, studied strange texts, and put up posters on their walls filled with weird symbols from an alien language.

Eventually they were told by their interplanetary friends to rent an airplane and rendezvous with a flying saucer that would take them from our atmosphere to the planet Mars. The two men, neither of whom was an experienced pilot, went to the

Gardena Airport in Los Angeles, and took off in a small plane, without filing the required flight plan. They have never been seen again. The FBI investigated, but never solved the case as far as anyone knows. The two were believed to have fled to Mexico, to escape various debts and other problems, but there is no proof that this is what actually happened.

Legend has it that the plane was never found, either. Of course, it could have crashed in the Pacific Ocean or even in the nearby mountains, simply by running out of fuel. A fascinating line in my detailed notes on this case states that the plane may have been found carefully and wilfully dismantled, but not damaged as in a crash. At this late date I have no idea where I heard this rumour, which I was never able to check out.

Hunrath and Wilkinson told a few close friends ahead of time about their plan to fly to Mars in a flying saucer. One of these friends was a former Army sergeant named Jerrold Baker, whom I met briefly in 1953 but came to know much better in later years. He finally died just recently. Baker was a key figure in the early California UFO scene, as he was involved not only with these two contactees but also with humourist Frank Scully, author of the classic *Behind the Flying Saucers* (1950), and with the events related in George Adamski's first and most famous book, *Flying Saucers Have Landed*.

Even today, many ufologists are aware of Adamski's first alleged space contact in 1952, near Desert Center, California, as related in the above-mentioned book. Although most of the pages were devoted to historical UFO sightings as told by British researcher Desmond Leslie, it was Adamski's few pages at the end of the book that received almost all of the nation-wide attention.

Baker was then living with Adamski and a hard core of UFO devotees on a small property on the road to Mount Palomar Observatory. He did not accompany Adamski and six others to the site where they were supposedly met on the desert by a Venusian; but he is credited with having taken one of the close-up photos in the book (taken elsewhere) – a picture which he later claimed was taken by Adamski himself and falsely credited to him just to make it look like Adamski was not the only one who could take such startling pictures.

I, of course, made it a point to meet George Adamski while on the West Coast. I spent a whole afternoon interviewing him at the little bar-restaurant on the property where he lived. Some people believed that he worked there, or that he owned the place. Actually, he was a Kato Kaelin sort of guy, whose landlady was a true believer, and allowed him to 'hold court' in the restaurant when friends, fans, or reporters came by. Some of these visitors were shocked to see that this great saucer guru would actually drink beer, right in front of them!

The George Adamski story is a long and complex affair, but suffice it to say that I interviewed not only the Master himself but also, separately, five of his six witnesses to the Desert Center contact. It turns out that no one but Adamski himself actually saw the Venusian or the 'scout ship' from which he emerged, as the others were all kept at a distance estimated to be a half mile to one mile away.

Worse, according to information I received from Jerrold Baker and others, the whole event was pre-planned rather than spontaneous, in that part of the group had listened to a channelled tape recording that told them just where to go, what to bring with them, etc. Adamski basically succeeded in hoaxing his own little circle of followers in order to better hoax the public!

And yet, Adamski was far from being an evil man, and he had a charisma which impressed me. He was a poorly educated Polish immigrant who became an American citizen by serving in World War I. In the 1930s and 1940s he ran various 'mystery schools,' then latched onto UFOs in the early 1950s when they first became fashionable.

Apparently Adamski sincerely believed much nonsense, such as the idea that the solar system consists of twelve planets, all of which are inhabited by benign intelligent beings physically similar to ourselves. In a letter to Jerrold Baker, of which I used to have a copy, he made the classic statement (regarding the photo falsely credited to Baker in the book): 'Sometimes you have to use the back door to get the truth across.' Adamski, who died in 1965, is buried in Arlington National Cemetery.

I found it amusing that most of the early saucer writers and contactees supported each others' stories, at least in public, though quiet back stabbing was as common in the field then as it is today. Thus Adamski, who saw beautiful live Venusians who looked just like us, accepted Frank Scully's accounts of dead little humanoids who had supposedly crashed their spaceships in various parts of the southwestern desert in the late 1940s.

Scully, author of *Behind the Flying Saucers*, had seen nothing himself but received his information from a friend named Silas Newton and from a mysterious 'Dr. Gee.' Scully and company were thoroughly exposed in a famous article in *True* magazine (September, 1952) by a professional writer named J.R. Cahn; but the true believers continued to believe, as always.

I met Frank Scully at his very comfortable home near Hollywood, and spent several hours with him there. People have never given enough thought to the fact that as a writer Scully was a professional humourist. His main claim to fame was a humourous column in *Variety*, the weekly showbiz newspaper. One can hardly help wondering whether he had his tongue firmly in his cheek when he wrote his ufological best seller.

In person, Scully was not very funny at all, but he did not seem particularly upset that Cahn had blown his story out of the water – partly by exposing Newton as a professional confidence man. 'Dr. Gee' was said to be a fellow named Leo Gebauer who was a partner of Newton's in the oil business, but Scully claimed that 'Gee' was actually a composite of eight different people who had given him information.

Cover for Frank Scully's discredited crash retreival book

If there was ever any doubt that Silas Newton was a confidence man, it was dispelled on December 29th, 1953, when he and Gebauer were found guilty of a complicated swindle involving fake machines that could locate underground oil. The trial took place in Newton's home town of Denver, Colorado; and by the wildest of coincidence, I arrived in Denver that very same day!

The banner front-page headline in the local paper read, 'Doodle-bug pair guilty.' I figured that it would be a difficult time to persuade Newton to do a UFO interview; but Newton, who was out on bail, was pleasant on the phone, though he did not know me at all; and thus that evening, while all of Denver was reading about the outcome of this long-drawn-out trial, I was sitting with Silas Newton talking about flying saucers, at the home of his son.

It is extremely interesting to note that neither the book *Behind the Flying Saucers*, nor Frank Scully in person, nor Newton, nor any of several other people I talked to about crashed 'little men,' ever mentioned the town of Roswell, New Mexico, or the military base near there. The crashes were given vague locations in Arizona, New Mexico and Texas, but none had details that would correspond properly with the now-famous Roswell crash of early July, 1947.

Roswell did not become a sacred shrine in the UFO religion until the publication many years later (1980) of *The Roswell Incident*, co-authored by Bermuda Triangle expert Charles Berlitz and ufologist William Moore. Actually, it was Moore, with some help from Stanton Friedman, who did much of the research for the book. In a sense, one could say that Moore 'created' Roswell, just as he 'created' the notorious MJ-12 documents a few years later (1987). It is amazing that Roswell, now the subject of numerous books, articles, TV presentations, etc., continues to grow bigger every year, while the similar stories told by Scully and his friends in the early 1950s are now all but forgotten.

The thing I always liked best about Scully's crashed saucers was the 'system of nines.' We were asked to believe that the saucers had dimensions like '99 feet, 9 inches,' which would supposedly indicate that these space people used nine rather than ten as the basis of their mathematical system. Of course this is ludicrous, since feet and inches are rather awkward, arbitrary measurements used only in certain parts of the planet Earth, and have nothing to do with any 'system of nines', if there ever was one!

And the part I enjoyed most during my interview with Newton was when he solemnly told me in great detail about a man from Venus who had walked up to a business man's desk and made a deep gouge in the desk with his thumb. It was the Maurice Beam story all over again, which I had already disproved – this time told by a man who had just been convicted of oil fraud that very day!

Not all the people I interviewed on my western trip were contactees, kooks, or con men, however. Among the saner voices were Al Chop and Edward Ruppelt, key figures in Major Donald Keyhoe's early UFO books. [Albert M. Chop, a civilian, was UFO press liaison for the Air Force Office of Public Information in the early 1950s; Captain Ruppelt, author of the classic *The Report on Unidentified Flying Objects* (1956), was head of the Air Force's UFO investigative agency, Project Grudge and later Blue Book, during the same period – eds.] When I met them together in Los Angeles, they had both recently retired from the Air Force and had gone into private industry. Although they disagreed on the validity of certain well-known UFO sightings, they were good friends, and neither was inclined to believe in the reality of interplanetary saucers.

Others I interviewed included

George van Tassel

scientists such as E. C. Slipher, a senior astronomer at Lowell Observatory in Flagstaff, Arizona; Dr. Frank Bowen, Director of the Mount Wilson and Mount Palomar Observatories; Dr. Walter Riedel, a senior project engineer at North American Aviation, and formerly chief designer at the rocket laboratory at Peenemunde, Germany, during World War II; and Dr. Clyde Tombaugh of the Lowell Observatory. Many years previously, Tombaugh had been the discoverer of the planet Pluto.

Naturally these men were not knowledgeable about crashed saucers or beautiful space people visiting us from Mars or Venus. Not too surprisingly, none of them believed in interplanetary flying saucers as a proven reality – though at that time I did, and I would have been delighted to obtain a strong positive statement from any of these gentlemen.

Over the years my own views have changed, and I now believe that UFOs are phenomena beyond our present knowledge and understanding – probably in some way part of the Earth's own environment, and probably part of the over-all spectrum of paranormal events – none of which are fully understandable or provable at our present level of science.

From my current perspective, I look back on my interview with Clyde Tombaugh as the most interesting and significant of all, though at the time I was frustrated because I could not get him to 'admit' that his famous sighting in August, 1949 was of an interplanetary saucer. This sighting had been written up in an important UFO article in *Life* magazine in 1952.

Dr. Tombaugh, interviewed at his home in Las Cruces, New Mexico, told me (as he had told many others) of the evening in 1949 when, while sitting outdoors, he saw an apparently solid object directly overhead, which then moved to the SSE in about three seconds, and disappeared at a height of 35 or 40 degrees above the horizon. It was yellowish-green in colour, and had about ten rectangular lights arranged in a symmetrical pattern. His wife was with him, and she noticed a faint glow coming from the object as a whole, though he did not; but he too believed it was one solid object because of the way the lights held their pattern and because of the symmetry.

It was a cloudless night, and Tombaugh had no way of knowing the size or height of the object. Interestingly, he stated that in spite of his scientific background, he was very unnerved by the experience, and therefore failed to study the object as carefully as he would have liked to do. He refused to express an opinion as to its origin.

There you have it, folks. Something is up there, or maybe even down here among us. But after almost half a century of the flying saucer era (going back to the Kenneth Arnold sighting in 1947), we enthusiasts are no closer to a provable, scientific answer than we were back then. Nonsense prevails, and the manure gets deeper every year. But my fascination with the subject continues, and I only hope that I – or any one of us – live long enough to solve the mystery.

IF FLYING SAUCERS WERE BRINGING RESIDENTS OF OTHER WORLDS TO VISIT OUR PLANET IN SUCH NUMBERS, IT COULD ONLY BE A MATTER OF TIME BEFORE CONTACT WOULD BE MADE BETWEEN US AND THEM. MANY THOUGHT THAT SUCH CONTACT SHOULD BE WITH HEADS OF STATE – NUMEROUS CARTOONS FEATURED LITTLE GREEN MEN CONFRONTING BEMUSED EARTHLINGS WITH THE REQUEST 'TAKE ME TO YOUR LEADER!' BUT IN FACT THE CONTACTEES TENDED TO BE JUST PLAIN FOLK. THEY CLAIMED TO HAVE BEEN CHOSEN FOR THEIR INDIVIDUAL ATTRIBUTES OF PERCEPTION, SENSITIVITY AND OPEN-MINDEDNESS, BUT TO OTHERS THEIR MOST NOTABLE CHARACTERISTICS WERE THE BRAZEN EFFRONTERY WITH WHICH THEY TOLD THEIR IMPROBABLE STORIES AND THE DOGGEDNESS WITH WHICH THEY STUCK TO THEM HOWEVER MUCH THEIR IMPROBABILITIES WERE POINTED OUT.

THE FIRST CONTACTEE TO MAKE A PUBLIC AFFIRMATION OF HIS EXPERIENCE WAS GEORGE ADAMSKI, A GENIAL, COLOURFUL CHARACTER WHO ACHIEVED WORLDWIDE FAME WITH HIS EXTRAVAGANT CLAIMS. IT MAY HAVE BEEN PRECISELY HIS EXTRAVAGANCE WHICH DISARMED SCEPTICS ON THE ONE HAND, AND GENERATED UNCRITICAL ADULATION ON THE OTHER. HIS BOOKS WERE WIDELY TRANSLATED: HE TOURED THE WORLD GIVING LECTURES AND SIGNING HIS BEST-SELLING BOOKS. ADAMSKI-ITE ORGANISATIONS SPRANG UP IN MANY COUNTRIES, NOTABLY GERMANY AND DENMARK.

MARC HALLET, A BELGIAN RESEARCHER WHO HAS SINCE BECOME ONE OF THE MOST PERCEPTIVE CRITICS OF THE UFO MYTH, BEGAN HIS CAREER AS A DEVOUT BELIEVER. HIS ACCOUNT OF HIS DISILLUSIONMENT THROWS A FASCINATING LIGHT ON HOW THE WORLD AT LARGE RESPONDED TO THE SENSATIONAL CLAIMS OF THE CONTACTEES.

ADAMSKI AND HIS BELIEVERS: A REMINISCENCE

by Marc Hallet

I was a young Belgian boy of twelve when I became interested in mysteries of every kind. In a public library I found my first book on flying saucers – as UFOs were labelled in those days. It was *Les soucoupes volantes viennent d'un autre monde*, published ten years earlier, in 1954, and written by the French science-fiction writer Jimmy Guieu. (An English translation, *Flying Saucers Come From Another World*, was published in London in 1956).

For me, the most attractive and interesting chapter contained Guieu's discussion of the American-Polish contactee George Adamski. The story Adamski told was simple but extraordinary: he had met a Venusian and 'spoken' telepathically with him at Desert Center, California. Six of his friends declared that they had witnessed the meeting from a short distance. More remarkable still, Adamski had successfully captured the Venusian 'scoutship' with his camera. So far as I could judge from Guieu's account, the story, though fantastic, had the ring of truth.

To learn more about flying saucers, I went to a larger public library. It took me a while to discover that here, flying saucers were classified as 'forms of transport'! There I found some of the 'classic' UFO books which had been written originally in French, by Aimè Michel, Michel Carrouges and Lieutenant Plantier, and French translations of books by Donald Keyhoe and Edward Ruppelt. I also

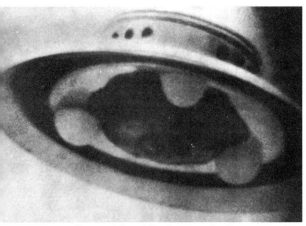
George Adamski's photograph of a supposed Venusian scout ship

found Jimmy Guieu's second non-fiction book. To my surprise, Guieu seemed to be the only one who believed in Adamski: the others dismissed him as a crackpot. However, as they provided no proof to support their assertion, I was inclined to think Adamski had been defamed. Unfortunately, I didn't at the time find a French translation of *Flying Saucers Have Landed*, written by Desmond Leslie and Adamski himself, and I was unable to learn more about this controversial case.

I became so deeply interested in flying saucers that, at the age of 14 or so, I decided to collect as much information about them as possible. In those days, xerox copies were not readily available, so I had to summarise my reading in notes on my little typewriter. How I worked!

In 1969, in a comic-strip magazine, a friend learnt there was a UFO group in Belgium: BUFOI-IGAP, an acronym standing for Belgian UFO Information – International Get Acquainted Program. Since I had, in the meantime, had found the French translation of Leslie's and Adamski's book, I wrote to this group, explaining that I was interested in saucers and especially in Adamski who, in my opinion, was by no means a crackpot. I was delighted by the answer I received, signed by Mrs May Flitcroft, the founder and President of the group. She explained to me that she was an old personal friend of George Adamski, and that IGAP was more or less the European branch of the George Adamski Foundation.

As I couldn't read English at this time, Mrs Flitcroft sent me a non-commercial French translation of *Inside The Space Ships*, Adamski's second book, published in 1956. It was a poor translation, but for me it was the most interesting UFO book I had ever read. Everything in it sounded simple and logical to me. The most exciting section was that in which Adamski describes the Moon, which he claimed to have observed in the course of a short space journey in a 'mother ship'. I was astounded by the fact that he used the same words as the Apollo 8 astronauts to describe the same things they had seen while orbiting the Moon. I decided to write a short text in which I made a precise comparison between Adamski's 1956 text and the astronauts' comments. Adamski's description was so accurate that I concluded he was telling the plain truth.

May Flitcroft published my text in her UFO bulletin. It was the first of a long series of articles I wrote to 'prove' Adamski was no liar.

Months and years passed. Little by little I learned to read English. At the same time, I became the most active co-worker of BUFOI-IGAP, and my work earned me access to all the group's archives, including the personal correspondence between May Flitcroft and George Adamski. In 1973 May asked me to write a book about Adamski; he had died in 1965, and she hoped to rehabilitate him in 1975. It was a challenge I was glad to accept.

In order to make a serious study, I decided to examine all the facts chronologically. First, my data had to be arranged methodically: this I did, and now for the first time I discovered some contradictions in Adamski's statements. I asked May Flitcroft, but to my surprise she was unable to answer my questions. She decided to ask help from Alice Wells, at the headquarters of the George Adamski Foundation in California. Alice Wells never answered these embarrassing questions.

May Flitcroft had two copies of some of the most interesting Adamski films which showed UFOs flying in different landscape settings. Convinced that these were genuine, she willingly gave them to me to conduct a serious examination. First, I showed them to a photographic expert who made some interesting comments. Then I examined some portions under microscope. This was the beginning of the end.

The microscope revealed a classic trick: two images had been superimposed. I was astonished, but not yet discouraged. Even though I was now sure that Adamski had not invariably told the truth, I did not consider this sufficient reason to reject everything he said.

At that time, May Flitcroft had gone to California, to visit her old friend Alice Wells at the Adamski Foundation. I suppose she told her that the films were about to be scrutinised by one or several experts; this is the only way I can explain her total change of attitude when she returned to Belgium. She demanded her films back, immediately. I copied them and gave them back to May, who seemed furious and anxious. I supposed that Alice Wells knew the films had been tricked, and had threatened May if her actions led to embarrassing disclosures.

After that it was impossible for me to continue to work for BUFOI, so in December 1976 I resigned. Some weeks later, I received a cordial letter from a young French publisher, Michel Moutet. He had read some of my articles and had been impressed by them. He offered to publish any articles or books I might write. I suggested a book on the Adamski case. He said yes, and asked me also to make a French translation of Adamski's second and third books, *Inside The Space Ships* and *Flying Saucers Farewell*.

I started work on a critical biography of Adamski. At this time, no one had written a UFO book based on the principles of historical criticism, so I had to work out my own method of approaching the subject. However, I made a fundamental error: any statement by Adamski which I did not know to be false, I accepted as true.

After some months I sent my finished manuscript to my publisher. My conclusions were that the first contact at Desert Center, together with the photographs of the Venusian 'scout-ship', were authentic, but that the later contacts and all the pseudo 'cosmic philosophy' were the fraudulent concoctions of Adamski himself, intended to make money and increase his reputation. My publisher was satisfied, and urged me to translate the two books which he proposed to publish before my critical book. This I did, but in the meantime Moutet ran into financial difficulties, and my book on Adamski was postponed.

Several years passed. I continued to collect information about Adamski. Gradually, I became convinced that the first contact and the earliest photos were as fraudulent as the rest. I told my ufologist friends of my disillusion, but when I proposed to completely rewrite my book, Moutet refused; the most he would allow me to do was to change the chapter where I explained how the films had been tricked. Consequently, when my book was eventually published in 1983, my acquaintances were disturbed to find that the views expressed in it were quite different from what I had communicated to them in private. I explained the situation in a privately printed publication *Choc en retour*, and subsequently published two further texts on Adamski: *The Adamski Sectarians* (1984) and *George Adamski: Last Synthesis* (1994). In the latter I demonstrated that Adamski had been a professional liar who had duped his followers throughout his life.

After my departure from BUFOI, May Flitcroft encountered difficulties publishing her UFO bulletin (since 1974 I had been its principal contributor). Her husband Keith, a longtime Adamski believer from Australia, tried to promote Adamski's 'Cosmic Philosophy' through the pages of the bulletin. But this soap philosophy, mixing Christianity, Buddhism, Theosophy and spiritism, was not to the taste of the members who had appreciated the articles I had been contributing. The number of subscribers fell off rapidly, and finally the bulletin came to an abrupt end. Some months later BUFOI itself was dismantled, and May and Keith left Belgium for Australia. I never heard from them again.

THE HEIRS OF ADAMSKI

When Adamski died in 1965, he left behind him many fans and personal friends. These friends chose Alice K. Wells as leader of the George Adamski Foundation, based in California, and recognised Major Hans Petersen, of Denmark, as leader of the IGAP in Europe. Many former followers who had already turned away from Adamski – such as Carol Honey (USA), Lou Zinsstag (Switzerland), Karl Veit (Germany), and Alberto Perego (Italy) – did not join these posthumous organisations. By the 1970s, the oldest and most loyal Adamski-ites were undoubtedly Alice Wells, May, Petersen, and Dora Bauer in Austria. None of them sought to take Adamski's place, but in the United States a bizarre contest sprang up.

After Adamski's death, several of his close acquaintances affirmed they had had contacts with the Venusian Orthon, whom Adamski had met at Desert Center, and with other 'space brothers'. This second wave of contactees included Madeleine Rodeffer, Steve Within, Fred Steckling and Charlotte Blodget, to mention only the best known. Steckling and Blodget came to Europe, as Adamski himself had done, to give lectures and to meet Flitcroft, Bauer and Petersen. Berlin-born Steckling even went so far as to publish a book, *Why Are They Here?*, dedicated to the memory of Adamski and with an introduction by Blob, including stills from a film he made in September 1966 of a fleet of saucers over Germany.

Each of these 'contactees' sought to persuade Adamski's followers that he or she was the one true successor. When Alice Wells refused to recognise any of them, they created their own more or less formal groups. Despite their quarrels and jealousies, each claimed to teach the 'universal cosmic brotherhood' taught by the Space Brothers!

The death of Alice Wells in 1980, at the age of 80, left a leadership gap at the George Adamski Foundation which Fred Steckling promptly filled. In the following year he published *We Discovered Alien Bases On The Moon* which enjoyed some commercial success. The book was based entirely on a study made by Major Petersen in Denmark during the 1970s, and which I had severely criticised at the time; needless to say, Steckling mentions neither Petersen's theories nor my criticisms in his book. Nor did he see fit to mention that he was a contactee and a follower of Adamski.

Steckling died in 1991. His son is said to have tried to take over the Foundation, but by now this institution had dwindled to nothing, for all Adamski's former followers had either died, drifted away or resigned in disgust.

For years, Adamski's faithful followers had waited, hopefully, for the coming of the Space Brothers. Little by little, their faith crumbled as they had to accept that their 'master' had not always told them the truth. One after the other, they were obliged to admit that there was no life on the Moon, nor on Venus, nor on Mars or Saturn. Yet Adamski had stated the contrary. To begin with, the Adamskiites speculated that he had lied in order to protect the Space Brothers' true origin. But protect them against what, against whom? Sadly, they had to concede that this explanation explained nothing.

HOW COULD THE BELIEVERS BELIEVE?

Some of my critics have asked me openly: How was it possible for me to believe the absurd claims of this ridiculous 'contactee'?

First of all: I was young when I discovered Adamski. At that time there was no historical criticism in the UFO field: cases were judged only by the standards of simple logic and scientific feasibility. When I began to exchange letters with May Flitcroft, and later when I delved into her personal files and library, I found so many apparent proofs that Adamski was not a liar, that I allowed myself to be convinced. In a short time, I learned that he had taken films 'impossible to fake'; that he had been congratulated for his work by a senior official of the U.S. Department of Cultural Exchange (the famous 'Straith Letter' which was later revealed as a hoax); that he had been granted a royal audience by Queen Juliana of the Netherlands; that he had been privileged to pass the message of the Space Brothers to Pope John XXIII and had been awarded the prestigious Vatican Medal in acknowledgement of his work. There were even suggestions that he had been taken seriously by the Secretary-General of the United Nations and by President Kennedy – how could I fail to be impressed?

Bear in mind, moreover, that the stories that Adamski told were far more believable than those being told today by the abductees, who claim to be raped by strange grey monsters who can pass through walls and land their spaceships wherever they choose without being seen.

On a scientific level, too, Adamski's claims had not yet been invalidated by the knowledge we have acquired by our space explorations. As recently as the 1970s, the possibility of life on Mars and Venus was still a matter for debate: a substantial literature existed about 'strange things on the Moon' and 'Transient Lunar Phenomena'. Some of the descriptions given by Adamski concerning the Moon and space itself were uncannily accurate. The 'fireflies' which he described, for instance, seemed to be the same as those subsequently reported by the astronauts.

It took me a certain time to discover that the fireflies reported by the astronauts couldn't be the same phenomenon as that described by Adamski. It took a while, too, to obtain certain proof that Adamski's 'Vatican Medal' was not an official award, because nobody before me had thought of directing an inquiry to professional numismatists at Rome. Above all, it took time to persuade May Flitcroft to lend me her precious films: Adamski had told her the CIA would steal them if anyone tried to make copies in a professional laboratory!

Adamski knew perfectly how to exploit the paranoia which was latent in the minds of his believers. May Flitcroft, like all his followers, was convinced that there existed a great conspiracy to suppress the truth about life on other planets. For her as for the others, the Moon photographs taken by the Ranger and Lunar Orbiters had been retouched by an army of professional silencers. The professional astronomers were either ignorant, or were accomplices of the CIA. Some of the robots, launched towards Mars and Venus, had been programmed by the

CIA to send back false data. But the true conditions of life on Venus were well-known to the U.S. authorities, for the Space Brothers had taken a 16mm camera to Venus, and then returned it to the U.S. government. Why was the truth about the Space Brothers suppressed? Because they knew the secret of free energy. And what would happen if the secret of free energy was released? The oil companies and the banks would face bankruptcy and a catastrophic collapse which would be the end of our monetary system. So the international bankers, and especially the Jews who had killed Jesus because he threatened the money order, were obliged to suppress the truth about our Space Brothers… these conspiracy theories formed the paranoid credo of the Adamski believers.

Never short of imagination, Adamski was always one step ahead of his imitators. He was the first contactee to go round the Moon in a spaceship. He was the first to visit Venus and to see there his dead wife reincarnated. He was the first to go to Saturn in a 'dematerialised' space ship, to attend a Universal Council where a Christus (who was not Jesus) was also present. He was the first contactee to speak of wonderful extraterrestrial crystals ; he had one with which he claimed to cure certain illnesses.

His own life history was continually changing to promote his 'philosophy' and earn him money. Back in the 1930s he had claimed to have been initiated in Tibet, and created a monastic order to diffuse his teachings. Later he published a science-fiction novel (written for him by Lucy McGinnis) based on space trips to Mars and the Moon. In this novel, a space 'Master' presents a 'cosmic philosophy' which anticipates that of the Space Brothers. When flying saucers became news, he claimed to have photographed them through his telescope. Then came his claim to have encountered a Venusian, which brought him a fantastic success. He told Charlotte Blodget stories based on his old science-fiction novel, which she summarised and published as *Inside The Space Ships*. Until his death, he continued to create stories of all kinds: in the 1960s he planned a huge Cosmic Village in Guadalajara, Mexico, from which his Cosmic Philosophy would be passed on to the world.

Of all his stories, there was one which particularly excited his followers. Many of the Space Brothers, he assured them, actually live on Earth, where they have 'missions' of all kinds to accomplish. So, for the Adamski believer, there was always the possibility one might meet a brother or a sister from space.

Imagine we are in the Sixties, and that a friend of yours, John Smith, is a dedicated Adamski believer. He has a desperate longing to meet a space person; the thought obsesses him. He even sends, through intersideral space, telepathic messages to the Space Brothers. Then one day John is queuing at his post office. Just to his left, in another line, there is a tall man, well dressed. His skin is tanned, his hair is brown, he has blue eyes. He wears no glasses, no hat. To you and me he looks perfectly normal; but to John he looks strange… there is something 'special', indefinable, about him. He thinks, 'Maybe he could be one of them'. He is flooded with a strange feeling; his feverish anxiety confirms the reality: this man is a Space Brother, for sure. The man looks around him. His eyes fall on John, who is so convinced he is looking at a space man that he smiles at him, like a child. The stranger is surprised, but politely he smiles in return. Now John is certain: He is one of them! He has captured my thoughts telepathically! The man looks at his watch, decides to leave. You and I would conclude that he has an appointment and can't wait any longer, but John interprets his departure differently. He knows that I know who he is, but for reasons of security he cannot make contact with me!

John is delighted by the episode. He has met a Space Brother. They have exchanged telepathic messages. A Brother has given him a sign. It is all proof that Adamski is right.

Incredible? Yet I heard many such stories in the 1960s and 1970s, from the friends and followers of George Adamski.

But do not think that those friends and followers had lost all their critical sense, that they believed every contactee story they heard. Quite the contrary. Adamski had warned them that many contactees were cranks and frauds who wrote about saucers only to make money. For he regarded contacteeism as his personal copyright: no one else could meet the Space Brothers without his blessing. One day he learnt that Elizabeth Klarer in South Africa had met a Space Brother. He exploded with fury and said, in the presence of contactee Laura Mundo, 'She has stolen my idea!'

When, in the sixties, he realised that his right-hand co-worker, Carol Honey, was speaking openly about his few contacts with the brothers, Adamski reacted violently. He created a new scenario. He wrote to all his colleagues and friends telling them that Carol had been contacted by a new group of space people, a group of evil space travellers who were here to invade our planet. The result was a schism. Many rejected Honey's claims, but a few decided that it was Adamski who was no longer credible, and chose to follow Honey. The controversy lasted until Adamski's death, after the two groups of followers went their separate ways.

Adamski's first book took his story to a wider audience

Some of Adamski's friends were intelligent liars who claimed contacts with the space people only to make money and to be cherished by naïve followers. Others deluded themselves and became the victims of the adventurers and intriguers. Some naïve women welcomed young men into their homes and gave them money because they told them they were Venusians, recently landed on Earth and, of course, without financial resources. In some cases, the young men would explain they were here to accomplish a special mission which consisted in 'crossing the energies' between Venus and Earth. This was effected by performing sexual acts with Earth-women. No doubt some of these ladies were delighted to make love with the young men in such a good cause.

Sex is often the means whereby the leader of a sect retains the loyalty of his female followers. George Adamski was an exception. Nevertheless, his personal fascination constituted a kind of amorous link, which captivated them and made them admiring, docile and obedient. I am sure that if he had wished it, many of the women who surrounded him would have happily fallen into his arms. But even though he was married, Adamski seemed to prefer young male adolescents, which is perhaps why he depicted the Venusian he met at Desert Center as a beautiful young man, why he met young 'extraterrestrials' only in hotels and why he had no more money on him after these meetings.

ALTHOUGH UFOS ARE ALMOST UNIVERSALLY ASSOCIATED IN THE CONTEMPORARY MIND WITH 'LIT-TLE GREEN (OR GREY) MEN,' IT WASN'T ALWAYS SO. MUCH IN THE UFO FIELD ISN'T ALWAYS AS IT SEEMS, AND THE EXTRATERRESTRIAL HYPOTHESIS IS NO EXCEPTION. LIKE ANY WORKING HYPOTHESIS, IT FIRST HAD TO EARN ITS WINGS, AS REVEALED BELOW.

ONE OF THE LEADING PROPONENTS OF ALIEN VISITATION, JEROME CLARK HAS BEEN INVES-TIGATING ANOMALOUS PHENOMENA FOR MORE THAN 30 YEARS. TODAY HE IS VICE PRESIDENT OF THE J. ALLEN HYNEK CENTER FOR UFO STUDIES (CUFOS) AND EDITOR OF THE CENTER'S QUARTER-LY INTERNATIONAL UFO REPORTER. HIS BOOKS INCLUDE THE ENCYCLOPEDIA OF STRANGE AND UNEXPLAINED PHYSICAL PHENOMENA (1993, REPRINTED IN AN ABRIDGED, PAPERBACK FORMAT AS UNEXPLAINED!), AND A MASSIVE, THREE-VOLUME UFO ENCYCLOPEDIA, CONSISTING OF UFOS IN THE 1980S (1990), THE EMERGENCE OF A PHENOMENON: UFOS FROM THE BEGINNING THROUGH 1959 (1992), AND HIGH STRANGENESS: UFOS FROM 1969 THROUGH 1979 (1996). CLARK HAS JUST COMPLETED A DIRECTORY OF UFO ORGANISATIONS, PERIODICALS, AND MUSEUMS SCHEDULED TO BE PUBLISHED LATER THIS YEAR.

MEETING THE EXTRATERRESTRIALS: HOW THE ETH WAS INVENTED

by Jerome Clark

It was Charles Fort who wrote the first UFO book (*The Book of the Damned*) and so created what would one day be called ufology, and it happened 28 years before Kenneth Arnold's June 24, 1947, sighting inspired the coining of the phrase 'flying saucers,' with all that implied. But before Fort others had won-dered, if only passingly, if space visitors had come to earth.

Widespread reports of 'airships' – cigar-shaped UFOs in modern parlance – between November 1896 and May 1897 had encouraged both speculation and hoaxers playing to the idea. Until *Damned*'s publication in 1919, however, such the-ories, with only the rarest and most obscure exception (for instance a 1909 letter in a New Zealand newspaper attributing local airship reports to 'a serious recon-naissance from Mars'), disappeared from print and popular consciousness.

In *Damned* and two successors (*New Lands* [1923] and *Lo!* [1931]) Fort created the first version of the extraterrestrial hypothesis (ETH), though the term itself would not be invented until the late 1960s, and by a man hostile both to it and to the idea that UFO reports represent anything at all. ('Extraterrestrial hypothesis' and 'ETH' were the creation of physicist Edward U. Condon, who headed the controversial Air Force-sponsored University of Colorado UFO Project in the late 1960s.) Fort's hypothesising, in any case, was done haphazardly, mostly in asides, and amid many jokes; he was, it should be stressed, foremostly a satirist. It is not always easy to tell when he was serious. His occasional letters to newspapers, composed in more straightforward style, indicate (if any readers of his books doubted it) a sincere conviction that extraterrestrial craft, artifacts, beings, and creatures have been and are present on earth.

Essentially Fort argued as follows:

Visitors from a multitude of worlds have come to earth over the centuries. They may have even affected the course of evolution and once been mistaken for gods, demons, or phantoms. These beings come here for a variety of reasons. Some have a profound interest in the human race. Some are little more than tourists. Some may be in communication with selected earthlings, while others seek open contact with all humans. Their ships are seen on or beneath the ocean surface and have been mistaken for sea serpents. The aliens may be responsible for mysterious disappearances of people and ships. Some strange forms observed in the atmosphere are themselves living entities.

In 1931 Fort's friend Tiffany Thayer founded the Fortean Society to continue what Fort had done: to collect and record reports of aerial and other anomalous physical phenomena. Fort himself died in 1932, but the society survived until 1960. Throughout the 1930s and into the mid-1940s its publication, *The Fortean Society Magazine* (later *Doubt*), was the only one to hold extraterrestrial visitation possible and to seek evidence for it. Its influence and visibility were negligible, though occasionally science-fiction writers made use of Fortean themes, most memorably Eric Frank Russell in *Sinister Barrier* (1939).

In the early 1940s articles on Fortean phenomena began to appear in two Ziff-Davis science-fiction pulps, *Amazing Stories* and *Fantastic Adventures*, owing to editor Ray Palmer's strange obsession with what he called the 'Shaver mystery.' Pennsylvania welder Richard Sharpe Shaver, who admitted to having been confined to mental hospitals and prisons, wrote to Palmer in 1943 to show him what purported to be an ancient alphabet from the lost (in fact never existent) continent of Lemuria. In due course Shaver's 'racial memories' of Lemurian life found expression in tales of an advanced race of giants called Atlans or Titans whom deadly solar radiation eventually forced either underground or (if they were lucky) into outer space, while others adjusted to the new surface conditions and became human. Most who remained in the caverns degenerated into sadistic idiots called deros, who torment surface-dwellers with death rays.

While Palmer's more rational readers sputtered, the more excitable, at Palmer's urging, sought 'evidence' for the continued presence of deros, teros (the embattled minority of good Atlans), and the space visitors with whom the subterraneans interacted. According to Palmer, the deros and their associates fly 'giant rockets that traverse in the upper air' and use them to travel to other planets when the occasion warrants. In *Amazing*'s April 1947 issue, Palmer even suggested an official cover-up; only the naïve could doubt, he said, that 'responsible parties in the world governments' know of 'spaceships visiting the earth'.

None of this means, as hyperbolic writers (notably John A. Keel and Roger Ford) would later assert, that Palmer 'invented flying saucers.' He did not depict the deros' 'rockets' as disc-shaped. Flying discs, it is true, do appear in an elaborate water-colour painting on the back cover of the August 1946 issue of *Amazing*, but they are not intended to represent anything more than illustrator Frank R. Paul's imagined 'scene on a planet circling Altair'.

Beyond his hold on his relatively minuscule audience of science-fiction and Fort enthusiasts, Palmer wielded no influence. When Arnold saw fast-moving flying discs over Mount Rainier, Washington, it did not occur to him that he might be viewing something from outer space. Rather he first assumed that this was a secret military test flight. Over the next few hours, however, he came to doubt that existing aviation technology could propel aircraft to the speeds (estimated to be between 1200 and 1700mph) at which the unknown objects were moving. Beyond that the unimaginative Arnold had no theories. Bill Bequette, the first reporter to interview him, recalled, 'Arnold never suggested that he had seen a spacecraft or anything like that. I believe he was just curious about what he had seen and wanted to know what it was.'

AFTER ARNOLD

Between Fort's and the first flying-saucer books in 1950, only R. DeWitt Miller's *Forgotten Mysteries*, released in the spring of 1947, put theories about space visitation between hard covers. In this thin work (in both the literal and figurative senses), culled from columns the author had written on psychic and Fortean phenomena for the popular digest *Coronet*, Miller devoted a single chapter to 'Enigmas out of Space.' Most of these 'enigmas' are unrelated to UFO reports, but he does take note of 'modern speculation' that 'conscious beings from other worlds have actually reached this earth and navigated our skies in space ships.' Miller, who credits the notion to Fort, goes on to recount three representative sightings from 1882, 1893, and 1913.

Though his book was little read, Miller would influence popular perceptions of 'flying discs' in the wake of Arnold's sighting. If we can judge from press accounts, alien spacecraft at first played no role in speculations about the identity and origin of the mysterious objects. On June 28 Bequette summarised the assorted theories in a feature for Pendleton's *East Oregonian*. The explanations ranged from 'heated circular exhaust pipes of jet airplanes' to guided missiles to light reflected off aircraft wings to war nerves to mirages to 'whisperings of Russian secret weapons'. As the days passed and the sightings continued, other solutions – 'transmutation of atomic energy',' meteors, 'red corpuscles of blood passing in front of the eyes', hysteria – were bandied about, along with growing suspicions about American and Soviet secret weapons.

A United Press dispatch on July 4 listed what it deemed the three leading explanations – meteorological phenomena, meteorites, aircraft from 'some foreign power' – and mentioned, in passing, 'a San Francisco layman's flat assertion that the [discs] were "space ships" from other planets.' This 'layman' may well have been associated with his city's active Fortean community, large enough to rival the New York-based Fortean Society. The next day, in a brief item, International News Service quoted an unnamed Detroit meteorologist's suggestion that the discs might be 'signals from Mars'.

July 7 and 8 were the breakout days for extraterrestrial hypothesising in press accounts. On the first date two press-wire dispatches out of Chicago, in implicit challenges to popular wisdom about the discs, noted that strange aerial objects were nothing new. Associated Press mentioned 'a rare book in Chicago's Newberry Library' – Fort's *Book of the Damned* – which revealed that 'reports of flying discs had similar counterparts in the past'. Though this story says nothing about Fort's theories about space visitors, the implications were clear enough. United Press reporter Claire Cox quoted R. L. Farnsworth, president of the

American Rocket Society and a member of the Fortean Society, on sightings 'in the last century, and plenty of other times, too. Nobody ever found out what any of the objects were.' After a brief review of nineteenth-century sightings by astronomers, Farnsworth remarks, 'I wouldn't even be surprised if the flying saucers were remote-control electronic eyes from Mars.'

Press enthusiasm for flying saucers had begun to diminish by July 10, either because sightings were declining or because the subject was losing its novelty. It was also being treated more and more as fit only for ridicule. That day, for example, President Harry Truman compared flying saucers to the notorious moon hoax (the 1835 creation of *New York Sun* journalist Richard Adams Locke, who regaled readers with stories about astronomers' alleged discovery of intelligent lunar life). A California psychic's claim of communication with the 'rulers of creation' and spaceships based in the 'dark of the moon' was widely circulated.

THE PUBLIC UNCONVINCED

This sort of discussion had almost no effect on public opinion. Nonetheless in later years a persistent myth would find expression in debunking treatments of the UFO phenomenon and become a sceptical article of faith: that nuclear-age anxieties caused the Americans of 1947 to imagine saviours from outer space. In reality, as Ted Bloecher found in a study of the 1947 wave, only two witnesses 'openly expressed the opinion that the objects seen could have been 'space ships'.' As the first Gallup poll on the subject, released on August 14 ('now that the uproar over the 'flying saucers' has subsided'), determined, outer-space explanations were so negligibly held that they were not even listed in the results. Asked 'what do you think these saucers are?', Americans responded as follows:

No answer, don't know: 33%
Imagination, optical illusion, mirage, etc.: 29%
Hoax: 10%
U.S. secret weapon, part of atomic bomb, etc.: 15%
Weather forecasting devices: 3%
Russian secret weapon: 1%
Other explanations: 9%

Gallup's accompanying press release indicates that extraterrestrial spacecraft did not register measurably even in the 'other explanations' category. It mentions a woman's Bible-based belief that the discs portended the end of the world. One man thought they were 'radio waves from the Bikini atomic bomb explosion,' and another suspected them to be a commercial product developed by the 'DuPont people.'

Gallup's next poll on the subject was taken in early 1950. This time space visitation squeaked in under the confusingly – even meaninglessly – titled category 'comets, shooting stars, something from outer space.' Of course believing that conventional astronomical phenomena cause UFO sightings is hardly the same thing as believing that spacecraft from other planets are responsible. And it is certainly not immediately evident that, given the context, those polled interpreted 'something from outer space' as representing the technology of civilisations from elsewhere. As Robert J. Durant remarks in his study of UFO polls, 'In retrospect, it seems nearly impossible that the ET hypothesis was virtually absent in the public mind as of May 1950, but that is what the poll shows.'

THE AIR FORCE AND THE SCIENTISTS

Nonetheless as early as October 1947 an Air Force intelligence directive noted that even within the military 'it is the considered opinion of some elements that the object may in fact represent an interplanetary craft of some kind.'

Project SIGN, the first known official UFO-investigative agency, commenced its work on January 22, 1948, under the Air Materiel Command (AMC) at Wright Field (now Wright-Patterson Air Force Base) in Ohio. At the outset project personnel had two operating assumptions. Some suspected that the discs were Soviet or American (perhaps Navy) secret weapons, while others were convinced that the phenomena would prove to be illusory. Meanwhile, though they got less newspaper publicity, sightings continued. In short order secret-weapon theories died for want of evidence, and investigators persuaded that the objects were real began to focus on the ETH.

A spectacular sighting over Alabama in the early morning hours of July 24, involving an Eastern Airlines DC-3 and a huge rocket-shaped structure with two rows of portholes, convinced the pro-ETH faction that its case was clinched. The Air Force Chief of Staff, General Hoyt S. Vandenberg, disagreed and had the radicals transferred out of the project. The episode so embarrassed the Air Force that for years afterwards it denied any UFO-project investigators had ever held such views. SIGN was reorganised and soon took on an anti-UFO tone under the new codenamed Project GRUDGE.

A formal report on Sign's findings, released on April 27, 1949, carried an appendix (E-2), consisting of the text of a letter by James E. Lipp of the AMC's Missiles Division. Addressed to Brigadier General Donald Putt, AMC's Director of Research and Development, it discusses, then rejects (for technological reasons that seem naive in retrospect), any links between UFO sightings and space travellers. Lipp, however, tries to envision a reasonable interplanetary-visitation scenario:

> Martians have kept a long-term routine watch on Earth and have been alarmed by the sight of our A-bomb shots as evidence that we are warlike and on the threshold of space travel. (Venus is eliminated because her cloudy atmosphere would make such a survey impractical.) The first flying objects were spotted in the Spring of 1947, after a total of 5 atomic explosions, i.e., Alamogordo, Hiroshima, Nagasaki, Crossroads A and Crossroads B. Of these, the first two were in positions to be seen from Mars, the third was very doubtful (at the edge of the Earth's disc in daylight) and the last two were on the wrong side of the Earth. It is likely that Martian astronomers, with their thin atmosphere, could build telescopes big enough to see A-bomb explosions on Earth, even though we were 165 and 153 million miles away, respectively, on the Alamogordo and Hiroshima dates.

In the 1940s and into the 1950s, knowledge of the surface conditions of the earth's neighbouring planets was still so nebulous that some astronomers deemed intelligent life on Mars, and possibly even Venus, as at least marginally plausible. The prominent astronomer Fred Whipple, for example, wrote that an intelligent race of Martians, through technological and evolutionary adaptation, may have survived 'the excessively slow loss of atmosphere, oxygen and water' and built structures to protect them from 'nights... much colder than our arctic winters.' In

1953, in his book *Flying Saucers*, Harvard astronomer Donald H. Menzel left open the question of life on Venus, remarking that 'had we ourselves developed on Venus instead of on the earth, it is not at all impossible that we might have developed into a race of mermaids and mermen.' He thought it at least possible that Mars harbours 'beings as intelligent as or more intelligent than we are' – though in common with other scientist-proponents of extraterrestrial life (such as, more recently, Carl Sagan and Frank Drake) he insisted UFOs had nothing to do with any of this. He urged scientists to try sending out signals to [Mars and Venus], or at least turning our great receiving antennas occasionally in the direction of these planets and listening for such signals as may come from them directly or indirectly. We might then hear in our receivers the Venusian or Martian equivalents of FM and television. In this way we could begin to check up on the habitability of the solar system, on the possibility of interplanetary communication, and perhaps, through exchange of intelligent ideas, even hasten that day when we ourselves shall be able to leave the earth and explore interplanetary space.

THE ETH IN 1950

Widespread popular opinion notwithstanding, flying saucers, flying discs, or – as the Air Force was already calling them – unidentified flying objects turned out to be no fleeting sensation. Sightings continued, in spite of official attempts (such as a GRUDGE-encouraged, debunking *Saturday Evening Post* piece in the spring of 1949) to discourage them. Only a tiny minority of people, however, believed UFOs to be of unearthly origin. Nonetheless popular perceptions were about to change.

In early May 1949 Donald E. Keyhoe, a much-published aviation writer and retired Marine Corps major, accepted an assignment from *True* editor Ken Purdy to look into the UFO mystery. On October 12 and November 27 *Variety*, the entertainment-industry organ, carried two sensational stories by columnist Frank Scully, who claimed that the U.S. government had recovered an extraterrestrial flying saucer and the charred bodies of its 16 diminutive but otherwise humanlike occupants.

Keyhoe's findings appeared in the January 1950 issue of *True*, then a widely read men's magazine, and it quickly became one of the most discussed magazine articles in history. 'After eight months of intensive investigation,' the article began, *True* had come to some dramatic conclusions: 'For the past 175 years, the planet Earth has been under systematic close-range examination by living, intelligent observers from another planet.' Over the past two years, having observed atomic-bomb explosions, the space visitors had stepped up their efforts. They were using three different types of craft, 'small, nonpilot-carrying disk-shaped aircraft', 'a very large... metallic, disk-shaped aircraft', and 'a dirigible-shaped, wingless aircraft.' The plan the aliens seemed to be following 'varies in no important particular from well-developed American plans for the exploration of space expected to come to fruition within the next fifty years.'

Keyhoe assured his readers that no evidence of 'belligerence' had come to light. He acknowledged a possible exception – the much-publicised 1948 crash of a Kentucky Air National Guard F-51 while in pursuit of an alleged flying saucer – but remarked that the craft's occupants 'could logically have feared they were in danger.' (In the 1950s the object was identified as a Skyhook balloon, launched as part of a classified Navy project.)

As for the UFOs' planet or planets of origin, Keyhoe had no strong opinion.

He mentioned neighbouring ones such as Mars and Venus (especially the former) as well as hypothetical ones elsewhere in the galaxy. But to Keyhoe this was a secondary issue; what mattered to him was that wherever the spacecraft came from, they were here, and the human race had to prepare itself to face the consequences. 'It might be a long time before they would try to make contact,' he wrote. 'But I had a conviction that when it came, it would be a peaceful mission, not an ultimatum. It could even be the means of ending wars on earth.'

Keyhoe had no idea what the beings looked like, and he assumed (wrongly) that no credible landing reports existed. A quick investigation of the crash/retrieval story being peddled by Frank Scully convinced him it was a hoax, and ever after Keyhoe paid little attention to any crash report and generally kept his distance from 'little men' reports of any sort, long after his colleagues had embraced close encounters of the third kind as an authentic aspect of the larger UFO phenomenon.

That same year Scully's *Behind the Flying Saucers* gave yet more currency to the growing belief in space visitors. Scully reported (on the authority of the pseudonymous scientist 'Dr. Gee,' subsequently identified as professional swindler Leo GeBauer) that three downed spaceships had been secretly recovered in the Southwest in the late 1940s. Their occupants, short and human in appearance, clothed in the 'style of 1890,' were presumed to be from Venus because they were too short to be Martians. This was not only untrue, of course, but laughably untrue, as Keyhoe had already discerned and as another *True* reporter, J. P. Cahn, would document in a savage expose two years later.

The third UFO book published that year (in December in Britain, the following April in the United States), Gerald Heard's *The Riddle of the Flying Saucers*, echoed Keyhoe's and Scully's belief that the visitors had benign intentions; they acted, after all, much like 'very circumspect, very intelligent gentlemen.' They could only be from Mars, where 'life is certainly far ahead of us.' Like Keyhoe, Heard assumed implicitly that no spacecraft had landed and no occupants had ever been seen. Thus speculation about the aliens' nature and appearance did not have to be tied to testimony from alleged observers.

In an off-the-cuff, probably tongue-in-cheek remark made to a *Los Angeles Times* reporter in March, 1950 – the astronomer (and life-long ufophobe) Gerard P. Kuiper speculated that conditions on Mars being what they are (or, in any event, were thought to be in 1950), the only intelligent beings that could exist there would be advanced insects. Thus inspired, Heard wrote that The Martians who piloted the flying discs were super-bees, 'of perhaps two inches in length... as beautiful as the most beautiful of any flower, any beetle, moth or butterfly. A creature with eyes like brilliant cut-diamonds, with a head of sapphire, a thorax of emerald, an abdomen of ruby, wings like opal, legs like topaz – such a body would be worthy of this 'supermind'... It is we who would feel shabby and ashamed, and maybe with our clammy, putty-coloured bodies, repulsive!'

In Heard's view their coming had to do with their concern that our atomic bombs and warlike ways could endanger their own safety. In his hyperbolic and somewhat hysterical way he continued:

When we twice struck Japan and then, not to slaughter, but to astound, made the Pacific spout – when we, time and again, sent up great super-thunderheads of smoke, spray and the wreckage of human industry and human bodies, right up into the stratosphere, then we put out a finger to beckon attention on any watching fellow-planet that we were out for trouble, and able to give it. They could hardly have failed to see that defiant, wanton signal... [T]hey could not have failed to conclude that the time for action had come.

THE NEW WAR OF THE WORLDS

A small but vocal minority of early ufologists feared that extraterrestrials, or some of them, were up to no good. Englishman Harold T. Wilkins, author of the alarmingly titled *Flying Saucers on the Attack* (1954); *Flying Saucers on the Moon* in its British edition), even thought he knew which UFOs were unfriendly:

> I have spoken of the apparent hostility of some types of flying saucers, particularly of the weird aeroform which has an insulated and non-rotary fusiform, or cigar-shaped center, around which revolves a singular ring, like the ring around the planet, Saturn. This ring is drawn out into an ellipsoid in order... to release satellite discs.

Wilkins linked flying saucers to natural disasters, fires, and disappearances of human beings. Unlike Keyhoe and Heard (who believed [Heard's emphasis] 'the visitor did everything... to avoid a contact, to keep clear of complications'), he assumed that the aliens knew what they were doing when they blasted Kentucky Air National Guard pilot Thomas F. Mantell out of the sky. As he read the incident, 'the entities in the weird and vast machine' directed a 'lethal ray of immense power... at Mantell and his 'plane... to demonstrate to terrestrial military power, with its anti-aircraft batteries, the folly of any close approach.' He compared the episode to scenes from H. G. Wells's classic interplanetary-invasion novel *The War of the Worlds* (1898). Though neither of his UFO books offers anything like a fully formed theory of alien hostility – the books are essentially compendia of saucer-lore, strung loosely together with occasional, generally eccentric commentary – Wilkins declares, in the title to a chapter of *Flying Saucers Uncensored* (1955), that the arrival of UFOs has brought us to 'The Earth's Gravest Hour.'

THE ETH THEN AND NOW

By the mid-1950s, then, the groundwork for most subsequent speculation about extraterrestrial visitation had been laid. There would be some modifications, of course. Space probes would eliminate any possibility that any planet in our solar system besides ours is inhabited, and so ufologists (not to mention astronomers) would have to look deeper into space for hypothetical advanced extraterrestrial races. In more recent years, as the abduction phenomenon has become an inescapable part of the larger UFO picture, theorists have had to consider the possibility of a more intimate association between earthlings and aliens than – aside from contactee literature – had been imagined heretofore.

Nonetheless, in most subsequent histories the basic notions set forth in the early years would continue to drive the discussion. From the 1950s to the present proponents of the ETH have held UFOs to be friendly, hostile, or merely curious, and they have sought (if sometimes naïvely or even crazily) to justify their speculations by linking them to current scientific theory about the likely nature of extraterrestrial intelligence.

Of the science-based examinations of the ETH, far and away the most important contributions are those by Michael D. Swords, professor of natural sciences at

Western Michigan University. In a series of well-informed, cogently argued papers, Swords has maintained that the phenomena reported by UFO witnesses, including the oxygen-breathing humanoids of CE3s, are entirely compatible with what could be expected of genuine spacefaring extraterrestrials. Swords argues that whether it is ultimately confirmed or disconfirmed, the ETH ought to be regarded as a respectable scientific theory.

Within ufology the ETH no longer holds the commanding role it once claimed. Though it is now challenged by other hypotheses, occult, natural, and psychosocial, it alone seems to offer an explanation for the physical phenomena associated with the most puzzling UFO reports. For this reason it is certain to endure as long as people continue to see mysterious phenomena in Earth's airspace and to wonder about their meaning.

AUSTRALASIA AND THE PACIFIC HAVE HAD THEIR FAIR SHARE OF REMARKABLE UFO EVENTS – FATHER GILL'S SIGHTING AT BOIANOI AND THE DISAPPEARANCE OF FREDERICK VALENTICH ARE JUST TWO OUTSTANDING EXAMPLES. FORTUNATELY THEY HAVE ALSO BEEN BLESSED WITH A NUMBER OF RESEARCHERS WHO HAVE MAINTAINED HIGH STANDARDS AND AN OPEN-MINDED APPROACH. PAUL NORMAN, A WELL-KNOWN FIGURE AT INTERNATIONAL CONFERENCES, HAS BEEN ASSOCIATED WITH MANY REMARKABLE INVESTIGATIONS, WHILE RESEARCHERS LIKE KEITH BASTERFIELD AND MARK MORAVEC HAVE MADE NOTABLE CONTRIBUTIONS TO OUR UNDERSTANDING OF THE PSYCHOSOCIAL DIMENSIONS OF THE UFO PHENOMENON.

A PARTICULARLY VALUABLE DEVELOPMENT OCCURRED IN 1982 WHEN BILL CHALKER OBTAINED DIRECT ACCESS TO THE UFO FILES OF THE ROYAL AUSTRALIAN AIR FORCE. WHILE HE CONCLUDED THAT, WHATEVER MIGHT OR MIGHT NOT BE THE CASE ELSEWHERE, THERE WAS NO ORGANISED OFFICIAL COVER-UP IN HIS COUNTRY, CHALKER DISCOVERED DOCUMENTS WHICH THREW VALUABLE LIGHT ON SEVERAL SIGNIFICANT CASES IN AUSTRALIAN UFO HISTORY.

BILL CHALKER MAY BE REACHED AT THE NEW SOUTH WALES UFO INVESTIGATION CENTRE (UFOIC), POSTBOX W42, WEST PENNANT HILLS, NSW 2125, AUSTRALIA; PHONE +61 294 844 680

THE 1954 UFO INVASION OF AUSTRALIA

by Bill Chalker

I n November-December 1953, the *Australasian Post* serialised Leslie & Adamski's *Flying Saucers Have Landed* in six weekly parts: the last three parts – Adamski's story – gave the Australian public their first major exposure to the bizarre world of the UFO contactee. The *Post*'s final issue for the year ensured that the subject of flying saucers would remain a talking point: in an article entitled 'Saucers have been seen here', Charles Hellier concluded, 'Whatever you think of saucers, the fact remains that enough reliable people see them to make certain that there is SOMETHING in the sky.'

The prelude was complete. The UFO 'invasion' of Victoria was about to begin.

Numerous reports came in from diverse locations in Victoria, prompting the Department of Civil Aviation (DCA) to make a public request for reports to be sent to them. Within a week they had received 59 cases spanning nearly 30 years. DCA officials indicated they were checking the reports and might turn them over to the Royal Australian Air Force for more extensive investigation. A spokesman said, 'Some highly qualified engineers in our department are convinced that there is something in the saucer mystery. We just can't ignore reports submitted by reliable witnesses…'

The RAAF made a series of seemingly open statements about UFOs during January, 1954. By the year's end they would retreat from their open-minded position and close the door, but soon after the New Year a RAAF spokesman was quoted as saying, 'People are definitely seeing something and we hope to find out what it is. The RAAF has an open mind on saucers. We haven't rejected them as impossible or accepted them as fact yet. There is a high ranking opinion in the Force that saucers do exist and you can't shake it. The RAAF has been receiving saucer reports and investigating them since the war'.

A 'high ranking RAAF officer' was even more outspoken. 'The RAAF is keeping an open mind on the objects, but I personally am convinced they have an Interplanetary source. People on this earth should be able to fly into outer space within about 40 years – why shouldn't people on other planets already have reached this stage?'

By the end of January the initial excitement in Victoria had all but died down, though sightings began to mount in other states. The pioneer Australian researcher Edgar Jarrold, of the Australian Flying Saucer Bureau, added fuel to the flames with a startling theory. In a press release dated 7 January, 1954, he stated that record waves of sightings had occurred in 1950 and 1952 during previous close approaches of Mars. He therefore predicted that record sightings would occur during 1954.

Jarrold was far from alone in his suggestion of a 'Mars connection'. During a visit to Australia that same year, a French Mars expert, Dr. Gerard de Vaucouleurs, was quoted as saying, 'There is something remarkable on Mars. If we could one day conclude there was activity displayed by reasoning minds on Mars, what a prodigious upheaval it would cause in human thought!' Referring to his Mount Stromlo observatory he made the remarkable statement, 'This is not only a learned probe for academic information. It is also a hunt for possible enemies from space'.

Curiously, the red menace was to loom large during 1954, for this was the year when the high tide of McCarthyism washed across the Australian scene, in the wake of the Petrov Affair. The 'red menace' was seen in two evocative forms. It stalked the corridors of power in Australia with the fear of communist infiltration, and it sported in the skies over Victoria in the taunting guise of the flying saucers. While a Royal Commission sought Communist reds beneath suspects' beds, the pressure was also on the intelligence community to determine the source of the saucer reports. Against the backdrop of hostile relations with Russia, the possibility that flying saucers might be of Soviet origin, either as hardware or as a psychological warfare weapon, was taken seriously. Just three days after the Russian embassy was withdrawn in the wake of the Petrov affair, the lull in flying saucer sightings was over and the 'invasion' of Victoria had resumed.

THE FLAP OF 1954

Most of the early 1954 reports had been distant, ambiguous observations. That was to change on the morning of 28 April 1954. It was a beautifully clear day. Along the Cressy-Ararat line, the country is very flat and the views are immense. Engine driver Ted Smith however, driving a Victorian Government goods train about 72 km west of Geelong, was unprepared for the immensity of the vision that was about to befall him and his fireman, Colin Beacon.

In the eastern sky, apparently some six or seven kilometres away, they saw a dark purple object diving and banking. 'It seemed to stop still for about a minute and a half and then dive at enormous speed. I nearly keeled out of the cabin when I saw the huge round mass plunging down at the train. It screamed down then suddenly raced up to the sky again.' Pulling out of the dive, the object seemed to bank at the same speed and then hung in the sky as if suspended.

The object was 'just colossal, obscuring the sun here and there by its bulk... not a clearly round object but somewhat covered in a haze – maybe caused by speed or design... I could see no windows or doors. Trees in the background looked like matchsticks against its bulk. It could have been a quarter mile (0.4 km) in diameter. We both saw it stand still in the air. It was frightening the way it just seemed to hang stationary – like a huge monster hovering over us unlike any possible aircraft. It came to within 300 feet of us, and I had a feeling it was driven. But it must have been by an amateur, the way it careered around the sky... We watched for four minutes before it disappeared behind a bank of trees... It was not like anything I had ever seen or read about. It was something out of a dream'.

A month later, on 30 May, East Malvern was the stage for a report which offered an additional feature: occupants. At about midday 'human-shaped shadows' were discerned in a 'flying football' which passed in a dive over six awed witnesses. One was a policeman, who said, 'Shadows of some people, I think could be seen for several seconds', and witness David Reese said, 'When it reached the lowest point, shapes, like human figures, could definitely be seen... I could distinctly see, inside it, dark shapes like busts'.

The suggestion of life aboard the saucers sparked a media sensation. The Malvern event was also one of the first sightings investigated by a scientist who authored a secret report to the Directorate of Air Force Intelligence. His role would become pivotal in the secret Australian defence and government investigations. He had interviewed David Reese and 'felt reassured as to the integrity of this witness'.

The Malvern sensation also prompted a further statement from the RAAF. Gone now was any suggestion of support for the 'interplanetary' theory of origin: political and intelligence considerations were muzzling the free wheeling opinions that had featured earlier in the year. Nevertheless the enigma was acknowledged when on 31 May Melbourne RAAF Public Relations Officer John Tyrrell said:

It would be stupid to ignore flying saucers. We believe there's something flying around which cannot be regarded as a figment of someone's imagination. We don't know what it is, we have no concrete evidence of saucers as such, but we simply can't discount certain reports from sane, seasoned RAAF and airline pilots.

On 26 June a writer described as an 'eminent Australian nuclear physicist, who has investigated 'saucer' reports since 1948' published a major article in the *Melbourne Argus*, entitled 'Saucers do exist and why!' It was indicated that the author's name 'must be withheld because of his link with high-level research'. For the period, the physicist wrote eloquently and knowledgeably:

From all corners of the world there have come thousands of reports of strange objects in the sky. They have been observed in ones and twos, in small groups, and even by the score, over cities, deserts, mountains and oceans, from distances of less than 50 yards to many miles. Radar pilots have checked with visual sightings. Jet fighter aircraft have attempted to intercept them and have been outmanoeuvred. The governments of the U.S., Britain, Canada and Australia have set up investigation centres. After eliminating all possible alternatives there remain several hundred reports that can't be explained by hallucinations, mass illusion, hoaxes, spots before the eyes, reflection, refraction, stars, meteorites, balloons or sun phenomena... An attitude of ridicule... has caused many people to refrain from making a report. This is not desirable if we wish to understand these mysterious phenomena…

Apart from this overview of the controversy, as it was perceived at the time, the scientist presented three hypotheses:

A certain remnant of reports may only be explained by the assumption that machines controlled by some intelligence are being observed… These machines are not manufactured on earth; that is, their origin is extraterrestrial… These machines originate from the planet Mars.

In retrospect, the last of these hypotheses seems somewhat naive, but at the time so provocative a speculation was, as we have seen, not totally out of step with the thinking entertained by some members of the scientific community.

The identity of the 'eminent Australian nuclear physicist' remained a mystery until I was able to identify him as scientist O.H. (Harry) Turner, at that time working in the physics department of Melbourne University, and who then and later was to play a distinguished part in several high-level undertakings.

The 'invasion' centred on Victoria in 1954 was the most significant of the early Australian sighting waves. In July the Australian Flying Saucer Investigation Committee (AFSIC) of Victoria released a study of 55 sightings, concluding, 'We are still far from deciding what these things are. It would be only guesswork to say they are actual spaceships from another planet. But we are fully agreed upon this – that these things are material objects. They cannot be put down to a person's hallucination or optical illusion. They are getting lower seemingly to land'.

THE CIVILIAN SCENE

While the RAAF was confronting 'the UFO problem', civilian research was in disarray following the perceived 'disappearance' of pioneer researcher Edgar Jarrold. The 'Jarrold mystery' was absorbed into the notorious Bender saga, and seemed to share many of its bizarre elements. Albert Bender's grandiosely-named International Flying Saucer Bureau, one of the earliest American flying saucer groups, closed suddenly. Many enthusiasts concluded he had been silenced and the weird affair was narrated in Gray Barker's book, *They Knew Too Much About Flying Saucers*. Bender fed the paranoia when he broke silence with his own *Flying Saucers and the Three Men*. Bender claimed three alien 'men in black' had coerced him into silence to prevent him revealing the truth about the Saucers which he had inadvertently stumbled upon. Now, Jarrold's 'disappearance' was used to swell the burgeoning 'men in black' legend.

However, a critical analysis of the Jarrold affair argues for a more prosaic explanation. By mid-1954 he was experiencing the high point of his ufological career. His prediction that there would be an increase in UFO sightings in June-July 1954, based on his Mars theory, appeared to have been borne out by events. The authorities were prepared to take him seriously and he had received an official invitation from the then Minister for Air, William McMahon, for a meeting with Air Force Intelligence in Melbourne.

In the event, while Turner, the 'eminent nuclear physicist', was given full access to the Directorate of Air Force Intelligence UFO files so as to undertake an officially requested classified 'scientific appreciation' of their contents, Jarrold was granted only a meeting with DAFI officer Squadron Leader Peter Birch: in addition, he was given a set of still prints from 94 frames of the controversial Drury UFO film. This was enough, though, to confirm Jarrold as the leading civilian

Australian UFO researcher of his day, so when he stepped out of the limelight, his 'disappearance' was attributed to sinister pressures. With hindsight, it is clear is that matters much more prosaic, such as the pressure of his dedication and increasing obsession with flying saucers on his own private life and family and their eventual disintegration, were the main factors for Jarrold's departure from the Australian UFO scene. Not only that, but he had not entirely 'disappeared'; a year later, in mid-1955, a feature article appeared in *People* magazine headlined

> The Australian Flying Saucer Bureau believes
> MARTIANS MAY LAND HERE NEXT YEAR

The article focused on Jarrold, confirming that whatever else may have changed in his life, his belief in his Martian theory remains constant.

THE TURNER REPORT

The burgeoning official files led the Directorate of Air Force Intelligence to ask Turner to undertake a classified 'scientific appreciation' of the official reports held on file. Turner recommended greater official interest, specific attention to radar/visual reports, and concluded that 'the evidence presented by the reports held by RAAF tend to support the conclusion that certain strange aircraft have been observed to behave in a manner suggestive of extra-terrestrial origin'. (This 1954 report remained classified until I discovered it during an inspection of classified DAFI UFO policy files with Squadron Leader Ian Frame during 1982).

The disposition of Harry Turner's controversial report is a revealing indictment of official handling of the UFO controversy. In studying the RAAF/DAFI UFO files, Turner made use of American researcher Donald Keyhoe's reports, concluding 'if one assumes these Intelligence Reports are authentic, then the evidence presented is such that it is difficult to assume any interpretation other than that UFOs are being observed'. He recommended that the RAAF seek official USAF confirmation of the legitimacy of Keyhoe's data.

Albert Bender's sketch of a MIB

The result was not encouraging. Australian Joint Service Staff (intelligence) in Washington replied, saying, 'I have discussed with the USAF the status of Major Keyhoe. I understand that his book is written in such a way as to convey the impression that his statements are based on official documents, and there is some suggestion that he has made improper use of information to which he had access while he was serving with the Marine Corps. He has, however, no official status whatsoever and a dim view is taken officially of both him and his works'.

This conclusion, not surprisingly, had the effect of undermining Turner's rec-

82

ommendations. The Department of Air concluded: 'Professor Turner accepted Keyhoe's book as being authentic and based on official releases. Because Turner places so much weight on Keyhoe's work he emphasised the need to check Keyhoe's reliability. (The Australian Joint Service Staff communication) removes Keyhoe's work as a prop for Turner's work so that the value of the latter's findings and recommendations is very much reduced.' Turner's findings, including his recommendation to set up a scientific 'investigating panel', were now found to be impractical and unjustified.

Sadly, this decision was based on an act of conscious or unconscious misrepresentation on the part of the US Air Force, who were up to their eyeballs in a misguided campaign to undermine the popularity of Keyhoe's books. While Keyhoe may have slightly 'beat up' his data, the USAF Intelligence reports he quoted, and which in turn were used by Turner to support his conclusions to DAFI, were in fact authentic, as the USAF themselves ultimately admitted. But by then it was too late to rescue Turner's initiative.

Thus political myopia, on the part of both the US and Australian military, effectively scuttled Australia's first serious flirtation with scientific investigation of UFOs. Meanwhile, unbeknown to Turner, a powerful example of the type of incident he recommended the RAAF concentrate on – radar cases – was already causing concern in military circles.

THE 'SEA FURY' ENCOUNTER

In August of 1954 there occurred one of the most controversial radar/visual reports of the decade. When the story leaked out in December it made front page headlines.

The official file on the event remained classified until the Directorate of Naval Intelligence released a copy upon my request in 1982. However, during his 1973 visit to Australia, Allen Hynek was able to interview the pilot involved in this famous incident, which became known as the 'Sea Fury' encounter. Dr. Hynek made his notes on this interview available to me during my 1984 visit to the Chicago headquarters of his organisation, the Centre for UFO Studies. In exchange I was able to provide Dr. Hynek with a copy of the official file on the incident.

Lieutenant James ('Shamus') A. O'Farrell was returning to Royal Australian Navy Air Station Nowra after a flight cross country in a Sea Fury aircraft. He described what happened as follows:

> At approximately 19.10 I noticed a very bright light closing fast from 'one o'clock'. This bright light crossed ahead of me and continued to a position on my port beam where it appeared to orbit. At the same time I noticed a second and similar light at 'nine o'clock', which made a pass about a mile ahead of me and then turned in the position where the first light was sighted.
>
> I contacted Nowra and asked if they had me on radar… they replied that they had 3 echoes and advised me to turn 180° to be identified… At this stage the two bright lights reformed at 'nine o'clock' from me and disappeared on a North Easterly heading.
>
> I saw no other lights and was only able to make out a vague shape with the white light situated centrally on top. Their apparent crossing speed was the fastest that I have ever experienced.

O'Farrell clarified for me that what really impressed him was, first, having the two objects in close proximity to his aircraft, at one point on either side of his wings, and second, the extraordinary speed at which they departed. He returned to base to find quite a reception committee awaiting him:

I came in and landed at 7.30 and when I got there there were quite a few people waiting for me. I thought it was a bit strange and so they came over, and they said, 'You sure you had aircraft out there?' The Surgeon Commander said, did I feel sick, or was I upset? I said no. After I was finished I went up to sick bay and he gave me a more thorough medical, and said, no, I appeared to be alright. I found out later that at the same time they checked to make sure I hadn't been drinking before I took off.

During Dr Hynek's 1973 Australian visit, O'Farrell was instructed to meet the American researcher. He demurred, explaining that after this length of time he was a bit hazy about the facts, whereupon he was sent some files to refresh his memory. To his surprise, they were not RAAF or naval files, but two substantial dossiers, one entirely about checks on him, and the other full of significant data, much of which he was unaware of – and this was supposed to have been his own personal experience! Here it was 1973, and he was reading classified Joint Intelligence Bureau files about his experience in 1954, that revealed to him for the first time that there had been ground witnesses to his famous encounter. The files even contained chinograph drawings of the Nowra radar screen tracings done by radar officer Jessop. To be still haunted by the 1954 encounter almost two decades later was both extraordinary and frustrating. (Fortunately the episode did not ultimately harm his employment. He retired from a distinguished career as an Air Naval Commodore and Naval Attaché in Washington.)

When I wrote of his experience in my 1996 book, *The Oz Files*, O'Farrell joined me in a book launch and gave a rich and compelling account of his encounter. His integrity, the supporting evidence of the ground radar and the testimony of independent eyewitnesses, ensure a lasting place in history for the 1954 UFO invasion of Australia.

IT'S NEVER EASY TO SEPARATE THE INDIVIDUAL FROM EVENTS, THE PERSON FROM THE PHENOMENON — OR THE UFOLOGIST FROM THE UFO. FOR ALL PRACTICAL PURPOSES, NEITHER EXISTED AS LITTLE AS 50 YEARS AGO. CERTAINLY THERE WERE NO UFOS RECURRING ON AN ALMOST DAILY REGULARITY, NOR WAS THERE A PROFESSIONAL POSITION, ACADEMIC OR OTHERWISE, THAT WOULD ALLOW ANYONE TO INVESTIGATE UFOS ON EITHER A FULL-OR PART-TIME BASIS. IRONICALLY, THE FIRST 'UFOLOGISTS' WERE PROBABLY LOW-LEVEL ENLISTED PERSONNEL IN THE UNITED STATES AIR FORCE WHO WERE SIMPLY OBEYING ORDERS, AND WHOSE NAMES ARE MOST LIKELY NOW LOST TO HISTORY.

NOT SO THAT OF MAJOR DONALD E. KEYHOE. ALTHOUGH HE RETIRED FROM THE MILITARY ALMOST 25 YEARS PRIOR TO THE ARNOLD INCIDENT, HIS NAME WILL BE FOREVER LINKED WITH FLYING SAUCERS. WOULD OUR PERCEPTION OF UFOS BE RADICALLY DIFFERENT TODAY IF KEYHOE HAD NEVER BECOME INVOLVED? WOULD THERE BE A CIVILIAN UFOLOGY? WE CAN ONLY SPECULATE.

THE AUTHOR OF OUR CAPSULE BIOGRAPHY OF KEYHOE IS MICHAEL SWORDS, A PROFESSOR OF NATURAL SCIENCES, BOARD MEMBER OF THE J. ALLEN HYNEK CENTER FOR UFO STUDIES, AND PAST EDITOR OF THE CENTER'S JOURNAL FOR UFO STUDIES. HE CAN BE REACHED IN WRITING AT: DEPARTMENT OF SCIENCE STUDIES, WESTERN MICHIGAN UNIVERSITY, KALAMAZOO, MICHIGAN, USA 49008-5033

DONALD E. KEYHOE AND THE PENTAGON

by Michael D. Swords

Major Donald E. Keyhoe (1897-1988) was arguably the most important and influential figure in modern ufology. His first article on the subject (*True*, 1949), regarded as one of the most widely read articles of all time, was quickly followed by two full-length books, *The Flying Saucers Are Real* (New York: Fawcett, 1950) and *Flying Saucers from Outer Space* (New York: Henry Holt, 1953). He was also instrumental in founding the largest civilian saucer organisation ever, the National Committee on the Investigation of Aerial Phenomena (NICAP).

Keyhoe proved singularly placed for his historical role. The Major was a graduate of the U.S. Naval Academy, who, due to an injury in a plane crash in Guam, retired from the Marine Corps in 1923. He maintained contacts with many military people, and some, such as the first director of the Central Intelligence Agency, Vice Admiral Roscoe H. Hillenkoetter, and the head of the Navy's guided missile program, Rear Admiral Delmer S. Fahrney, operated at the highest levels of the Pentagon. Keyhoe's major employment was as a freelance writer whose work appeared in such periodicals as the *Saturday Evening Post, Reader's Digest,* and *American Magazine.* He was quite successful in this profession, making, as he would later lament, far more money than he ever managed as a writer in the 'UFO business.' Investigative journalism was his profession; UFOs were a writing assignment that got out of hand.

Although Keyhoe had heard a lot of press talk and rumour about flying discs (and had been at least mildly interested), his real involvement began on May 9, 1949, when the editor of *True* magazine asked him to investigate same. Several magazines were tackling the subject and one, the *Saturday Evening Post,* had just published the first of two parts of an Air Force-assisted article by Sidney Shalett. The previous year had seen three unusually well-publicised sightings: the Thomas Mantell crash, the Chiles-

Donald Keyhoe, author of some of the most important UFO books ever published

Whitted flying fuselage, and the George Gorman dogfight, all three of which continued to cause comment.

Rumours of crashed disks and little men began to enter into public awareness about this time, as well. Within the Air Force and the Pentagon there was a raging disagreement about whether the disks could be interplanetary. Project SIGN had recently written its famous pro-UFO 'Estimate of the Situation', and an opposing Pentagon group released a countering report that the whole business was either bunk or perhaps some foreign technology.

True had been given a tip that there was some 'official secret' being covered up here. The editor and the reporter assigned to it initially had run into a stone wall. Keyhoe was called in because he was a good journalist, had written for *True* before, and had the connections which might split the stone wall. He was intrigued and began a six-month investigation that would culminate in the most widely read *True* article of all time – one which, expanded, would become his first UFO book.

The Flying Saucers Are Real was essentially the retelling of Keyhoe's 1949 investigative odyssey. It is almost, but not quite, in perfect temporal order. In terms of the facts associated with specific UFO cases, it is uncannily accurate. Checks of Keyhoe's details against actual Air Force case investigations show no tendency to exaggerate in order to tell a better story. Thus the volume is an invaluable and honest guide to the era from a position just outside the doors of secrecy. Not that the work is purely objective, however. Keyhoe made many deductions and speculations (always easily distinguishable from his factual reporting mode). Many of these were correct; many were wrong. All were honest, sober attempts to puzzle out the riddles (both ufological and military) that he was being fed. He was particularly weak when he attempted scientific matters, a failing which he humbly admitted (thereby enhancing his believability and likeability with the reader). But he was always intelligent and reasonable as he took on the various options. As to his writing style, it is a matter of taste. It reminds me of 1940s pulp detective fiction, with its 'just the facts, ma'am' reconstructed conversations and silent mental musings on aeroplanes and in taxi cabs. I find it terrifically effective. You feel as if you are sitting right at Keyhoe's shoulder as he peels away one of the greatest stories ever told.

What did he find? Why was he so impressed that he spent the rest of his life hooked on UFOs? Other than the mountain of oral and written reports, and suggestive conversations with people in the know, we can pick out two primary sources of Keyhoe's interest: (1) the Air Force press release of April 27, 1949 ('Project Saucer'), and (2) the Thomas Mantell crash case. Of these, the Project Saucer document was of greatest importance, as it lent strength and sustenance to the reality of the flying disks in many ways, but Mantell's plane crash and death fascinated Keyhoe for years. The Project Report was the center of his interest, the Mantell case the heart of his obsession.

The release of the Project Saucer report by the Air Force was probably a bureaucratic foul-up. Shalett's draft of his (unwelcome) *Saturday Evening Post* article had reached the Pentagon in late February 1949 and Gen. James Cabell's Air Force intelligence office did not approve. Still, with the backing of Secretary of Defense James V. Forrestal, it was going to go through. A solution was to create an official Air Force press release to appear simultaneously with the first half of the article in the magazine. A statement of 50 pages or more on flying disks was supposedly being prepared for this purpose. Somehow this never happened, and the Project Saucer report was released instead. This report was a condensed version of the formal Project SIGN report written by Wright-Patterson AFB personnel.

The report is 22 single-spaced pages of case condensations, speculation on extraterrestrial life, and possible alternative explanations. Although coming to no conclusion, any objective reader would realise that there have been some amazing and mysterious experiences, that technology was apparently involved (rather than weather balloons, pranks, and stars and planets), and that the extraterrestrial hypothesis was still very much an option. Certainly the Air Force was still interested in investigating the reports, and in no way considered them to be all bunk. Keyhoe was amazed at what he was reading. The public pronouncements of the Air Force did not cohere with this liberally objective report. He was especially puzzled as to why this essentially positive report was released simultaneously with Shalett's Air Force-assisted and essentially negative article. As a good investigative reporter he suspected something unusual and probably important behind the scenes. It created in his mind the belief that someone in authority was trying to cleverly manage the news about flying disks. But who? And why? And what did this have to do with whether or not they were real?

Although Keyhoe could have chosen better cases to focus on, it was the Thomas Mantell case which dominated his early thoughts. The case took place on January 7, 1948, just as Project SIGN was formally starting. A UFO was sighted over Godman Field, Kentucky, when a flight of fighters was passing nearby under the command of 25-year-old Kentucky Air National Guard Captain Thomas F. Mantell, Jr. They were asked to investigate. Mantell alone got close. He radioed that it was metallic and of tremendous size. Shortly, his F-51 crashed into the Kentucky countryside, taking his life. Many ground witnesses saw the object high in the sky. All of them were puzzled. The report electrified many military people. Was a flying disk responsible for the destruction of a U.S. military plane and the death of its experienced pilot?

People are interested in and trust their own. Military men respect military men. Pilots respect pilots. Keyhoe was a military man and a pilot. Mantell's death was an emotional thing for him, and brought with it a validation about the saucers that the case probably did not deserve. Still, one can hardly blame him. Project SIGN and the

Pentagon botched the case by announcing that Mantell had chased the planet Venus. The ground witnesses and many military people were, of course, outraged. Keyhoe made the only logical conclusion: it was a cover-up, more evidence of manipulating the news. And a cover-up of what? Something metallic and of tremendous size that can outrun planes and disappear high in the stratosphere. Now he was reading in 'Project Saucer' that the thing was not Venus at all. It was an 'unknown.'

Three months after the press release, the military decided that it had been a great mistake. Shortly thereafter the much more negative Project GRUDGE report (as Project Sign had been renamed) was finished at Wright-Patterson AFB and sent to the Pentagon. Another battle promptly ensued about its release. At that time, an official request for an opinion on the psychological-warfare potential of flying disk reports was prepared inside the Air Force intelligence establishment. When Keyhoe's *True* article appeared (they had alerted the Pentagon to it, like good patriotic Americans), the Air Force immediately released a prepared statement that flying disks did not exist, and that the Wright-Patterson AFB project had been closed.

Keyhoe experienced all this second-hand, but in an intensely focused fashion. *The Flying Saucers Are Real* documents the reluctant falling away of all alternative explanations. He felt forced to conclude that 'the The Air Force was puzzled, and badly worried, when the disks first were sighted in 1947... [and that] Project 'Saucer' was set up to investigate and at the same time conceal from the public the truth about the saucers. During the spring of 1949 this policy, which had been strictly maintained by Forrestal, underwent an abrupt change. On top-level orders, it was decided to let the facts gradually leak out, in order to prepare the American people. While I was preparing the article for the January 1950 issue of *True*, it had been considered in line with the general education program. But the unexpected public reaction was mistaken by the Air Force for hysteria, resulting in their hasty denial that the saucers existed...

'In regard to the flying saucers themselves,' Keyhoe continued, 'I believe that in the majority of cases, space ships are the answer:

1 The earth has been under periodic observation from another planet, or other planets, for at least two centuries.

2 This observation suddenly increased in 1947, following the series of A-bomb explosions begun in 1945.

3 The observation, now intermittent, is part of a long-range survey and will continue indefinitely. No immediate attempt to contact the earth seems evident. There may be some unknown block to making contact, but it is more probable that the spacemen's plans are not complete.

I believe that the Air Force is still investigating the saucer sightings, either through the Air Materiel Command or some other headquarters. It is possible that some Air Force officials still fear a panic when the truth is officially revealed. In that case, we may continue for a long time to see routine denials alternating with new suggestions of interplanetary travel.'

In *Flying Saucers From Outer Space*, Keyhoe starts intensively with the summer of 1952, but he does jump around a bit and provides some earlier information. He notes that Dr. Urner Liddel had attempted to explain away all UFOs as Skyhook balloons in February 1951. Since this included the Mantell case, Keyhoe was suspicious. He knew that Liddel was chief scientist at the Office of Naval Research, and perhaps this explanation was a cover-up. Keyhoe didn't dwell on this, however, because another insider scientist, Dr. Anthony Mirarchi of the Air Force, was quoted in the press saying that Liddel was wrong and that some UFOs might be foreign missiles. Whether this was accurate or not, Keyhoe considered it to have been bad judgment and a potential source of public anxiety.

Prior to July 1952, the Major recorded several other intriguing developments. The Canadian government seemed to have a serious flying-saucer investigation going. (Keyhoe had talked personally to the man who became its chief proponent, Wilbert B. Smith.) Also, there seemed to be moments of surprising cooperation between our own project and the media – *Look*, *Life*, and Keyhoe himself. This again convinced him that a huge debate was raging in the Pentagon. Finally came a story of a crashed saucer on the northern European island of Spitzbergen. True or not, this would surely create more of a 'Red scare' among those who believed the saucers were Soviet, and who perhaps remembered Mirarchi's warning.

All this became moot when the saucers put on their biggest public show of all time: what Ruppelt called the 'Washington Merry-Go-Round' that occurred on two successive weekends in July 1952. The case was huge. It made banner front-page head-lines. Radar at Washington's National Airport had tracked a cluster of objects over restricted airspace near the Capitol building. Visual confirmation came from commercial flights and jets scrambled by the Air Force. The government was agog from the Pentagon to the President. A major statement had to be made.

The incident caught the Pentagon and its chief of intelligence, Major General John A. Samford, with their pants down. A press conference was called, but there was insufficient time to prepare a carefully worded statement. On July 29, two days after a second set of radar-visual sightings had taken place, Maj. Gen. Samford, under orders from his superiors (no one knows exactly whom), faced the nation. He brought with him several Project Blue Book personnel (including Ruppelt and James), and Major General Roger Ramey, chief of the Air Defense Command. It was an imposing show of force, but Keyhoe said that only Ruppelt really looked relaxed.

Keyhoe's first work – one of the most influential UFO books ever

Reading the transcript is a strange experience. The press conference was awkward for Samford, who was apparently a man used to providing direct answers. This situation was totally different. Some of the odd phraseology and wandering ellipses give the reader the impression of a man struggling to tell you very little, but still forced to say something that you will happily accept as true. It was an impossible task. The literal bottom line of the message was that the recent happenings were a mistake caused by unusual weather conditions; the Air Force takes the UFO problem very seriously and in no way denigrates those persons who think they have seen UFOs; and yet they have found nothing so far in any reports that calls for alarm.

Keyhoe came away from the press conference convinced that Samford had done his best under difficult circumstances to debunk the saucers, allaying the public's fears while keeping any overt lies to a minimum. In a way, it was a somewhat ingenious performance for the days before spin control and deniability. The major newspapers and wire services soon reported that the Washington sightings were due to temperature inversions playing tricks on radar. This did not convince Keyhoe or anyone else interested in UFOs, but it seemed to calm the general public.

Strangely enough, shortly thereafter Keyhoe began getting astonishingly helpful information from the Pentagon regarding their UFO investigations. Given its extent and the level of its approval, it is the one element in this whole story which I cannot completely understand. Fournet explained his view as follows:

> I had a couple of open-minded superiors in Col. Adams and Col. Smith. We all became convinced that, because of some of its past practice, the USAF public image on UFOs was very tainted, and some action had to be forthcoming to remedy this. We also felt that there was absolutely no harm in admitting that we didn't have any conclusive answers but were working assiduously on it. Basically, these views were bought at higher levels, and I was told to work with PIO [the Public Information Office] (specifically, Al Chop) to see that everything that was legitimately declassifiable was to be released to the press... The entire press had the privilege of requesting this info; Don Keyhoe happened to be one who found out quickly about this policy and took maximum advantage of it.

Fournet added that pressure for such a policy had been building for some time because of the huge increase in UFO reports in the summer of 1952 and that it was finally triggered, not by the Washington radar/visual sightings, but by the Tremonton, Utah, film. Nevertheless, Keyhoe was still confused by this open policy.

Almost immediately after the press conference, Keyhoe went to the Pentagon where he was told that the Air Force wanted to hold back nothing about the UFO sightings, and that he was the person that they were most anxious to convince. Since the chief of the Public Information Office, Colonel Dewitt Searles, was now acting like a completely closed-minded debunker, Keyhoe found this hard to believe. However, he was introduced to a civilian employee who was to play a major role. This was Al Chop.

Chop became Keyhoe's liaison to higher authorities. Chop told him bluntly, 'I have been instructed to help you.' Through Chop, Keyhoe began to get access to almost any case report that he had heard about and had an interest in. Sometimes he did not even have to ask about a case. All this boggled Keyhoe's mind. What was he being set up for?

During September 1952, Chop fed Keyhoe choice radar cases that seemed chosen to negate the temperature-inversion theory of Samford's press conference. Finally, he provided Keyhoe with an Air Force radar expert who essentially said that temperature inversion could not have accounted for the Washington sightings. Baffled, Keyhoe asked Chop point-blank to tell him who was responsible for this cooperation. With his typical openness Chop replied: 'General Samford himself decided it.'

Why this was happening was a mystery that Keyhoe never confidently felt he solved. He finally concluded there must be three groups in the Pentagon, each with a different attitude towards UFOs: an 'interplanetary' group that believed all data should ultimately be released; a group that believed flying saucers were real, but that release of such information would cause serious problems; and a sceptical group that thought any UFO publicity caused problems.

Keyhoe saw the oddly changing Air Force public attitudes as ebbs and flows in the battle between these groups. He thought that group three was in the ascendant between 1948 and 1951 but that group one held a tenuous supremacy in 1952.

Although Keyhoe's scenario comes close to describing the situation in those days, it surely doesn't offer a complete roster of the schools of thought on UFO reality, the extraterrestrial hypothesis, or the wisdom of releasing UFO information to the public.

And it does not explain General Samford. What in the world was motivating him to contradict his own statements at the press conference? Samford was a Pentagon heavyweight, a major general, director of Air Force Intelligence, and chief of the National Security Agency. He was a powerful, intelligent man. What was he thinking of?

What neither Keyhoe nor Chop realised was the extent to which the CIA had progressed in decisions on UFO policies. Dr. Marshall Chadwell and Mr. Fred Durant had organised the now-famous Robertson Panel which, led by former CIA chief scientist Dr. Howard P. Robertson, had met with Wright-Patterson and Pentagon UFO experts in January 1953. They decided upon a debunking public stance on flying saucers for reasons of national security. All that Chop or Keyhoe learned at the time was that the CIA was beginning to apply its muscle in the matter of UFOs, and that some Air Force intelligence personnel were 'mad as hell' about the intrusion. In the meantime, many of the key UFO-sympathetic personnel were leaving the Air Force. In the natural course of his career Fournet was released from duty, Chop was also about to leave, and Ruppelt was in the last months of his upbeat leadership of Project Blue Book.

Having cleared all the exceptional UFO cases, especially the information on the Tremonton film, for the book, Chop and the UFO proponents were rapidly in decline. But they were not dead yet. Chop cleared one last thing for Keyhoe through his superiors: a remarkable letter acknowledging that the Air Force was not ruling out an extraterrestrial explanation for UFOs and declaring that 'if the apparently controlled manoeuvres reported by many competent observers are correct, then the only remaining explanation is the interplanetary answer.' Keyhoe's publisher reprinted the letter in full on the back of the dust jacket of *Flying Saucers From Outer Space*.

The publication of *Flying Saucers From Outer Space* ended, unfortunately, a period of naïve, almost purely joyful exploration of the UFO phenomenon by Donald Keyhoe. After the departure of the open-minded Fournet, Chop and Ruppelt, Keyhoe began to receive hints that the new Pentagon authorities were out to discredit him. Keyhoe believed these tips and defended himself, often calling on Ruppelt and Chop for support. This began an escalation of enmity between Keyhoe and the Air Force. His third book, *The Flying Saucer Conspiracy* (1955), tells this saga and turns decidedly sour. In 1956, the founding of the National Investigations Committee on Aerial Phenomena (NICAP), largely Keyhoe's creature, produced a popular civilian organisation at war with the Air Force over UFOs. Now the Air Force had a constant irritant on its hands and a good reason to shed itself of the responsibility for UFO investigations. This would not happen for another thirteen years, when the rigged University of Colorado 'scientific study' of UFOs finally allowed them to dump Project Blue Book.

When considered alongside the early reports and the Air Force analyses themselves, Keyhoe's early books serve as the foundation of the study of UFOs. Keyhoe is a founding father of ufology, perhaps the most important one. He certainly was a major sustainer of ufology as he and NICAP battled through the 1950s and early 1960s to keep the subject alive. As the extraterrestrial sirens sang to him, he, as did many others, became engulfed by their enticement. . . a somewhat reluctant U.S. Marine sailing very strange waters for the rest of his life. Ufology owes more than we can say to Donald Keyhoe, a good man, a talented man, who was in the right time and place to crack the door, and give the rest of us a little look inside.

THE 1960s

BECAUSE OF ITS CONTROVERSIAL — ONE IS TEMPTED TO SAY, TABOO — NATURE, FEW SCIENTISTS HAVE
WANTED TO BE EVEN REMOTELY ASSOCIATED WITH THE UFO PHENOMENON, LET ALONE CLOSELY
IDENTIFIED WITH IT. ASTRONOMER J. ALLEN HYNEK WAS ONE WHO EVENTUALLY BRAVED THE WAVE
OF AVOIDANCE, ATMOSPHERIC PHYSICIST JAMES E. MCDONALD ANOTHER. A THIRD WAS THE FRENCH
COMPUTER SCIENTIST, JACQUES VALLEE, WHO SERVED AS THE ROLE MODEL FOR THE UFO INVESTI-
GATOR PORTRAYED BY FRANCOIS TRUFFAUT IN STEVEN SPIELBERG'S CLOSE ENCOUNTERS OF THE
THIRD KIND (IN WHICH HYNEK HIMSELF HAD A CAMEO ROLE).

WHILE VALLEE'S OWN CONTRIBUTIONS TO THE FIELD HAVE BEEN BOTH SEMINAL AND LEG-
ENDARY, THEY'VE ALSO MANAGED TO GENERATE A FAIR AMOUNT OF OPPOSITION AND CONTROVERSY
WITHIN UFOLOGY ITSELF. CONSERVATIVE STUDIES OF THE SUBJECT SUCH AS ANATOMY OF A
PHENOMENON (1965) AND CHALLENGE TO SCIENCE: THE UFO ENIGMA (1966, CO-AUTHORED WITH
WIFE JANINE) WERE FOLLOWED BY PASSPORT TO MAGONIA: FROM FOLKLORE TO FLYING SAUCERS
(1969) AND MESSENGERS OF DECEPTION: UFO CONTACTS AND CULTS (1979). MESSENGERS, IN PAR-
TICULAR, WITH ITS WARNING OF THE POTENTIAL MANIPULATION OF SOCIETY'S PERCEPTION OF THE
UFO PHENOMENON, LEFT MANY UFOLOGISTS SCRATCHING THEIR COLLECTIVE SCALPS.

AFTER A DECADE OF MAINTAINING A RELATIVELY LOW PUBLIC PROFILE, VALLEE ERUPTED IN
PRINT AGAIN WITH WHAT IS KNOWN AS THE "ALIEN CONTACT TRILOGY," CONSISTING OF
DIMENSIONS (1988), CONFRONTATIONS (1990) AND REVELATIONS (1991). UFO CHRONICLES OF
THE SOVIET UNION: A COSMIC SAMIZDAT APPEARED IN 1992, THE SAME YEAR AS FORBIDDEN
SCIENCE, VALLEE'S JOURNALS FROM THE YEARS 1957-1969, FROM WHICH THE FOLLOWING EXCERPT
IS EXTRACTED. FASTWALKER, A NOVEL IN COLLABORATION WITH TRACY TORMÉ, WAS PUBLISHED LAST
YEAR. IN RECENT PUBLIC AND PRIVATE ANNOUNCEMENTS, VALLEE HAS LET IT BE KNOWN THAT HE
NOW CONSIDERS HIMSELF RETIRED FROM THE FIELD.

DAYS IN THE LIFE: DIARY ENTRIES FROM MAY 15 TO JULY 9, 1966

by Jacques Vallee

CHICAGO. SUNDAY 15 MAY 1966

Hynek called me this morning, with much bitterness in his voice. He was the guest speaker at the Midwest astronomers banquet in Madison last night, on the theme: "Flying Saucers I Have Known." He quoted the cases most susceptible to intrigue an audience of scientists. Yet Northwestern students who were in attendance later told him they had heard many negative comments among their colleagues. People were waiting for funny stories of naive witnesses and stupid farmers who confused Capella with a space-craft and marsh gas with an extraterrestrial mother ship. Instead he described the Mount Stromlo case, in which all the witnesses were astronomers, and the MIT case, and the sighting at Monticello by the two anthropologists we had interviewed in Madison, too close for comfort. And the explanations for these sightings? There were none, he said courageously. The audience didn't like it.

Personally I am sceptical about the possibility of any genuine research in this country even if the Air Force does create a special commission. It seems obvious that such a group will be dominated by sceptical people. I can imagine it conducting very costly statistics like Battelle Memorial Institute did in the days of Report 14. They can easily bury the problem in technical jargon while pretending to study it.

MONDAY 16 MAY 1966

A Northwestern graduate student has overheard a conversation about Hynek among two astronomers in a Tucson restaurant: "With all the money he makes as Air Force consultant, it wouldn't be surprising if he turned out to be the one who has been starting all those silly rumours about flying saucers!"

TUESDAY 24 MAY 1966

My written examination is finally over; I have submitted a book of answers 150 pages thick and my committee has accepted it, clearing me for the oral part and my dissertation itself. Relieved, I wrote to Alexander Kazantsev to confirm I would travel to the Mathematics Congress and to give him the dates of our trip to Moscow, then I drove to the beach to look at Lake Michigan. I sat at the edge of the water and started writing a new article about the patterns behind the landings for the *Flying Saucer Review*. I have read the Valensole file again. I imagined what it would be like to stand with Maurice Masse in his field in Provence. Perhaps I will do it some day. The clouds rushing around the skyscrapers of Chicago and the howling airliners which seemed to hover on their way to O'Hare brought me back to reality. Lake Michigan was very quiet today. Miles away to the north I could see the two white domes of the new observatory.

WEDNESDAY 25 MAY 1966

Harvey Plotnick has just returned from New York. He tells me that the recent success of *Anatomy* has opened up a new genre and triggered a chain reaction among the big publishers. The people who had written off the whole subject as utterly dead have revised their opinion now that they have seen the reviews. Every major New York house has a UFO book on its list of forthcoming titles, Harvey says, to capitalise on the market we have revealed. For example, G. P. Putnam is bringing out a book entitled *Incident at Exeter*, by John Fuller, which is the best of the bunch.

WEDNESDAY 8 JUNE 1966

A major event has happened in the last few days. A friend of Brian O'Brien has launched a bold new campaign that is taking everybody by surprise. His name is James McDonald, forty-five years old, professor of atmospheric physics at the University of Arizona. Having suddenly become interested in the subject, he read many books, including *Anatomy*, and decided to do his own research. Through O'Brien he asked to be authorised to spend two days at Wright Field. He began by requesting to be shown all the cases of 'globular lightning'. He was amazed and horrified at what he saw: case after case that obviously had nothing at all to do with electrical discharges in the air. So he asked to see more and started reading the general files, getting increasingly upset as he kept on reading.

McDonald moved very fast once he realised, as he told us bluntly, 'that the explanations were pure bullshit. So he bypassed the Major and went straight to the

General who heads up the Base, to tell him exactly what he thought of Blue Book. After forty-five minutes, which is much longer than Hynek ever spent with the General, they were talking about the humanoid occupants! Then he flew back to Arizona and started contacting all the amateur investigators, one by one, from APRO to NICAP. He made an appointment to see Hynek.

We have just had lunch with McDonald today, and it is clear that an entire era has come to a crashing end. This man has many contacts, many ideas, and he is afraid of nothing.

He reached the campus about 11:30 and Hynek took him on a tour of the observatory. At noon I went to pick them up, and I drove them back to Hynek's office, where we all sat down. McDonald signed the guest book, and I presented him with a copy of *Phénomènes insolites*. After that the serious business began, with a forceful attack against Hynek:

> "How could you remain silent so long?"
> I jumped in before a fight could erupt.
> "If Allen had taken a strong position last year the Air Force would have dropped him as consultant and we wouldn't be here talking about the phenomenon."
> McDonald brushed aside my comment.
> "I'm not talking about last year. It's in 1953 that Allen should have spoken out! Public opinion was ready for a serious scientific study."
> "In 1953 I was nothing, a negligible quantity for the Air Force," replied Hynek. "Ruppelt regarded me with considerable misgivings, as a first-class bother. He didn't like to have a scientist looking over his shoulder."
> "Yet he says some nice things about you in his book."
> "That didn't stop him from playing very close to the vest whenever I was around. He didn't let me see his cards."

The debate remained on that level, with McDonald insisting that Hynek had a duty to say something while Hynek would only concede that he had been 'a little timid.' Bill and I kept trying to explain to McDonald that any forceful statement by Hynek would have thrown him out of the inner circle. It could even have precipitated a decision by some General to put the files into the garbage.

Eventually we set aside our differences and the four of us went to lunch. At the restaurant the discussion became more constructive. Hynek retraced in detail the real history of Project Blue Book, truly an incredible tale. Thus he explained how, following Ruppelt's departure, he had seen a succession of unqualified, uninterested officers at the head of Blue Book. He was almost never invited to give an opinion. Hardin neglected his duties completely, he said. He spent all his time following the stock market while waiting for retirement – indeed, today he runs a brokerage office. McDonald was astonished, although he ought to have some experience of how the military runs. I can see how difficult it will be for the public to understand the situation, when the history of this incredible period finally gets written down.

THURSDAY 9 JUNE 1966

Two o'clock, and my oral examination is over. Things had started very badly this morning. I woke up too early and I was seized with nausea. I managed to drive all the way to Evanston. When I called my adviser to tell him I might be late, he said, "If that can make you feel better, you should know your written examination was

The astronomer and ufologist J. Allen Hynek (centre)

outstanding, we're all impressed...' Another professor told me my responses were among the best he had seen at Northwestern, and the oral part went well.

Afterwards Hynek bought me lunch. He assured me the road was clear for my thesis work. Naturally we compared notes about McDonald, and we discovered we had the same impression: extremely positive and enthusiastic at first, then a certain feeling of mistrust towards the man, an uneasy reaction that was hard to define.

SUNDAY 12 JUNE 1966

Tomorrow Hynek goes to Wright Field to meet with the Base Commander, General Cruikshank. He wants to find out just how impressed he was with McDonald's arguments. He has also written to Harold Brown, telling him frankly how he felt about the whole issue. In his answer the Secretary of the Air Force says he has 'carefully studied' his ideas: indeed the Air Force will go ahead with university-based investigations, which McDonald wanted to scratch as academic, worthless and irrelevant. The whole project is now in the hands of General James Ferguson in the Pentagon. Hynek and the Dean of the Northwestern Faculty of Sciences have an appointment with him. Other universities are being approached but it seems that Northwestern is the only one with enough guts to look seriously at the problem.

John Fuller is trying to set up a meeting with U Thant, the UN Secretary-General.

FRIDAY 17 JUNE 1966

I am trying to visualise what our research centre could do, how it would be organised physically. But I am not sure I want to go on living in Chicago and raising our son here. We do have many acquaintances on campus, and we are close to a few people with whom we have dinner occasionally, or go to a party or a movie. But apart from these few friends we see nothing but an emotional desert all around us.

TUESDAY 21 JUNE 1966.

Hynek returned to Evanston today with some important news. He had gone off to New York to see Fuller and U Thant, who was anxious to know what the United States is going to do about the UFO question, because some of the member nations had expressed concern. Hynek assured him that the Air Force had firmly decided to create an independent scientific commission, the only remaining question being to know where it would be located. This could be a step towards the UN setting up their own study, under the Space Committee.

'You know that I am a Buddhist,' said U Thant. 'We believe there is life throughout the universe.'

'Most astronomers would agree with you,' replied Hynek. 'The question is to know how "they" would ever come here, given the enormous distances involved.'

'Perhaps their lifespan is measured in centuries rather than years. Coming here could be as simple for them as going around the block is simple for us!'

They went on to discuss the possibility of alien bases on Mars. U Thant also wanted to know about observations made by pilots. Hynek quoted *Anatomy*, adding in his usual cautious manner that such observations 'had indeed been reported.'

Finally they discussed possible action points. U Thant explained that the initiative could only come from member nations. It is their government which must bring the subject up before the General Assembly.

Hynek has requested my help in this. I will ask Aimé Michel if he can set up a meeting with a French government representative, and I will write to Fontes to get him to initiate similar action with Brazilian authorities.

While we were thus talking in Hynek's office a long letter arrived from the Secretary of the Air Force, and he read it to us. Brown said that Hynek's recommendation to turn the problem over to scientists was now getting the highest priority.

We also learned that Lyle Boyd, Menzel's co-author, would be happy to move to Evanston if we were to get the research contract. Finally, a group of unnamed scientists said to be from Wright Field has asked Hynek to supply his "twenty best cases." Who are these people? I advised him not to send them anything until we know for certain where these friendly strangers come from and what kind of hidden agenda they may have.

WEDNESDAY 22 JUNE 1966

What I heard today has left me very puzzled. Hynek and the Dean just came back from Washington, where they had conferred with General Giller, who serves on Ferguson's staff. Ferguson himself belongs to Air Force Research and Development. And Giller told them categorically that under no circumstances would Northwestern get the contract. The Air Force, he patiently explained, is looking for a university that has not had any previous involvement with the problem. Hynek says it is like opening a restaurant and looking for a chef who has not had any previous involvement with cooking!

The real reason is perfectly clear. They are only looking for a rubber stamp, and the last thing they want is the intellectual independence of Hynek's team. There may be a small silver lining here: perhaps the Air Force will give us the task of organising the historical data, while the major contract aims at future cases only. Another relatively positive aspect is that Hynek will now be free to speak out without an 'Air Force' label. He will begin by writing a carefully worded preface for *Challenge*. I also recommended that he push harder towards the creation of a UN commission, where he would be the logical leader. And I added:

'Let's see how those who get the award will explain away the UFO Phenomenon. They don't know what they are getting into.'

SUNDAY 26 JUNE 1966

Jim McDonald called me yesterday from Tucson to get more data about power failure cases. We ended up spending an hour on the phone talking about the general situation of the field. He confessed to me that his radical campaign bore little fruit so far. It seems all he has accomplished is to antagonise the Wright Field people. He acknowledged he had not succeeded in convincing Kuiper either. Even his friend Brian O'Brien, with whom he had another meeting last Friday, remains sceptical. One would think he would learn something from this. Yet he continues to claim that the lack of interest in the subject among scientists is all Hynek's fault. He has clearly been indoctrinated by the folks at NICAP, especially Keyhoe and Hall. In a conversation with McDonald, Hall has even insinuated that Hynek didn't really know much about the UFO problem, and that he had only done research on "five or six cases," which is patently false. Hynek's only interest in the whole thing, Hall told McDonald, is the money he gets from the Air Force! It is not surprising that the field makes no progress, mired as it is in this kind of unfounded rumours, bitter infighting and deliberate calumnies.

Jim tried to recruit me for his camp.

"If it wasn't for your influence, and all the research you brought over from France, Hynek would still be arguing that ninety-nine percent of those reports are due to Venus or to marsh gas!" he said. "It's time for you to move on."

Yet I don't see what good McDonald's approach will do, if he keeps behaving like a bull in a china shop.

Atmospheric physicist James McDonald

TUESDAY 28 JUNE 1966

While I was typing the appendices to *Challenge* the phone rang and I heard Allen's joyous voice. He was calling me from Colorado to report on a direct request by Quintanilla: he now wants to have our proposal for data reduction of all the Blue Book files as soon as possible. This would be a parallel effort to the main contract the Air Force has not yet awarded. The Major stated that Northwestern had the highest chances of getting the job, since both Allen and I were there. This would not be a sole source contract, however. At least one other university would be consulted to provide healthy competition.

Allen was elated at this news, and he seemed ready to jump back on the barricade and fight. He was reading the end of

Challenge, he told me, and he congratulated me: 'Reading it, I realise better than ever that the phenomenon embodies an authentic mystery. It shows up in your graphs with the hourly distribution of sightings,' he said. We made grandiose plans for the Autumn.

FRIDAY 8 JULY 1966.

On Wednesday morning I went to O'Hare with Janine and with the observatory administrator to greet Hynek as he flew in from Denver. We held a meeting in the TWA Ambassadors' Club to review the proposal in detail, far from the ringing telephones of the office or from his busy house in Evanston.

If the history of all this gets written some day, I take pity on those who will try to extract the deeper meaning and the actual motivations of the protagonists. The Air Force wants to get rid of the responsibility for a mystery it obviously can't cope with. If they lean too heavily towards the sceptics' side, turning all UFOs into marsh gas and globular lightning, the witnesses will have good reason to feel insulted, and they may complain to their Congressmen. But if they were to confess the truth, namely that many sightings go unexplained, the American public may simply get scared and feel unprotected. This is one battle the Air Force cannot win, especially when the scientific community looks down its august nose at the whole thing and refuses to get its hands dirty. The new concepts that started to evolve in our own minds five or six years ago have not spread among our colleagues yet, not even among the best informed of the ufologists. But sooner or later these new concepts will become the dominant framework. Historians will take them for granted. It will be very hard for those who will look back on this period to understand our hesitations, our painstaking manoeuvres.

Hynek received the proposal on Monday. He had only a few changes to suggest, mainly in the budget section. I proposed that we add Lyle Boyd to the team. After all, Boyd wrote Menzel's book and would be an excellent source of knowledge to balance the staff of our project. Driving back to Evanston we rushed to a typewriter and we had the document polished up in time for Hynek to leave for Dayton. He promised to call as soon as he had anything new.

I was at home and asleep when he called last night about 11p.m. The Air Force had already started to process our document. There was general confusion in Dayton, because they didn't know yet which university would get the main research contract: 'The right hand of the Air Force doesn't know what the left hand is doing,' he said, laughing. Our only competitor for the data analysis contract is Battelle Memorial Institute in Columbus, not far from Dayton. Many years ago Battelle compiled Special Report #14. It is said that they were paid the sum of $600,000 for it, a very large amount in 1953, showing that the Air Force was seriously looking for answers at that time.

Hynek did present our database proposal at a 10a.m. meeting attended by Quintanilla, four Colonels and the Wright Field chief scientist, Dr. Cacciopa. The briefing was well-received, he said: 'If it was up to the Dayton people we would already have the contract.'

The Air Force is eager to get on with the job. They are getting a little anxious because another one of the universities they contacted has turned them down, and two leading scientists have told them they wouldn't touch the UFO research business with a ten-foot pole, no matter how much they were paid. Hynek keeps over-reacting to the criticisms voiced by McDonald. I have had to advise him against writing a strong UFO manifesto and sending it to *Science* magazine: 'Let's at least wait until we have a signed contract,' I recommended.

Jim Lorenzen called Hynek during his stay in Boulder. He told him that he and Coral were thinking of dissolving APRO. They are looking for someone to buy the files for fifteen thousand dollars.

SATURDAY 9 JULY 1966.

Anatomy will soon be out in paperback. It will be in every airport and every drug-store in America, from Maine to Oregon, sandwiched between the latest report on teenage sexuality and some Western novel of cowboys and Indians. What good will that do?

I went to the edge of the lake alone, to think. What are we trying to accomplish? I came to the sad conclusion that our efforts are childish and probably hopeless, because this is a very shallow, desperate world that has no vision and takes no chances.

LOCAL GROUPS ARE THE LIFEBLOOD OF UFOLOGY. TO PROPERLY EVALUATE A REPORT, LOCAL KNOWL-
EDGE IS INDISPENSABLE; EXPERTS FROM AFAR, UNFAMILIAR WITH THE LIE OF THE LAND AND THE HABITS
OF THE RESIDENTS, CAN EASILY JUMP TO FALSE CONCLUSIONS WHICH MAKE A MYSTERY OUT OF A
MOLEHILL. TENS OF THOUSANDS OF SUCH GROUPS HAVE BEEN FORMED DURING THE FIFTY YEARS OF
UFO HISTORY. SOME FADED QUICKLY FROM THE SCENE, SOME ENDURED AND FLOURISHED: BUT
SHORT- OR LONG-LIVED, THEY PROVIDED THE BROAD BASE ON WHICH THE NATIONAL ORGANISA-
TIONS STOOD.

FEW SUCH GROUPS HAVE PLAYED SO SIGNIFICANT A ROLE AS THE MERSEYSIDE UNIDENTIFIED
FLYING OBJECTS RESEARCH GROUP, CREATED IN MAY 1966 IN LIVERPOOL, IN NORTH-EASTERN
ENGLAND. THE GROUP WAS TO CHANGE ITS NAME FROM TIME TO TIME, AND IS TODAY KNOWN
WORLDWIDE UNDER ITS MAGONIA BANNER: BUT THROUGHOUT ITS LIFE IT HAS MAINTAINED A CON-
SISTENT ROLE AS THE WATCHDOG OF BRITISH UFOLOGY. THE OPENING WORDS OF ITS VERY FIRST
BULLETIN SET A TONE IT HAS NEVER LOST:

THE RECENT PRESS COVERAGE OF UFOS HAS NO DOUBT CAUSED MANY UFOLOGISTS
MUCH REJOICING. CATS WILL HAVE BEEN NOTED PEEPING OUT OF BAGS EVERYWHERE, AND
THE GREAT TRUTH TO BE ON THE VERGE OF REVELATION. OTHER UFO INVESTIGATORS WILL
HAVE VIEWED THE PUBLICITY WAVE WITH MIXED FEELINGS...

'MIXED FEELINGS' HAVE BEEN WHAT JOHN RIMMER AND HIS COLLEAGUES HAVE OFFERED THE
UFO COMMUNITY FOR MORE THAN THIRTY YEARS, DRAWING VITUPERATION FROM A FEW, BUT
RESPECT FROM MOST SERIOUS UFOLOGISTS. FOR ALL ITS TINY CIRCULATION, FEW UFO JOURNALS
HAVE BEEN ATTACKED SO FIERCELY OR PRAISED SO LAVISHLY: IT IS HARDLY EXAGGERATION TO SAY
THAT WHAT MAGONIA THINKS TODAY, THE UFO COMMUNITY WILL THINK TOMORROW. IN 1968 IT
DESCRIBED ITSELF AS 'ONE OF THE FEW PUBLICATIONS IN THIS FIELD WHICH DOES NOT SEEK TO BLUD-
GEON ITS READERS INTO THE ACCEPTANCE OF THE PROPOSITION THAT UFOS ARE SPACESHIPS FROM
OTHER PLANETS'. TODAY, AS THEN, MAGONIA DOES NOT BLUDGEON ITS READERS: IT SIMPLY INVITES
THEM TO EXAMINE MORE CLOSELY THE PROPOSITION THAT FLYING SAUCERS COME FROM OUTER
SPACE, THAT ABDUCTIONS ARE PHYSICALLY REAL, OR THAT WARMINSTER IS THE UFO CAPITAL OF
ENGLAND.

JOHN RIMMER CAN BE CONTACTED AT JOHN DEE COTTAGE, 5 JAMES TERRACE, MORTLAKE
CHURCHYARD, LONDON SW14 8HB: PHONE +44 (0)181 876 7246

A UFO FLAP AREA

by John Rimmer

From the beginning of UFO research in the early 1950s, through to the
1980s, ufologists have studied the phenomenon of the 'flap' or 'wave'.
These terms denoted concentrations of UFO reports within a limited period of time, or in a limited geographical area. 'Wave' usually referred to a
gradual increase in sightings over a wide geographical spread across a period of
weeks or even months. Notable waves occurred in France in 1954, in the USA in
1965-66, and in Britain in 1968. The term 'flap' usually refers to a more localised
phenomenon in quite a small area, and maybe centred on a few percipients.

Throughout the sixties and seventies, some ufologists devoted a considerable amount of time to attempting to discern some pattern within and between the major waves. They linked them to a variety of other periodic phenomena, ranging from the sun-spot cycle and close approaches of the planet Mars to sociological stresses in American society. Gradually, with the concentration of interest on such aspects of ufology as crash-retrievals, abductions, and military involvement, and the consequent lessening of interest in 'lights-in-the-sky' types of cases, the wave phenomenon seemed to fade out of public consciousness in the 1980s. Perhaps the Belgian mystery triangles of 1989-90 are the exception to prove the rule, as the interest in these objects was largely promoted by the very strong military overtones to the reports. Many researchers regarded them as sightings of test-flights of 'Stealth'-type technology.

The more localised type of flap, however, continues to be reported and recorded. This is often because of the involvement of a particular individual or research group in a specific location. A large number of cases reported throughout 1994 and 1995 in the Central Region of Scotland can be traced to the enthusiasm of a number of local researchers. They not only publicised nationally and internationally reports which might otherwise have been confined to the local press, but also provided an accessible and sympathetic reporting point for local people, whose puzzling experiences might otherwise have gone unrecorded. This makes it difficult to say whether such flaps are the result of an objective increase in the number of strange events actually taking place in a locality, or a result of the increased activity of locally-based researchers. This prompts one to ask whether any area could become a flap area if a group of keen ufologists who were skilled in handling the media began operating in the area.

Perhaps the most famous flap area in Britain is the small Wiltshire market town of Warminster, situated on the main road and rail links between the tourist centres of Bath and Salisbury. From 1962 to the late 1970s, the town and its surrounding countryside was a focal point of UFO activity. As in many other flaps, many of the events seemed to centre around a single charismatic personality; in this case a local journalist, Arthur Shuttlewood, who died on September 12, 1996, at the age of 76.

The Warminster phenomenon built up gradually, beginning with reports of a strange noise, which would move over the town at night. Local residents reported a phenomenon which shook the tiles on their roofs and rattled the windows of their houses as it passed. Local concern grew so great that at one point the Town Council organised a public meeting for citizens to air their worries and hear 'explanations' from a variety of self-appointed experts, many pushing their own agendas. It is significant that Warminster adjoins an area of Salisbury Plain that is closed to the public, and used for military exercises. Warminster itself is surrounded by military camps and ranges. In this early stage of the phenomenon most local residents, if not visitors, were prepared to put 'The Thing' down to military activity.

The Warminster reports gained a focus in 1965 when a photograph taken by Warminster resident Gordon Faulkner was published in the mass-circulation tabloid The *Daily Mirror* showing a classic circular 'saucer' allegedly hovering over the town. This image rapidly gained recognition as the 'Warminster Thing', and was reproduced on the cover of the first of Arthur Shuttlewood's books, *The Warminster Mystery*.

With continued press interest, and Shuttlewood's energetic promotion of the town in a string of later books, Warminster rapidly became the centre of UFO activity in Britain for the rest of the decade. The town appeared to be a place where a UFO sighting could be virtually guaranteed to anyone prepared to take the trouble to look, helped largely by the continuing military activity on Salisbury Plain and other Army ranges closer to the town. A visit to Warminster became almost a rite of passage for a generation of British ufologists.

Shuttlewood's first book was basically a collection of anecdotes about the 'Thing' and a wide range of other odd stories which were reported from around Warminster. They included such events as birds falling dead from the sky, ghostly figures leaping out in front of car drivers, cars mysteriously stopping, and unexplained light phenomena in the hills around the town. Later books, with titles like *The Flying Saucerers* and *Warnings From Flying Friends* put the author much more in the tradition of the saucer contactee, alongside figures such as the American, George Adamski. At these hilltop vigils Shuttlewood would provide a running commentary on the sights and sounds of the Wiltshire night.

Most visitors would spend a night skywatching at one of two major vantage points just outside the town: Cley Hill and Cradle Hill. Both gave good views across the surrounding countryside, including the Army ranges which stretched from Cradle Hill to the deserted village of Imber. As ufologists met during the day in the pubs and cafes of the town, informal itineraries and skywatching parties would be arranged. Sometimes these would be more organised, as the major national UFO organisations would from time to time coordinate national skywatches. As night fell a small convoy of cars would drive out of town to the hill-top sites. Most nights Arthur Shuttlewood would be at the site to put his own spin on the subsequent events.

A typical Warminster skywatch would see a dozen or so people huddled round parked cars at the top of a lane leading to the summit of Cradle Hill, next to a gate which marked the limits of the Army land. One of the things which is most surprising to newcomers at UFO skywatches is just how much there is to see in the darkness. Headlights of cars several miles away seem surprisingly bright. At night it may be impossible to see the horizon or the outline of other hills, and most people are very vague when it comes to estimating the angular elevation of objects, so lights actually on the ground may seem to be well above the horizon. Arthur Shuttlewood, however, was very familiar with the topography of his part of the world, and he was able to calm down over-excited first-time skywatchers who tended to claim every passing car as a UFO. This matter-of-factness made him more convincing when he was describing the amazing sights that he and his small coterie of Warminster-based colleagues claimed to have witnessed. His spoken commentaries, like his books, were full of lavish descriptions: lights never 'shone', they were always 'corruscating'; their trajectories were never 'from horizon to horizon', but 'coursing across the vault of the heavens.'

The groups who stood on the Warminster hilltops listening and watching came from across Britain and Europe, and they brought with them their own contributions and experiences, stories which then became part of the Warminster ethos. Events did not have to be particularly strange to be imbued with the Warminster magic – one story, followed breathlessly by a group of skywatchers, boiled down to the apparent claim that the needles in a ball of knitting-wool were mysteriously reversed whilst in the glove-compartment of a visitor's car!

The improbability of many of the stories mattered little however, compared with the atmosphere they created. Arthur Shuttlewood himself was a natural storyteller. No doubt many of his narratives had been honed through repetition to countless groups of skywatchers, but they were told with a quiet and fluent authority, no 'ums' or 'errs', his voice modulating as a revving car engine broke the nocturnal silence. After a while the whole skywatching experience would take on an almost hypnotic character, with a combination of sensory deprivation in the darkness, the steady murmur of Arthur's voice, and the self-reinforcing gossip of a small group of enthusiasts. Wild rumours would circulate around the hilltop: at one point it was said that Army personnel had orders to shoot Arthur Shuttlewood if he strayed onto Ministry of Defence property!

At the height of the flap the summer Bank Holidays would see hundreds of would-be UFO spotters in the town. Although many local residents were resentful of the notoriety their home town had gained, others welcomed the significant extra revenue it brought into the local economy.

The Warminster 'flap' probably peaked as a phenomenon in 1967 or 1968, although it continued as a ufological experience well into the next decade. An event which was perhaps influential in demythologising events in the town took place in 1970. A group of ufological sceptics associated with a Surrey-based society SIUFOP (Society for the Investigation of Unidentified Flying Objects) staged a well-planned but basically simple hoax. It involved a car with a flashing light standing on the roof which was parked on a hill about ¾ of a mile from the regular group of skywatchers on Cradle Hill. One of the hoaxers was planted amongst the watchers, with a camera containing previously prepared photographs showing a light shape superimposed on a photograph of the landscape. After the group had noted the flashing light the 'plant' announced that he had photographed the phenomenon, and asked if any of the others present would take the film and have it developed. The film was taken by one of the skywatchers, who was associated with the magazine *Flying Saucer Review*, which at the time was the largest circulation UFO-related magazine in Britain, with an international circulation.

The pictures were developed and the images revealed were published in *Flying Saucer Review*. For two years a debate continued in the pages of that magazine, which discussed the possible motive power of the 'object' photographed, its direction of travel and its size. The fact that the photograph bore no similarity to the light seen by the skywatchers (they were not even in the same positions) was explained by suggestions that the 'object' was emitting ultraviolet radiation or was surrounded by ionised air.

Besides the fact that the image on the photographs was quite different from the observed light, and in quite a different location, the hoaxers had introduced a number of other deliberate discrepancies into the photographs which they thought investigators would notice. These were not noticed. One researcher who examined the negatives reported 'there is nothing about these photographs which suggests to me they have been faked in any way'. The Director of Research at the Astrophysical Institute at the French National Centre for Scientific Research declared: 'In my opinion there is no question of the object photographed being in any way the result of faking...'

SIUFOP had intended to let the experiment run for several years, monitoring discussion and comments on the affair in specialist magazines. However through a coincidence, the editors of *Flying Saucer Review* found out about the deception after about two years. and the story was dropped by the UFO press.

Besides any possible effects of this incident on the ufological community, many researchers were independently becoming disillusioned by the Warminster phenomenon. Events in the town were increasingly being centred around a cultist group called the Star Fellowship, and Arthur Shuttlewood's books were growing even more opaque and occult-flavoured. His 1971 title, UFOS, *Key to the New Age*, seemed to epitomise the changes that were taking place at Warminster, which was becoming a destination on the New Age pilgrimage route around the West of England: a suitable stopping-off point on the way back from the Glastonbury Festival.

Eventually Warminster died as a major centre of UFO interest, the brief UFO boom passed and the tourist economy of the town relied once again on visitors to the neighbouring attractions at Lord Bath's stately home at Longleat. One disillusioned visitor in 1971 noted that the inexpensive rooms over the Farmer Giles pub where ufologists stayed had been transformed into the upmarket 'Farmers' Hotel'.

Although there was still a UFO/New Age group operating from the town, Warminster rarely featured in the UFO literature throughout most of the seventies and eighties. The 'Thing' had gone elsewhere, and Arthur Shuttlewood's stream of books dried up.

Interest returned in the late eighties, with the growth of the corn circle phenomena. Warminster was in the middle of the Wessex region where the majority of circles appeared. The town's earlier history was dredged by both mystery circle proponents and sceptics. Critics pointed to the absence of anything resembling a sharp-edged corn-circle during the town's heyday, when it was full of ufologists looking for anything strange or mysterious. Believers, on the other hand, found descriptions of circular markings and disturbances recorded in Shuttlewood's books and articles in small circulation specialist magazines published at the height of the Warminster flap.

Perhaps a line can be drawn under the Warminster events with the confession in 1992 by a former Warminster resident that the original photograph of the 'Thing', which had featured in a double-page spread in the *Daily Mirror*, was a hoax. Roger Hooton told the British UFO Research Association that he, the photographer Gordon Faulkner, and another man had faked the photograph by throwing a small model into the air and snapping it. Like the more methodical experimental hoaxers of SIUFOP a few years later they had incorporated a number of deliberate inconsistencies into their story. Again, none of the investigators had picked them up. Two of the principle hoaxers were connected with the *Warminster Journal*, the local paper which Shuttlewood also worked for. In his confession Roger Hooton claimed that the *Journal's* editor and publisher, Charles Mills, was aware of the hoax at the time and published it as a joke. Certainly the coverage of the story in the newspaper – half a column on page seven – seems remarkably restrained compared to the centre page spread it merited in the *Daily Mirror*.

Perhaps the town's last gasp of publicity came at the end of 1996, when a film company chose to hold a promotion event there to publicise the UFO blockbuster *Independence Day*, and unveiled a plaque proclaiming Warminster as Britain's 'UFO Capital'.

Warminster is just one UFO flap area amongst hundreds around the world. Although it accounts for thousands of individual UFO sightings, its growth as a significant part of UFO history is probably accounted for by the intense activity of just one man. Media interest in a cluster of UFO reports and accounts of other odd events would have faded out within a few months, except for the appearance of one hoaxed photograph, fortuitously linked to the local paper, and the energetic promotion given to it by the local stringer for a national tabloid. From that a ufological legend was born.

As the most visible government and military agency ever established to investigate the UFO phenomenon, America's Project Blue Book came under increasing scrutiny and criticism from civilian ufologists. Was it really interested in UFO investigation, or little more than a public relations ploy? Was it a source of reliable information, or merely an outlet for anti-UFO propaganda. Conspiracy theories abounded. What can't be denied is the fact that, without the Blue Book files, ufology would be seriously impoverished today, both publically and scientifically.

From April of 1963 until December of 1969, when the United States Air Force officially closed the covers of Project Blue Book, Hector Quintanilla was its commanding officer. The picture that emerges from this excerpt of his unpublished memoirs, UFOs: An Air Force Dilemma, clearly contrasts the military viewpoint of such matters against that of the civilian UFO culture of the time.

PROJECT BLUE BOOK'S LAST YEARS

by Colonel Hector J. Quintanilla (ret.)

n April 1963 I was informed of a new assignment at Wright-Patterson Air Force Base. Nobody mentioned UFOs and probably nobody knew at the time that I was to become the new (and the last) Project Blue Book Officer. I arrived at Wright-Patterson during the latter part of July 1963. My sponsor was Lt. Col. Robert Friend, chief of Project Blue Book from 1959 to July 1963. Bob Friend had done a tremendous job with the UFO program, but very few people knew it. He did his job, did it well, and stayed in the background. Bob took me around the base, showed me where all the essential buildings were located and then introduced me to all his contacts. In this business, contacts are essential in order to get the job done in the minimum time. When the formality of processing was all over, I was introduced to the man who in some ways changed my life and in a way also changed the destiny of UFOs. This gentleman was a man who stood six foot, three inches tall, walked straight as an arrow, had a commanding voice, was a West Point graduate, a native of California, *persona non grata* in some circles, and a full Colonel who went by the name of Eric de Jonckheere.

Colonel de Jonckheere wasted no time in telling me that he had selected me to be the next UFO officer. He had reviewed my record and considered me qualified to handle the job. He needed an officer with a physics degree, with maturity, tact, drive, and one who could stay cool under fire. I shook my head – hell, he couldn't be talking about me. I had a physics degree and I was mature, but the rest of the stuff was not part of my make-up. He asked me to try it for a couple of weeks and then come back and give him a briefing. Bob Friend briefed me on the program and I occupied myself daily by doing background reading and research.

On 5 August 1963, we got a call from the newspaper office in Fairfield, Illinois. The *Wayne County Press* was having a field day. The first paragraph of the paper that day read as follows: 'An 18-year-old boy was chased home Sunday night by a flying saucer or some other unknown heavenly body. The whole neighbour-

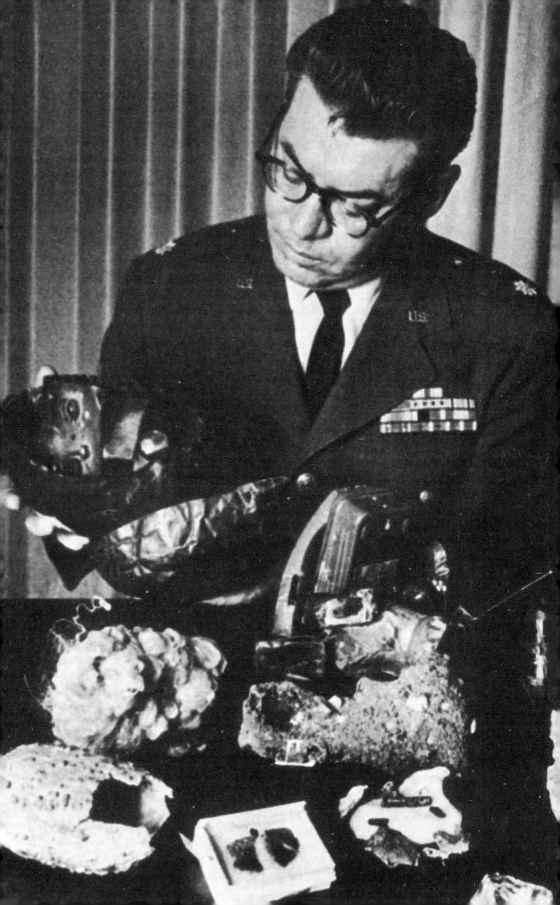

hood out this way is talking about it.'

MY FIRST UFO CASE

This report triggered other reports, so Bob said that I could cut my teeth on this one. I'll have to admit that I was apprehensive and probably scared, so I was most happy that Bob was heading the team. The other member of the team was Sgt. Charles R. Sharp, who would be our photographer. We left for Fairfield immediately and arrived at our destination late at night. The following morning we visited the Sheriff's office and he briefed us on what had transpired. The sheriff wasn't excited at all and he wasn't the least bit concerned at what had happened. We went to the newspaper office and they gave us names of some additional witnesses.

First off, we contacted the young man who had experienced the frightening event. The newspaper reporters had been interviewing him so much that his mother at first refused to let us talk to him. The young man's grandfather interceded for us and then we were able to proceed with the investigation. We started at the beginning where he first experienced the event, on the road from the drive-in movie. We measured angles, distances, times, etc. We went over the same route and reconstructed the event as closely as possible. I was taking most of the notes and Bob was asking most of the questions. We had a star chart with us and the clincher came when the young man told us that he and some friends had stayed up until four o'clock in the morning watching the saucer. The saucer disappeared all of a sudden at day break.

In order to complete the investigation, we had to talk to the young man's girlfriend. She had been in the car with him as they were driving back from the drive-in movie. The young lady was bothered by a toothache and wouldn't sit adjacent to the driver. She was in no mood to be cordial and this possibly bothered the driver to no end. She wasn't excited about her boyfriend's experience. Two days after her boyfriend had experienced the event, her toothache was gone and she didn't know what all the excitement was about.

Before we left Fairfield, we had concluded that the flying saucer chasing the young man was really the planet Jupiter. We had two other sightings to check while we were in Fairfield. We determined that the second sighting was a meteor. We had other witnesses to verify our conclusions. The other sighting was an air-to-air refuelling operation which we verified as soon as we returned to Wright-Patterson.

Back at the base, Colonel de Jonckheere asked for a full report. Bob told me to write it up because I'd have to brief the 'ol' man.' I briefed the Colonel and gave him a full account of what had transpired, our conclusions, etc. He nodded his head in satisfaction and said, 'You're my new UFO officer.' At that time I didn't think I was ready for the responsibility and I told him so. Colonel de Jonckheere looked me straight in the eye and said: 'You take this job and do it well or I'll bust your ass.' And that, ladies and gentlemen, is how I became a UFO investigating officer.

THE SOCORRO CASE

From July 1963 to April 1964 there was very little publicity about the UFO program. I had just come on board as project officer, so the UFO hobby clubs were not yet picking on the program again. Public relations were routine, such as answering letters and furnishing information to students for their science projects or term papers. Things were going so well, that I remember I stopped smoking that January.

But all hell broke loose on 24 April 1964, and I started smoking again. On that date at approximately 17.45 hours, at Socorro, New Mexico, police officer Lonnie Zamora was headed south chasing a speeding automobile when he suddenly heard a roar and saw a flame in the sky to the southeast. He decided to let the speeder go in favour of investigating the flame, because he knew there was a dynamite shack in the area and it might have blown up. He turned onto a gravel road that led by the shack.

As he was driving slowly along the road, Zamora saw above a steep hill just ahead a funnel shaped flame, bluish and sort of orange. The base of the flame was hidden behind the hill; there was no smoke connected with the flame. He had trouble getting his car to the top of the hill because of loose gravel; he had to try three times before he made it. As he reached the top of the hill, he saw a shiny object to the south, this side of the dynamite shack, about 150 to 200 yards away. It was off the road to the left in the arroyo, and at first glance it looked like a car turned over. But when he drove closer, it appeared to be aluminum clay, not chrome, and oval-shaped like a football.

Zamora drove about 50 feet along the hill crest, radioing back to the sheriff's office, '10-44 [accident], I'll be 10-6 [busy out of the car], checking a wreck down in the arroyo.' From this point, seated in the car, he could not see the object over the edge of the hill. As he stopped the car, he was still talking on the radio, and as he was getting out, he dropped his mike. He picked it up and put it back and started down towards the object.

Just then he heard a very loud roar, not exactly like a blast, but also not steady like a jet engine. It was of low frequency at first and then became higher. At the same time he saw a light blue flame, sort of orange at the bottom. Zamora believed the flame came from the underside of the object; he could see no smoke but he did see some dust in the vicinity. He panicked, thinking the object was going to blow up.

ZAMORA'S REPORT

The following is Zamora's report, slightly rearranged for the sake of clarity: 'As soon as I saw flame and heard roar... ran away from object but did turn head towards object. Object... was smooth – no windows or doors. As roar started, it was still on the ground. Noted red lettering of some type... Insignia was about two and one half inches high and about two inches wide, I guess. Was in the middle of object... Object still like aluminum white.

'[Running], bumped leg on car back fender area. Car facing southwest... fell by car and [sun]glasses fell off, kept running to north, with car between me and object... rose about level of car, about 20 to 25 feet, guess. Took, I guess, about six seconds when object started to rise and I glanced back... it appeared about directly over the place where it rose from.

'I was still running... [then] about 50 feet from car, I ducked down, just over edge of hill... I stopped because I did not hear the roar. I was scared of the roar, and I had planned to continue running down the hill. I turned around toward the object and at the same time put my head toward ground, covering my face with my arms... when the roar stopped, heard a sharp tone whine and the whine lasted maybe a second. Then there was complete silence about the object.

'That's when I lifted up my head and saw the object going away from me... in a southwestern direction... It did not come any closer to me. It appeared to go in straight line and at same height – possibly 10 to 15 feet from ground, and it cleared the dynamite shack by about three feet. Shack about eight feet high. Object was travelling west fast. It seemed to rise up and take off immediately across country.

'I ran back to my car and as I ran back, I kept an eye on the object. I picked up my… sunglasses, got into the car, and radioed to Nep Lopes, radio operator, to look out the window to see if he could see an object. He asked, 'What is it?' I answered, 'It looks like a balloon.' I don't know if he saw it. If Nep looked out his window, which faces north, he couldn't see it. I did not tell him at the moment which window to look out of.

'As I was calling Nep, I could still see object. The object seemed to lift up slowly, and to get small in the distance very fast. It seemed to just clear the Box Canyon or Mile Canyon Mountain. It disappeared as it went over the mountain. It had no flame whatsoever as it was travelling over the ground, and no smoke or noise.

'Feeling in good health. Last drink – two or three beers – was over a month ago. Noted no odours. Noted no sounds other than described. Gave direction to Nep Lopes at radio and to Sergeant Chaves (of New Mexico State Police at Socorro) to get there. Went down to where the object had been, and I noted the brush was burning in several places. I got my pen and drew a picture of the insignia on the object.

'Then Sgt. Chaves came up, asked me what the trouble was because I was sweating and he told me that I was white, very pale. I asked the Sgt. to see what I saw and that was the burning brush. Sgt. Chaves and I went down to the spot and Sgt. Chaves pointed out the tracks.

'When I first saw the object (when I thought it might be a car) I saw what appeared to be two legs of some type from the object to the ground. At the time, I didn't pay much attention to… the two legs. The two legs were at the bottom of the object, slanted outwards to the ground. The object might have been about three and a half feet from the ground at the time…'

MY INVESTIGATION

Lonnie Zamora experienced an event which left quite an impression on him. He was a serious officer, a pillar of his church, and a man well versed in recognising airborne vehicles in his area. He was puzzled by what he saw, and frankly, so was I. And yet, I've always had some doubt about this case, even though it is the best documented case on record. In spite of the fact that I conducted the most thorough investigation that was humanly possible, the vehicle or stimulus that scared Zamora to the point of panic has never been found.

During the course of the investigation and immediately thereafter, everything that was possible to verify was checked. The communications media must have been waiting for a case like this, because after Zamora reported his sighting all hell broke loose. The telephone at my house was ringing off the hook. I went to my office so that I could direct the investigation from there and at the same time contact Kirtland, Holloman, and White Sands via our telephone communications system. As I walked into our building, and turned into the hallway towards my office, I could hear the telephone ringing, ringing, ringing.

The operator informed me that I had 10 or 12 calls waiting for me. I decided not to accept the calls until after I had talked with my UFO investigating officer at Kirtland. Major Connor was my primary investigator at Kirtland, but he was

Landing traces at Socorro

inexperienced. Fortunately, my chief analyst, Sgt. David Moody, was on temporary duty at Kirtland. I asked Major Connor to get in touch with him and for Moody to get in touch with me regardless of the hour. It was hours before the investigation could be organised and on its way. A Geiger counter had to be found and the base photographer had to be called. The staff car, which had been provided for the investigation had a flat tire midway between Albuquerque and Socorro. Socorro is located 55 miles south of Kirtland Air Force Base.

The Stallion Range Officer had already conducted a preliminary investigation and had also interviewed Zamora. This information was turned over to the Air Force investigators as soon as they began their interview with Zamora. Connor and Moody kept in touch with me and provided me with good information, but there was nothing from which we could draw a definite conclusion or a decent evaluation. The news media was on SAFOI's back and SAFOI [Secretary of the Air Force Office of Administration - eds] was on my back. I didn't have any idea as to what Zamora saw and reported, but by God, I was going to find it. Because of the pressure from the news media, I decided to send Dr. J Allen Hynek, Project Blue Book consultant, to Kirtland to help with the investigation. I felt that Hynek could concentrate on Socorro while Connor and Moody could check all other activity at the other bases in New Mexico.

In the meantime, Marilyn Beumer Stancombe, my secretary, and I began checking for some sort of possible activity. Radiation had been checked by Connor and Moody and the readings were negative. I checked the Holloman AFB Balloon

Control Centre for balloon activity. All local weather stations and Air Force bases in New Mexico were checked for release of weather balloons. Helicopter activity was checked throughout the state. Government and private aircraft were checked. The reconnaissance division in the Pentagon was checked. I checked with the immigration division hoping they might help. Finally, I was at my wits end, so I told Marilyn: 'Get me the White House Command Post.'

She looked at me with those beautiful blue eyes of hers like I was nuts. I said, 'Yes, Marilyn, the White House Command Post.' She never asked me a question, she just started dialling. I was afraid she would ask me how she could reach them, but she didn't. It took her five or six calls, but she got me the Command Post. A Major General answered and I explained to him my situation. He was very sympathetic, but off-hand he couldn't recall any type of activity in my area of interest. However, he said he'd check and call me back. Fifteen minutes later the General called back and told me that the only activity which he had was some U-2 flights. That was of no help, so I thanked him for his cooperation and put my thinking cap on again.

It took days for us to check all of these agencies and activities. I finally received Dr. Hynek's report. It was one of his typical reports which contained few technical details and added practically nothing to what had already been submitted by Connor and Moody. Though Hynek added very little to the investigation, his typical press interviews added more flame to the fire. The more press coverage the sightings got, the greater the number of sightings which were reported throughout New Mexico.

I was determined to solve the case and come hell or high water I was going to find the vehicle or the stimulus. I decided that it was imperative for me to talk to the Base Commander at Holloman AFB. I wanted to interview him at length about special activities from his base. I needed help to pull this off, so I called Lieutenant Colonel Maston Jacks at SAFOI. I told him what I wanted to do and he asked, 'Do you think it will do any good?' I replied, 'God damn it, Maston, if there is an answer to this case it has to be in some hangar at Holloman.' He went to work from his position at the Pentagon and the approval for my visit came through.

Colonel Garman was the Base Commander during my visit. He was most cooperative and told me that I could go anywhere and visit any activity which interested me. I went from one end of the base to the other. I spent four days talking to everybody I could and spent almost a whole day with the down-range controllers at the White Sands Missile Range. I left Holloman dejected and convinced that the answer to Zamora's experience did not originate and terminate at that base.

On my way back to Wright-Patterson, I hit upon an idea. Why not a lunar landing vehicle? I knew that some research had been done at Wright-Patterson, so as soon as I got back I asked for some briefings. The briefings were extremely informative, but the lunar-landers were not operational in April 1964. I got the names of the companies that were doing research in this field and I started writing letters. The companies were most cooperative, but their answers were all negative.

It was now time for me to pass judgment on the case after a careful review of all the information at hand. I hate to use the word 'judgment,' but that is exactly what it boils down to. As President Truman used to say, 'The buck stops here,' and in the world of UFOs my desk was the end of the line. It was time for the Air

Force to make a formal decision on the sighting at Socorro, New Mexico. I reviewed the Air Force Materials Laboratory analysis of the landing area. Conclusion: no foreign residue. Laboratory analysis of the burned brush revealed no chemicals that could have been propellant residue. Radiation was normal for the alleged landing area and for the surrounding area. There was no unusual meteorological activity, no thunderstorms; the weather was windy, but clear.

Although we made an extensive search for other witnesses, none could be located. There were no unidentified helicopters or aircraft in the area. Radar installations at Holloman AFB and at Albuquerque observed no unusual blips, but the down-range Holloman Moving Target Indicator Radar, closest to Socorro, had been closed down for the day at 16.00

Police Officer Lonnie Zamora

hours. All the findings and conclusions were negative. The object was travelling at approximately 120 miles per hour when it disappeared over the mountains, according to Zamora's best estimate.

So I labelled the case 'Unidentified' and the UFO buffs and hobby clubs had themselves a field day. According to them, here was proof that our beloved planet had been visited by an extraterrestrial vehicle. Although I labelled the case 'Unidentified' I've never been satisfied with that classification. I've always felt that too many essential elements of the case were missing. These are the intangible elements which are impossible to check, so the solution to this case could very well be lying dormant in Lonnie Zamora's head.

SAFOI and I had been most fair with the communications media. We gave them everything we had on the case. We even let the reporters review the official file for themselves, but we still took our lumps from some of them. Reporters are a unique breed. They are impatient, offensive, and they don't like to read voluminous reports. Time and time again I offered them the official reports, only to have them ask for my opinion and what I thought of the incident. I had good rapport with most of the reporters, but three of four of them were real stinkers. It's not really a bad percentage if you take into account the total number of reporters that I dealt with.

DOCTOR TROUBLES

I had never heard of Dr. J. Allen Hynek prior to my assignment as the Project Blue Book Officer. My predecessor, Lt. Col. Robert J. Friend, introduced me to Dr. Hynek in July of 1963. I'll have to admit that I was awed and impressed the first time that I met Dr. Hynek, but that feeling diminished proportionally with the number of contacts I had with the good doctor. I was the one in charge of the Project and therefore, had to answer to my Commander, the Vice-Commander, the Chief Scientist, the Air Force Systems Command, and numerous people in the Pentagon for the operation of the Program. My ass was in a sling and on a number of occasions, because of Hynek's flare for publicity and off-hand remarks, it was bent all out of shape. I was called to task much more often to answer for his remarks and comments, than I was to answer for mine.

Prior to April 1964, I had very little trouble with Hynek. He complained to me that Dave Moody was not treating him according to his scientific statute or some crap like that. I talked to Dave about it the first couple of times and Dave would come back that he was too busy to baby-sit or kiss the doctor's ass and that if he would get busy and evaluate the cases that were referred to him, that he wouldn't have time to worry about scientific statute. Dr. Hynek and Dave had a thing going and I decided to study it. After I analysed the situation, I had to agree with Dave. Dr. Hynek would come into the office and he would spend the first couple of hours socialising or gossiping or telling us a lot of nonsense about who was writing books, articles, etc. It was during one of these distracting sessions that I raised my voice and asked Dr. Hynek to confine his visits to case studies and let the rest of the staff proceed with their work.

Our philosophy as to how the program should be administered differed and we began to polarise during the Socorro investigation. I wanted publicity kept at a low key until we could finish the investigation, but he managed to stir up a hornets' nest by making irrelevant remarks. During the first few days of the investigation, the telephone lines to my office were backed up for 40 minutes and the lines to the base were backed up for 10 to 15 minutes. By this time the switchboard operators were wishing that I'd move my base of operation to Venus or Mars. They were really very nice and sympathetic, but it created chaos for them on a number of occasions. Sending Hynek to investigate the Socorro incident was my mistake and I began to regret it almost immediately. His part of the investigation didn't add anything significant to the overall report, but he was now in the national limelight and he managed to stay there for quite a while because the news media depicted him as the 'expert UFO Air Force consultant.' This prestigious title gained him publicity and recognition which he couldn't possibly get as the chairman of the Dearborn Observatory. Up to this time, Hynek had taken a fairly stable stand with regards to UFOs and the associated phenomena. As the wind changes the desert, so Hynek began to change and I never knew what was coming next. He embarrassed me and the Air Force on a number of occasions, but I kept my cool in public and wasted no words with him in private. But by 1966 I had become convinced that Hynek had lost his usefulness to the project.

THE MICHIGAN FLAP

I had weathered a few controversial flaps in the past and I was just about to get involved in another. The weather around Dayton in March 1966 had been unseasonably mild. The rest of the Midwest was getting weather just like ours. I normally braced myself at that time of the year because invariably something always happened. Jack Jones of the *Dayton Journal Herald* calls the spring 'the silly season' and I agree with him.

I had expected something to happen, but I was totally unprepared for Frank Mannor's sighting at Dexter, Michigan on 17 March 1966. When I got up to my office the following morning, the switchboard lines were already backing up. News of Frank Mannor's sighting reached the American people via the national wire services and the newspapers were calling for an instant evaluation. I had decided not to make any comments except that we were investigating.

Then I got on the line with Selfridge AFB and told them that I was sending

Dave Moody to assist them in checking out flight activities, radar, experimental work, and laboratory work at the university. I also decided to send Dr. Hynek to conduct an on the spot investigation of the area, the witnesses, and to make contact with the law enforcement officers in the area. I would stay at Wright-Patterson and guide the operation from my office and wait for the information to filter in. In the meantime, I would check with the national centres for unusual activity.

The next day Woody called with a negative report. He had checked out the radar antenna and we decided what couldn't have been the cause. Hynek called early in the morning and told me that reporters and TV cameramen were dogging him everywhere he went. I told him he'd just have to put up with it and do the best he could, but I could tell he was pouting. He claimed that he just couldn't do the job with so many people around. He asked me if he could have a news conference and I said no. This was setting a precedent and I didn't like it.

The next day Hynek called again and informed me that he had a possible solution to Frank Mannor's sighting and I asked him for the details. My secretary, Marilyn Beumer Stancombe, was on the line taking all the information in short hand. He told me that the solution was 'Swamp Gas.' I told him to check this out with his colleagues at the university and let me know their reaction. In the meantime, I would check it out with the chemists and botanists on the base. He also wanted me to arrange for a press conference from the Information Office at Selfridge AFB. I was against this from the beginning, but he was insistent and I told him I'd check it out with the Pentagon.

I talked to Major Davis and Sara Hunt of SAFOI about the press conference and neither one of them was enthusiastic about the idea, however, in this particular case it could have its merits. Since it was setting a precedent, the decision would have to be made at the top. That evening at 6:30 pm I got a call from the Pentagon. It was Major Davis, and General Garland had made an affirmative decision with regards to the press conference. This time it would be an exception; however, I was not to submit requests of this type in the future. Hynek called me at the house at around nine o'clock that night and I gave him the news. The first thing the next morning I called up Selfridge and told them to arrange the conference. Someone suggested the Detroit Press Club as the site of the conference and I couldn't see any objection to that.

I did not have specific instructions for Hynek. I wanted to see a copy of his news release before he distributed it to the reporters. I also wanted him to read his release to Sara Hunt and SAFOI, two hours before the conference, so that we could prepare copies for release to the national media from the DOD press desk. Hynek read his release to Sara and his copies were ready for distribution at the designated time. While Hynek was holding his news conference in Detroit, the Pentagon was releasing his finding to the media in Washington, D.C.

The Project took its lumps because many people had not heard of Swamp Gas, Foxtails, Jack O'Lanterns, Will O'the Wisp, Foolish Fire, or Ignis Fatuus. The news media played this sighting to the hilt. The publicity that this sighting received was unbelievable. Hynek became an instant celebrity and the sightings started pouring in. We had a total of 1,112 sightings in 1966 and that total has never been equalled since.

THE 1970s

Sketch of the five spinning objects seen over Edwin Fuhr's Saskatchewan farm

ONE OF THE EARLIEST AND MOST INFLUENTIAL UFO SIGHTING CLASSIFICATION SYSTEMS WAS THAT DEVELOPED BY DR. J. ALLEN HYNEK, FOUNDER OF THE CENTER FOR UFO STUDIES AND FORMER SCIENTIFIC CONSULTANT TO PROJECT BLUE BOOK. THE HYNEK SYSTEM WAS BASED PRIMARILY ON PROXIMITY OF OBSERVATION. DISTANT SAUCER-SHAPED OBJECTS SEEN BY DAY WERE REFERRED TO AS DAYLIGHT DISCS, WHEREAS REMOTE LUMINOUS OBJECTS REPORTED BY NIGHT WERE CATALOGUED AS NOCTURNAL LIGHTS. A THIRD CATEGORY WAS RESERVED FOR THOSE REPORTS IN WHICH VISUAL AND RADAR CONTACT OR OBSERVATION WAS MADE SIMULTANEOUSLY.

BUT WHAT OF THOSE OBSERVATIONS WHEN THE WITNESS OR WITNESSES CLAIMED TO HAVE BEEN APPROACHED TO WITHIN 500 FEET BY AN UNKNOWN OBJECT? HYNEK NAMED THE FIRST OF THESE, IN WHICH NO OTHER INTERACTION OTHER THAN OBSERVATION OCCURRED, CLOSE ENCOUNTERS OF THE FIRST KIND. CE-II, OR CLOSE ENCOUNTERS OF THE SECOND KIND, INVOLVED SOME SORT OF PHYSICAL TRACE LEFT BEHIND BY THE OBSERVED OBJECT, EITHER ON THE ENVIRON- MENT, OR ON THE WITNESS, OR BOTH. CE-III, CLOSE ENCOUNTERS OF THE THIRD KIND, REFERS TO THOSE CASES IN WHICH BOTH UFOS AND ALIEN ENTITIES WERE REPORTED (HYNEK, THE UFO EXPERIENCE, 1972).

THE FOLLOWING IS ONE OF THE MORE CLASSIC CE-II EPISODES OF ALL TIME. ITS AUTHOR IS A CANADIAN ASTRONOMY EDUCATOR AND SCIENCE WRITER (BSC, MED) CURRENTLY ACTIVE IN UFO RESEARCH. HIS ARTICLES HAVE APPEARED IN THE MUFON UFO JOURNAL, INTERNATIONAL UFO REPORTER, FLYING SAUCER REVIEW AND THE JOURNAL OF UFO STUDIES. HE HAS CON- TRIBUTED TO SEVERAL UFO-RELATED ANTHOLOGIES AND HAS TWO BOOKS OF HIS OWN, WITH OTHERS IN PROGRESS. HE IS THE EDITOR OF THE LONG-RUNNING SWAMP GAS JOURNAL, WHICH BEGAN IN 1978 AND BECAME AN ELECTRONIC JOURNAL IN 1990.

RUTKOWSKI IS ALSO ACTIVE ON THE INTERNET AND HAS BEEN AN INVITED GUEST ON NUMEROUS INTERNET RELAY CHAT (IRC) CHANNELS DEVOTED TO UFOS AND RELATED SUBJECTS. HIS E-MAIL ADDRESS IS: RUTKOWS@CC.UMANITOBA.CA

THE LANGENBURG CE2 CASE: WHEN UFOS LEFT THEIR MARK

by Chris A. Rutkowski

L angenburg, Saskatchewan, is a small town located about eight miles west of the Manitoba border and about 130 miles north of North Dakota. The area is flat, open prairie and is known for its wheat production. Nearly all resi- dents of the region are farmers or are somehow involved in agriculture.

In early September, 1974, word spread through the community that something strange had occurred on the farm of Edwin Fuhr, a 36-year-old man who grew rapeseed on some acreage north of the town. The story broke into the media when a detailed article appeared in the *Regina Leader-Post* (10 September, 1974, p.3). Soon, the story was carried across Canada.

On 18 September 1974, Dr. J. Allen Hynek of the Center for UFO Studies

(CUFOS) in Illinois received a newspaper clipping about the Langenburg incident from a CUFOS correspondent in Winnipeg, Manitoba. He conferred with Ted Phillips, who then contacted Bill Cameron, a news editor with the Canadian Broadcasting Corporation's radio station in Regina. As it seemed like a good case, arrangements were made for Phillips to travel to Langenburg on 21 September. He arrived in Regina that morning and was met by Bill Cameron. The two immediately drove to Langenburg to begin the CUFOS investigation. Over the next two days, Phillips conducted an extensive investigation and interviewed the witness, Edwin Fuhr, as well as Fuhr's mother and the investigating RCMP officer, Ron Morier.

The case has become one of the most classic and most often-cited 'UFO landings' in the history of ufology.

DETAILS OF THE CASE

It began like an episode of *The X-Files*.

Around midnight on Saturday, August 31 and extending through until about 3:00 a.m. on September 1, a babysitter in a farmhouse next to the Fuhr homestead was frightened by the sounds of dogs barking and growling outside. Because they were usually quiet unless provoked, the babysitter wondered if there was somebody or some animals prowling outside the house.

On Sunday morning, September 1, 1974, rain drizzled from the overcast sky, it was 43 degrees F and the wind was NW at 12 mph. In other words, it was a typical early fall day on the Canadian prairie.

That morning, the Fuhr family was preparing to go to church, except for Edwin Fuhr who had to attend to some farming chores. He left home at about 10:00 a.m. and began harvesting his rapeseed crop in a field located about 1,500 feet from his home and about 5½ miles northeast of Langenburg. After operating his swather for approximately one hour, he neared a slough at the south end of the field. As he approached the slough, he slowed down and checked his position. He was about 75 feet from the slough and was forced to stop because of the soft ground.

However, he was surprised to see a dome-shaped object about 50 feet away from him in the grass between the slough and his crop. At first, he thought it was a metal goose blind.

'I thought someone was playing a trick on me,' he told Ted Phillips, 'I took it for granted. I have a neighbour who will play tricks, and when I saw it I thought, 'What the devil's he doing now?'... And I thought, 'Well, I'll walk up there and scare him,' and it scared me, instead!'

He stopped the swather, got off and began walking through the four-foot-high crop. He walked to within 15 feet of the object. As he approached, he noticed that the grass around it was moving, and realised that the object itself was spinning at a high speed. Frightened, he backed away until he reached his swather. 'I never turned my back on it once,' he later told investigators.

He climbed on board and from this vantage point could see the spinning object as well as four more similar objects off to his left. 'I sat there like I was froze,' he said. 'I couldn't move nothing. I didn't know what the devil to do. I sat there for... it could have been 15 minutes or 20 minutes.'

The five objects all seemed to be spinning and hovering approximately 12 to 18 inches above the ground and were arranged in an arc around the slough. They all appeared metallic, 'like a brushed stainless steel.' Fuhr said he could see slightly darker 'grooves' on the domes: 'they were darker gray... a dark gray... like it had been hot at one time, like steel that gets hot and cools off.' No other surface details were visible. Each object was about five feet in height and about 11 feet in diameter. They each appeared to have a bottom 'lip' which was a slightly different shade than the rest of the 'body.'

One object appeared to be exhibiting some kind of activity, although Fuhr wasn't sure what was occurring. He explained: 'That one looked like there was something [coming] out of it... probing around in the grass. He described it as about 'the size of a fifty-cent piece.

Fuhr said that at one point, he tried to put the swather into gear and escape, but he couldn't move the throttle or the steering wheel. He admits, however, that he wasn't sure if this was because it was actually inoperative or if he was too weak in his panicked state. 'I know the swather throttle was wide open; I had never slowed it down.'

Several minutes passed before the objects suddenly rose into the air, one by one, in a 'step' formation, the nearest one leading the pack. They climbed until they were about 200 feet above the ground. 'If you had winked, you would have missed the take-off from the ground to where they stopped,' Fuhr noted.

At this time, a puff of grey 'vapour' was exhausted from two 12-inch 'ports' on the underside of each object. Fuhr felt a strong downward blast of wind and a 'pressure' which flattened the grass and crop beside the swather and nearly knocked off his hat. 'Oh, hell, here goes my crop!' he thought.

The objects stayed in position for a few minutes, then abruptly ascended into the clouds and were gone. Bewildered, Fuhr stayed on top of his swather for several minutes, expecting them to return.

When they did not come back, Fuhr jumped off the machine and walked over to where the objects had been. He discovered five rings of depressed grass. The grass was swirled in a clockwise direction; it was not dead and did not appear to have been heated or charred. Inside the number two ring were the 'probe marks.' The grass there was laid flat in three-foot-long strips leading away from the ring on one side.

Fuhr said that he recalled hearing the sounds of agitated cattle in a neighbour's pasture. Later, he learned that they had been so upset they had broken the fence in three places.

WORD GETS AROUND

Fuhr was bewildered by what he had seen, and was not sure what others would think about his experience. So, while he mulled over what had just happened, he fired up the engine and continued swathing. He told Phillips that he didn't know what he was going to tell his family when he got home, but eventually went for lunch about 12.30, more than an hour after the UFOs had disappeared.

Phillips also interviewed Fuhr's mother. She had just returned from church, and said that Edwin was acting 'altogether different. He was so worked up that he couldn't hardly eat dinner... He said, 'I don't want nothing; I'm not really hungry.' I said, 'Why?' And he said, 'I saw something this morning.'"

His family, particularly his father, insisted that he tell them what was wrong. Edwin reached for a small stainless steel bowl on the table and said, 'That's what it looked like.'

'You gotta be nuts,' his family responded. 'That's impossible.' He told them to see for themselves, finally coaxing his father to accompany him to the site. The elder Fuhr was amazed at the marks, especially those left by the 'probe.' 'He was crawling around on his hands and knees all Sunday afternoon in that one spot there,' Fuhr noted.

The family discussed the objects and the rings throughout the day. That evening, Edwin's brother-in-law came over for a visit and was caught up in the excitement. He was sceptical, and called the Royal Canadian Mounted Police to see if anything had been reported that day. Constable Ron Morier took the call and reported that nothing was on file.

Morier told Phillips that Fuhr's brother-in-law hesitated before telling him what had occurred, as if he was embarrassed about the incident. But Morier went out to the Fuhr farm early the next morning and was impressed with what he saw.

He explained: 'I could see that [Edwin] was still, it appeared to me, to be quite shaken, you know, about this whole thing. He was jumpy and you could see by just looking at the guy that he had been scared. But he took us out there and sure as hell there they were, five circles. I was sceptical too, but I was curious. There they were; I had never seen anything like them before...'

Morier called his Corporal and suggested that he come out as well and get some photographs of the rings. They could see no obvious way that the rings might have been hoaxed; the surrounding grass was still long and undisturbed. Pictures and measurements were taken, and a package was dispatched to the National Research Council (NRC) of Canada.

EXPLANATIONS

In those days, the NRC had an arrangement with the Royal Canadian Mounted Police in which UFO reports were to be forwarded in the expectation that some were sightings of fireballs and meteors and might therefore lead to the recovery of meteorites for scientific study. The reports which did not seem to be meteors were ignored and simply filed away without further investigation. The NRC's 'Non-Meteoric Sightings Files' are available for public viewing in the National Archives of Canada, and date back several decades. They contain many RCMP investigations of UFOs, including many for which there are no obvious explanations. For budgetary reasons, the NRC's collection of such reports was halted in 1995.

The official explanation of the case was given by arch-sceptic Dr. Allen MacNamara of the NRC, and published across Canada on 27 September, 1974. MacNamara was a researcher with the Herzberg Astrophysical Institute in Ottawa, and was often the first person to examine official UFO reports received at the NRC. He made no secret of the fact that he thought the subject of UFOs was ridiculous.

MacNamara, who admitted he had not investigated the case but had only read the RCMP reports, stated publicly that the rings on the Fuhr farm were:

> ... exactly the same as the 'fairy rings' which can vary in diameter from a few feet to a good fraction of a mile. The grass will be healthy and rich on the inside and dead on the outside... The dead grass would fall over with the slightest disturbance. [*Regina Leader-Post*, 27 September, 1974]

What was not emphasised in MacNamara's description of the fungi is that they do not form circles over a very short period of time, they do not form in cultivated crops and they themselves do not leave grass flattened in the manner found. Most ufologists with experience in unexplained ground markings (UGM)

One of the swirled crop patterns found on Edwin Fuhr's farm

cases are familiar with examples of crop pathology, and fairy rings definitely do not account for the 'saucer nest' variety of UGMs. Other crop growth effects such as lodging are more likely as possible explanations, but the fairy ring explanation, used most often by uninformed debunkers, is not viable in most circumstances.

Of course, the Fuhr circles were not found actually in the rapeseed field but in a soggy, unseeded area of a slough, left untouched because of its rocky, boggy soil. This means that under some circumstances, fairy rings possibly could form there. In fact, reporters trying to support MacNamara's theory noted that mushrooms were found underneath some of the flattened grass. Nevertheless, the appearance of the Fuhr rings was clearly unlike typical fairy rings and we still are left without an agricultural cause. Even if we were to disregard Fuhr's observation of the objects, one criticism is that the 'thickness' of the rings averaged about 2½ to 3 feet. This is very uncharacteristic of fairy rings, which usually have very narrow effects compared with their diameters. Also, the rings were relatively uniform in size and geometry, an effect which would be untenable in nature.

MORE CIRCLES

The Langenburg circles had all the characteristics of the later British crop circles, except one: they were made in grass, not cultivated crops. However, what is not generally known about the Langenburg case is that there were several more circles found in the immediate area and throughout Saskatchewan around that time, and that some of these were in cultivated crops.

During the evening of 2 September dogs were again barking excitedly on the Fuhr farm. One dog which normally roamed freely around the farm refused to go near the field where the objects had landed. The Fuhrs also noted that their television was 'acting up' that night.

The morning of 3 September, 1974, two days after the original encounter, Fuhr found a new, sixth crop circle in formation with the original five. The dogs barked again in the evening of 14 September, and, in the morning of 15

September, a seventh circle was found, again in a formation resembling an arc with the other six circles.

On 14 September, 1974, three more rings were found on another farm about a mile east of the Fuhr site, this time in a cultivated crop. They were of comparative size to the Fuhr circles, but had no associated UFO activity. Also on that day, a strange circle of wheat was found flattened and twisted counter-clockwise near Young, Saskatchewan, more than 200 miles northwest of Langenburg. The diameter of that ring was 14 feet, and its width was 24 inches. Additional rings were found at sites near Peebles, Lake Lenore and Dinsmore, Saskatchewan, over the next few weeks, all in wheat. Altogether, no less than 15 circles were found (or rather reported) at seven different sites in Saskatchewan.

The area around Langenburg has an extensive history of both UFO cases and crop-circle-like UGMs. For example, in the fall of 1967, farmers near Willen, Manitoba, only about 50 miles southeast of Langenburg, found several rings while swathing their wheat field. On 4 September, 1977, not far away, near Rossburn, Manitoba, a farmer came upon as many as 25 circles as he was swathing his wheat field. UFOs were not associated with either of these discoveries.

OPINIONS AND COMMENTS

The discussion of the Langenburg evidence by Ted Phillips echoes the remarks by cerealogists today, more than 20 years later. The Langenburg case was #746-20-74 in his immense files on UGMs and trace cases. Regarding the Langenburg case, he wrote:

> It would be impossible to imagine the creation, by nature, of even one of the Langenburg rings. As indicated by measurements taken at the site, the rings are almost perfectly circular. When one takes into consideration that we are dealing with not one, but seven such areas [at the Fuhr site], a natural cause seems rather far removed. One must remember that the sites were all swirled in the same clockwise pattern, all were of very nearly the same dimensions and all had the same type of undisturbed central section.
>
> It is obvious that these characteristics make the fairy ring theory very implausible. Fairy rings tend to be very irregular in shape, and the likelihood that seven would be so uniform is well-nigh impossible.

On the possibility of a hoax, Phillips commented:

> The perpetration of such a hoax would have involved a great deal of time. Fuhr, like all the farmers in the area, depends on his crops for income. I cannot believe that he would have taken the necessary time during harvest to create even one ring, certainly not seven. The last thing a farmer wants at harvest time is several thousand people walking through his crops and that is exactly what he had. He did not contact the news media and was even hesitant to relate the event to his own family. The RCMP was satisfied that no device had been driven or rolled into the area as there were no marks in the high grass other than the rings.

The Langenburg case is listed as N74-067 in the NRC's Non-Meteoric Sightings file. The RCMP report on the case is included in the file, and gives a basic description of Fuhr's story, with only a few comments. One point that is made, however, is Morier's opinion of Fuhr:

> The witness Fuhr has been known by a member of this detachment for a period of four years, and during this time he has not been known to materialise any such stories. He is a responsible person and his information is considered reliable.

It is possible, though, that Fuhr was a victim of a hoax, rather than a perpetrator, although his observation of the five objects would still need interpretation. It is certainly possible that the sixth and seventh rings were created by copycat hoaxers, however.

The UFO or ETH theory is generally advocated in this type of experience because of the observation of physical craft. Taken at face value, Fuhr's story seems to definitely suggest that aerial vehicles of some kind created the markings in the field.

A third interpretation is that the rings were created by a 'plasma vortex' of ionised particles which somehow flattened the grass and were visible to Fuhr for a short time. Proponents of the plasma vortex theory of crop circle formation suggest that observations of apparently physical flying craft (UFOs) creating landing traces can be construed as proof that ionised plasmas may seem to be solid objects. It is debatable whether or not the Langenburg case could be attributed to this mechanism. Since Fuhr approached to within 15 feet of one of the UFOs, it should have been possible, at that short distance, to easily distinguish a plasma from a 'real' physical object.

PHILLIPS' TRACE CASES

In his report on the Langenburg case, Ted Phillips noted that he had at that time (1974):

> 756 reports of observations of unidentified flying objects involving physical traces…
>
> 12% involve landing sites described as rings…
> 10% [have] a depressed ring surface…
> 22% [had] ring diameters between eight and twelve feet…
> 20% [had] ring width between one and two feet…
> 18% [had a] disc-shaped object seen at [the] site…

He noted of Langenburg in particular:

> The Langenburg event is almost totally unique in one respect – of the total landing-trace cases, only one other report involves the landing of more than two UFOs at a given site. That one report took place near Trancas, Argentina, on 21 October, 1963, with the landing of six UFOs.

Phillips cited the Langenburg case when he addressed the First International UFO Congress in 1977 in Chicago. He described his investigation and impressions of the case as follows:

> There had been an estimated four thousand people walking through the area

by the time I got there, so it was kind of like going to a carnival ground and trying to find one footprint. What I was able to observe showed no discolouration or burning. Analysis of the soil and other plants didn't indicate anything unnatural. I was able to observe that the UFOs seemingly landed in an area that was not visible from the farmhouse or from any other farm in the area. They picked a perfect spot to go unnoticed for a prolonged period of time.

RECENT STUDIES OF THE LANGENBURG CASE

In the intervening years between 1974 and the present, several more UFO and physical trace reports have originated in the Langenburg area. These have been duly recorded by civilian groups such as Ufology Research of Manitoba (UFOROM) and government/military personnel such as the RCMP and NRC.

In June, 1991, John Timmerman of the Center for UFO Studies brought the CUFOS travelling UFO exhibit to a mall in Yorkton, Saskatchewan, not far from Langenburg. There, Chris Rutkowski and Jeff Harland of UFOROM assisted him with the display and also in interviewing new witnesses of UFOs who came forward as a result of the display. Arrangements were made for Edwin Fuhr to come to the mall to meet with the three ufologists. An extensive interview resulted, reviewing the case and adding some possible new information.

First of all, Fuhr now believes that the objects were not quite featureless; he claims that he had the impression of 'something on the outside like rivets of some kind, but you couldn't tell if there was a window in it or not.'

Second, Fuhr claimed that the sixth circle found was partly on top of a large rock. He said that 'scientists dug the rock out' and took it away. We have no record of such a rock in any other account, and Phillips' notes do not include anything about a rock. However, since thousands of people visited the Fuhr site, any one of them could have described him- or herself as a scientist and taken the rock away.

A very significant comment by Fuhr during the 1991 interview related to another previously-unreported effect. He claimed that a man from Russell, Manitoba, who had allegedly worked at a nuclear research institute, brought a Geiger counter to the Fuhr site during the 1980's. He told Fuhr that the slough was radioactive. In addition, Fuhr related that 'undercover RCMP' later visited the site with him and that he was shown that radioactivity was detected on their own geiger counters.

This issue of radioactivity seemed quite easy to clear up. Fuhr was asked by John Timmerman if he could lead the three back to the site to get more soil samples. He agreed, but there was a problem; he said he'd 'have to go to the RCMP to get a release for it.' He said others had tried to take samples away, but were somehow blocked from doing so by the RCMP. Fuhr went on to note that he had 'signed papers that no soil can be released unless they [the RCMP] release it.' Fuhr stated that the order to prevent soil material from leaving the site was written by Constable Ron Morier, the original investigating officer from whom Ted Phillips had received outstanding co-operation.

Finally, after considerable review of his memories regarding the incident, Fuhr believes that he experienced some 'missing time.' From his original interview by Ted Phillips in 1974:

P: From the very first observation until they disappeared into the clouds, how long did you see them?

F: The most it could have been was 15 to 20 minutes, it could have lasted more or less, I can't be sure.

P: What would have been the shortest time?
F: 10 minutes, maybe. I just don't know, I don't know how long I sat in the swather, I can't remember that part. After it was over I looked at my watch, it was fifteen after eleven. When I first saw them I didn't look at my watch, it could have been around 10.30, I just don't know. I knew I had went out about 9.30... How long I watched them I don't know, I do know that I stood there, my feet wouldn't move, for two minutes. How long I was in the swather I don't know. I was like, I guess, in shock. I just kept staring at those things, I couldn't take my eyes off them.

(later in the interview)

P: After the objects left, you waited two minutes; then what did you do?
F: After I looked at the marks I continued to swath for quite a while because I didn't know how to tell those guys at home, that was my problem. When I got home they asked me 'what's the matter?' – I was all pale in the face, I didn't say nothing. I washed and tried to eat and I was trying to think how I could tell them about this thing. I went in for lunch about 12.30.

However, during the 1991 interview with Timmerman, Fuhr said he had sat on the swather a much longer time and did not arrive home until about 2.00p.m. He estimated the time he spent watching while sitting on the swather was 'about an hour and a half.' He claimed that his relatives had waited a long time for him to come home.

In 1991, Fuhr commented that he believed 'something' might have happened to him while he was observing the objects, but he could not recall any details. Because of some discrepancies in the chronology of events, Fuhr was asked:

R: Did anyone ever suggest that you had some 'missing time' and that there is more to what happened?
F: Some fellows did and that I should go under hypnosis, and I won't go under hypnosis.

T: Do you have some special reason for not doing that?
F: I got that from professionals. They told me not to.

Pressed for details, Fuhr would say only that among the many, many people who had visited him since his experience, some 'UFO experts' had told him not to undergo hypnosis. Reassurances of controlled clinical tests performed under the supervision of registered psychologists (who have worked with UFOROM on several occasions) did nothing to change his mind.

Clearly, the case has become embellished after years of 'poking around' by dozens of self-proclaimed 'experts.' Today, Fuhr relates stories of 'investigators' loading their station wagons full of soil from the site, and of people claiming to be 'from the government' doing seemingly redundant tests and measurements.

There is no question that over the years, Fuhr's memory of the 1974 event has faded and also been influenced by the many people who have spoken with him about his experience. This would be expected, given his celebrity status in the eyes of some people. Some embellished details are possibly manifesting themselves, but his original story remains essentially intact.

During the 1989 wave of UFO sightings in Canada, Fuhr was one of many Langenburg-area residents to have witnessed more UFOs, mostly nocturnal lights. He is regarded as somewhat of a local celebrity, though he has yet to actively seek any publicity. He remains a meek, yet stubborn, individual who is showing signs of weariness from coping with the continuing interest in his experience.

What really happened to Edwin Fuhr in 1974? On the surface, it would appear that he had a chance or deliberate encounter with five small, bowl-shaped flying saucers – perhaps remote-controlled drones.

Although some local townspeople were originally sceptical of the incident, in later years it appears that there has been an appreciation of the worldwide attention given to the area. Recently, when the town created its own WWW page on the Internet, the developer included a section on local UFO sightings, including the Fuhr case. Not surprisingly, perhaps, it managed to get some of the details wrong.

ABDUCTIONS ARE TYPICALLY A SOLITARY AFFAIR IN WHICH THE EXPERIENCER REPORTS BEING TAKEN FROM HIS OR HER BEDROOM OR AUTOMOBILE LATE AT NIGHT, FROM WHERE THEY ARE 'BEAMED' INTO A WAITING UFO AND THEN SUBJECTED TO PHYSICAL EXAMINATION. THE LAWS OF PHYSICS ARE FREQUENTLY VIOLENTLY VIOLATED IN SUCH ACCOUNTS. GRAVITY IS ALLEGEDLY OVERCOME, USUALLY VIA A BRIGHT BEAM OF BLUE OR WHITE LIGHT, AND SOME EXPERIENCERS RELATE PASSING THROUGH SOLID OBJECTS SUCH AS WALLS AND WINDOWS. AN EPISODE OF 'MISSING TIME' MAY ALSO BE RECOUNTED. FOR THESE AND OTHER REASONS, MANY RESEARCHERS HAVE TURNED AWAY FROM A LITERAL, PHYSICAL INTERPRETATION OF THE ABDUCTION EVENT TOWARD A WHOLLY PSYCHOLOGICAL EXPLANATION, REASONING THAT IF THE EXPERIENCE INDEED TAKES PLACE AS DESCRIBED, THEN IT MUST, OF NECESSITY, TAKE PLACE IN THE EXPERIENCER'S MIND AND NOT IN 3D SPACE-TIME AS WE KNOW IT.

DEDICATED SCEPTICS TEND TO DISMISS EVEN THE EXPERIENCE ITSELF. AT BEST, THEY ATTRIBUTE IT TO 'BAD DREAMS' BROUGHT ON BY PERVASIVE MEDIA INFLUENCES, INCLUDING SCIENCE-FICTION IMAGERY AND THE SENSATIONALISTIC 'TABLOID' TV PROGRAMMES WHICH HAVE GROWN IN NUMBER IN RECENT YEARS. WHERE ARE THE INDEPENDENTLY WITNESSED ABDUCTIONS, THEY ASK, OR EVEN MULTIPLE ABDUCTIONS, IN WHICH MORE THAN ONE PERSON IS INVOLVED?

ONE OF THE FIRST MULTIPLE ABDUCTION CASES TO SURFACE IS RECOUNTED BELOW. THE AUTHOR, RAYMOND FOWLER, HAS BEEN INVOLVED IN UFO RESEARCH FOR WELL OVER A QUARTER OF A CENTURY AND IS PRESENTLY DIRECTOR OF INVESTIGATIONS FOR MUFON, THE MUTUAL UFO NETWORK, THE WORLD'S LARGEST MEMBERSHIP UFO ORGANISATION. HE IS THE AUTHOR OF NUMEROUS BOOKS ON THE SUBJECT, BEGINNING WITH UFOS: INTERPLANETARY VISITORS (1972) AND THE ANDREASSON AFFAIR (1979), FOLLOWED BY THE ANDREASSON AFFAIR – PHASE TWO (1982), CASEBOOK OF A UFO INVESTIGATOR (1981), THE WATCHERS (1994), THE ALLAGASH ABDUCTIONS (1993) AND WATCHERS II (1995). HIS BOOKS HAVE BEEN REPRINTED IN JAPAN, GERMANY, POLAND, HUNGARY, BRAZIL AND TAIWAN. THE ANDREASSON LEGACY IS SCHEDULED TO BE PUBLISHED IN 1997.

THE ALLAGASH ABDUCTIONS

by Raymond E. Fowler

On Friday night, 20 August, 1976, four young art students in their early twenties left Boston, Massachusetts for a canoe and camping trip in a wilderness area of Northern Maine along the Allagash River. The group consisted of identical twins, Jack and Jim Weiner, and their friends Charlie Foltz and Chuck Rak. Upon arrival at a staging point, they hired a pontoon airplane which flew them and their canoes to Telos Lake on the Allagash Waterway. During the next several days they canoed and camped along the Waterway.

On Tuesday, 24 August, they and a number of other campers were puzzled by a bright object that suddenly appeared in a clear black clear sky punctuated with twinkling stars. Jim took out his binoculars and focused them on the glowing intruder, which appeared to be a few miles away and only a couple of hundred feet

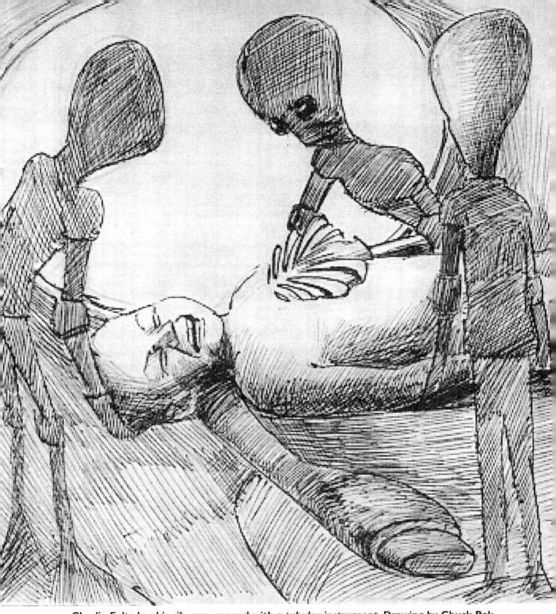

Charlie Foltz has his rib cage opened with a tubular instrument. Drawing by Chuck Rak

above the treetops. He was studying ceramics at the time and compared the peculiar light to that 'one sees inside a pottery kiln at… approximately 2,350 degrees Fahrenheit… It hovered perfectly still for a few seconds and then extinguished from the outside edge of the light to the centre. I did not really think much about it, except that I had never observed a light implode like that before.'

The incident was soon overshadowed by the tasks of setting up camp and planning for the next day's activities. On the evening of Thursday, 26 August, they reached a lonely site on Eagle Lake and decided to go night fishing for trout. The utter darkness of the area necessitated building a huge bonfire to mark their campsite. Shortly after beginning to fish, Chuck became aware of an eerie feeling of being watched. He turned and saw 'a large bright sphere of coloured light hovering motionless and soundless about 200-300 feet above the southeastern rim of the cove.'

Chuck yelled for the others to look behind them. There, rising above the trees was a huge oval glowing object. As their eyes became adapted to its intense brightness, a gyroscopic motion was noted, as if there were pathways of energy flowing equatorially and longitudinally from pole to pole. This divided the sphere into four oscillating quadrants of brightly coloured light. The colour changes were liquid and enveloping, as if the entire object had a plasmatic motion to it, like a thick sauce does as it starts a rolling boil.

Charlie grabbed a flashlight and blinked it at the object. Instantly, the thing came to an abrupt halt and began to slowly approach the canoe. Simultaneously, a tube-shaped beam of light erupted from the object and hit the water. A glowing ring with a dark centre reflected on the water's surface, indicating that the beam was hollow. The object and its beam of light began moving toward the canoe. Terrified, the campers paddled frantically toward their bonfire as the beam swept across the lake and engulfed them.

It was from this point on that the conscious memories of the four differed according to each witness' vantage point. Charlie Foltz remembered paddling for shore and suddenly finding himself standing at the campsite with the others, watching the object move away. Chuck Rak remembered staying in the canoe after the others had piled out in panic onto the shore. Transfixed, still holding his idle paddle, he could not take his eyes off the object.

Jack Weiner remembered a sinking feeling that they were not going to be able to outrun the beam of light. 'Holy shit! This is it!' he said. 'We'll never get away.' The next thing he knew, they 'were on the shore getting out of the canoe, looking directly at the object which was now about twenty or thirty feet above the water... It hovered there, right in front of us, completely silent for what seemed like four or five minutes.' The beam of light was then directed into the sky and the object began moving away, shooting into the stars and disappearing in an instant. Jim Weiner also recalled the beam of light, then standing on the shore, watching it hovering, and its rapid disappearance. 'We all seemed to be in a state of shock,' he said. 'We just stood there, unable to move or talk.'

When the strange anaesthetising effect wore off, Chuck got out of the canoe and joined the others as they trudged dreamily up the beach to their camp. Even in this state, they were dumbfounded when they saw the remains of their bonfire. 'When we left to go fishing,' Jim Weiner explained, 'we set very large logs on the fire to burn for a good two to three hours. The entire experience seemed to last, at the most, fifteen or twenty minutes. Yet the fire was completely burned down to red coals.'

At that time, they had no conscious memory of what had happened during the time it took for their huge bonfire to burn down. This would remain a puzzle to them for years.

A few years later, Jim suffered a head injury which caused tempero-limbic epilepsy. During treatment at the renowned Beth Israel Hospital, Jim's doctors were concerned that he was not getting enough sleep and asked him if he were encountering any sleep disorders. He was embarrassed to tell them he had been experiencing strange visitations, during which, while paralysed, strange creatures would probe him in his bedroom. Ultimately, he confided in his personal physician, who was familiar with the UFO abduction literature, especially references to missing time. He was reluctant to pursue this approach, too, though, until his doctor noticed an announcement of a speech I was giving in nearby Waltham, Massachusetts, and suggested that he attend.

133

After the lecture, Jim approached me and described what he and his friends had experienced. Ordinarily I would have just referred him to the local chapter of the Mutual UFO Network for investigation. But, the fact that multiple witnesses (all artists), including twins, were involved piqued my curiosity. Thus, in January of 1989, I initiated a formal investigation.

The investigation team consisted of MUFON investigator and CEIII/IV specialist David Webb (solar physicist), MUFON hypnosis consultant, Anthony (Tony) Constantino (professional hypnotist) and myself (MUFON National Director of Investigations). Later, I would involve members of the J. Allen Hynek Center for UFO Studies and a private detective.

All witnesses were interviewed and interrogated. Each was given standard MUFON UFO report forms to fill out and sign. In order to establish both witness and sighting account credibility a number of careful enquiries were necessary. First, I conducted character background checks with friends, neighbours and employers. Secondly, I contacted a number of persons who the four had told about their experience. These included relatives, friends and even the chief forest ranger who had received their initial report. I examined the witnesses' maps and notes about their camping trip and the incident as well as checking out the astronomical and weather data against what they had reported.

Everything indicated that the witnesses were telling the truth and accurately remembering what had happened to them. The next step was to attempt to discover what had occurred during the hours of missing time. This was done through a series of hypnotic regression sessions.

It was obvious to us that the period of unaccounted for time had to be sandwiched between sighting the object and reaching shore. The beam of light hitting the canoe seemed to be the dividing point between memory and amnesia. During the first of a long series of hypnosis sessions, it was decided to concentrate on this segment of their terrifying encounter. The four witnesses promised not to reveal the contents of their hypnosis sessions to each other until a special meeting to be held at the completion of the sessions.

Under hypnosis, all four percipients relived detailed and traumatic UFO abduction experiences during the period of missing time. All were transferred, one at a time, into the UFO by the hollow tube-like beam of light. On board, they encountered strange humanoid creatures that exerted some kind of mind control over them so that they could not resist their demands.

All were made to undress and sit on a plastic-like bench in a misty area filled with diffuse white light. Each was then taken from the bench and given a physical examination. This consisted of looking at their eyes and in their mouths with a pencil-sized rod with a light on its tip. The aliens also placed them in a harness and flexed their arms and legs. Then, one by one, they were made to lie on a table where each was examined by a number of strange hand-held and larger machine-like instruments that were lowered over their bodies. The alien entities also removed samples of saliva, skin scrapings, blood, faeces, urine and sperm from each of them.

After the examinations, the abductees were made to dress and enter another room which had a round portal in one of its walls. They were lined up and made to walk into the opening. Strange sensations surged through their bodies as they found themselves floating down the hollow beam of light into their canoe, which was now in shallow water near their campsite. The tube-like light seemed to hold the canoe steady as each was placed in it in the same seating positions they were in prior to the abduction.

As the hypnosis sessions continued, much detail was recovered about their on-board experience. Also, it was discovered that the twins had had bedroom visitations by alien creatures and abduction experiences since early childhood. The bedroom visitations were remembered without the use of hypnosis. The twins, their brother and parents had attributed the entity visitations to a ghost. A UFO connection was the farthest thing from their minds!

Hypnosis revealed more details about Jim's current adult bedroom visitations. Incredibly enough, during our investigation, both Jack and his wife Mary reported being abducted from their remote mountain home in Townshend, Vermont.

During the night of 20 May, 1988, Jack's dog woke him up when it scratched at the door wanting to go out to relieve itself. When Jack got up to put him out, he was shocked to see a blue light shining through the kitchen window. He went out to look and saw a glowing object hovering over the field adjoining his house. He only remembered bringing the dog back in. In the morning, he thought he had dreamed everything.

However, under hypnosis, he relived a shared abduction experience with his wife in minute detail. Mary only consciously remembered dreaming about deer with big eyes coming to their bedside and staring at them. She did not respond well to hypnosis. Each time she was brought to the point of seeing the deer (screen memories of the entities?), she brought herself out of hypnosis.

The events the couple reported were not uncommon to abductees. Jack and Mary were brought to stand in front of a huge house-sized glowing object sitting on a blue light that enveloped its underside. The glow around the object itself was changing colours from white to yellow to orange and purple and back to white. No noise emanated from the object, but the air was filled with the acrid smell of ozone.

Jack and Mary were made to walk into the blue light under the object. Instantaneously, they were transferred inside of the glowing craft. Mary was then separated from Jack, who was made to undergo an examination similar to the one that he and his brother and friends had experienced twelve years earlier. After the examination, Mary was reunited with Jack. Both were literally floated across the lawn from the craft to their house, through the unopened front door and to their bedroom. There, they went back to bed in a strange lethargic state of mind.

This experience left physical evidence behind in the form of burns on the bottom of Jack's feet. Jack had also received a scoop-shaped scar above his ankle during still another abduction.

During our examination, I noted another very prominent scar just below it and asked him how it happened. Jack told me that it was from an operation to remove an anomalous lump that had appeared overnight several years prior. His doctor thought it was a cyst, but was unable to drain it. She then referred Jack to a surgeon who removed it. In a post-operative examination, he was told that the local pathologists did not know what it was and had sent it to the Center for Disease Control in Atlanta, Georgia for further analysis.

Curious, I asked Jack to obtain copies of his medical records. When he asked the records clerk for them, she remarked that he must have been in the military, which he hadn't. She found this odd because the thing removed from his leg had been sent to military pathologists in Washington, D.C. Puzzled, Jack glanced at the pathologist's report and was amazed to see that the pathologist had been a United States Air Force Colonel!

Attempts for further information about the anomalous lump were thwarted as Jack's surgeon would not cooperate with our enquiry. When I phoned the Armed Forces Institute of Pathology (AFIP), I was simply told by the public information officer that the AFIP occasionally assisted civilian doctors. When Jack asked why the lump was sent to the AFIP rather than the Center for Disease Control, he was told by his surgeon's secretary that it was less costly even though Jack was covered by insurance!

Our investigation took the better part of two years to complete. The sixteen hypnosis sessions alone took place over a period of sixteen months. Our enquiry revealed that each of the witnesses exhibited the typical benchmarks characteristic of other abductees as ascertained by a detailed correlation of their accounts with an exhaustive survey of 270 reported UFO abductions compiled by Dr. Thomas E. Bullard of the University of Indiana.

Another follow-on enquiry into the witnesses' veracity was conducted by the J. Allen Hynek Center for UFO Studies which provided a battery of tests to ascertain the psychological profile of each witness. These include a test for fantasy-prone individuals and the Minnesota Multiphasic Personality Inventory (MMPI) test. The written results of these tests are confidential but they did not reveal any mental aberrations that would negate the testimony of the witnesses.

One of the interesting things that occurred in the aftermath of Jim and Jack's abduction experiences was the radical changes in both their interests and artwork. Prior to the Allagash abductions, neither had any interest in mathematics or computers, Jim's prior interest having been in ceramics and Jack's in landscape painting. Now both became heavily involved with computer-generated art. In fact, Jim now teaches computer art at a local university and Jack runs a part-time computer art business out of his home. Such sudden changes in the interests and abilities of abductees have been noted before in the aftermath of UFO abduction experiences.

Up until this time in the enquiry, no lie detector tests had been administered because of the expense involved and because we felt that every facet of our investigation indicated that the witnesses were honest and accurate individuals. However, when the producer of *The Joan Rivers Show* offered to pay for polygraph tests if the four would appear on her show, I reluctantly agreed.

I say reluctantly because I was not sure how Joan Rivers would treat the four abductees. She was a well-known comedian and I did not want them to become the focus of ridicule on national television. Also, none of the four had ever appeared on a television show. I was afraid their emotions and nerves would be at an all time high travelling to New York, waiting to go on TV, and then taking a lie detector test prior to the show.

Sorry to say, my worst fears were partially realised. I say partially, because in the end Joan Rivers treated them royally and seriously. She made them feel at home and let each tell their story in an objective fashion on the show, which first aired in May 1993. However, the polygraph test was a different story. The already anxious witnesses waited for the polygraph examiner well into the evening hours but he did not show up. Then, after they had retired for the night, he arrived abruptly and said that he had only time to do two persons. Jack Weiner and Chuck Rak volunteered. Later, they told me that the examiner was very aggressive, bordering on hostile. He would not tell them the results of the tests. Late that evening he hurriedly packed up his equipment and left them in a state of anger and anxiety.

As I said, the show went extremely well. But, when I phoned the producer and asked him why the polygraph tests were not mentioned, he referred me to the

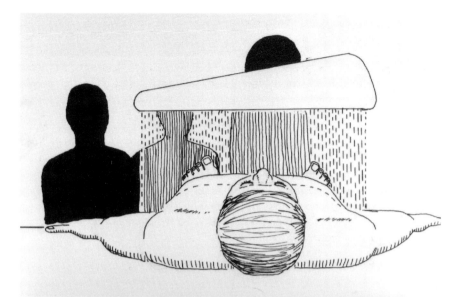

Charlie Foltz's recollection, under hypnosis, of his abduction experience

examiner. I phoned him several times and left messages but received no reply. When I finally reached him, he told me that Chuck Rak had failed the test and that Jack was a borderline case. I asked him to send me a copy of the complete test for each subject, including the polygraph tapes, as I had been promised them. He refused. He also would not admit that the tests could be flawed because of the already anxious state of Chuck and Jack and their being abruptly and unexpectedly called from their hotel rooms at such a late hour.

I was very angry. Everything pointed to the honesty of all four individuals. Conversely, everything pointed to the worst of environments for an expertly performed polygraph test. A well administered polygraph test should provide a calm and neutral environment. The subject should be well-rested and feel relaxed and at ease. Also, a polygraph examiner must not be biased or even appear biased to the person being tested. The worse thing an examiner can do is to appear abusive to the subject being tested. This attitude in and of itself can negate the accuracy of the test. Regretfully, both Jack and Chuck felt hostility from the examiner and in turn both felt hostile toward him.

I was in a quandary. My book on the case was in the last phases of production. Any new data was restricted to adding a page at the end of the book. My report had already been sent to a number of researchers. The polygraph examiner refused to let me have the tests' tapes for independent analysis. I felt that the tests were terribly flawed and refused to compromise the case by publishing their results without further investigation. I was now obligated to arrange new polygraph tests not only for Jack and Chuck but for all four individuals. This was not only to give me peace of mind about fully documenting this important case but also to assuage the hurt feelings of Jack and Chuck. They were terribly upset at their honesty being called in question. I was most pleased when all four unanimously agreed to follow-on tests under scientifically accepted conditions to clear their reputations.

Since Charlie Foltz and Jim Weiner lived in the Boston area, they were the first to be tested by Ernest C. Reid, CPE, a Certified Stress Analyst with an office in Dedham, Massachusetts. While waiting until I could afford to have Chuck Rak and Jack Weiner tested, the producers of *Unsolved Mysteries* stepped into the picture and kindly paid Mr. Reid's expenses for both. Each of the four witnesses were subjected to three types of examinations and all four passed their tests. Mr. Reid found nothing to indicate that they were lying about what they had experienced.

The polygraph tests essentially completed my investigation of this fascinating multiple witness abduction case. The final report consisted of 702 pages in a 10-volume format which was provided to UFO researchers for peer review. As in other cases that I have investigated, my final report was reduced to a book for general public information.

My evaluation, stemming from the overall results of the investigation, concluded that the moral character of the witnesses, the graphic reliving of their experiences under hypnosis, and the extraordinary correlations between their experience and that of other abductees provided overwhelming evidence that their experiences were objective in nature.

UFOLOGY, BY DEFINITION, IS THE STUDY OF UNIDENTIFIED FLYING OBJECTS. FOR THE FIRST HALF OF ITS EXISTENCE THE SUBJECT MATTER WAS OBVIOUS AND RELATIVELY STRAIGHTFORWARD. BEGINNING IN THE LATE 1960S AND EARLY 1970S, HOWEVER, UFOLOGY EXPANDED TO INCLUDE A NUMBER OF OTHER ALLEGEDLY ANOMALOUS PHENOMENA WHOSE CONNECTIONS WERE NOT ALWAYS IMMEDIATE OR APPARENT. AMONG OTHERS, THESE INCLUDED UNUSUAL ANIMAL DEATHS, UNMARKED HELI-COPTERS, RUMOURS OF SECRET UNDERGROUND MILITARY BASES, AND, MOST RECENTLY, SO-CALLED CROP CIRCLES. A DEBATE CONTINUES WITHIN UFOLOGY TODAY AS TO WHETHER THESE ARE DISCRETE EVENTS, CONNECTED PARTS OF SOME MYSTERIOUS WHOLE, OR, IN THE CASE OF CROP CIRCLES, SIM-PLY EVIDENCE OF WIDESPREAD HUMAN HOAXING. ARE THE REPORTEDLY RELATED EVENTS REALLY AN OUTGROWTH OF UFO ACTIVITY, MERELY AN ATTEMPT TO EXPLAIN ONE MYSTERY BY REFERENCE TO ANOTHER, OR MYTH-MANIA IN THE MAKING? AS LONG AS THE UFO IS IMBUED WITH AN AURA OF INVINCIBLE MYSTERY (AND UNLIMITED ABILITIES), IT SEEMS CERTAIN TO CONTINUE GROWING TENTA-CLES LIKE A MANY-HEADED HYDRA.

ANIMAL MUTILATIONS ARE A SPECIFIC CASE IN POINT, SOMETHING THAT DAVID PERKINS HAS BEEN EXAMINING FOR THE PAST 20 YEARS. A GRADUATE OF YALE UNIVERSITY IN AMERICAN STUDIES AND POLITICAL SCIENCE, PERKINS IS THE AUTHOR OF ALTERED STEAKS, THE FORTHCOMING THE CATTLE MUTILATION CASEBOOK (WITH TOM ADAMS) AND PARANORMAL PHENOMENA AND THE EVOLUTIONARY IMPERATIVE. HE FOUNDED SPIRIT – THE MAGAZINE OF THE ROCKY MOUNTAIN SOUTHWEST, AND IS PRESENTLY A STAFF WRITER FOR SAME. HE CAN BE REACHED IN WRITING AT 111 EAST SANTA FE AVENUE, SANTA FE, NEW MEXICO, 87501.

DARKENING SKIES, 1979-1980: OF DEAD COWS AND LITTLE GREEN MEN

by David Perkins

'I can't see what the attraction of a bull's ass would be to a UFO.' Toronto Star (12-17-79)
'We're looking for humans doing these things [cattle mutilations] not UFOs or
little green men,' Edmonton Journal (11-26-79).

Both quotes by Corporal Lyn Lauber, Royal Canadian Mounted Police.

'If little green men are responsible for the mutilations, I'll bring them in by the ears.' Ex-FBI
Agent Kenneth Rommel, Project Director of Operation Animal Mutilation statement to
Albuquerque TV Station KOB (5-26-79)

W hile RCMP Corporal Lauber and Ex-FBI agent Rommel were cracking 'little green men' jokes in 1979, thousands of ranchers throughout the American West and Canada were demanding answers from their politicians and law enforcement officials. Who or what was mutilating their animals and when was it going to stop? Local law-men were describing the situation in their communities as 'near hysterical' or 'total

panic' or 'somebody's going to get killed.'

The cattle mutilation phenomenon had simmered up from the American Heartland in the early 1970s. By 1973, Minnesota, Oklahoma, Wisconsin and Kansas had reported similar incidents. In most cases there appeared to be a consistent pattern. Ranchers reported finding their animals dead, with sexual organs removed, blood drained, and missing some combination of ear, tongue, eye, udder or patch of skin. Rectums were frequently described as 'cored out'. In the so-called classic 'mute' [for mutilation] case, the incisions were often described as being performed with 'surgical precision.' In addition, the animal would show no signs of struggle, no tracks or evidence would be found at the scene, and common predators were said to avoid the carcass.

Initially, the seemingly senseless crimes were seen as the work of vandals or pranksters. By the autumn of 1973, however, the situation was reaching near-epidemic proportions. In a six-week period, Kansas lawmen received 44 mutilations reports. Some authorities speculated that the cattle killings were the handiwork of cultists who needed the blood and body parts for their rituals. Local ranchers armed themselves and took to patrolling the back roads in continuous shifts.

By the end of 1975, the phantom surgeons had struck in virtually every state west of the Mississippi. Mutilation reports were numbered in the thousands and losses were being estimated in the millions of dollars. Governor Lamm of Colorado called it 'one of the greatest outrages in the history of the Western cattle industry.' Newspapers fuelled the explosive situation with sensational headlines such as:

'BOY SAYS UFO LANDED, LEFT BLOODY COW BEHIND'

'BORED RICH CULTISTS BLAMED IN CATTLE DEATHS'

'INTROVERTS BLAMED FOR MUTILATIONS'

'MUTILATIONS PRELUDE TO HUMAN SACRIFICES?'

Most theories centred around the litany of saucers, Satanists or the CIA. Many communities divided into four camps: (1) Those who believed the mutes were the work of space aliens in flying saucers, collecting cow parts for reasons unknown. (2) Those who felt blood-thirsty cultists were responsible. (3) Those who thought that some branch of the US government was responsible, perhaps clandestinely testing chemical/biological weapons. (4) Those who were certain that the 'mutilations' were the work of common predators such as coyotes and buzzards.

It was against this strange backdrop that then US Senator from New Mexico, Harrison Schmitt, convened the first multi-state mutilation conference, in Albuquerque on 20 April, 1979. The already existing network of mute investigators was perplexed. Why would Senator Schmitt, an Apollo 17 astronaut who had walked on the moon, extend his neck in such a politically risky move? According to Schmitt, the mutilation problem was one of the first issues with which he was confronted by his constituents upon taking office. As he told the conference: 'There are few activities more dangerous than an unsolved pattern of crime. Such a pattern... is the mutilation killings of thousands of cattle, horses and other animals over the past several years throughout many states. The economic losses suffered by individuals probably have reached 2.5 million dollars or more.'

For reasons unknown, I was to be the first speaker. The tension in the auditorium was so thick you could have cut it with a scalpel. As I looked over the crowd, I pondered: What other topic could possibly draw this motley crew into one room? A moon-walking astronaut, FBI agents, state police, sheriffs and local police from around the country, Indian pueblo governors, tribal police chiefs, Los Alamos scientists, veterinarians, New Agers in robes, hippies, news media, politicians, spooky agent types, dusty ranchers in beat-up cowboy hats, independent researchers and, of course, ufologists of all stripes and colours.

I told the diverse assembly that I was a Yale-trained sociologist with an interest in 'the study of cults, mass delusions and belief systems which lie outside the mainstream.' I went on to say that I'd been researching the mutilation phenomenon since 1975, after incidents had occurred in my neighbourhood in the mountains of Southern Colorado. What I didn't say was that the first reported mute in my county had happened a short distance down the road from my house. The only evidence at the scene was a few drops of blood leading toward my home. I learned later from my local sheriff, that since I was a relative new-comer to the area, I was briefly considered a suspect. I had my doubts that the audience would appreciate the humour and irony of that scenario.

As the attendees fidgeted in their seats, I told the group that I had amassed a considerable amount of information on the mutilations, which I would be glad to share with anyone interested, and that I'd 'never run across a phenomenon which has presented more of challenge to the rational mind.' After more general remarks and exhortations, I asked that the group seriously consider the possibility that UFOs and mutilations were related phenomena.

What followed was a parade of speakers who filed to the podium to regale the audience with UFO/cattle mutilation correlations. At one point, Senator Schmitt reminded the group that although this was 'not specifically a UFO conference, it is an issue that has been associated with the cattle mutilation incidents from the beginning.' The Senator also related a case from his files involving the disappearance of a calf after a 'helicopter' had been heard at four a.m.

On the same subject, Texas researcher Tom Adams gave a summary of 'mystery helicopter' cases involving over 200 incidents where unmarked, unidentified helicopters had been observed in the vicinity of mutilation sites. The expanded report was published as *The Choppers – and the Choppers: Mystery Helicopters and Animal Mutilations* (1980). Adams also edited the *Stigmata* newsletter, the flagship mute publication of both lawmen and the independent research community.

Local lawmen weren't sniggering at the mention of mystery helicopters and UFOs. Their files contained reports of the same admixture of bizarre aerial phenomena. As Colorado Sheriff Lou Girodo later told me: 'It's possible that these mutilations are being done by creatures from outer space. Maybe the strange helicopters are really spacecraft camouflaged as helicopters.'

A report from the files of Sheriff Richards of Cochran County, Texas read: 'The people all tell the same story. It [the UFO] is about as wide as a two-lane highway, round and looks the colour of the sun when it is going down and has got a blue glow around it. When people see this thing, in two or three days we hear about some cows that have been mutilated… It sure has got everyone around here uptight.'

Sheriff 'Tex' Graves of Logan County Colorado had also been frustrated in his attempts to apprehend the elusive mutilators. Graves, whose county suffered 72 mutilations between 1975 and 1977, noted tripod marks near some mutilated animals. In 1977, his department expended considerable time and effort pursuing an unidentified craft known as 'Big Mama.' The large UFO would park itself over Logan County and disgorge 'a baby UFO' which would fly off and 'disappear.' Undersheriff/pilot Jerry Wolever and news reporter Bill Jackson took several distant photos of Big Mama and her baby but their attempts to get a closer look from the air were futile. According to Wolever: 'We can never get close to her because she plays games. She always paces us, just so far away, or disappears altogether.'

Perhaps the most bizarre files of anyone at the conference belonged to Captain Keith Wolverton, a deputy sheriff from Cascade County, Montana. During the mute onslaught of 1975 Wolverton had been assigned full-time duty investigating the incidents. In a slight departure from cases elsewhere, many of the incisions appeared 'serrated.' Some of the neat, bloodless cuts seemed 'burned' or 'cauterised,' leading Montana lawmen to speculate that a form of 'laser surgery' might be involved. Between August of 1975 and May of 1976, Wolverton recorded over 100 mutilation incidents. During this time he also logged 130 reports of mysterious helicopters and/or UFOs. Many of the anomalous events centred around Malmstrom Air Force Base and the string of ICBM Minuteman missile bases strung out through the neighbouring counties.

The cult theory received a brief boost with the discovery of a 'ceremonial site' near Butte, Montana. A fellow lawman theorised to Wolverton that the cows were being tranquillised with PCP (a hallucinogen). The 'witches' would then remove the blood and 'trip out' on the strange brew. In 1978, the lab at Oklahoma State University found mescaline, another hallucinogen, in the pericardial fluid of a mutilated Arkansas cow.

As Wolverton's investigation wore on, reports coming into his office gave new meaning to the term 'high strangeness.' Two young women reported an encounter with a seven-foot tall 'creature' with a face that was 'dark and awful, not like a human's.' One of the young women fired a .22 rifle into the air in an attempt to frighten the critter. The beast fell down, theatrically pulled itself along the ground and then stood erect again. The women fled in a blind panic.

Another man reported spotting a 'tall, hairy creature' carrying an object about the size of a bale of hay with what appeared to be 'a piece of dark plastic' flopping from the ends. For reasons unknown, reports of Bigfoot-type creatures during mute/UFO waves are not uncommon.

Still, Schmitt's conference did not have the desired result of getting the FBI actively involved. Citing 'lack of jurisdiction' unless the crimes happened on Federal or Indian land (which they did), the FBI claimed to have no authority in the matter. The political hot-potato was then picked up by District Attorney Eloy Martinez in Santa Fe. Martinez applied for and received a near $50,000 grant from the federally funded Law Enforcement Assistance Administration to finance a year-long probe into the mute problem to begin in May 1980.

Kenneth Rommel, who had spent 28 years with the FBI, was hired as Project Director of Operation Animal Mutilation. Senator Schmitt and the mute investigation network were sceptical. Many doubted the motivations and objectivity of Rommel and Martinez. The District Attorney told visiting journalists: 'We were out to discredit each of these theories [UFOS, cults, etc.]. Our goal was to put to rest once and for all the extreme ideas about cattle mutilations.'

In a breakfast meeting with Rommel, I offered him the use of my files. He had no interest in seeing the files or talking to any of my sources. 'But what about solid evidence of cult involvement from Iowa, Montana, Idaho, Arkansas and Canada?' I pressed. 'Listen,' Rommel said, 'the only cult activity comes from people like you... people who need aspects of mystery in their lives.'

'Yes, I'm a naturally curious person,' I admitted, 'but what about the evidence of clamp marks and broken bones that have been reported?' Rommel retorted that the death throes of sick animals can be quite violent and that 'someone might have slipped into the pasture to apply the clamp marks as a joke.' He confided that his main concern upon taking the job was that panicky ranchers would start shooting at helicopters again as they had in 1975. Rommel gleefully added that his final report would 'screw a lot of people to the wall, including some very high public officials.'

When Rommel's report came out in June 1980, he claimed to have personally investigated 15 'so-called mutilations,' concluding that all had been the work of natural predators. The notion that ranchers couldn't tell the difference between natural and unnatural animal deaths was 'simply not true.' Senator Schmitt called the report 'not definitive,' saying that 'apparently Rommel had reached his conclusions before he began his investigation.' Even Rommel's counterpart in Canada, Corporal Lyn Lauber of the RCMP (who was still hot on the trail of the cultists) remarked that Rommel's report 'appeared to have an ulterior motive.' Lauber told one reporter, 'I'd like to see him write off our confirmed cases as predators.'

From a public safety point of view, Rommel's probe and its 'findings' were entirely understandable. *Newsweek* (30 September, 1974) reported that over-anxious vigilantes in Nebraska had fired two shots through the canopy of a utility company helicopter and that the National Guard had ordered its pilots to fly at higher altitudes to avoid being fired upon. Yet the report was not generally well-received by the rural ranchers and lawmen caught up in the mute maelstrom. The cowmen, many from generations of ranching families, were insulted that they were being accused of being so ignorant that they couldn't tell the difference between the work of a coyote and a scalpel. 'We ought to get out of business if we can't,' one rancher told me.

Mutes were temporarily knocked off the front pages of newspapers. Oddly enough, the main thrust of the phenomenon moved to the western provinces of Canada during the year of Rommel's investigation. As in the US, the strategy for dealing with the mutes was blame the media, whittle down the actual numbers involved, down-play the situation and hope that it goes away.

Over 150 cattle mutilations were reported in Alberta during 1979. Dr. David Green, a veterinary pathologist working with the RCMP, was able to do complete necropsies on only 24 of these cases, concluding that three could be confirmed as actual mutilations. By early August 1980, another 100 cases had been reported. Green necropsied 20 and again found only three of them conclusively mutilated. Although the RCMP had a policy of not talking to the media about the mutes, the Canadian press stated that there had been over 550 cases reported in western Canada during 1979-80. The RCMP found a novel way out of this conundrum. Of the six 'real' mutes, all were determined to have died of natural causes before they were mutilated. Since it was technically not a crime to mutilate a dead animal in Canada, there was no law enforcement problem!

The Colorado Bureau of Investigation took a similar approach to the numbers game. Of the 203 reports recorded by the CBI during 1975-76, 35 had actually been examined by Dr. Albert McChesney and his staff at the College of

144

Veterinary Medicine. Of the 35 cases, 11 were determined to be 'real' mutilations. According to McChesney's summary: 'Most affected cattle died from some natural cause... subsequent to death, some carcasses were mutilated and parts were amputated by unknown persons using sharp tools.' Again, the animals were already dead before they were mutilated, so what's the problem?

Just for the sake of discussion, let's play our own numbers game. Assume that the proportion of 'real' to reported mutilations indicated by McChesney's findings (roughly one-third) holds true with the total number of reports (203). In other words, one-third of the 203 were 'real,' say about 70.

Using the one-third proportion against the total number of reported mutes during the 1970's and early 80's (my tallies show a very low-end number of 2,500) we get a total of roughly 850 'real' mutilations. This is not an 'insignificant' number of mutilated animals. Just for the record, my files show closer to 400 mute reports in Colorado during the period the CBI claimed 203. As in Canada, that is double what the official sources claimed. If the actual number of cases across the board (as opposed to the number reported through official channels) is roughly double, we're now looking at about 1,700 'real' cases.

Regardless of how anyone plays with these numbers, local lawmen and independent investigators had good reason to mistrust the findings of state agencies and their government-sponsored laboratories. Sheriff Yarnell of Elbert County, Colorado related a revealing story to me. During the wave of 1975, he had meticulously taken samples from mutilated cows and sent them to the College of Veterinary Medicine lab for testing. The results always came back: predator damage. To test their accuracy, Yarnell took his own knife, cut a section from a dead cow and submitted it. 'Hell, I was really obvious about it. I even cut little notches in it,' the Sheriff said. The report came back: predator damage. 'I called 'em up to chew 'em out,' Yarnell said. 'The lab guy just laughed and said, we're human too. Everyone makes mistakes.'

Sheriff Leroy Yowell of Lincoln County, Colorado had a similar tale to tell. In 1975 he had fruitlessly chased mystery helicopters in a plane. Yowell's personal theory was that chopper pilots from the Army base at Fort Carson were doing the mutilations 'just for a lark.' The Sheriff's theory was bolstered when a blue government-issue valise was found containing a bloody scalpel, soiled plastic gloves, a cow's ear and part of a cow's tongue. The day before, a CBI agent had investigated a nearby mute. In the agent's opinion, the animal had been mutilated 'with a sharp instrument after death.' Trouble was, the cow parts in the valise didn't match the mute, or any other animal reported mutilated during that time.

Yowell submitted the satchel to the CBI criminology lab technicians who were unable to obtain any finger prints from the items. Incredibly, the crime lab was unable to determine even what species of blood was on the scalpel.

Carl Whiteside, Deputy Director of the Colorado Bureau of Investigation, candidly told one journalist that the study of mutilations was 'like trying to nail jelly to a wall... Everybody who has gotten involved with the mutilations has come away more confused than when they went in, including us.' He accused the 'UFO contingent' of taking over the conference 'to use cattle mutilation reports to prove that UFOs and space aliens visit the earth.'

Mutes and UFOs were strange bedfellows indeed. By the mid-1970s, the major US UFO groups were scrambling to dissociate themselves. In 1974, writer/researcher Jerome Clark, a protégé of America's pre-eminent ufologist, Dr. J. Allen Hynek, began corresponding with a federal prisoner who claimed firsthand knowledge that the mutilations were the work of a nation-wide Satanist organisation.

Clark took the prisoner's dubious information (later totally discredited) to Donald Flickinger, the Minnesota-based special agent of the Treasury Department's Bureau of Alcohol, Tobacco and Firearms. In 1975, Flickinger launched an investigation into the supposed Satanist network. His subsequent widely leaked 'confidential' report stated that the mutilations were the responsibility of a nation-wide 'religious occult.'

Shortly after the Flickinger Report was leaked, Hynek, a former Air Force UFO consultant who had recently founded the Center for UFO Studies (CUFOS), issued his own statement: 'The press has speculated that UFOs are in some way responsible for cattle mutilations... not one documented report exists in which a UFO sighting is directly connected to a cattle mutilation. Research has been done... and a confidential government report has found that a Satanic cult is responsible.'

The Aerial Phenomena Research Organisation (APRO), which had endorsed the UFO/mute connection in the famous Snippy case, issued their own statement which cleared away 'the suspicion of UFO involvement in the grisly mutilations... Our study has provided a glimpse into a Satanic organisation... which has grandiose plans of bringing about a 1,000 year reign of terror and darkness.' Mainstream ufology, in its continuous struggle for scientific legitimacy, clearly did not want to alarm the skittish American public, or further muddy the turgid waters of UFO research.

However, ufology's efforts to keep its orphan stepchild at arm's length during the 1970s ultimately failed. In 1980, the mutes came home to roost, at least for awhile.

A seminal event in the metamorphosis of the mutes was a UFO/abduction case investigated by Albuquerque businessman and APRO investigator, Paul Bennewitz. A Cimarron, New Mexico woman, Myrna Hansen, and her son consciously recalled seeing UFOs and two white-suited 'men' 'working on' a bellowing cow near Cimarron on the evening of 5 May, 1980. A four-hour period of 'missing time' followed. Bennewitz called in Wyoming hypnotherapist Dr. Leo Sprinkle (who had worked with numerous abductees) to regress Hansen. In a hypnotic state, Hansen revealed that she and her son had been taken aboard a craft manned by small gray beings and tall hairless humanoids. Hansen further recalled the aliens mutilating a live cow and being taken to an underground cavern near what she thought was Roswell, New Mexico. After enduring a painful vaginal procedure, she saw a vat of red liquid in which she observed a floating humanoid figure and what she assumed to be various animal parts. Hansen and her son also stated that 'they [the aliens] mean to control the earth.'

A similar story of a Texas woman who claimed to have been abducted into a UFO with her daughter and witnessed a cattle mutilation performed by aliens was reported in a documentary film *Strange Harvest*. Again, the information was retrieved under hypnosis by Dr. Sprinkle.

Strange Harvest, produced by Linda Moulton Howe with CBS-affiliate KMGH TV in Denver (first released in May 1980), was probably the single most influential piece of media coverage ever presented on the mutilation subject. Howe had contacted me in 1979 when she was beginning work on the project. I provided her with copies of my files and lists of contacts, and also travelled with her for much of the filming of the show, appearing in two different segments (never mentioning UFOs).

The documentary received wide national exposure and MUFON, the world's largest UFO organisation, enthusiastically embraced Howe's UFO/mute connection and made her a sort of unofficial spokesperson on the topic. But by the time the film was aired, my own research was leading me away from a strict UFO/mute correlation. To my mind, the mute question had become an infinitely complex equation. Even the Extraterrestrial Hypothesis could not adequately explain all of the evidence surrounding the phenomenon.

Meanwhile, myth and manipulation became curiously intertwined. In the follow up book, *An Alien Harvest* (1989), Howe gave considerable space to the ideas of ex-Naval petty officer Bill Cooper, who claimed that a 'secret government' controlled the country. According to Cooper, this shadow government had signed a treaty with the aliens allowing them to mutilate animals and abduct humans to obtain the necessary blood, enzymes and genetic materials they needed to survive. In exchange, the government supposedly received advanced alien technology. Cooper appeared to have gotten much of his information (if it could be called that) from John Lear, an ex-airline pilot with a background in the CIA.

When I first met Lear, he provided me with documents of dubious origin purporting to show the interior of an underground alien/government base near Dulce, New Mexico. There were drawings of large vats with 'pale meat' floating in them and chambers where 'hybrid embryos' were in various stages of development. According to Lear, the aliens were using genetic material taken from abductees and cattle organs to create 'almost human beings.' The documents alleged that the aliens put their hands in cow blood for nourishment: 'It's not just food they want, the DNA in cattles (sic) and humans is being altered.'

The Lear/Cooper paranoid, conspiratorial vision came to be known as 'the Dark Side Hypothesis.' Lear picked up many of these ideas from Paul Bennewitz, who had been deeply influenced by the Cimarron abduction case, and who claimed to be in contact with the aliens on his computer. Beginning in the early 1980's, an Air Force Office of Special Investigations (AFOSI) officer named Richard Doty, based at Kirtland Air Force Base in Albuquerque, had fed Bennewitz a steady stream of bogus documents and other inducements to reinforce the Dark Side Hypothesis. In an arguably classic misinformation campaign, Doty and his military intelligence cohorts sucked in Linda Moulton Howe and several of ufology's most prominent researchers. Bennewitz was driven to the brink of insanity, and eventually hospitalised with a massive nervous breakdown.

In his history of the UFO phenomenon, *Watch the Skies!* (1994), Curtis Peebles claims that by the early 1980s the 'flying saucer myth' consisted of three distinct components – crashed saucers, abductions and mutes. Gradually, these three threads were interwoven to make a new mythology, which he calls 'the alien myth.' According to Peebles, 'It was from the mute myth, with its images of death, dismemberment and conspiracies that the alien myth would first emerge. In the end, the alien myth would itself become submerged in a witch's brew of fascist conspiracy theories, hate and paranoia.'

Peebles, a UFO sceptic, uses the word myth to mean something imaginary, fictional or unreal. I prefer Joseph Campbells' definition in *The Hero With A Thousand Faces* (1949): 'Myth is the secret opening through which the inexhaustible energies of the cosmos pour into human cultural manifestations. The prime function of mythology is to supply the symbols that carry the human spirit forward, in counteraction to those other constant human fantasies that tend to tie it back.' As

Carl Jung reminds us, all myths have some basis in reality.

Meanwhile back in the Heartland, mutilations are still being found, though infrequently reported. 'Why bother?' the cowmen say. Ranchers' reactions to these events vary wildly. In one case, I arrived at night to investigate a mutilation report in Colorado only to find the rancher furiously at work burying the carcass with a backhoe. His wife intercepted me and quickly escorted me back to my car. 'Please go away,' she implored. 'My husband thinks this is the work of the devil!'

While pondering another Colorado mute with a grizzled and laconic old rancher, I asked him, 'What do you think did this to your cow?' He chewed, spit and shrugged his shoulders: 'I dunno… I guess somebody just needed some parts.'

The flip side of this coin was my visit to Elsberry, Missouri in 1978. The whole town was seeing 'your traditional flying saucers', mutes were dropping like flies, mystery helicopters prowled the hills, 55-gallon drums flew in formation, Bigfoot creatures picked through the dump and little people wearing 'glowing suits' were seen at the lake. Someone had printed up T-shirts saying: 'Elsberry Missouri – Mutilated Cow Country'. The image on the shirt showed a cow on its back with one leg missing. A flying saucer hovered over the cow containing a grinning little alien holding a bloody knife.

At night the roads were jammed with parked cars. People had driven from miles around to watch for the saucers. With binoculars in hand, folks sat in lawn chairs, drank beer and sodas and ate picnic meals. Children frolicked and dogs cavorted. At first, the scene struck me as rather pathetic, the epitome of folly. But the more I watched, the more absorbed I became. Eventually, I wanted to see the saucers, too.

THE 1980s

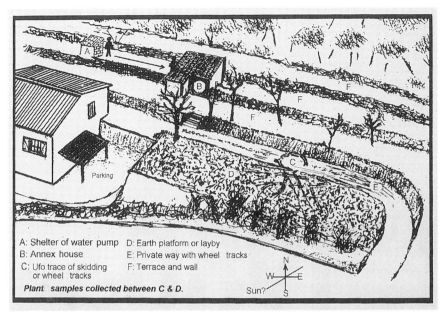

A: Shelter of water pump
B: Annex house
C: Ufo trace of skidding or wheel tracks
D: Earth platform or layby
E: Private way with wheel tracks
F: Terrace and wall

Plant samples collected between C & D.

Sun?

Drawing of the site of the famous Trans-en-Provence UFO case by Eric Maillot

For many years, France was the only country outside the United States to maintain an official, authorised organisation for the investigation of UFOs. GEPAN (Groupe d'Étude des Phénomènes Aerospatiaux Non-Identifiés), a section of the National Centre for Space Studies (CNES), though sometimes accused of being little more than a public-relations exercise, conducted a handful of in-depth investigations which were perceived as neutral and scientific.

Of these, none achieved greater international prominence than the apparent landing at Trans-en-Provence. In itself this single-witness case seemed to present few features of outstanding interest: if it was taken seriously, this was because the official French organisation took it seriously, coming up with seemingly 'scientific' evidence that an alien spacecraft had briefly visited this obscure French homestead. At the same time it has been the subject of investigations by many private groups and individuals, the latest that of Eric Maillot, the author of this article. He and Jacques Scornaux, who translated it, are veteran researchers whose early interest in the physical aspects of ufology gradually extended to its psychological aspects. Eric Maillot may be reached at 20 rue J Moulin, 08800 Montherme, France (phone +33 3 24 53 68 06); Jacques Scornaux at 6 rue Lekain, 75016 Paris (phone +33 1 45 25 42 74)

TRANS-EN-PROVENCE: WHEN SCIENCE AND BELIEF GO HAND IN HAND

by Eric Maillot and Jacques Scornaux

'On the shore of the unknown, we found the print of a strange foot. We built scholarly theories about it. Eventually, we succeeded in reconstituting the creature who left this print, and now we acknowledge that the footprint is our own.' Jean-Paul Sartre

Every ufologist has heard of the Trans-en-Provence case: French- and English-speaking commentators alike do not hesitate to present it as the scientifically-supported UFO case, the one indispensable reference. Was it not chosen to lend weight to the briefing document submitted by CUFOS, FUFOR and MUFON to the U.S. Congress? Yet though there are many self-styled 'experts' in the Trans case, very few have studied the dossier in its entirety, and rarer still are those who took every detail into account.

To give just one example: not one ufologist, scientist or expert described the supposed landing trace exactly as it was! Even the drawing made by the gendarmes on the site was not true to the facts. You will read of 'two concentric circles' or 'two ring arcs', but you will never find mention of a distinct straight print, closely linked to the trace. Yet this structural feature, as clear as it is disturbing, can be seen on detailed photographs which have been published many times, from the journal *Lumières dans la nuit* shortly after the event to the 1992 brochure presenting the findings of the inquiry made by SEPRA (the government organisation which, on a reduced scale, replaced GEPAN). It is hardly an exaggeration to say that it is as if everyone has insisted on describing a plate though a frying pan was before their eyes!

How did this single-witness CE2 case come to be both so well and yet so incompletely known? The answer is simple: for a UFO case to achieve classic status, it does not have to involve an extraordinary story, it is quite sufficient that 'science' should take a hand in it.

Our story really begins a few months before the sighting itself. In 1980, however incredible it may seem for an official body, GEPAN did not know how to find a biologist who could analyse samples in the event that a UFO landing were to take place. Then, thanks to an engineer, Jean-Christophe Vève, who was also a ufologist, GEPAN heard of Michel Bounias, a biochemist who worked at Avignon. Bounias happened to be Vève's neighbour: that is the way official ufology works in France. A contract was signed between Professor Bounias and GEPAN: and it was not to be long before that contract was invoked in regard to an actual case.

On 9 January 1981, GEPAN received a telex from the Gendarmerie at Draguignan, a town in the hills above Cannes, near the Côte d'Azur. Its main paragraph read as follows:

> On 8 January, the witness, having heard a faint whistling sound, saw from a distance of 50m an object above his garden. It continued down to about 1m from the ground. When the witness approached, the object then went east. Total duration: 1 minute. Ovoid shape, dull grey colour, neither porthole nor aerial, no effect on the witness, no beings seen. Traces: two circle arcs like tyre skidding traces, length: 80cm, width: 10cm.

Later, when Bounias quotes this telex, the arc length is curiously reduced to 40cm. But contradictions appear even during the first hour of the investigation. In that first telex we have a UFO 'motionless at 1m above the ground', but when the Gendarmerie come to make their official report it will be described as 'seen on the ground'. The same report contradicts the telex, and also later statements from the witness, by referring to dust seen when the object takes off. Moreover, the words 'tyre skidding traces' used in the Gendarmerie telex mysteriously disappear from the official report of the witness' statement. Later, we shall find the word 'tyre' missing from GEPAN's Technical Note number 16 (hereafter NT16) which constitutes the definitive report on the investigation so far as the French authorities are concerned: instead we read of 'a sort of skidding trace'. The 'tyre skidding' is referred to only in newspaper accounts: it is omitted from those accounts which constitute a supposedly scientific inquiry.

Well, what did the witness himself have to say? His story (though it was to vary somewhat in later versions) can be summarised as follows:

> On 8 January 1981, around 5p.m., Renato Niccolai, a 52-year-old technician of Italian origin currently on sick leave due to a heart condition, is building a shelter for a water pump on an earth terrace at a higher level than his house. His attention is aroused by a whistling sound. Turning his head to the east, he sees a dull disk surrounded by a thick ring coming down from above the trees bordering his garden. This disk lands on a lower terrace and the witness, some 50m away, loses sight of it. He walks some 20m up to a little building

on the same terrace as the pump shelter. From there, he observes the craft which he describes in these words: 'It's a somewhat bulging disk like two plates glued to each other by the rim, with a central ring some 20 cm wide'. The object, which has landed very near the upper terrace wall, is perhaps 2½ m in diameter, 1½ m high and rests on two (or four) feet (or jet-pipes) like 'a mason's buckets upside down', protruding some 20cm. The witness only sees two 'buckets' facing him. After some four seconds, the object takes off rapidly towards the east. Two protruding buckets and two others retracted can be seen beneath it. The total duration of the sighting is some 30 to 40 seconds. He goes up to the landing site and finds what seems to be skidding traces. He resumes working. When his wife comes back from her job around 9p.m., he tells her about his sighting and the traces. She does not believe him and says he's playing a joke. However, next day, she is convinced when he shows her the traces, and she speaks about it to their neighbour, Mme Morin. This lady is interested in UFOs and alerts the Gendarmerie.

As investigations and publications on the case multiplied, other versions of the story were to appear. *Flying Saucer Review* located the case in the wrong department: the official report by SEPRA speaks of a UFO which landed for more than a minute! Setting aside such gross distortions, let us concentrate on internal inconsistencies in the testimony.

Even if we accept Niccolai's estimate of the object's shape and size, we need to explain why the two or four 'buckets' under the UFO left no visible trace on the ground. (Some people claimed that infrared photographs did show circular traces left by the buckets, without expressing surprise that these showed no sign of movement whereas the skidding traces do indicate movement) Moreover, the UFO could not leave two arc traces without contradicting the witness's testimony (Niccolai stated 'it was not rotating')

Even if he was mistaken, and the object was rotating, the buckets are wider than the arc traces and their position under the craft does not match the trace diameter. But if we increase Niccolai's estimate of its size so that the buckets fit the trace, the UFO becomes so wide that it hits the wall.

Niccolai hears no impact sound, although he describes the UFO as 'falling like a stone'. Nor does he perceive the noise that the grinding and crushing of the gravel by the UFO should have made (GEPAN estimated the object's weight at several tons). Yet he hears a faint humming or hissing sound both when it drops onto the terrace and when it takes off again.

Finally, from where he was standing, Niccolai would not have been able to see the UFO hitting the ground, because at this stage it would have been largely hidden by the terrace wall.

Neither GEPAN, SEPRA nor any scientist who studied the case saw any reason to question Niccolai's testimony; yet these inconsistencies provide good grounds for arguing that the witness, who saw the trace only a few moments after the sighting (from 30 seconds to five minutes, depending on which version we accept), was mistaken when he identified it as the landing site. He had only an incomplete view of the landed UFO and had only four seconds to memorise the landmarks: moreover he was moving with respect to those marks. How many of us, in such conditions, would be able, at a distance of 50m, to locate an object within one metre? Even the GEPAN investigators locate the trace incorrectly on some photographs in their NT16, as well as shrinking its size by half on two of them.

Trans-en-Provence in a French UFO journal

If we go by the very first Gendarmerie report, and surmise that the UFO did not actually land but hovered at 1-1½ m from the ground, these inconsistencies disappear. Why was this version set aside? Perhaps because, if this were the case, GEPAN would have found itself in an awkward position. For officially, GEPAN's mandate was that it would intervene only (1) when it had access to the site within 48 hours of the incident ; (2) when there was more than one witness ; and (3) when physical traces existed.

In practice, GEPAN did not stick to these guidelines in many other cases. But in the Trans case its investigators did not reach the site until 40 days after the sighting, and there was only one witness. With only the traces to justify its intervention, GEPAN had good reason to favour their reality. So they accepted Niccolai's testimony, without asking inconvenient questions such as why the extraterrestrials should land so close to the wall when there was plenty of space on the wide terrace.

Instead, the investigators chose to concentrate their analysis on the plant samples, which allowed them to set aside the physical trace, which, though useful for promoting the case, was potentially embarrassing. Samples were taken by the Gendarmerie, not very carefully, one day after the event, again after 15 days, and yet again by GEPAN when they eventually arrived 40 days later. Unfortunately, they were not collected in accordance with a strict and scientifically tested protocol. Instead of making sampling using an orthogonal frame covering the whole trace area, the Trans trace was studied asymmetrically, with sampling on only one axis and on one side from the centre, the test plant (a wild medick) being collected wherever it happened to grow. A bunch of amateurs could hardly have managed things more clumsily.

Nevertheless, that's how it was. And so it came about that on the basis of improperly acquired samples, Professor Bounias, who possessed no knowledge of the ufological investigation and no expertise in plant pathology, became the expert in the analysis of plant traumata caused by mysterious craft of unknown origin.

Bounias' study on the Trans plants concluded that they had undergone accelerated ageing, inversely proportional to the square of their distance from the centre of the trace. This ageing was measured mainly by the variation of pigment concentrations (chlorophylls, carotenoids). Without explaining in any detail why he excluded every other possible cause (disease caused by a pathogen, action of a chemical, UV radiation, lightning, heat or water stress, etc.), Bounias offered the hypothesis that this effect 'might be linked to the action of an energy field of an electric kind; later he added that the cause might more precisely have been a beam of pulsed microwaves. Though he never explicitly said that this beam could be emitted only by an extraterrestrial craft, this was clearly implied.

Now another scientist enters the scene. It happened that, during his investigation, Bounias became acquainted and shared his findings with Dr Jean-Pierre Petit, a well-known French physicist and ufologist who is noted for his thesis that UFOs are craft propelled by a magnetohydrodynamic (MHD) engine emitting – guess what? – pulsed microwaves! The presence of two recognised scientists, Bounias and Petit, was very influential in promoting the Trans case in the mass media. As for GEPAN, it was only too happy to be able to offer a seemingly scientifically-substantiated case to the supervising authorities who were only too prone to cut its budget, so it did nothing – to say the least – to encourage a more prudent approach. As recently as 1993 Jean-Jacques Velasco, head of GEPAN's successor SEPRA, co-authored a book with the flamboyant journalist and UFO believer Jean-Claude Bourret in which the 'official' version of the Trans case was trotted out once again.

So it was that Trans-en-Provence became one of the great classics of ufology, to the great delight of ufologists worldwide who could at last point to a case that was supported by academic scientists and even a government body like GEPAN. However, not all UFO researchers allowed themselves to be blinded by science. Some inquiring minds pursued the investigation further and proposed experimental checks or pragmatic explanatory hypotheses.

In 1984, Michel Monnerie, a well-known French ufologist whose investigative experiences had led to his becoming more and more sceptical, proposed a psychological hypothesis to explain the Trans case which might be entitled 'Beyond his control' or 'The snowball effect'. It can be summarised as follows:

> Mme Morin believes in UFOs and speaks enthusiastically about them to her neighbours M and Mme Niccolai. Renato Niccolai then plans a practical joke. He has heard that ufologists are fond of physical evidence, and it happens that vehicles, manoeuvring on the way to his house, have left odd traces which he decides to exploit. He has only a limited acquaintance with ufology, but he has a hazy knowledge of the classic UFO shape and he throws in jet-pipes and a whistling sound for good measure. When his wife comes back home, his first words to her (which tend to support the joke scenario) are 'Your cat is back, extraterrestrials brought him home' (their cat had not been seen for some days) and only then recounts his sighting. At first sceptical, she believes him when he shows her the trace. The following day, she mentions it to her UFO-believing neighbour Mme Morin, and no doubt Niccolai is pleased to have fooled people of a higher social status than his own.
>
> But when he embarked on his little game, he never imagined what might follow. Mme Morin insists that the Gendarmerie must be alerted. Confronted with the gendarmes, Niccolai is afraid to go back on his story, fearing to be charged with contempt for law enforcement officers. So he feels bound to stick to his initial statement, and more and more so as the case gains momentum. So he tells his story again and again, to gendarmes, GEPAN, ufologists and the popular media; the variations in his story, far from weakening his credibility, speak rather in his favour, for they imply that he did not plan an elaborate hoax and had no time to prepare a consistent scenario. He agrees with what investigators say to him, because they know so much more than he does about UFOs. Do they ask whether there were bolts? All right, there were bolts.
>
> And so, little by little, he completely loses control of his own story. He tries to protect himself by saying 'I don't believe in UFOs, I saw a strange craft, it was surely a military one', though we know from his words to his wife that the idea of extraterrestrials was in his mind from the very start. Feeling initially compelled to stick to his story, perhaps as the years passed it became a source of satisfaction for him – an Italian technician who was no longer able to work because of health problems and who spoke poor French – to be visited by experts of all kinds who assure him that, thanks to him, 'science

progresses', to quote the book by Bourret and Velasco…

This hypothesis is the most economical of all the possible explanations. It calls for no faking of a trace by the witness and explains the variations and inconsistencies in his relation of the events. But it is not the only possible down-to-earth hypothesis, as we shall see. And it goes without saying that it is totally unacceptable to the true believers and the proponents of a 'scientific' UFO.

In that same year, 1984, the results of the Bounias analysis were submitted to Professor A., a Belgian plant pathologist, a member of the scientific council of SOBEPS, the main Belgian UFO group, and a man with an open mind as to UFOs. Bounias refused a scientific debate, even at a private level, with Professor A., and never answered the justified criticisms made by the Belgian. Instead, he preferred to continue to promote his work to the popular media, where nobody would ask him embarrassing questions. GEPAN and Velasco, though informed of Professor A.'s conclusions, saw no reason to seek the advice of other experts to settle the dispute and hushed up the very existence of a scientific difference of opinion: almost nobody in ufological circles was aware of the matter, and it sank into oblivion.

Yet Professor A. was able to point out numerous gaps and errors in Bounias' work. The methodology of sample collection was defective, and many checks and searches were not made at all. Often the samples were too few for meaningful conclusions to be drawn, and frequently the data was inadequate or even non-existent. Certain comparisons (for example between a germinating crucifera and an adult medick) did not make much sense, and altogether Professor A. concluded that a lot of work had been done to little purpose, and that the results were inconclusive. Indeed, the same might be said of GEPAN's participation as a whole, which could be seen as a huge waste of time and the French taxpayer's money.

It was only in 1995 that I acquired all these facts, and I then decided to review all the data which, according to Bounias, seemed to show a UFO effect. I was surprised to find flaw after flaw in his procedures. Many of them are too technical to describe here, but one which we can all understand relates to samples, categorised as 'exhibiting abnormal values' and which are also described as 'dried, browned and crushed' . Simple visual inspection confirms that these samples were indeed 'affected', but by what? May it not have been simple trampling, something that is never taken into account in Bounias' hypotheses? Might not a heavy foot mimic a UFO effect?

It is quite possible that the first investigators, or M and Mme Mrs Niccolai showing the trace to their neighbours, trampled the plants that subsequently became 'scientific' samples. Footprints are visible on the photographs taken less than 48 hours after the event.

In January 1984 Bounias made another surprising pronouncement. He told the media that some effects on plants were persisting even after two years, though less strongly. Yet the implication is clear: any effect which persists for so long must result from soil characteristics or other site conditions, for the young plants did not exist at the time of the supposed landing. Though Bounias tried to protect his position by speaking of a 'remnent effect' he had to admit the possibility of an 'anterior effect' and acknowledge that 'several anomalies seem fortuitous', repudiating some of his 1981 findings. It is a half avowal. At a UFO congress at Lyon in 1990, Bounias admitted that some of the variations observed in 1983 were not statistically significant, and as for embarrassing data, he even suggested humourously that a rat urinated on a plant… Unfortunately, he did not go further, to propose another prosaic explanation: that one or more vehicles might have manoeuvred and parked for a rather long time above the grass, imposing light deprivation which altered the chlorophylls, and causing the crushing, wilting and ground traces.

Some years later, Bounias had the opportunity to perform another analysis of plant samples allegedly exposed to the mysterious radiation of a UFO. At Nort-sur-Erdre (Loire Atlantique) in 1987, a young boy claimed to have recorded the sound emitted by a UFO hovering above trees. Leaves were collected and – are you really surprised? – Bounias found traumata similar to those observed in the Trans plants. Alas for him, in-depth investigation by Renaud Marhic demonstrated beyond any doubt that this case was a hoax: there was no UFO, and therefore there could be no UFO effects.

My object in all this is not to question Professor Bounias' expertise in topics where he is genuinely a specialist, such as the analysis of very minute quantities of substances by thin layer microchromatography. But today's science is a very specialist business, and a scientist who goes outside his own field of expertise is hardly more competent than an intelligent layman. It is to be feared that, as has happened to other scientists who happen also to be UFO believers, Professor Bounias allowed his beliefs to guide his judgment.

Let's go back to 1984. In that year Michel Figuet, a widely-respected researcher who co-authored the landmark *Dossier Complet* of close encounters in France, opened investigations to test the hypothesis that the observed effects and traces may have been caused by cement leaking from a concrete-mixer or by the drilling equipment which a neighbour claimed to have seen on the spot some days before the sighting. Spurred by critics who suggested that he had overlooked this factor, Bounias hurriedly offered a demonstration that the concrete-mixer hypothesis was wrong. But again, methodological shortcomings – for example, dilution effects by rain are ignored – render his demonstration valueless.

In 1989 one of the most eminent of all ufologists made his appearance on the Trans scene. Jacques Vallee, having received the complete dossier from Michel Figuet and discussed the case with him, sought to restore its credibility by instituting further experiments in the U.S. He obtained from GEPAN two samples from the trace ring (though no control sample) and produced findings which allowed him to dispose of Figuet's embarrassing hypothesis. Vallee concluded that no trace of cement, oil or chemical pollutant testified to the presence of a vehicle. Yet the laboratory had been given no information regarding the nature of the sample, being told only that 'they were not hazardous in terms of radioactivity or toxicity'; consequently no specific tests were performed for cement, oil and other potential plant toxics such as pesticides or weed-killers. The use of a scanning electron microscope and energy-dispersive X-ray analysis no doubt impressed credulous non-scientists, yet such procedures were inadequate to test for the really interesting substances.

In many other respects, Vallee's results are so at variance with those of GEPAN that we might well ask if these samples were really collected at the same site. However, this does not prevent him claiming that his analysis tends to support the findings of French laboratories. True, where GEPAN saw traces of a major event, Vallee sees nothing particular: only ordinary soil. But he tries paradoxically to use this ordinariness as an argument for a real UFO and so invents a new kind of proof: proof by absence of evidence! What he is saying, in effect, is that since there is no evidence of soil perturbation by, say, a concrete-mixer or a drilling machine, there must have been a UFO!

In the event, it was Figuet himself who invalidated the drilling hypothesis: he established that the drilling had been carried out months earlier, in August 1982. The site does not match, moreover work of this kind is never conducted less than 2m from a wall. As for the cement hypothesis, we must bear in mind that most of the chemical constituents of cement were indeed found at the site, but the traces would have been very difficult to identify as due to cement since most of them are natural soil components which would have been there anyway. A purely qualitative determination makes little sense: only a statistically significant quantitative difference from a control sample would be relevant.

It was Michel Figuet's determination to make a really thorough re-evaluation that led me to reconsider the dossier in more depth. A careful examination of the photographs revealed features no investigator had taken into account. Everyone had chosen to ignore the traces which suggested trampling and, above all, the tyre traces clearly visible on the path, in the grass and crossing the 'UFO' trace in all directions, notably at the centre of it or connected to the arcs. The likelihood that there was a tyre trace, unrelated to Niccolai's UFO, is supported by the presence of carbon black-like residues. One laboratory guessed these might come from a primer paint, but other paint components are lacking. On the other hand, carbon black is used in tyre tread rubber (which also contains many other substances found at Trans by GEPAN).

Noting this, I conducted a little experiment with my car. I found that skidding while braking, or slipping while starting on a clayey limestone, produced effects very like those seen at Trans – that is to say, polishing or abrasion of gravels, fine ferrous striae and a little black deposit left by the tyres on rock grains. Under the microscope, the deposit is identical in appearance with the GEPAN photographs. Try it for yourself! It is to be feared that GEPAN failed to make a number of elementary checks and comparisons of this kind, for fear of having to acknowledge that the trace could have been made by a rolling object with tyres. Yet Niccolai himself mentioned the presence of vehicles on the terrace, some weeks before the sighting, in connection with the construction of the little annex house.

Why did GEPAN so single-mindedly pursue the idea that an extraterrestrial object had really landed at Trans? Is it possible that the case was seen as a lifeline which might save GEPAN from imminent wreck? At the end of 1983 a restructuring took place which reduced GEPAN's mandate: henceforward, it was no longer to be responsible for the scientific study of UFOs, but only for 'making investigations' with no resources. So it is likely that in early 1983, and perhaps before, GEPAN had been anxious about its future. Then – by a happy coincidence – in March 1983 it was able to publish its report on Trans. Three weeks later, a second strong case, in which the witness was himself a scientist, was published. Earlier, in its NT 14, GEPAN had demonstrated its ability to expose fake UFOs and to assign a place to meteorological phenomena such as lightning effects. This triple synchronicity suggests a political dimension to the official investigation of Trans which could account for the way it was conducted.

It may also explain why GEPAN failed to spot an aspect of the case which was noted only recently by researcher Raoul Robé. He pointed out that the Trans incident did not occur, as has all along been generally supposed, in full daylight: no, it was twilight.

According to Niccolai, the sighting took place around 5p.m.; moreover, a hill, 100m higher than the site, stood between him and the sun. Since sunset that day was 4:58p.m. local time, it is likely that the sun was no longer visible and that lighting conditions were less than perfect.

On the other hand, perhaps Niccolai was wrong in his estimate of time? This seems not unlikely in the light of his somewhat surprising statement that after the sighting he carried on working. What if the sighting took place half an hour sooner, before sunset, around 4:30p.m.? Well, in that case another interesting factor enters the scenario, for it so happens that about this time, according to GEPAN, a military helicopter, from one of the several bases in the region, flew over Trans at an altitude of no more than 200m. Could this have been the basis of the story, the witness's attention having been awakened by a whistling sound, which he himself described to Michel Figuet as 'like that of a helicopter'.

If so, two possibilities suggest themselves. First, staying with the practical joke scenario, we may hypothesise that Niccolai, surprised by the helicopter (whose passage he does not mention in his testimony), thinks of a UFO which inspires his practical joke. Or second; that, under the influence of the medical treatment he is taking for his heart condition, he fails to identify the helicopter and its oblong shadow passing across the terrace and over the trees. After this fugitive vision has disappeared, he finds an odd trace which convinces him that the object came down to the ground. (Indeed, GEPAN itself had in 1979 investigated a case in which the witness's perception had been altered by medicine).

If Niccolai was indeed mistaken about the time, and if a real UFO did visit his property, the helicopter pilot could have seen it. But GEPAN never explored the possibility. Why not? Isn't it strange that, during 16 years, no one thought of asking what possible reason the UFO had to make its brief appearance on Niccolai's land? But if he was mistaken about the time, the reason becomes crystal clear: the UFO was hiding from the helicopter!

So, ironically, instead of abandoning Niccolai's UFO as a figment of his own imagination and GEPAN's wish-to-believe, we find that GEPAN's sloppy procedures actually point to a way of bringing back to life this UFO which was on the point of losing its nuts and bolts, its paint – and its credibility!

CONCLUSION

What happened at Trans-en-Provence was that, from a single, uncertain and inconsistent testimony, GEPAN, with the help of some other scientific actors, all of them linked to ufological circles, succeeded in creating a case which achieved classic status. Regrettably, it now appears that the Trans case is far from being as solid as its champions would like it to be.

Let me, in conclusion, hand the mike to the witness himself, who stated, at the end of a TV programme devoted to his sighting, 'The little word I wish to say in concluding, it's... Maybe I saw something, maybe it is a story. The proof, one can find it there on the ground... people, scientists may find something there, that's something else. I say, I too, during the night, I dream'. On another occasion Niccolai confessed to Michel Figuet 'There are so many silly people in the world. On some future day, I shall tell you the whole truth'. I look forward to that day with confidence.

If you wish to learn more about this very complex and thrilling case, the comprehensive existing dossier (in French) published by SERPAN is obtainable from Michel Figuet, La Roche, 71520 Dompierre-les-Ormes, France.

MANY RESEARCHERS HAVE NOTED THAT THE UFO PHENOMENON SEEMS TO WALK HAND-IN-HAND WITH THE ODD WORLD OF COINCIDENCE AND SYNCHRONICITY, THE PARANORMAL, AND THE CONUNDRUMS OF ZEN. THE FOLLOWING EXAMPLE COMES TO US FROM RICHARD F. HAINES, WHO HAS BEEN INVESTIGATING UFOS FOR MORE THAN 30 YEARS. A SPECIALIST IN THE PSYCHOLOGY OF PERCEPTION, FOR MANY YEARS DR. HAINES WAS EMPLOYED AT THE NASA-AMES RESEARCH CENTER IN CALIFORNIA, FROM WHICH HE RETIRED IN 1988 AS CHIEF OF THE SPACE HUMANS FACTOR OFFICE. HE IS THE EDITOR OF UFO PHENOMENA AND THE BEHAVIORAL SCIENTIST (1979) AND THE AUTHOR OF NUMEROUS ARTICLES AND BOOKS ABOUT UFOS. THE LATTER INCLUDE OBSERVING UFOS: AN INVESTIGATIVE HANDBOOK (1980); MELBORNE EPISODE: CASE STUDY OF A MISSING PILOT ABOUT FREDERICK VALENTICH (1987); ADVANCED AERIAL DEVICES REPORTED DURING THE KOREAN WAR (1990); AND PROJECT DELTA: A STUDY OF MULTIPLE UFO (1994).

THE QUESTION

by Richard F. Haines

L ife has a wonderful way of humbling us humans. I hope that this true story will illustrate this fact. One of the many clients with whom I had worked in the area of Close Encounters of the Fourth Kind (i.e., alleged alien abductions and visits) involved a mother with two sons who was living in Los Angeles and whom I had been working with for several years. She claimed to have been visited periodically by little creatures very unlike human beings. Let us call her Bonny. The details of their (let us call them Visitors) very frequent visits to Bonny's suburban apartment are really not important here but, suffice it to say, were quite typical of the visits many others continue to describe to this day. What is important to describe is one particular event which involved me.

My phone rang one evening at about eight o'clock. It was Bonny, and she seemed a little more depressed than normal. A word is in order about this brave woman to set the context for the story to follow. She was divorced from her husband several years earlier and was now trying to raise her two sons (Daniel, eight years old; Frank, 16 years old) (all names are fictitious) on her income from a medical secretarial job. In fact Frank was giving her real problems and had moved out on his own. Bonny possesses a higher than normal intelligence and has the kind of personality that one could not help but like – fresh, creative, witty. She is a vivacious and outgoing person who makes friends easily. But periodically, Bonny would describe Visitor visits to her apartment, always after dark, usually at about the same time of night, and always involving some kind of tingling sensation followed by spreading body paralysis preceding the event and partial or almost total amnesia afterwards.

These visit events had been going on for so long (I had worked with her for several years keeping track of them and had counted over 100 by this time) that I felt justified in thinking that Bonny was being far too personally submissive, no, absolutely passive, toward these uninvited 'guests.' I don't wish to get into these details here. It was this attitude of mine about her which actually set the stage for the weird events which were to follow and which I wish to recall here leading up to the question.

During this telephone call (note: made late in September 1988; this and sub-sequent narratives are transcribed from telephone taped interviews) I said, 'Well, Bonny, I have been thinking about your experiences for a long time now and it seems to me that you really should be taking more initiative when they are with you if you can. It is not right for them to be able to do anything they want and you nothing. I have been thinking about what you can do to change this situation. Here is something that I want you to do if they ever do come back.'

Bonny tried to object but I persisted. Finally she agreed to hear my request. 'I want you to ask them, what is the atomic weight of lead, that's all,' I replied.

She seemed puzzled. 'I don't even know what that means,' she said. We talked about the question for several more minutes, however I didn't explain it in any detail. That could come later if necessary. At length she agreed to do this and finally jotted my question down on a piece of paper. We said our goodbyes and hung up. I was surprised when the phone rang about an hour later. It was Bonny. She said, 'Dr. Haines, I just have to ask you one more question about the atomic weight of lead.'

'All right Bonny, what is it?' I said.

'How big a piece of lead?' she asked. I was relieved as I heard these words because they signified that she did not know much about the physics involved. Of course I had chosen this question for several reasons: (1) I did not know the answer myself and so could not be accused of mentally transmitting it to her during our phone conversation and (2) It is a number which is known to some accuracy which could be looked up in a textbook if necessary.

'Bonny, believe me. It doesn't matter how big the piece of lead is. Just ask them the question exactly like I asked you,' I replied. Soon we hung up and I smiled to myself, half wondering whether I would ever hear from her again.

It was not until 25 October 1988 at 9.45p.m. that Bonny called me to say that she had been visited again the previous night and that she had asked them my question. She was clearly excited. By then so was I. What follows is a word for word transcript of our telephone call that night; all of the key details are accurate. I have left out some of her comments which are not directly related to my question and its answer. B = Bonny, H = Haines

B: Anyway, the next thing I knew, I had the two more familiar beings by my side of the bed.
H: OK.
B: And I remembered thinking, 'Oh, God! No! Just don't paralyse me!'
H: Uh-huh.
B:...I began to get heavily sedated...And as I began to...That's when I remembered, when I became aware that there was going to be an encounter, you told me, try to keep my eyes open, and not...not look away. And that's why I looked. (She laughs) And I, Oh, my God! This is a tall one!
H: Uh-huh.
B: But I looked. And I don't know whether it was my own mind telling me then to put my face down in the pillow, or whether it was an instruction, my interpretation was that it was an instruction...Whether or not that's true, I don't know.

And just as that effect was...that sedative-like effect began I remembered, 'Oh! There was one more part to what I was supposed to do, if this ever happened again.'

H: Yes.

B: And so with what I had in me, I desperately eked out the question... and I was desperately (unintelligible). And you know it was getting harder and harder, because what this, whatever they did was, like drugging me.

H: Yes.

B: Um, from as an awake a state as I am now. And I did eke out the question. And, they knew already. As I was trying to... this I remember clearly. Now, again, for the record, I'm not saying for a fact, these beings told me this number (she laughs)... But I believe they did.

H: OK.

It was at this point that Bonny asked the Visitors the question, 'What is the atomic weight of lead?'

B: They said very firmly, first of all, 'Why are you asking what's already known?' That was part one... And the second part was... Now, because I've had a very disturbing day as a result of all this, I want you to know, the second part of the answer they gave, there were three parts to this, the second part was that Auger knows.

H: What? I guess I didn't hear you.

B: (she laughs) You're never going to talk to me again after this. You're going to think I am committable. Some name, a German name. Auger. 'Why do you ask what's already known? Auger knows.' (She laughs)

H: 'A-U-G-E-R?' I spelled out.

B: Yeh. I don't know if an auger is a thing or I had a feeling it was Mr. Auger, or a Dr. Auger. But it was, it was... 'Why do you ask what is already known? Auger already knows.' (she laughs)... and I remember trying to say in my mind, 'Please, Dr. Haines wants to know!'... and I was getting groggier and groggier. And I couldn't completely... I guess they were trying to put me under, like that one other time when...

H: Uh-huh.

B: Put me out. And I was so desperate to get an answer to this question, I couldn't succumb. And it was like to placate me, they gave me a number. When this was over, I had that same crackling (sound) in my ear. It was 3.00 in the morning. I'm sitting on the edge of the bed, and I (unintelligible) that I had a pen and paper right then. (she laughs)

H: Hum.

B: As crazy as this number is, I could have written it down, and at least had one series of numbers. But I didn't. And I waited 'til morning, like 7.30 today. And rather than having the number in my mind fresh, I was all mixed up. I had two sets of numbers. And I know they make no sense at all. They can't possibly be. And so (she laughs) I've been walking around with these two crazy numbers in my pocket all day long.

H: (laughs) Tell me what they are.

B: And...this number makes no sense. Because if this number... I know they aren't the correct numbers.

H: How do you know that?

B: But I do remember the sequence that, that I got them in. The numbers I know are completely incorrect. I've lost them.

H: How do you know that?

B: Because I'm all mixed up now. Because I... they're not what I had fresh in my mind, whatever felt fresh when I first was on the edge of my bed.

H: Are you saying that the numbers you're going to tell me are just made up then?

B: No. They're... I just think they're mixed up. But the sequence is definitely the way... I mean, it's not like saying something weighed 50 pounds, just 50. And this is what's so crazy, and I know you'll... now you're going to know I'm crazy 'cause an atom can't weigh as much as what I have in my mind.

H: I see.

B: It said, it was like... These are the two series of numbers I have. And I know neither of them are correct. They're jumbled up. But I'll give you an example of one. (It) is like 16, like the teens, but with a dot. (she laughs)

H: Now say that again. A sixteen...?

B: Like 16 point... ah, 2338, like that!

H: OK.

B: An atom can't weigh sixteen pounds! (Both laugh) And so, see? And then the other one was, that I had in my mind as the course of the day went on, it was like the same... It was like 11.2333. And this, this you know. That was the layout. It was like two digits, a dot, and then four digits, or five digits.

H: OK.

B: And originally, when I first snapped out of this whole thing, I guess I had a clear picture of whatever those numbers were.

H: Uh-huh.

B: But I know, I know... they are completely wrong. And I doubt I ever was... I must not have been told anything that really mattered. It just doesn't make any sense. But... it's troubled me terribly all day long.'

H: Well, I'm sorry to hear that, because they shouldn't have. There's no reason for you to be troubled about that.'

What follows in the transcript is Bonny's honest concern that she wanted to keep her promise to me not to look up any information about the chemistry or physics of lead. In her own words, 'Cause I swore to God to you, I wouldn't. And I wanted (to) desperately. Just to relieve myself, even to see, this makes no sense at all. Just to have something, you know what I mean?... And I couldn't even open up a dictionary, 'cause I made you that promise... So now I, I have these things in my mind, and I can't even get feedback from the dictionary on whether I'm completely nuts, or what.'

The two numbers which Bonny claimed came to her were 11.2333 and 16.2338.

After we hung up I looked up the atomic weight of lead in my *Handbook of Chemistry and Physics* (44th edition), page 401. The 1961 international atomic weight is 207.19 (atomic no. 82). I was disappointed but not particularly surprised that the numbers did not agree. Curious, I began looking up other numbers in the handbook which were characteristic of lead. I discovered on page 2186 that its specific gravity in vacuum-distilled form (at 20°C) is 11.342. This number is only 0.109 units from the number she told me. Interestingly, both of her numbers have the identical numeric sequence, two digits, a decimal point and four more digits! I called Bonny back and told her these findings. She was neither sad nor glad at the news, further reinforcing my view that she did not look up this number in a book before calling me.

Perhaps the real Zen aspect of this story happened the next morning when I went to work. Our San Francisco Bay area had experienced an earthquake previously and the two story concrete building I worked in had been damaged so that the two entry doors at each end of the building were blocked shut for repair. Everyone had to enter the building from the single front door. I was about 15 minutes late to work that morning and was walking down the sidewalk from the parking lot on the west side of the building as I saw a friend who worked in the same group I was in. He was approaching the front door from the opposite direction. We entered at the same exact time, meaning that he too was 15 minutes late! Before coming to work at the institute he had worked in the science office at the White House and before that at Lockheed. Even before I had a chance to say good morning he smiled at me and said, 'Hi... I have good news.' At this moment the events of the previous night were a long way from my mind. He continued, 'You know the project that I've been working on for a long time... well it's finally been approved. Our new organisation is a reality.' He was obviously proud and could not wait to tell others about this genuine accomplishment. He went on, 'We call it the Affiliation for University and Government Environmental Research (A.U.G.E.R.).' When I realised that this acronym was the same one Bonny had told me, I almost fell over. I had to tell my friend about my phone call.

He listened intently, trying to conceal a slight smile, as I described the key events of Bonny's encounters and my question to 'them.' As I described the numbers she gave for the atomic weight of lead and the similarity to the specific gravity for lead he said, 'That's very interesting. Did you know that there are many different isotopes of lead (actually 16). Perhaps your question to her was ambiguous.' He didn't comment further. I thought to myself, perhaps they gave us a better answer than my question deserved!

As I look back on this entire episode I am not yet sure what the real message is for Bonny or for me. But I do know that it is a valuable to keep on asking questions. And, after asking Bonny the question, I find myself a little humbler than before.

THE SMALL COUNTRY OF BELGIUM WAS THE SCENE, IN 1989-1990, OF ONE OF THE GREATEST CLUS-
TERS OF UFO SIGHTINGS EVER CHRONICLED. BUT IT WAS NOT ONLY THE NUMBER OF SIGHTINGS
THAT WAS IMPRESSIVE: IT WAS THE CONSISTENCY OF THE REPORTS, WHICH SEEMED STRONG EVIDENCE
OF UFO ACTIVITY OF A VERY SPECIFIC KIND — HUGE, BLACK TRIANGULAR-SHAPED FORMS, MOVING
SLOWLY THROUGH THE BELGIAN AIRSPACE, CHALLENGING ANY LOGICAL EXPLANATION.

THE WAVE WAS ALSO CHARACTERISED BY AN UNUSUAL DEGREE OF CO-OPERATION
BETWEEN THE AUTHORITIES AND BELGIUM'S MAJOR UFO ORGANISATION, SOBEPS (SOCIÉTÉ BELGE
D'ETUDE DES PHÉNOMÈNES SPATIAUX), A WIDELY-RESPECTED GROUP FOUNDED IN 1971 WHOSE
JOURNAL INFORESPACE HAS MADE AN OUTSTANDING CONTRIBUTION TO THE UFO DEBATE. THE
TWO VOLUMES RELATING TO THE WAVE PUBLISHED BY SOBEPS, THOUGH IN HINDSIGHT THEY CAN
BE SEEN AS SOMEWHAT UNCRITICAL IN THEIR ACCEPTANCE OF EVIDENCE AND PREMATURE IN THEIR
JUDGMENTS, REMAIN MONUMENTS OF DEDICATED RESEARCH, TESTIFYING TO THE DILIGENCE AND
ENTHUSIASM OF THE BELGIAN INVESTIGATORS.

WIM VAN UTRECHT IS A LONG-TIME AND WIDELY-RESPECTED RESEARCHER WHO HEADS THE
CAELESTIA PROJECT: HIS 1994 ANALYSIS (WITH FRITS VAN DER VELDT) OF THE 1975 ZWISCHBERGEN
PHOTOGRAPH IS ARGUABLY THE FINEST CASE STUDY IN THE UFO LITERATURE. HE CAN BE REACHED
AT KRONENBURGSTRAAT 110, B-2000 ANTWERPEN, BELGIUM.

THE BELGIAN
1989-1990 UFO WAVE

by Wim Van Utrecht

PRELUDE

For nearly a decade all had been quiet on the European front. Then, on 9
October 1989, the Soviet press bureau TASS launched the story of a UFO
landing in a park in Voronezh, some 500 km southeast of Moscow.
According to the report, a pair of three-eyed giants and a mechanical dwarf
had emerged from the landed craft and fired some sort of laser gun at a boy, ren-
dering him temporarily invisible. The story was repeated in newspapers all over
the globe, probably not so much because the editors regarded the bizarre tale as
proof of an alien act of aggression, but because the publication of this UFO story
in the Soviet Union's leading paper *Pravda* illustrated the political changes taking
place in the former USSR since the beginning of Gorbachev's perestroika.

The story of the Voronezh landing was the first UFO news for a long time to
hit the papers in Western Europe. It seemed to act as a trigger for further reports. On
the weekend of 25-26 November, alarmed citizens from the Dutch-speaking part of
Belgium reported seeing a luminous disc circling their homes. Later it turned out that
the sightings had been caused by a light-show from a disco, whose owner had been
trying to attract youngsters by projecting a rotating xenon lamp onto the cloud-deck.
Despite the fact that the culprit had been identified, the light-show continued to spark
off UFO reports in the area until 16 December, when, after the Belgian Air Force had
sent two aircraft into the air to identify the 'mysterious disc', the Public Prosecutor's
Office ordered the disco manager to switch off his installation.

Artist's impression of the mysterious 'black triangle' seen repeatedly over Belgium in 1989-1990

THE COMING OF THE TRIANGLES

Four days after the reports had started to trickle in from Limbourg, and only 70 km southeast of Halen, another UFO incident occurred. This time the events were to create waves far beyond the borders of the small Belgian state. On 29 November 1989, two members of the Eupen gendarmerie – in the German-speaking part of the country – had the experience of a lifetime. At 5.24 that evening, as they were driving their patrol car from Eupen to Kettenis (province of Liège), the two gendarmes spotted a bright light over a field bordering the road. Observing that the light was following a course parallel to theirs, they quickly drove to a point that would take them under the object's predicted trajectory. However, as the unidentified aircraft flew over the puzzled witnesses, it stopped, made a full turn and left in the opposite direction.

The two men could now discern 'a dark solid mass in the shape of an isosceles triangle'. Underneath were three blinding white lights, one in each corner: a pulsating red light glowed in the centre. They decided to follow the strange craft which was now heading back for Eupen. In the village they paid a quick visit to their headquarters and rang the nearest airfield and a nearby military base. They were told there was no air traffic or military activity in the region that could account for the sightings.

At 6.30p.m. the two witnesses returned to their patrol car and decided to head for a place which they were sure would offer a clear panoramic view over the area and the nearby lake of Gileppe. Upon arrival they once again saw the object. It now seemed to be hovering motionless directly over the watch-tower of the lake. In an early interview, one of the witnesses said that, at this time, they 'had the unclear impression that, every now and then, there were beams of light shooting out from the sides'. In later interviews, however, the witnesses were quoted as having described 'a stationary white ball which repeatedly, but always simultaneously, emitted two clearly visible but very thin beams of a reddish light in opposite directions'. The latter source also speaks of 'small fire balls that appeared at the extremities of the beams, detached themselves and returned to the object after having circled the white ball a few times'. While observing this unusual display, a series of lights emerged from behind a nearby row of trees. Behind the lights the gendarmes distinguished the dark greenish silhouette of a triangle that rose into the air and executed a sharp turn. During this manoeuvre an upper structure could be seen with what appeared to be illuminated windows, 'like a train wagon lit from the inside'. The object then followed a spiral trajectory before taking off in the direction of the German border. At 8.39p.m. it disappeared from view.

Throughout the three-hour incident, the policemen had been in constant contact with their headquarters in Eupen. Greatly to their relief, the dispatch officer informed them that he too had seen the object and that additional sightings were being received from patrols in nearby communities. One colleague, patrolling the area northwest of Eupen, confirmed that not only had he seen an object carrying three blinding white lights and a pulsating red light, but he had also noticed 'something at the back of the craft that was turning round, like a turbine'. Other witnesses – some 150 eyewitness accounts were gathered that night – mentioned a distinct sound that reminded them of a ventilator. Researchers sceptical of an extraterrestrial interpretation of UFO reports have pointed out that these descriptions could be of an ultralight motorised aircraft or a blimp. They further point to the fact that three white lights and a red flashing light are consistent with standard lighting configurations for aircraft. Earlier, several independent witnesses had spotted, in broad daylight, an oval- or cigar-shaped object travelling slowly just south of the lake of Gileppe. Could the nocturnal object over Eupen have actually been a blimp, reported as triangular simply because of the position of the three 'corner lights'?

It was only in 1996 that an independent researcher discovered that the planet Venus had been at exactly the spot where the gendarmes had situated the 'bright ball of light' over the watch-tower of the lake of Gileppe. My verification revealed that Venus had reached its maximum magnitude that day and was only five degrees above the horizon. The planet's azimuth also matched that of the presumed UFO. Moreover, the sky was crystal clear that evening and the witnesses had not mentioned a second bright light near the UFO. These circumstances make it very likely that Venus was indeed responsible for this phase of the sighting. As for the 'unclear impression of beams of light shooting out from the sides', this could have been the well-known atmospheric effects that occur when light sources are observed low on the horizon. If the Venus interpretation is correct, there is no longer a reason to believe that more than one unidentified object was in the Belgian skies that evening.

SOBEPS COMES INTO PLAY

The next day the story of the 'Eupen triangle' was highlighted on various Belgian television stations, and on 1 December Michel Bougard, president of SOBEPS, visited Eupen to interview the two principal witnesses. Soon other investigators, most of them SOBEPS members, followed in Bougard's footsteps. In their search for additional witnesses, a SOBEPS team not only installed itself in a local press bureau, but also went from door-to-door, asking people if they had previously seen something unusual in the sky. A praiseworthy reflex, but one that also marked the beginning of the group's monopoly on the events that were to follow.

December 11-12, 1989, was another memorable day for Belgian ufologists. That night numerous people in the regions round the cities of Liège and Namur were baffled by a mysterious illuminated contraption that sailed over their homes. The sightings came to a strange end when, shortly after 2a.m., a man in Jupille-sur Meuse, woken by a deep, pulsating sound, saw an egg-shaped object that seemed to have got stuck in a spruce-fir. The object carried three bright spotlights underneath and something that looked like a rudder at the back. It took a few seconds before the contraption managed to tear itself loose, after which it headed towards the witness, flew over his house and finally disappeared in the distance. Immediately thereafter, a bright vertical beam of light came on from behind the houses facing the witness. The next day the area was searched by journalists, gendarmes and military. According to the witness, even a helicopter was employed. The description of the unknown object strongly suggests that some sort of motorised blimp got into trouble that night. The beam of light may have been a searchlight, possibly coming from someone guiding the blimp from the ground. However, no one ever came forward to claim responsibility for such an incident.

As UFO reports kept pouring in for more than a year and a half, the popularity of SOBEPS increased at an equivalent pace. Interviews with members of the group were published in almost every newspaper and magazine in the country: UFOs became a regular topic in talk-shows on television and radio. Usually the address and phone number of SOBEPS were given in case readers wanted to report a personal experience. By such means the group collected some 2,000 eyewitness accounts during the two-year period, many of them in the form of tape-recorded phonecalls. During the years that preceded the UFO wave, SOBEPS had been struggling to keep its head above water. Now, in the space of only a few days, new life was breathed into the organisation by attracting new volunteers who were prepared to go into the field and check as many reports as possible. Incredible as it may seem, SOBEPS succeeded in obtaining investigative reports on approximately 450 cases. Most of these are detailed in the group's journal *Inforespace* and in their two books, each about 500 pages thick.

How reliable is the evidence collected by SOBEPS? The lack of training and experience of some of these new recruits inevitably resulted in ill-documented reports of no scientific value. Sceptics also criticised SOBEPS' predisposition to look for an extraterrestrial origin. Investigators acquainted with the writings of leading SOBEPS members know that this is the case, yet the fact remains that this well-organised society, with its neatly arranged office in the Belgian capital, managed to earn respect from both ufologists and non-ufologists, including the Belgian Air Force. During the first weeks of the wave, the BAF had been swamped with phone calls, and it was decided that SOBEPS was better placed to deal with this type of report.

This marked the beginning of a short but intense relationship which reached its peak during the period of Easter 1990. During this prolonged holiday weekend of 14-17 April a Hawker Siddeley and a Brittan Norman reconnaissance airplane were put at stand-by during a skywatch organised by the group. The code-name of this historic collaboration was 'OPERATION IDENTIFICATION OVNI'. Many military men, civilians, investigators and newsmen took part: the only absentees were the UFOs themselves. In a recent interview, Major-General De Brouwer regretted that the BAF was never given a political mandate nor official instructions to start an in-depth inquiry into the Belgian reports. This meant that the Air Staff had to deal with the situation within its own already chock-full agenda. The Major-General personally assured us that no special UFO service exists within the Belgian Army.

In March 1991 there was a final upsurge of the number of reports. Then sightings became rare, with the exception of disco lightshows that continued to stir the imagination all over Europe.

POLITICAL AND SOCIO-CULTURAL ASPECTS

On 21 December 1989 the Belgian Minister of Defense, Guy Coeme, issued an official statement about the growing number of UFO reports emanating from the province of Liège. With regard to a possible military explanation, the Minister stated that the Army had no idea what the UFOs were, but that:

– they were not AWACS-type aeroplanes, because these are subject to radar control when they fly over Belgium;
– they were not F-117A aeroplanes, as was confirmed by the US Air Force;
– they were not remote-control military machines, because none was used during these particular weeks;
– they were not ultralight motorised aeroplanes, because they produce a different and specific sound.

Official statements by politicians or military people are not usually taken seriously by ufologists. This time something was different: instead of the ufologists, it was now the sceptics who were crying 'cover-up', suspecting that the Air Force was taking advantage of the UFO excitement to draw public attention away from their test flights of state-of-the-art experimental aircraft, probably of US design. Aviation magazines were scrutinised for the latest news on black projects such as the Black Manta, the Avenger, the Aurora, the Senior Citizen and, more recently, the LoFlyte. What most sceptics failed to take into account was that most of these presumed wonderplanes were supposed to be supersonic aircraft, not capable of hovering close to the ground as was described in the best-documented Belgian cases. Another unanswered question was why such aircraft would fly over a densely populated region carrying blinding spotlights if they were executing covert military test flights. However, one thing was clear: the newest trends in aviation design were being reflected in contemporary UFO descriptions.

Because of the proportions the Belgian wave had taken on, UFOs were now being regarded as a serious problem at the highest levels. Throughout 1991-1993, the possibility of establishing a European Centre for UFO Reports was on the agenda at no less than ten meetings of the European Parliament. The idea for a co-ordinated UFO centre came from Belgian's vice-premier Elio Di Rupo. A scientist by training, he wanted clear answers, but in the end the British – always a little averse to European collaboration – crashed the dream of many a ufologist when they suggested that the Community's money could be spent in more useful ways.

Occasionally, UFOs were reported from neighbouring countries, but the majority of the sightings occurred within Belgium, and from an area only about 200 kms long and 100 kms wide. Apart from the first series of reports, which came from the Dutch- and German-speaking areas in the east of the country, almost all cases emanated from the southern, French-speaking area (Wallonia). When plotted on a map, the dissemination of the reports indicate that the wave began in the east, then shifted to Liège and finally to Brussels, where SOBEPS has its head-quarters. It is hard to escape the implication that cultural factors and the location of UFO investigators had a major influence on the reporting process.

The flap lasted 16 months but it took only a fortnight to transform the traditional nuts-and-bolts image of the flying saucer into a new high-tech UFO, one that pops up almost exclusively at night, looks like a dark, angular structure and carries several bright lights, sometimes accompanied by a panoply of luminous 'special effects'. Triangle- and boomerang-shaped UFOs had occasionally been reported in the past, but only in the 1980s did they come to dominate the international scene. Today, anyone who claims to encounter a domed metal saucer is liable to meet with scepticism even from ufologists: it will take something like the huge discs of the film *Independence Day* to turn back the clock.

THE RADAR EVIDENCE

On 11 July 1990, Lieutenant-Colonel Wilfried De Brouwer (later promoted to Major General, Deputy Chief of Airstaff, Plans, Operations and Personnel) held a remarkable press-conference at the NATO headquarters at Evere, Brussels. In the presence of a considerable crowd he acknowledged that something highly unusual had occurred in the night of 30-31 March 1990. On that date several gendarmes from a location just south of Brussels had observed inexplicable lights in the sky. Most thought the lights were stationary, though some reported possible movements. At about the same time, a radar station had picked up a fast moving target. Immediately, two F-16 fighters were scrambled: one pilot was to videotape the radar screen while the other opted for a direct head up display.

Unfortunately, the latter plane's camera had not been adjusted for a nocturnal operation, and as a result its images turned out totally black: so the only evidence pertaining to the chase were the radar images recorded by the other F-16. At first sight these were quite spectacular: there had been no less than 13 lock-ons on an unidentified target. Apparently one or more objects had crossed the F-16's path, executing the most uncanny manoeuvres. Ufologists welcomed this announcement as evidence that something strange was indeed occurring in our skies, even if the rapidly jumping and diving blips hardly matched the slow flight that most eyewitnesses described.

To the sceptical community it seemed more probable that the spooky radar images could be ascribed to computer malfunction, a misinterpretation of the computer data or a refraction of radar waves caused by atmospheric effects. The critics also emphasised that the radar returns did not positively correlate with the radar trackings obtained from the groundstations. I myself was told by an acquaintance of the pilots that at no time during the scramble had they witnessed anything unusual, nor were they impressed by the freakish radar blips.

In the end the sceptics proved right: the lights that baffled the gendarmes were identified as bright stars and planets, while a military study of the radar tapes revealed that at least one of the lock-ons (probably three) occurred when the F-16's radar mistakenly locked onto the second F-16. The others were almost certainly 'ground clutter' resulting from refraction of the radar beams by irregularities in the atmosphere, causing surface objects such as cars to appear as airborne targets on the radar screen.

Major-General De Brouwer now regrets that the press-conference took place before all the data had been properly analysed. He recalls having allowed a French reporter to photograph two sequences of the radar tape. Shortly thereafter the photos appeared in the popular weekly *Paris Match*. This brought the indignant Belgian media to exercise so much pressure that the Air Force was left with no other choice than to present a detailed account of what had happened.

In the early stages of the wave the Minister of Defence, Guy Coeme, had stated that the affair should be treated with total openness. Top Air Force officials, including Lieutenant-Colonel De Brouwer and Chief of Staff General Van Hecke, supported this view. However, the Army Chief of Staff, General Charlier, was not too happy with the way things were developing. To him UFOs were just a load of nonsense and there was a serious risk that military secrets would be leaked. Weaknesses in the country's radar system were being exposed in the popular media.

THE PHOTOGRAPHIC EVIDENCE

One can understand that most SOBEPS members were over the moon when they heard about the incidents of 30-31 March, especially when they also received word that, in the early hours of 31 March, only minutes after the F-16s had returned to base, a Brussels man had captured the famous triangle on video. The images, shown on television in many countries, depict the well-known configuration of three white lights and a central red flashing light. But the truth is that this recording did not remain a mystery for long. SOBEPS, after first endorsing the document, made follow-up inquiries which revealed that the film showed an ordinary airliner preparing to land at Zaventem airfield. I later learned that the witness also claimed to have encountered UFOs and 'space beings' on many other occasions, both before and after he took his video.

The next day, All Fool's Day 1990, an umpteenth skywatch organised by SOBEPS finally payed off as three group members had the privilege of witnessing a trapezium- shaped platform with rounded corners fly over their heads. The object was equipped with two sets of blinding 'searchlights', flanked by smaller lights. Underneath was a red glow. The only sound was a humming which reminded the trio of a jet engine. Fortunately, SOBEPS' photographic expert was among the witnesses and four photographs were made. However, when the film returned from the photolab the skywatchers were in for a major disappointment: only four microscopic white dots could be distinguished, and these in only one of the shots, although the photographer had used a tripod, a 300 mm telephoto lens and highly sensitive 1600 ASA film. Moreover, just before the UFO came into view, he had taken several pictures of aircraft lights and all these turned out right. As I have pointed out, the position of the spots on the one successful photo are characteristic of the two headlights and two wingtip lights of an ordinary aeroplane. Could the UFO experts have been misled in the excitement of the moment? The General Secretary of SOBEPS, who was among the witnesses, admitted that 'on that day we were tiptoe with expectation' but their final conclusion was that infrared radiation from the unknown craft had erased the photographic image on the film.

As in any recent UFO flap, the investigators were confronted with dozens of videos and photographs, none of which depicted anything more than a varying number of white lights. Most turned out to be aircraft lights and bright stars or planets: in one instance the reflection of sunlight in distant windows was taken for a low hovering UFO. Often the electronics of the videos had fooled the witnesses. The autofocus system of most camcorders cannot cope with bright points of light against a dark background. This usually results in large transparent blobs of light with strange indentations, which in reality are reflections of components within the optical system of the camera.

Only one document, a colour slide, proved more difficult to explain. It was also the only piece of evidence that actually revealed the presence of a triangular structure. The colour slide in question was taken early April 1990 by a young man from Petit-Rechain, not far from Liège. It depicts a black triangle silhouetted against a dark bluish background. There are white lights in each corner and a fourth light, surrounded by a reddish aura, in the centre (the other lights also display an orange colouring but to a lesser extent). The photographer, who is a member of a local photography club, took his photograph using a Praktica BX20 equipped with a 200 mm telephoto lens: SOBEPS investigators are convinced of the photographer's integrity and point to the unusual aspect of the white lights. These can best be described as clusters of smaller lights, each depicted as a small sinuous stripe, each cluster running in a different direction. A scientific consultant to SOBEPS suggests that the lights are plasma jets, part of the object's propulsion system.

There are other problems with the Petit-Rechain slide, such as that it shows no background details which allow verification of the object's actual size and distance. The exact date on which it was taken remains unknown, meaning that astronomical and meteorological data cannot be verified. We are told that a second photograph was made of the object, but was subsequently thrown away 'because there was nothing on it'. The 'good' slide was put in a drawer and surfaced four months later only when a journalist convinced the witness that his slide could well be important evidence.

The slide was analysed by various experts and at various institutions, with no conclusive results. So I personally made an experiment to see how easily such an image might be obtained, using a small triangle of black card glued onto a larger grey-blue card. Tiny holes were pierced with a needle in the corners and centre of the triangle. The entire construction was then placed in front of four spotlights and photographed. A deliberate shake of the card created trails of light which, as in the Petit-Rechain photo, do not – contrary to what one might expect – all run in the same direction. While not conclusive, my experiments suggest that the photo could be simulated with everyday materials.

OTHER PHYSICAL EVIDENCE

Old-time ufologists have told me they were sure the Belgian UFOs were not 'the real thing'. They point to the low number of entity reports and daylight sightings, and to the absence of electromagnetic effects – the stalling of car engines, compass-needles running mad, interference with radio and television – all of which for them characterised the 'genuine' flaps of the past.

Also markedly absent during the Belgian wave were reports of traces on the ground or on vegetation. Only four cases were recorded throughout the period. In one incident mention was made of twelve circular patches in some grass, but no mention was made of any unidentified objects or lights and it is likely that the patches were 'fairy rings' caused by fungi. In two other cases, no one besides the witnesses of a UFO incident saw the strange traces described. One witness even insisted that the traces were still clearly visible while none of the investigators and gendarmes who accompanied him could see anything out of the ordinary.

STATE OF AFFAIRS ANNO 1997

The Belgian wave produced hundreds of fascinating eyewitness accounts but not a single piece of conclusive physical evidence. Yet even sceptical researchers have to agree that trivial everyday phenomena cannot explain those incidents in which independent witnesses reported seeing a UFO on the same day and within a well-defined area, as occurred on the three peak days 29 November 1989, 11-12 December 1989 and 12 March 1991. In addition there have been several isolated incidents, some of them related in great detail by reliable observers, but unconfirmed by independent witnesses and with no shared characteristics which would permit further analysis.

The triangular shape is generally regarded as the 'trademark' of the Belgian wave, but surprisingly it does not always feature in the reports themselves. Moreover, in those cases where a triangular structure is mentioned explicitly, the sighting is generally at night. So what remains is the description of a low flying dark object, estimated to be hovering no more than 150m above the ground, capable of changing its course abruptly, yet producing no downdraft and only the soft humming sound of a motor, and carrying a lighting configuration which matches standard safety regulations for aircraft.

For those in search of a down-to-earth explanation, two possibilities suggest themselves: an ultralight motorised aircraft or a blimp. As in the 1980s Hudson Valley 'triangle' flap, a rumour circulating in aviation circles claims that an Air Force pilot, flying a home-built ULM without the knowledge or permission of his superiors, was responsible for the 29 November sightings: no confirmation of this claim has been obtained. Since most witnesses described the phenomenon as 'huge', the ultralight hypothesis implies that the witnesses made grotesque errors in their estimates of sizes and distances.

The alternative is airships. What are the chances of a motorised airship being flown over our country? Do such blimps, equipped with bright spotlights exist? Well, they do, and the man who rents them – we will refer to him as 'K' – lives in Brussels.

In 1991 a SOBEPS investigator, who is also an airline pilot, started an inquiry in aviation circles. It led him to K, who admitted that his contraptions had indeed been responsible for the majority of the sightings. We were later told by Major General De Brouwer that K had even contacted the Air Force, offering to sell them the solution to the UFO problem for a substantial sum (an amount of the order of a million US dollars has been mentioned). The proof consisted of an envelope containing all the dates and locations of the flights of the airship concerned.

What do these blimps look like? K's main invention is a radio-controlled steering mechanism for motorised airships equipped with either a set of spotlights or a camcorder. These craft are rented to add lustre to concerts, for advertising purposes or to videotape major indoor events from above. Flyers received from K contain photographs of classical cigar-shaped blimps equipped with a video camera and small spherical balloons carrying three spotlights. One of K's patent designs shows a traditional blimp with a projector and a moviescreen mounted under the hull, bringing to mind the many accounts of a giant rectangular object sailing the sky at low altitude. All this makes K a good candidate to explain the Belgian UFO wave: however we could never find any proof of K's actual involvement. What is worse, K now denies having ever flown his lighter-than-air craft outdoors.

Is that the final word on the Belgian Wave? Perhaps not. Late in 1996, investigator Jan Van Eetvelt and myself addressed a detailed parliamentary question to our present Minister of Defence, Jean-Pol Poncelet. The question focused on incidents in which military involvement was reported. Major General De Brouwer, now retired, kindly provided assistance and advised us how we could best approach the Army. On 17 December the text was tabled before the Chamber of Representatives. We now await the Minister's written reply, in the hope that it will help us to continue our search for explanations.

THE 1990s

Photograph of a supposed **UFO** near the Canary Islands on 5 March 1979 – probably
the vapour-trail from a submarine missile launch

THERE IS PROBABLY NO COUNTRY IN THE WORLD WHERE INTEREST IN THE UFO PHENOMENON IS MORE VARIED AND MORE WIDESPREAD THAN IN SPAIN: YET THE SUBJECT IS TAKEN SERIOUSLY AND STANDARDS ARE GENERALLY HIGH. EVEN THE COUNTRY'S POPULAR MAGAZINES – ENIGMAS, MAS ALLA, ANO CERO – PUBLISH ARTICLES BY IMPORTANT RESEARCHERS SUCH AS STILLINGS, STRAND, MÈHEUST AND RING. AT A MORE SERIOUS LEVEL THEIR UFO JOURNALS ARE OF THE HIGHEST STANDARD: THE MAGAZINE STENDEK WAS, DURING ITS LIFETIME, ONE OF THE WORLD'S FINEST UFO PERIODICALS, AND TODAY CUADERNOS DE UFOLOGIA MAINTAINS THE TRADITION. SPAIN IS ALSO THE HOME OF THE LAST GRAND OLD MAN FROM THE 'CLASSIC' ERA OF UFO RESEARCH, ANTONIO RIBERA, ONE OF THE BEST-LOVED FIGURES ON THE UFOLOGICAL SCENE.

INVESTIGATION IN SPAIN IS INEVITABLY ASSOCIATED WITH VICENTE-JUAN BALLESTER OLMOS, WHO, ALONE OR WITH COLLABORATORS, HAS AUTHORED A SERIES OF OUTSTANDING BOOKS WHICH REFLECT MORE THAN TWENTY YEARS OF DEDICATED WORK. HIS 1987 ENCICLOPEDIA DE LOS ENCUENTROS CERCANOS CON OVNIS (WITH JUAN FERNANDEZ PERIS) IS PROBABLY THE BEST-DOCUMENTED COLLECTION OF CLOSE ENCOUNTER CASES IN PRINT. BALLESTER OLMOS'S ATTENTION REMAINS CHIEFLY DIRECTED AT STRONGLY EVIDENCED UFO SIGHTINGS, AS OPPOSED TO ABDUCTIONS, WHERE EVERY LOCAL CASE HE HAS INVESTIGATED PROVED TO BE EITHER A HOAX OR CAPABLE OF SOME ALTERNATIVE EXPLANATION.

DURING RECENT YEARS HIS MAIN ACTIVITY HAS BEEN CO-OPERATING WITH THE SPANISH GOVERNMENT IN THE RELEASE OF OFFICIAL DOCUMENTS. IN 1995 HE PUBLISHED A BOOK CONTAINING HIS FINDINGS TO DATE, EXPEDIENTES INSOLITOS, AND HERE HE PRESENTS SOME NOTABLE CASES FROM THE MILITARY ARCHIVES.

VICENTE-JUAN BALLESTER OLMOS CAN BE CONTACTED AT APTDO DE CORREOS 12140, 46080 VALENCIA, SPAIN PHONE +34 6 361 3108 (HOME): FAX +34 6 179 2600

DECLASSIFICATION! MILITARY UFO RECORDS RELEASED: THE SPANISH EXPERIENCE

by Vicente-Juan Ballester Olmos

In the history of UFO research in Spain from 1947 to 1997, one event is of outstanding importance: the release by the Spanish Ministry of Defence of previously secret Air Force UFO archives, a process which started in 1992. I was privileged to play a part throughout this process which has made the official files literally an open book which anyone may read.

NO SECRET LASTS FOREVER

Friday, 8 November 1996. 13.30 hours. Torrèjon Air Force Base, near Madrid. Lieutenant Colonel Enrique Rocamora walks briskly along the corridors of the Aerial Operative Command (MOA) heading for the commander-in-chief's bureau. This is no routine dispatch: he carries with him the proposal for declassification of the last UFO file waiting for release.

It was during 1990-1991 that I started to induce the Air Force to review the classified matter policy applied in 1979 to UFO information (before that it had been considered Confidential). Step by step I watched the process proceed. In May 1991 the Air Safety Section, responsible for matters concerning UFOs and custodian of the UFO files, submitted a memo proposing to declassify the archives. In March 1992 the Joint Chiefs of Staff decided to downgrade the classification level imposed on UFO documents, leaving to the Air Force Chief of Staff the authority to fully declassify them.

Angel Bastiola & Ballester Olmos

The documents transferred to MOA comprised 62 files of UFO reports covering the period 1962 to 1991; procedures and memos shaping official Air Force policy on UFOs, 1968 to 1991; and UFO information requests from civilians addressed to the Air Force over the same period.

MOA's Intelligence Section took on the declassification task. The actual workload was handed to Lieutenant Colonel Angel Bastida. An open-minded individual and the prototype of the 21st century military man, Bastida formulated a new procedure detailing the involvement and investigation of UFO reports by the Air Force, and an analysis of all available historical information with arguments favouring full disclosure of existing and future UFO files. Incidentally, Bastida also authored the best paper ever written by the military on the Air Force and the UFO problem

In September 1992, the first files were declassified. They were cases from 1962, 1967 and 1968. By the time Bastida moved to another military post he had declassified 22 files. His successor, Lieutenant Colonel Enrique Rocamora – a strong and sharp staff officer – declassified a further 53 files. The process was carried out as speedily as possible, given the fact that declassifying secret UFO files was only one part of these officers' work.

SIGHTINGS: STRANGE AND LESS STRANGE

The military UFO reports contain descriptions of several different kinds of seemingly anomalous phenomena. They include examples of lights or uncorrelated radar echoes which seem to defy a rational explanation. My colleagues and I are painstakingly analysing all pieces of information to determine if these cases can be solved, or whether they become true UFOs. The entire files are available to whoever may contribute his/her know-how to this endeavour.

In the majority of cases, investigation, whether by the Air Force or by independent civilian ufologists, has revealed a misinterpretation of some kind. These cases show us, on the one hand, what kinds of anomalous features may occur; and on the other, how easily people, puzzled by the sighting of unexpected luminous phenomena in the sky, can jump to erroneous conclusions.

24 NOVEMBER 1974: ALARM IN A RADAR SQUADRON

Grand Canary is one of the five Spanish islands in the Atlantic Ocean which form the Canary archipelago. At about 19.30 hours on 24 November 1974, Air Force Lieutenant Colonel E.L. and his daughter were driving by the North Freeway, when they saw a bright white light in the sky leaving a short trail, travelling at great speed and disappearing a few seconds later. His statement described it as a meteorite or bolide flying horizontally in a northwest direction at some 1,000 metres.

Fifteen minutes later, at 19.45, an Iberia Fokker-27 took off from Tenerife airport en route to Las Palmas (Grand Canary Islands). On a clear night, it was flying over a stratus cloud layer to its flight level of 2,000 metres and turning northwest when the pilots sighted a powerful light just in front of them, in a flight corridor typically used by regular air traffic from Las Palmas to Tenerife. Iberia captain Saura called Canary Flight Control to tell them they were passing 'traffic proceeding from Las Palmas'. By now the light had descended to 1,800 metres, the standard flight level for airplanes. Captain Saura was surprised to be told there was no reported flight at that position. He insisted that he had it in sight, well silhouetted against the stratus layer, at a range of some 25 km, and he asked for a check from the military radar.

The radar operator on Grand Canary duly reported that he had only the Fokker's echo on screen: he saw no other traffic. At this point, the airliner's crew realised to their amazement that the light had been stationary at 'three o'clock' for more than a minute: any normal aircraft should have sailed past by now. Full of curiosity, the Fokker's pilot started to change course in the direction of the light. As he did so, the light seemed to shift rapidly away from the aircraft, emitting intermittent orange and yellow flashes as it vanished.

By now, the radar station had been placed in 'alert' situation, and their personnel started to scrutinise the skies with special care and attention. At 20.20 hours an echo was detected at 20° (NNE), 56 km distant, approaching directly towards the radar site at 500 knots; they were unable to determine its altitude.

The trace disappeared when it entered the 'blind cone' (vertical) of the antennae, and did not reappear. Out of doors, a light of more than 1st magnitude was sighted, fixed in the firmament (according to one witness), slowly moving around the site (according to another), while a third declared it to be nothing more than a star.

At 20.30 hours, radar detected a trace at radial 356° (north), 58 km away, which correlated with Iberia flight 281 Madrid to Tenerife. At the same time, it recorded an uncorrelated track at 326° (northwest), 74 km away, heading south. After changing direction, it remained stationary until passed by IB-281, whereupon it suddenly vanished. No other traffic was scheduled at that time and location.

Taken together, these observations seem to indicate that a mysterious luminous object was hanging above two of the Canary Islands for more than an hour. However, it is also legitimate to divide the complex series of events into several individual occurrences: (1) a meteor-like sighting of brief duration, (2) a light in the clouds which a nearby military radar system did not recognise, but which disappeared as soon as the pilot altered his angle of vision, (3) in an excited environment (radar operators were requested to search for UFOs with extreme care), they detected a first echo which mysteriously disappeared without a trace, another trace in the proximity of a commercial aircraft (not seen optically by the aircrew), and finally a fixed light in the celestial vault not different from a star. In summary: a case offering radar traces which are not confirmed visually, and visual sightings which are not confirmed by radar.

No final conclusion has been adopted to date by the research team.

23 DECEMBER 1985: A UFO IN THE LOG BOOK

The merchant vessel *Manuel Soto*, owned by Transmediterranea Co., was sailing on December 23, 1985 from Las Palmas (Grand Canary island) to Arrecife (Lanzarote Island). At 03.10 hours, the third officer on duty observed in the horizon by the bow what seemed to be the rising of a heavenly body. He identified it as the star Antares. Checked ten minutes later, however, the light's position did not correspond either with Antares or any other star or planet. The officer took measurements of the altitude and azimuth of the light, which remained stationary until 03.25 when it suddenly began to move quickly. Other members of the crew came to see what was happening.

The light approached the ship, passing directly over the vessel two minutes later. As it did, all the witnesses could perceive the object's profile, which did not resemble that of a typical aeroplane or helicopter. The object had a very intense white light on its central part, a weaker red light near it, and another white light – not as strong – set apart. The separation between the lights made the witnesses think the object was flying low, but they could hear no sound.

The shipping company passed the log book entry to the Spanish Navy. The Navy Staff submitted it to the Air Force, but Canary Islands Air Command reported that their investigations showed no UFO observed on that date. No further investigation was made.

And so this second sighting from the Canary Islands also remains unidentified. Sadly, nothing was reported about how the object was lost out of sight. In principle, the behaviour of the object – approaching from the horizon, flying at a constant altitude and speed – is consistent with that of an aircraft. Nevertheless, lack of additional detail – including the actual silhouette of the craft – prevents us from developing any specific hypothesis.

8 DECEMBER 1980: AIRCRAFT ON FIRE?

A brief file reports – just two telephone messages – received in the Cadiz Maritime Captaincy General from merchant vessel *Conquistador* and fishing ship *Besugo*. At 20.50 hours on December 8, 1980 the first ship was navigating 35°27' N/ 7°50' W bearing northeast, when it reported a disintegrating object over the vessel at some 20° altitude which was sighted by the captain and the radio operator.

Additionally, at 20.45 hours, personnel from the second ship, sailing in position 33° 52' N/ 8° 55' W, observed a fiery phenomenon in a north direction at sea level. Their impression was that it might be a passenger plane with a fire on its left engine.

In isolation, those two incidents off the Morocco coast might never have received an explanation. However, consulting our files we discovered that a significant flap of 'UFO sightings' originated at that time in southwest Spain. Thousands witnessed a series of incandescent objects flying in a group passing slowly overhead. The general trajectory of the luminous trail was southwest to northeast.

As described, the phenomenon is absolutely compatible with a meteor shower or a space junk re-entry: the second alternative can be discarded as no decay is known to have occurred at that date, so meteors seem the preferred explanation.

An aircraft and a UFO over the Canaries on 22 May 1980, from Spanish Air Force files

25 DECEMBER 1980: JET PROPULSION UFO

On 25 December 1980, at 22.05 hours, an Air Force captain was driving along the Tudela-Arguedas road when he saw an unknown flying object with a large central body with a 'powerful jet propulsion system'. In addition, he saw a few more tiny luminous objects manoeuvring in formation with the large one. He estimated their altitude at some 1,000 metres, course 20° (north-northeast): the speed was similar to a commercial airplane. He saw it disappear behind the mountains, leaving a smoke trail much wider than that of a plane.

In the absence of any supplementary information, this would have been simply another unidentified. But there was a thick dossier in my archives to put this event into its proper perspective. That night, a giant, fiery phenomenon was sighted over Spain and other European countries a few minutes past 21.00 GMT (one hour later in Spain) skyrocketing on a rough south-to-north course.

North American Air Defense Command (NORAD) reported the re-entry into the atmosphere of the rocket used in the launch of Soviet satellite Cosmos 749. It was travelling from southwest to northeast on an arc that would have taken it over Portugal, Spain, France and southern England. There is little doubt that this is what the officer witnessed.

19 AUGUST 1982: A ROTATING FLYING SAUCER

A civilian witness reported an unusual experience on 19 August 1982, at 22.30 hours, seen from an apartment block facing the sea in the summer resort village of Blanes (Gerona). He was with seven other people, who also watched the aerial show in astonishment. The first witness was on the terrace when he heard the sound of an aircraft and just above him he saw a circle of lights blinking regularly. Through binoculars he distinguished the shape of a 'cylindrical disc' which was rotating clockwise: he estimated its size as twice that of a DC-4 airplane. Speed and altitude were constant, then it made a turn so he could see it both from underneath and from the top. It had seven or eight illuminated 'windows'. The sighting lasted around three minutes. Then and there he made some drawings of what he thought he had seen and some days later he sent a letter to Air Force Headquarters with a full description of the events and some impressive sketches.

The official report presents no conclusion at all as no investigation was ever conducted. However, a review of newspapers for August and September 1982 disclosed similar sightings in many towns of eastern and northern Spain. Not only that, the press, confirmed by Barcelona Air Control, reported that advertising aircraft carrying luminous publicity panels were active during that summer in such locations, giving rise to surprise observations and misinterpretations with UFOs. Again, we may be confident that this was what the witness saw at Blanes.

FACTS AND FIGURES

The Spanish declassification process imposes no restriction as to date. Over the years, several current incidents, whether reported to the Air Force by civilian witnesses or by military personnel, were declassified immediately after investigation – an example which other countries would do well to follow.

Since 1992, a number of UFO observations have been added to the MOA archives, both old and new, so that the original 62 files have now become 75. They amount to 1,900 pages, which anyone can read (and copy) in the Library of the Air Force Headquarters in Madrid.

The files cover a total of 97 separate events between the years 1962 to 1995, which averages about three cases per year. But we find that certain years – 1968 (23), 1969 (7), 1975 (7), 1977 (6), 1978 (8), 1979 (9) and 1980 (7) – seem to deviate markedly from the mean. However, examination often reveals simple down-to-earth explanations. The 1968-69 wave was clearly due to a press release by the Ministry of Air asking the public to report UFO sightings, combined with the highly visible night-time appearance of the planet Venus, plus giant meteorological balloons carried by wind from France. 1975 is conspicuous only because one file includes several cases originating with a single and unreliable informant. A 1977 file, likewise, describes a succession of contactee-type stories allegedly experienced during a three-month period. The 1978 peak is due to a photographic fraud which involved several dates. 1979 contains some good cases, but we notice that half of them occurred in November: for this we can look to the media impact of the incident of 11 November when the crew of a Supercaravelle reported strange lights. Finally, 1980 shows a chance accumulation of varied events, totally unrelated to one another. In short, none of the fluctuations constitutes a real 'wave' of true UFOs.

The reports reveal 20 radar detections, 15 scrambles or launches of jet interceptors, 10 close encounters, 13 instances where photographic material exists, and 28 civilian pilot witnesses (figures not mutually exclusive). Apart from the Air Force, other official bodies making reports included the Navy (9 reports), the Civil Guard (7), the Army (5) and the Police (3).

If we look at time of day data, the following table appears:

	12-18 Hrs	18-24 Hrs	00-06 Hrs	06-12 Hrs	Not Known
IFOs	11%	57%	17%	12%	3%
UFOs	6%	50%	31%	13%	

It is somewhat dismaying to find that, contrary to what we might expect, UFOs follow the same time-of-day distribution as IFOs.

As soon as files were declassified, a multidisciplinary team of experts, coordinated by myself, rushed to analyse the information. The research is not finished, as some reports present complex problems which make analysis difficult. The absence of inquiry at the time, the absence of corroboration, and insufficient information add to the complications. Nonetheless, our investigative efforts proved fruitful and we have been able to draw an array of general conclusions.

IFOs comprise 85% of the total. They break down to:

Astronomical explanations – the most frequent error stimulus: four out of ten observational mistakes involve Venus, other planets and stars, meteors and fireballs, or even the Moon.

Hoaxes explain two out of ten reports.

Meteorological balloons emerge as misperception culprits in one in ten cases (mostly from the French CNES programmes of 1967-1970).

The Miscellaneous cluster includes a variety of reasons for misinterpretation: three of every ten IFO cases are due to rockets and missiles, aircraft, reflections and temperature inversions, space junk re-entries, false radar echoes, fireworks or light projectors.

These proportions are consistent with those found in other samples, for example by Allan Hendry in *The UFO Handbook*. This suggests a world-wide pattern.

Nevertheless, 15% of the reports released by the Air Force remain to be resolved. One case (January 1, 1975, Burgos) defies every explanation and arises as a true anomaly. Nine others present outstanding abnormal features and they are under further study. Finally, five cases have insufficient data to be evaluated.

CHRONOLOGY

My role in this process has had two well-defined stages. During 1990 and 1991 my task was to meet with the Air Force's Public Relations commanding officer and with the Colonel in charge of the Air Safety Section, seeking to convince them that UFO information poses no threat to National Security; that keeping UFO reports secret gives a false image that the State is concealing 'special knowledge'; that restriction of access to UFO files from students is hardly compatible with a truly democratic nation. I pointed out parallels such as the US precedent in freeing the Blue Book files, the initiative of the Australian Air Force, and GEPAN/SEPRA in France.

One of my objectives was to get all official UFO reports to a centralised location before declassification began, and in 1991 I persuaded Colonel Alvaro Fernandez Rodas – an intelligent, well prepared officer – to ask all Air Regions to submit any UFO information they had on file. By this means the archives grew from 55 to 62 files.

That was a useful start: but what was the next step? One day in June 1992 I was approached by Lieutenant Colonel Bastida. It happened by chance while I was visiting a General in the Air Force Headquarters, and that evening I had my first meeting with the man from MOA.

I found that he was aware of my UFO work and I could feel he respected it. In fact, he had used my books as a guideline for designing case summaries, procedures and methodology involving statistics and a computer catalogue of UFO cases. This meeting was the first in a long series: mutual communication between civilian and military 'ufology' became a reality.

This relationship continued with Rocamora, Bastida's successor. Frequent visits and other contacts permitted me to:

1. – closely monitor the declassification process, including incoming new material, and ensure that any information on record was made public totally uncensored (except for witness names).

2. – stimulate an official search by Air Force bases, radar stations, etc. for both past and recent cases: this led to more than 25 additional case sources (to be released shortly).

3. – obtain the declassification of policy documents, directives and instruction texts prepared by the Air Force over the twenty-five year period.

For myself, as a civilian investigator, the achieving of these goals has been a dream come true. It would not have been possible, however, without a progressive attitude within the Air Force, and the determination of a group of military men to achieve one of the major targets of the ufological community in any country: to have the 'secret' stamps removed from the Air Force's UFO reports.

Acknowledgements The author wishes to recognise the able assistance and cooperation of Mr. Joan Plana, Vice-president CEI (Barcelona) and expert in defence issues, and the author's co-worker since 1988. Thanks also to Sra. Carmen Romero Asensio, for a professional word-processing of a difficult hand-written text.

When in 1974 Ion Hobana & Julian Weverbergh published the English translation of their UFOs in Oost en West (as UFOs from behind the Iron Curtain), it was a dramatic revelation to ufologists in the West. Documentation of cases in Bulgaria, Czechoslovakia, Hungary, Poland, Russia and Yugoslavia, and particularly from Hobana's native Romania, showed that UFOs were not, as some Soviet critics insisted, a malicious fabrication of the capitalist West, but a phenomenon which transcended political and ideological frontiers.

Nevertheless the 1974 book featured, for the most part, discs, other structured shapes and luminous phenomena seen in the skies. Though in France and Italy a great many landing cases had been reported, only one such was reported from Romania, and even that one was considered by Hobana to be of dubious value.

Perhaps significantly, this case from the 1990s is also notable for its extraordinary light display; so extraordinary, it justifies the author's comment that 'we are confronted with one of the most amazing cases in UFO history'.

Ion Hobana can be contacted at 24 N Bälcescu Boulevard, 70122 Bucharest, Romania: phone +40 1 6 14 68 98

BALLET OF LIGHTS IN THE CARPATHIANS

by Ion Hobana

On the night of 13/14 August, 1991, a Romanian passenger plane crashed in the Retezat Mountains, while en route to Timisoara. All the six men aboard were killed. The Deputy-Minister of Transport, in a statement to Rompres news agency, stated that the tragic accident had been caused by a powerful storm.

I contacted the experts at the Meteorology Institute. They assured me there had been no unusual atmospheric phenomena in the Retezat Mountains that night. The synoptic maps, updated every hour from on-the-spot information, recorded no heavy rainfall nor high gusts of wind in the area of the accident. The testimony of an eye-witness, who reported that one of the engines was on fire, was not confirmed by examination of the wreckage.

More than a year later, the press published the findings of the aeronautical and judicial inquiry. The principal conclusion was that the accident was not due to malfunction or any other technical cause, but to a loss of orientation by the crew, following an initial miscalculation of the time taken to cover the various legs of the route. The error, estimated as ten minutes, corresponded to a deviation of 50-60 kilometres.

Wanting to know the whole truth of the matter, I had a lengthy discussion with some members of the inquiry commission. They told me that the accident was due to a fatal set of circumstances: an improvised crew composed of individuals who had not previously flown together; a ground radar out of order; the misinterpretation of a message from the control tower. I had no way of checking these assertions, but they seemed quite convincing.

But the accident had been the subject of a strange coincidence. On the morning of 14 August, before any news of the accident had been published, the Petrosani journal *Zori Noi* printed an article under the headline 'A Mysterious Phenomenon'. It recounted the extraordinary experience of a group of seven persons during the night of 4 August: the incident took place only two kilometres from the scene of the air crash ten days later.

Subsequently, the local correspondent of the influential newspaper *Adevarul*, Constanta Corpade, secured an interview with one of the witnesses: Domokos Martin is a member of Salvamont, a mountain rescue association, who for thirty years has travelled the Retezat Mountains, at all seasons and in any weather conditions. Finally, in October 1991, at my request, Mihaela Muraru-Mândrea travelled to the scene of the adventure and tape-recorded her conversation with Domokos and his colleague George Resika. Relying on these sources, I have drawn up this account which convinces me that we are confronted with one of the most amazing cases in the history of the UFO phenomenon.

THE SIGHTING

On that night of 4 August, the mountain rescuers Domokos Martin and George Resiga were accompanying five tourists on the road from the Pietrele chalet to the Salvamont base near Bucura Lake. The sky was cloudless. A group of four tourists, including two girls, were walking about half a kilometre ahead of the others. At 10.45 pm, by which time they were one kilometre ahead of their companions, they saw a rapidly-moving light. Thinking it might be a tourist who had lost his way, they began to shout and wave their flashlights. The speed of the unknown light increased and its path changed from linear to zigzag.

The girls became frightened, and the group halted to let the others catch up with them. All seven were together when the light, red in colour, approached to within some tens of metres, hovered stationary for a while, then returned to Valea Rea where it had seemed to come from.

As the party resumed their walk, they saw, also in the direction of Valea Rea, an intense white light, and then a third one, this time pale blue. After some minutes, they reached higher ground at Curmatura Bucurei. From here they no longer saw isolated lights: instead there were a multitude of luminous points, green, bluish, turquoise (the most dominant colour) but also yellow-red and pink. These points were gathered in an oval shape, lying on the upper-right part of Valea Rea.

From an oval, the shape changed into a clearly outlined cylinder, then into a parallelogram all of whose sides were lit, then into a giant heart! Finally the lights multiplied further until they made up something like a town. The seven witnesses had the impression of being in an aircraft flying at night, at a low altitude, looking down on a splendidly illuminated settlement with avenues, streets and crossing.

Remembering that in their food knapsacks they were carrying some powerful binoculars, they pulled them out. Taking it in turns to use them, they could now see that each of the lights was a disc shape, with a phosphorescent porthole.

The mountain-rescue men were equipped with a radio-transmitter. When the very first light, the red one, made its appearance, they had tried to contact their colleagues at the base near Bucura Lake. Unfortunately the Curmatura peak was between them and the base, and they were unable to make contact. Now that they had reached the peak, they signalled with their flashlights towards their colleagues at the base, shouting at them to switch on their radio. When contact was established, they drew their attention to the lights: whereupon the lights changed their configuration once again, turning into something like airport landing lights, seen in a row; then reverting to the oval shape which, suddenly intensifying its brilliance, began to rise and eventually disappeared upwards.

Immediately after this, the perfect visibility, which had permitted such clear observation of the phenomenon, gave place to a dense fog. The seven travellers were unable to see more than two or three metres around them. This can hardly be due to the displacement of fog patches to the right and left of Valea Rea, because the night was still without a breath of wind.

At first the staff of the Salvamont base expressed suspicion of the seven witnesses, guessing that it was either a deliberate joke or a hallucination of some kind. But the genuine astonishment of the witnesses, and the consistency of their accounts, eventually convinced them to take the affair more seriously.

The following morning, Romania Radio News announced that a UFO had been observed over the Danube, at the Iron Gate. Only at this point did they decide to send a brief account of the sighting to the local newspaper.

OTHER LIGHTS IN THE AREA

I must add that the events of 4 August 1991 were not entirely unique in the Retezat Mountains. A friend of Domokos Martin once saw an orange light moving about two kilometres away, on the ridge of Stanisoara Mountain. A man from Bucharest told George Resiga that, while standing on the plateau in front of the Petrele chalet, he had seen a very powerful light moving in a zigzag.

The 'nocturnal lights' chapter of the UFO file includes many cases which are puzzling not only for the witnesses but also for those who try to analyse them. Few, however, present such a high strangeness index as the phenomenon of 4 August 1991. Did the changing shapes have significance, and if so, were they seeking to communicate a message? Was it coincidence that, soon after radio contact was established with the base, the 'light show' was terminated?

Finally, what about the coincidence with the air crash ? I have been told by a well-informed individual, who wishes to remain anonymous, that the accident was caused by powerful electromagnetic forces which rendered the controls unable to function. Since, as the weather report indicates, there were no natural forces active that night, maybe we should blame some such luminous manifestation as that seen by the walking party. There is even the possibility that the aircrew, like the tourists, saw the likeness of a town, and thinking they had reached their destination, lowered their altitude and hit the side of the mountain. Well, it's a possibility.

Artist's impression of the UFO car-stop near Vejle, Jutland, on 19 September 1995

MANY UFO SIGHTINGS OCCUR WHILE WITNESSES ARE OUT AND ABOUT IN THEIR MOTOR CARS, AND THERE HAVE BEEN MANY CASES WHERE THE VEHICLES ARE THEMSELVES AFFECTED. A PHYSICAL EFFECT MUST HAVE A PHYSICAL CAUSE, AND CAR-STOP CASES ARE IMPORTANT INDICATIONS THAT THE UFOS POSSESS PHYSICAL REALITY. THE AMERICAN INVESTIGATOR JAMES MCCAMPBELL HAS DONE VALUABLE RESEARCH INTO THE FORCES WHICH MIGHT CAUSE EQUIPMENT TO BEHAVE ERRATICALLY, BUT THIS PROMISING LINE OF APPROACH HAS NOT YET RECEIVED ALL THE SCIENTIFIC ATTENTION IT DESERVES.

KIM MØLLER HANSEN, AUTHOR AND LIBRARIAN, WHO REPORTS THIS RECENT INCIDENT, HAS BEEN A COUNCIL MEMBER OF SCANDINAVIAN UFO INFORMATION (SUFOI) SINCE 1980. HE DIRECTS THE SUFOI PICTURE LIBRARY AND EDITS THE TWO DANISH MAGAZINES UFO-NYT AND UFO-VISION. HE MAY BE CONTACTED AT PRIVATE, EILEKIERSVEJ 14, BENLØSE, DK-4100 RINGSTED, DENMARK, FAX +45 53 61 94 57.

CAR-STOP ENCOUNTER IN DENMARK

by Kim Møller Hansen

n his Account of Denmark as it was in the year 1692 the English minister to that country, Robert Molesworth, wrote that 'in Denmark you will not meet any people with extraordinary abilities or qualifications. No one will distinguish himself by exceptional studies or occupations. None is enthusiastic, furious, mad or a dreamer. The Danes always keep to the beaten track.'

This description may be true today – so far as witness accounts go, at least. SUFOI (Scandinavian UFO Information, founded in 1957) has never been troubled by agonising abductions, cattle mutilations or similar alarming incidents. In most cases the reports we investigate involve nocturnal lights and daylight discs – though once in a while a more interesting case will turn up, such as the famous car stop experience of police officer Maarup in August 1970, which I reported in Evans & Spencer, *UFOs 1947-1987*.

More recently we had another dramatic stopping of a car, where a very large disc with a powerful light hovered over the vehicle. This account of the event of 29 September 1995 is based on the witness's written report and the investigation by Torben Birkeholm, SUFOI's Field Investigator in Jutland.

'THE ENGINE WENT COMPLETELY DEAD...'

It was Friday evening. A 24-year-old man was driving southward from Brande towards Vejle in Jutland, on his way to visit his parents. He was driving a 1981 BMW 320: his only companion was the black Labrador lying on the back seat. There was hardly any traffic.

It was dark with dry, clear weather: the external temperature was over 10°C. The young man was approaching a left turn in a forest area. He slowed down and drove past a side road on the right that leads to Billund. As he turned his speed was approximately 60 km/h. The car's clock was showing 21.30, when suddenly he saw the speedometer shoot straight round to maximum and the other instruments started to go wild. The rev counter also went to maximum and the thermometer shot up into the red, where the needle stood vibrating. At the same time the windscreen wipers started going at great speed – though they were not even switched on! In bewilderment he tried flicking the wiper switch, but this had no effect.

The dog started to become agitated on the back seat, and the witness had to tell it to lie down. As he approached a lay-by on the right he noticed that his headlights were also behaving oddly, changing in strength, and that the engine had started to misfire as though it was flooded. He tried to keep some life in it and pumped repeatedly on the accelerator, but to no avail. Finally the engine went completely dead and the car came to a stop – in complete darkness – out in the middle of the country road.

A POWERFUL LIGHT EXPLODES OVER THE VEHICLE

While the witness nervously peered through the windscreen and glanced repeatedly in the rear-view mirror, for fear of any cars that might be approaching, he tried immediately to re-start the car. He turned the ignition key, but nothing happened. The ignition light did not come on, there was no power. Everything was dead.

However, he noticed that the car's clock was faintly lit. To his amazement it was not showing the time, but 88.88.88! He felt as if time had stopped as he tried several times to start the engine. 'There must be a small current if the light is on,' he thought. But after three or four fruitless attempts he suddenly became aware of a strange, oppressive sensation 'from above', like some sort of physical influence that he found hard to describe.

Apart from the restless dog, everything was completely quiet, and he looked around in wonder while he continued trying to start the car. Less than twenty seconds had passed since the first indication that something unusual was happening.

Without warning – and without a sound – an enormously powerful light practically 'exploded' over the vehicle. The light came from above, and it was blinking or pulsing quickly at regular intervals. The witness saw the light through the windscreen, looked up and saw a huge disc above him. He was scared, but immediately opened the door, put his left foot on the road and leaned halfway out, his left hand on top of the door and his right hand on the steering wheel. His dog was whining and trying to hide, trying vainly to 'bury' itself under the front seat.

THE LIGHT SOURCE

The light was dazzling and he had to squint to see anything. He saw a large disc, 12-15 metres in diameter, just three or four metres above the car. The disc's outer edge was dark against the background of the starry sky. A little further in he could see a number of concentric circles of light, which were closer together the nearer they were to the centre of the disc.

Each light-circle consisted of 'lamps' that were equally spaced all the way around. Each 'lamp' consisted of two circles, like a bulb in the middle of a reflector. The light itself seemed like neon and each 'lamp' shone as brightly as a halogen lamp.

Near the centre of the disc the light was so strong that the witness could make out no details, or see whether there was a single light source or a cluster of small ones. He observed that the light's boundary was very sharply defined, going straight down rather than spreading out to the sides as would be normal.

Consequently, the circumference of the light field on the ground corresponded to that of the disc above.

Shortly after, as he sat back inside and shut the door, he saw that the light was now illuminating the whole road on both sides of the car, including the verges though no further. As before it was very sharply defined. The road at that point was wider than usual, as there was an extra lane for motorists turning off towards Billund.

The colour of the light was white and indigo, somewhat reminiscent of the light from a welding torch, but not nearly as strong. It 'quivered' in a strange fashion.

THE LIGHT GETS DIMMER AND THE DISC MOVES

The man rolled down the window and put his arm and head outside. He looked up again, though keeping a lookout for any cars coming from behind, turning his head rather than using the mirror.

After a short time he saw that the intensity of the light was slowly diminishing, as if someone were operating a dimmer. Soon it was as weak as a car's indicator light, but it continued to blink or 'quiver'. Through the windscreen he saw that the disc was slowly moving forwards ahead of him. It carried on towards the trees nearby, still very low down, and as it reached the first trees it literally had to 'tip' its left-hand side up to avoid them. It carried on with a faint light and disappeared out of sight in a matter of a few seconds, still without a sound.

As the disc glided towards the front of the car he could see that it was not flat. It looked peculiar, with something like 'triangles' or 'spikes' which he estimates were approximately one third of the disc's diameter, or about three metres high. The outer edges were rounded off, like a parasol. The disc had tipped its left side up by at least 20 degrees, and he could see the underside at the same time. He could not tell whether it righted itself again before it went out of sight.

For a short while he simply sat in the car, trying to calm his still agitated dog while he collected himself after what had happened. After maybe three or four minutes he turned the ignition key to check if there was any power. The headlights came on and he noticed straight away that the digital clock stood at 21.31. He turned the key completely: the engine started immediately. Lights and instruments were functioning normally.

He was still feeling afraid – his legs were trembling – but he drove off. For a while he did not drive over 70 km/h, but he speeded up when he had calmed down a little.

After driving 35 km the witness reached his parents' home and immediately told them what had happened. The experience was still affecting him and he was shaking. His parents asked him to contact someone – there must be some 'UFO people' he could ring. But he was too frightened and upset and did not phone anyone.

ENTER SUFOI

Later, the witness told a friend about the experience, who likewise urged him to report it. He thought the matter over a lot, but could not bring himself to contact anyone till some weeks later he saw a Danish TV documentary about UFOs. A few days afterwards he phoned SUFOI.

We immediately sent him a report form: when we got it back, it was clear that it dealt with a Close Encounter of the Second Kind. A meeting was arranged and we recorded a lengthy interview.

The local press was used to trace witnesses to the incident. SUFOI received a number of responses from local residents regarding various sightings, but there was no 'star witness' who could be tied in with the car's stopping. One sighting, however, did occur the same evening, only a few kilometres from where the car stopped.

Around 19.20 a young couple were standing in the kitchen on a farm. The woman was standing facing the window which looked out over the farmyard. Suddenly a beam of light appeared from above and shone down onto some flagstones in the yard in front of the window.

The beam of light was very sharply defined and around one metre in diameter, as was the area where it hit the flagstones. The light beam did not move and after about five seconds the woman drew her friend's attention to it. He was standing with his back to the window, but turned in time to see the light for about three seconds before it vanished. The duration was about ten seconds in all.

The farmyard is surrounded by high trees, so the couple excluded things such as light from neighbouring properties as an explanation. They did not go outside.

It was obviously not possible to tie this case in with the car stopping, as there were several hours between the two incidents and the second light beam was much smaller. But this too was an interesting sighting, and the coincidence of the two events on the same evening may be significant.

DURATION OF THE SIGHTING

How long did the young man's encounter last? In the his original written report the witness stated that it lasted 30 seconds, maybe longer. During the interview he was asked to state the duration of each phase of the incident. Later he was asked to close his eyes and recall the events while being timed. Without being told the result, he was asked once again to close his eyes and try to re-live each phase in turn. The results of these accounts are shown here:

Phase	Own statement	Blind test with phases	Blind test – complete sighting
1st phase: car starts to behave strangely, light appears	20 secs	15 secs	
2nd phase: witness leans out: shuts door again	20 secs	11 secs	
3rd phase: rolls down window, looks up and out, until light begins to dim	10 secs	5 secs	
4th phase: light dims to lowest level, disc moves away	12 secs	11 secs	
Total time	62 secs	42 secs	41 secs

It is remarkable that the two blind tests are so nearly identical. This could be pure coincidence, but it speaks in favour of a genuine sighting. Note that the witness originally stated an overall duration of at least 30 seconds, while his phase-by-phase account indicated a good minute. We may reasonably suppose that the true figure lies somewhere between 30 and 60 seconds.

Is that a little or a lot? Try timing it yourself – a lot can happen in that time, and a great number of details can be noted.

THE WITNESS

The 24-year-old man lives in Aalborg (northern Jutland), where he is a student nurse. He originally comes from around Vejle, where he has many acquaintances who interest themselves in the UFO phenomenon in their spare time. He has himself heard about UFO sightings, read about them in newspapers – not books – and seen TV programmes on the subject. He has also seen the film *Close Encounters of the Third Kind*.

He comes across as a surprised and honest person who gives no impression of being other than very normal.

He has spoken further about his thoughts in connection to the experience. He especially noticed the strange 'oppressive' feeling just before the light appeared. In a way it was like just before a thunderstorm, but very physical. Just as the light appeared he noticed a sort of 'pleasant' feeling that he has never experienced before. He was scared but nevertheless did not feel 'threatened' in any way. He did not feel it was anything that wanted to harm him.

While the object was present it seemed as though 'time stood still' in the space where the light was. At the same time it was unbelievably quiet; he found it striking and totally incomprehensible that there was not the slightest sound, despite the enormous 'machine' hovering just above him.

He also felt as if he should 'go up'. In any case he imagined that it might happen, but the thought did not frighten him. In fact he hoped that more would happen – that 'someone' or 'something' would come and show itself. He wanted to know what it was, and felt in some way 'drawn' to the disc above him.

While it was there he did not notice any sort of heat from the intense light. On the contrary, he felt a sort of 'coldness' (it was also chilly outside), which he could compare a little to a feeling from his hospital work. He had recently been on practical training in a department with an NMR scanner (which produces a powerful magnetic field). There one feels that one's body seems to be registering something unusual. He imagined in fact that the powerful light was taking some sort of 'photograph' of him.

THE CASE IS NOT CLOSED

SUFOI has not succeeded in tracing other witnesses through the local media. We have considered ringing doorbells in the area, or using the national media in the hope of finding a motorist from out of the area, who might have noticed the light or even the 'disc' from a distance.

Furthermore we need answers to a number of technical questions concerning the car. It would be interesting to define the physical conditions which might cause the instruments to behave as described. For example, what level of current is required to activate the digital clock, and under what circumstances will it show 88.88.88? The car should have been examined by qualified technicians immediately after the incident: unfortunately this was not possible, due to the time that elapsed before SUFOI became involved and because of the cost.

As work on the case has progressed, a number of questions have arisen that require further interviews with the witness. The young man has made himself available to SUFOI throughout the investigation, and it is only the fact that the investigators must use their spare time that is delaying bringing the case to a full conclusion.

AFRICA SEMPER ALIQUID NOVI — THERE IS ALWAYS SOMETHING NEW COMING FROM AFRICA, COMMENTED PLINY IN HIS NATURAL HISTORY, AND IT'S AS TRUE IN THE TWENTIETH CENTURY AS IT WAS IN THE FIRST. NO DOUBT WE HEAR OF ONLY A TINY FRACTION OF THE INCIDENTS WHICH OCCUR BETWEEN THE MEDITERRANEAN AND THE CAPE: BUT, LARGELY THANKS TO THE ENERGY AND ENTHUSIASM OF CYNTHIA HIND, THE AFRICAN CONTINENT IS NOT ENTIRELY TERRA INCOGNITA SO FAR AS UFOS ARE CONCERNED.

HOW DOES THE AFRICAN EXPERIENCE OF UFOS COMPARE WITH OTHER PARTS OF THE WORLD? UFO REPORTS FROM UNDEVELOPED OR DEVELOPING COMMUNITIES ARE ESPECIALLY INTERESTING BECAUSE THEY PROVIDE A YARDSTICK WHEREBY HAPPENINGS IN MORE SOPHISTICATED REGIONS CAN BE MEASURED. THEY RAISE THE QUESTION TO WHAT EXTENT UFO EVENTS ARE NOT ONLY INTERPRETED BUT ACTUALLY SHAPED BY THEIR CULTURAL CONTEXT.

THIS QUESTION HAS BEEN THE LONG-RUNNING THEME OF CYNTHIA'S CAREER AS AFRICA'S LEADING UFOLOGIST. AFRICA-BORN, SHE DIVIDES HER TIME BETWEEN INVESTIGATING AT HOME AND REPRESENTING AFRICAN UFOLOGY ABROAD: A POPULAR FIGURE RENOWNED FOR HER LIVELY PRESENTATIONS AT INTERNATIONAL CONFERENCES, THERE IS NO ONE BETTER PLACED TO EVALUATE THE AFRICAN EXPERIENCE IN THE GLOBAL CONTEXT.

CYNTHIA HIND CAN BE REACHED AT POSTBOX MP49, MOUNT PLEASANT, HARARE, ZIMBABWE: E-MAIL <GEMINI@MANGO.ZW>

UFOS IN AFRICA: CHANGING WAYS IN CHANGING DAYS

by Cynthia Hind

I t has been interesting for me, over the years, to note the cultural perception in Africa of what UFOs are. Initially, when people were mainly distributed in the rural areas, their attitude to the possibility of life in space, be it humans from the United States or Russian astronauts, would be total non-acceptance. How could anyone, even people from our Earth, reach the heights that belong only to God? It was an impossibility! Once, talking with a group of workers at the Forestry Commission in La Rochelle, Zimbabwe, someone mentioned the word 'astronaut': but when we discussed it, I found that they had no definite idea of what an 'astronaut' could be. They only one knew that it was 'someone who could fly very high in his aeroplane'. As for the idea of men walking on the moon, that was totally unacceptable! 'Only God can walk on the Moon,' they said, and this sentiment was re-iterated by Irene Granchi's Brazilian-Indian cook in Rio de Janeiro (Irene is President of C.I.S.N.E. in Brazil).

A frequent identification of entities is that they are 'ghosts'. Ghosts are well-known in African culture and a variety of ghosts exist in their beliefs. They range from the benign ancestor ghost who visits his descendants merely to show them something in a gentle way, or point out an omission on their part as far as his burial is concerned, to the more evil ghost who takes over a dead person's body to harass, even harm a villager against whom he has a grudge. (The recipient of these visitations often becomes ill to the point of death.) These appearances may be greeted with fear, but at least they are accepted and understood. Not so the alien beings of UFO-lore, although one can understand why they are given the all-embracing 'ghost' label.

Today in Africa, the rural people, unless they are successful farmers or ranchers, are moving in thousands towards the bright lights of the cities. The prospect of employment, becoming street vendors with a ready sale of vegetables, of shops filled with goods (some virtually unknown only a few years ago), cinemas, sophisticated bars and pubs: all this is an attractive lure to those who have never previously known this excitement. And with it come television and the journalists' revelations in the tabloids and magazines.

Sometime ago I was interviewed about my UFO investigations for a magazine published for the customers of a large clothing store, with branches throughout southern Africa. Maria Sullivan, who works with me, and I received about 300 letters from school-children, mostly in the rural areas, asking eagerly for more information. It certainly gave me an insight into how the rural African people were progressing in their search for knowledge. Some of the letters were sad (lack of money, lack of family) and others quite amusing. I quote: 'I'm a boy of 16 and interested in studying UFOs. It has been believed that UFOs are superstitious but I would like to be well versed about these things since I had seen one like the one described in the magazine (a glowing space-craft)'. – 'I was very happy to hear of you. I did not believe it at first but now I'm starting to see the lighter side of things.' – 'Please help, do me a favour and write relating your story and many more. I have not much to say. Sorry for breaking the Queen's language here and there.' – 'I want to know more about UFOs and why they exist?'

Since independence African children – certainly in Botswana, South Africa, Zambia and Zimbabwe – are becoming aware of what the world says and thinks about UFOs. I am no longer dealing with tribal taboos and cultural stigmas: instead, I meet with enquiring minds. On balance I'm sure this is a good thing, even though I will never again encounter that naïve, innocent approach I have long come to expect. On the other hand, perhaps I will find thousands of new cases, no longer identified as 'ghosts', but a verification of what is going on here and in other Third World countries.

One morning in 1994, 62 children at Ariel School in Ruwa, about 30 km from Harare in Zimbabwe, saw several shining objects land adjacent to their playground at about 10 am, during the morning school break. The date was 16 September, two days after a controversial aerial sighting in the form of a magnificent pyrotechnic display over southern Africa. (This was later identified as the nose-cone of a Russian satellite, sent up on the 26th August, 1994, which had come to earth in our area.)

The children were in the playground in noisy play. The teachers were all in the staff-room at a monthly meeting, and the only other adult on the premises was inside the school tuck-shop, minding her wares. A young boy rushed in to tell her something was landing near the school and that a little man with a band around his head was running up and down. The mother in the tuckshop did not believe the boy and refused to leave her stores. So, for several good reasons, there were no adult witnesses.

The children had watched the objects (four or five of them) come in along the electricity pylons and come to earth, or hover, near the third pylon. Almost immediately, two small humanoid figures emerged through a doorway. They were about one metre high and were dressed in black. They had long black hair; large, rugby-ball-like eyes, hardly any nose and a small slit for a mouth. They ran across the unkempt, bush-covered field next to the playground (where the children for safety reasons were not allowed to go unaccompanied by an adult) in slow motion, and in a confused way. The children were transfixed, not only by the unfamiliar scene before them, but by the eyes of the small creatures, as was discovered later by Dr. John E. Mack, Professor of Psychiatry at Columbia Medical School.

It later emerged from Mack's discussions with the children that they had received telepathic messages, although the word 'telepathy' had no meaning for them. For the first time, there was an underlying similarity in the interpretation of the messages. The children at the school were black and white African, Asian, and coloured (from a mixed marriage of black and white). A 10-year old white girl said she felt 'we would bring harm to life on Earth as we were becoming too technologised.' A black boy said he had received a message about the pollution around us. A small coloured girl, aged about nine years, thought that perhaps we were being warned that the end of the world was coming. She was especially anxious about it all and was disturbed by the whole event.

Not all the children had seen the same things. I discovered later that some had climbed onto packed logs in the playground, which gave them an elevated view of the craft, so that they drew legs on the machines in their pictures. Others, who stood on level ground, could not see the tripod type legs from their vantage point. The children also found it difficult to describe the clothing worn by the little men. Without wanting to lead them, I suggested they wore a suit like their headmaster. No. Well, what about a track-suit like they wore to gym? No, not like that either. Did they recall seeing men in diving suits ... and before I could finish, several children chorused, 'Yes, like that, tight-fitting and shiny.'

On sensitive investigations like this, I am always wary of leading the witness. But there is a problem, particularly when interviewing children or unsophisticated people in the bush. I am dealing with images and conceptions which are totally unfamiliar in Africa. When a BBC interviewer asked the children what happened when the craft eventually left, they said, 'It just went.' I knew at once that they meant it literally disappeared. The craft lifted up about three metres and then disappeared. The reporter did not understand and despite his questioning, all the children repeatedly said was 'It just went.'

In the La Rochelle case of 1981, I wanted to know the colour of the craft. Clifford Muchena, the main witness, said it was 'shining'. I persisted, 'Shining – what?' Only later was I told there is no word in Shona (the local dialect) for 'silver', but when I pressed Clifford what he meant by 'shining', he drew a silver 20-cent piece from his pocket. So it is difficult, among so many varying cultures, to learn what witnesses mean without putting words into their mouths.

What about the schoolchildren at Ariel School: were what they told John Mack the basic thoughts of 9-12 year olds? Or did they indeed receive these messages telepathically? There was no physical evidence for investigators to work on. Two young boys said there were burn-marks on the ground, but when they went back a few hours later with a BBC cameraman there was nothing to show. Gunter Hofer, a technologist who assists me with most cases. had little reaction on his Geiger counter and none on the metal detector.

Imagination on the part of the children? When the headmaster took the children to their respective classrooms and had them draw what they had seen, the drawings, although showing what most of the 62 witnesses had seen, were hardly the results of collaboration. Mass hysteria? This has occurred in Africa, but the three mass cases I know of involved girls at puberty. The Ariel school children ranged from 6 – 12 years, which certainly does not fit the pattern,

Also, it is a fact that some of the children were traumatised by the experience, suffered from nightmares and needed counselling, although the majority, despite the excitement of what they had seen, carried on quite normally. But, surprisingly there has been no reaction from local people and government officials to these dramatic events. I know African culture allows for 'ghosts', but perhaps the concept of visitors from other planets, other dimensions, or other times, is still unacceptable and therefore more comfortably ignored.

In November 1996 Gunter, Maria and I went out to Bindura, some 90 km from Harare, to interview a 17-year-old boy, Lloyd Karambakuwa. He is a student at the Hermann Gemeiner Secondary School, busy studying for his 'O' levels. This is the story he told us:

At between 01:00 and 01:30 hours on the 6th March, 1996, Lloyd woke and decided to do some homework. It was quiet at that time and he knew he would not be disturbed. While thus engaged, he heard a 'clicking' sound, not unlike a telephone – except that there are no telephones in the area. It continued for some minutes so Lloyd decided to check what it could be. He opened the front door and looked outside. He could hear the sound coming from up the road and when he glanced in that direction, he saw something very strange. He quickly went outside and hid behind the front hedge of his house and was able to observe a small figure (about one metre high) with a head like a rugby-ball, dressed all in white overalls. On its back, the creature had a small satchel, attached to which was an aerial with a flashing red light. Lloyd was terrified; he told me he was 'asphyxiated with fear' and ran back into the house, jumped into bed and covered himself with his blankets. He slept fitfully for the rest of the night.

At 06:00 the next morning he went to look where the creature had walked and found several footprints which he could not identify and which he attributed to the creature. When he arrived at school, he told his friends about the ghost in the night, but one of his friends suggested that it was a UFO. Lloyd is now under the impression that the creature is the UFO.

Lloyd thought there might be another witness, a security guard at the Teaching Centre opposite his house. Inquiries led me to the security firm responsible, and I learnt that one of their guards, a woman, had been on duty at the centre when she had seen a ghost. She had been so disturbed by the event, she had refused to do further night-duty and found herself another job. When I traced the woman, Kumbadzai, she told me that after first sighting the 'ghost' she had hidden herself behind a wall. She too had heard the clicking noise and been afraid when she saw the figure in white. It had passed her on the road twice, and on the second time round, the figure had been covered in 'rainbow colours.' Both Lloyd and Kumbadzai, who is illiterate, were unsophisticated in their relationship to UFOs, and yet their reports matched, and compared favourably with similar incidents in other parts of the world!

Presently, I am dealing with several new cases. One, which took place during an October evening in 1996, concerns two men on a lonely farm road. One of them, a white man, slightly disabled, was driving back to where he lived on a farm about 20 km from Harare. He saw a light in the sky and watched with astonishment and apprehension because the leaves and branches had not moved at all when the 'craft' took off. He could not recall any noise, merely a faint humming sound as the craft left. It had been a very hot day, around 32°-33°C and the night was clear and calm. If this was something ordinary, it certainly behaved in a most peculiar fashion; and if it was something extraordinary, how would one ever prove what it was?

Another case I am currently investigating concerns a couple returning home in the dark who saw a craft of some type approaching them; at the very last moment it swerved upwards and out of sight within seconds, but not before they had been able to observe a very clear Star of David on the underside of the machine. Without interrogation and using my own estimate of the situation, it was either an Israeli aircraft come game-hunting in Zimbabwe, or a Biblical visitation!

On the 28th August, 1966, South Africa also had its share of excitement. At 04:00 in the early hours of the morning, an unusual object was seen over Pretoria. Apparently, it was recorded on video by a police sergeant, and not only that, was pursued by both a police car and a police helicopter. The object was disc-shaped and slightly pulsating, with lights flashing on the dome of the machine.

At first, everyone thought it was a hoax, or a publicity stunt for the film *Independence Day* which was due to open the following day in Johannesburg. But Superintendent Viljoen, who piloted the helicopter, which followed the object for quite some time, was surprised at its speed and the fact that it moved in an undulating fashion. The police car chased it for 100 km to the town of Cullinan, a town famous for the diamond of that name.

Recently I set off from Harare with Gunter, Doug and Maria on a fine Saturday morning to make the 150 km journey to Featherstone, to the farm where Johnny R. had had a strange experience. This is an area of ex-South African Afrikaans farmers whose families had trekked originally from South Africa. It is not a wealthy area and Johnny told me he felt they had been neglected by earlier governments who had not bothered with the roads, nor built a good dam for the farmers.

Johnny is 31 years old, sturdy and good looking: he runs a farm of cattle, sheep, pigs and vegetables for his mother. On the night of 5 February 1996, he woke from a disturbed dream just after midnight when he heard a car go past. He got up and looked out of the bedroom window which faces onto the front of the farm. He watched as two cars passed each other, one moving much more slowly than the other. This in itself was surprising, as it is a very isolated area where few vehicles are seen and especially not at that time of night. The slow car pulled into his gate and Johnny thought immediately, 'Oh no, these guys are coming to pinch my new engine on the borehole!'

He rubbed his eyes and his face to make sure he wasn't asleep and looked at the car again. It was long and wide and made a low humming sound. He could see lights at the back; a row of red lights and a front light which shone high to the top of the msasa trees (about 15 metres high.)

The object stopped at the gate for a good 30 seconds and then drove on as if the gate had been opened. And that was it: it was gone! Johnny said. 'I watched for about half a minute and then I ran into my Mom's room to tell her. She begged me not to go out but I said I'll go and fetch some of the workers. I'm not going to let them pinch my engine.'

Johnny took his torch, his rifle and his dogs and together with four workers, he went to the gate. Despite the fact that it had rained and cleaned the ground, there were no tyre marks, nor human or animal tracks. As they approached the gate, Johnnie could feel heat coming up from the surface of the road; a really oppressive heat radiating from the ground. Even his ears were flushed with the heat and he and the workers were soaked with perspiration. It was about 12:30 hours by now so when they found nothing further, they all went back home.

It was the only the following morning that it occurred to Johnnie that when they reached the gate, it had been closed. This meant the car had disappeared through a closed gate, because he had been looking at it when it had disappeared.

The next day, Johnnie sent one of his workers to fetch some sheep who were lost in the bush and on his way hack in the early evening, the worker said he saw something straddling the road. By the time he reached there, it had gone, but strangely enough, the sheep would not walk over the area where the object had been. They divided round it, although they did not appear to be unduly disturbed.

Johnny told us of other experiences with light-balls at night, especially when he had been out hunting buck. But this latest experience was nothing like that; this 'thing' had scared him and he had no idea what it was. His workers told him they had seen something similar before, but they felt it was a ghost. Johnny agreed with them. 'I'm a Christian myself, ' he said, 'and I'm telling you, it's a phantom, a spiritual phenomenon. I don't believe in UFOs and visitors from beyond this planet.' *Et tu, Brute.*

Ghosts? Or Entities from another dimension, time travellers or whatever? I think the phenomenon has not really changed, even though Africa has changed. It does seem to appear more frequently recently, but perhaps that is because people report more readily. The actual reportage, when analysed, seems to remain the same, but with much more detail. This last six months, I have had more serious reports than I have in five or six years!

In 1981 at La Rochelle, the entities were identified by Clifford Muchena as 'ghosts of my ancestors'. When I pointed out that his ancestors would hardly wear silver suits instead of leopard skins and monkey-fur hats, he thought for a moment and then said 'Well, times change!'

ASPECTS

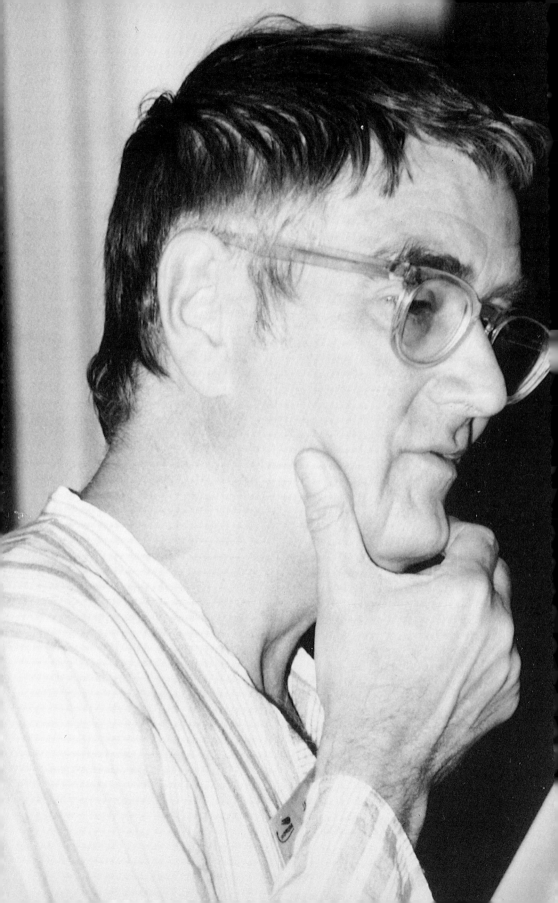

ONE OF THE FUNDAMENTAL PARADIGM SHIFTS IN THE 50-YEAR HISTORY OF UFOS HAS BEEN THE MOVEMENT AWAY FROM THE CLASSIC DAYLIGHT DISC CASE TO THOSE INVOLVING REPORTED ALIEN ENTITIES, ESPECIALLY THOSE CASES IN WHICH PEOPLE CLAIM TO BE ABDUCTED ABOARD THE UFO BY ALIENS. FOR MANY, ABDUCTIONS ARE THE 'ANSWER' TO THE 'UFO PROBLEM' BECAUSE THEY SEEM TO EXPLAIN WHY THE SAUCERS ARE HERE, AND TO INDICATE AN EVOLVING LINE OF INTENTIONAL ACTIVITY, BEGINNING WITH REMOTE RECONNAISSANCE, THEN SOIL AND PLANT SAMPLING, AND ENDING IN ACTUAL PHYSICAL ABDUCTION OF THE EARTH'S INHABITANTS.

FOR THE SCEPTICAL COMMUNITY, THE ABDUCTION ACCOUNTS ARE THE HEIGHT OF ABSURDITY. EVEN UFOLOGISTS DISAGREE AS TO WHETHER ABDUCTIONS REPRESENT A REAL PHYSICAL EVENT, SOME SORT OF PREVIOUSLY UNRECOGNISED PSYCHOLOGICAL EXPERIENCE, OR MERE FANTASY. HOW THE ABDUCTION EXPERIENCE CAME TO OCCUPY CENTRE STAGE IN THE UFO CONTROVERSY IS THE SUBJECT OF THE FOLLOWING ESSAY BY SCIENCE JOURNALIST PATRICK HUYGHE, AN EYEWITNESS TO THE EVOLUTION. HUYGHE'S ARTICLES ON UFOS AND OTHER SUBJECTS HAVE APPEARED IN OMNI, THE NEW YORK TIMES SUNDAY MAGAZINE, NEWSWEEK, SCIENCE DIGEST AND FORTEAN TIMES. HE CO-EDITS THE ANOMALIST. HIS MOST RECENT BOOK IS THE FIELD GUIDE TO EXTRATERRESTRIALS (1996), ILLUSTRATED BY HARRY TRUMBORE. PATRICK'S E-MAIL ADDRESS IS PATRICK@CLOUD9.NET.

THE BEST KEPT SECRET

by Patrick Huyghe

Anything can happen in New York. I thought I knew what that meant until I arrived in the Big Apple in 1977, fresh out of journalism school. Within a couple of weeks, I witnessed a shoot-out between a handful of policemen on the sidewalk and someone inside a store on Second Avenue. The scene unfolded in front of me as the city bus I was riding nonchalantly made its regular round of stops down the Avenue. My face was glued to the window as I tried to follow the scene receding quickly behind us. It was then that I realised, that no matter what happens, life goes on.

During those first few weeks in New York I also learned that the apartment I had moved into was just a block away from one of the legends of the early days of UFO research, Ted Bloecher. He had founded Civilian Saucer Intelligence of New York back in 1952 with Isabel Davis, worked for a time at the National Investigations Committee on Aerial Phenomenon, produced the Report on the UFO Wave of 1947, and had begun compiling the 'Humanoid Catalog' with David Webb. Bloecher and I quickly became friends and he soon introduced me to a New York artist who had become interested in UFOs.

AT THE BIRTH

His name was Budd Hopkins. Hopkins' apartment and studio became the meeting ground for a handful of investigators, UFO witnesses, and other interested parties, such as myself. On a monthly basis, if I recall correctly, we would met at Hopkins' place, drink white wine, eat cheese and crackers, and discuss UFOs. Actually, what we discussed the most was the abduction phenomenon. That was Hopkins' abiding interest. He was convinced that the aliens were able to block the memories of those they abducted and that these hidden events could then usually be revealed through hypnosis. Hand in hand with that conviction came Hopkins' belief that just about anyone could be an abductee. You didn't need to have a conscious memory of being abducted. You didn't even need to recall a UFO sighting. All you needed was a nagging feeling that 'something may have happened' at some point in your past.

Actually, you didn't even need that much. Curiosity about UFOs was enough to mark you a potential abductee in Hopkins' eyes. He thought that my own interest in the UFO phenomenon might be motivated by a forgotten but real abduction experience. He offered to have me hypnotised to ferret out my abduction episode, but I refused. Sure, I'd seen a strange orange object in the sky as a nine-year-old growing up in Newport News, Virginia, but 'unidentified' is all it was. I had no 'missing time' episode. (If I did, it was missing.) No, I could barely bring myself to believe that abductions were real. To think that someone was an abductee on the basis of one's interest in UFOs seemed patently ridiculous.

I was not the only one to think so. Peter Gersten, a criminal lawyer from the Bronx who had been attending the gatherings and who would later file a landmark Freedom of Information Act lawsuit for the U.S. government's UFO documents, thought that Hopkins had a one track mind and was on the wrong track at that. Disagreements erupted and soon the once-congenial meetings of that core late-1970s group were no more. Bloecher became increasingly uncomfortable with the subject and soon dropped out of the field altogether. Having landed my 'dream job' as a staff writer at *Newsweek* and being disappointed by the experience, I decided to move to the serene setting of a farmhouse near Charlottesville, Virginia to continue my writing.

A year later Hopkins came out with his first book, *Missing Time*, and forever changed our concept of the UFO phenomenon. When the 1961 abduction episode of Betty and Barney Hill became public in the second half of the 1960s, it seemed like a unique case. By the late 1970s, with the Travis Walton, Pascagoula and other cases having made national headlines, it became obvious that the Hills were not the only ones to have experienced a 'UFO abduction.' Then came the early 1980s with Hopkins sending chills down our spines with the suggestion that many people who had been abducted were probably not aware of what had happened to them. And so Hopkins began his crusade to let them – and the rest of the world – know exactly what had happened to them.

I was back in the New York metropolitan area by the second half of the 1980, at a time when the public seemed seized with alien fever. Huge triangle-shaped objects were being seen over the Hudson Valley where I was living and a well-known horror novelist, Whitley Strieber, confessed to his own bizarre UFO abduction experiences in upstate New York in a best-seller called *Communion*. By that time Hopkins had figured out what the aliens were doing with the humans they were abducting. His second book, *Intruders*, detailed the cases he drew upon to support his conclusion that the human species was the subject of a genetic experiment conducted by alien beings. It was the summer of 1987 and for a while I got caught up in alien frenzy. On some very hot days I found myself almost believing that the aliens were here.

Though Hopkins and I were still friends, I was no longer welcome at regular gatherings, which were now largely comprised of abductees. The once informal get-togethers had become support group meetings with Hopkins acting as counsellor. He took a lot of flak for this. But he had no choice but to take on that role, he argued, as therapists and other social scientists were reluctant to deal with the problems facing abductees. Hopkins was now even hypnotising his own subjects. Given the number of abductees who had come forward since *Missing Time*, it had become too time-consuming and costly to find psychologists to conduct all the regression sessions that needed to be done. While I understood the constraints under which Hopkins was operating, I felt that he was doing irrevocable harm to his case by putting his own subjects under hypnosis. Who was to say that the subjects were not telling Hopkins exactly what he wanted to hear?

A TELLING SURVEY

Then, as the 1990s unfurled, the most unsettling revelation to date about the abduction phenomenon was unveiled. The aliens seemed to operate on a scale that was previously unimaginable. Unimaginable to everyone, perhaps, but Hopkins.

The news emerged in a roundabout way. By the start of the decade Hopkins' crusade had finally attracted the attention of a couple of wealthy individuals – one being Las Vegas real estate tycoon Robert Bigelow – who were willing to fund a professionally conducted national survey to learn the extent of the abduction phenomenon. But if Hopkins' thesis that most abductees did not even know they were abducted was correct, the poll takers could not simply come out and ask people 'Are you a UFO abductee?' and expect to get an accurate count of those who had been taken by the aliens. Instead, Hopkins – along with Temple University historian David Jacobs, who had followed in Hopkins' footsteps as an abduction researcher – devised a set of questions about people's unusual experiences which their research indicated was closely associated with abduction histories.

In 1991 the Roper Organization surveyed 5,947 adults nationwide using a battery of 11 questions. Nine of these eleven abduction-related questions had been thoroughly pre-tested by Hopkins and Jacobs. Those nine were questions most frequently answered positively by abductees, and negatively by non-abductees. The other two questions simply tested the reliability of the poll. The first asked respondents if they had seen a UFO, and since answers to that question have been collected since the 1950s, too high a response rate would indicate there was a problem with the polling. There was no such problem. The other question was a fake query, which gave the pollsters an idea of how many people had the impulse to answer positively no matter what was asked. The responses from the one percent who responded positively to this question were not included in the final results.

But when the results of the survey came in, Hopkins and Jacobs found the numbers 'outlandish.' The raw statistics suggested that a 'ridiculously high' seven to eight per cent of the

David Jacobs

population had had an abduction. Feeling that these results would be 'politically unacceptable,' Hopkins and Jacobs decided to only look at the answers to the best five questions, those they considered to be the highest indicators for an abduction – seeing unusual lights in a room, having missing time, experiencing flying through the air without knowing why, being paralysed in the presence of strange bedroom figures, or discovering puzzling scars on their body. Unless someone answered positively to at least four of these five questions, they were not considered 'potential abductees.' A person could conceivably answer positively eight of the 11 questions and still not make the cut.

Even on that basis, the Roper Survey came out with some stunning numbers: 119 adults, or two per cent of the survey population, revealed they had had experiences suggestive of a typical UFO abduction. Extrapolating that result to the entire population of the United States translated to a staggering five million abductees across the country. In other words, one out of every 50 Americans seem to have had experiences consistent with what abductees have reported.

CASE HISTORIES

Those numbers confirmed – or exceeded – Hopkins' worst fears. But where was the evidence for this industrial-scale quantity of UFO abductions, I wondered? From their beginning in the 1960s abductions always seemed to be an occasional 'there's one, let's get 'em' sort of thing, as Jacobs put it during an interview I did for *Omni* magazine in 1994. But an exhaustive analysis of 300 published abduction accounts by University of Indiana folklorist Thomas Bullard found that only one in four abduction cases involved more than one person. And of those, about half involved only two people. A case involving seven people was the greatest number of people taken in a single episode and a clear oddity in the published literature. Bullard's analysis clearly failed to confirm the numbers developed by the Roper Survey.

If the Roper Survey was correct, mass abductions had to be taking place somewhere, regularly. But where was the invasion? Was it a total secret? Not quite, as it turns out. As difficult as is it to believe that vast numbers of humans are being abducted in this way on a regular basis, there is, surprisingly enough, anecdotal evidence to support the survey results. Hints of just such a dastardly covert program lie in many an abduction case file, mostly dating from the late 1980s to the present.

One appears in Hopkins' most celebrated case, the Linda Cortile 'Brooklyn Bridge' Abduction, which has been dubbed the 'Case of the Century.' This case, recounted in minute detail by Hopkins in *Witnessed*, involves the abduction by several alien figures of a married mother of two from her 12th floor apartment near the Brooklyn Bridge on November 30 1989. Not only is former United Nations Secretary General Perez de Cuellar said to have witnessed this abduction – and even been abducted himself – but the event apparently involved a mass abduction of humans right from the middle of the City that Never Sleeps – New York City.

On the same date and time as Linda Cortile's abduction, a woman in her thirties claims to have been abducted from her own Manhattan bedroom located further up town in the middle of the night. She consciously remembers being outside that night, moving along the streets involuntarily, and seeing 15 or 20 other women all moving zombie-like toward a UFO on the banks of the East River. At one point she looked down the East River and saw two other UFOs in the sky, one a bright orange object at the southern end of Manhattan, ostensibly the one that abducted Linda Cortile. With claims such as this one, it's not surprising that some critics dubbed the case the 'Manhattan Transfer'. Were the aliens out that night abducting Manhattanites in droves? Anything can happen in New York.

The underlying notion of a massive covert program is also present in the 'Catherine' abduction case, which occurred on March 6, 1991. Driving home after work late that night, Catherine, for some reason, got lost in some woods north of Boston and ended up getting home about 45 minutes later than it should have been. The next day she heard on the news that dozens of people in the northeast had spotted a UFO that night, including a policeman and his wife who had seen an object stop overhead and shine a light on them. But astronomers were convinced the object was a shooting star.

A few weeks later, still troubled about that evening, Catherine decided to contact the Harvard psychiatrist John Mack, who had become interested in abductions through Hopkins. When Mack began probing into the events of that night, Catherine remembered that at one point her car had come to a stop and her body had gone numb. Suddenly her door opened and a long thin hand with only three fingers reached in for her. Catherine was then swooped up in a beam of light toward a huge metallic ship lit up like a Christmas tree. Everyone should be able to see this, she thought.

The alien abductor then led Catherine into an enormous room 'the size of an airplane hangar'. In it she saw rows and rows of tables about five feet apart. A third to half the tables had humans on them and, Catherine noted, 'they're all having things done to them.' She estimated there were between one hundred and two hundred people there. To the left of Catherine's table was a black man with a beard. The beings then began running their fingers down her spine. The examination had begun.

The rest of Catherine's traumatic UFO experience appears in John Mack's controversial book, *Abduction: Human Encounters with Aliens*, and is rather typical of such stories. But one detail in her story stands out – like a Gulliver in Lilliput – that bit about the hundreds of other humans she saw aboard the alien craft that night. And it seems that Catherine is by no means alone among alleged abductees in remembering the presence of large numbers of humans aboard the alien craft.

Just about every contemporary UFO abduction researcher has a case of this kind in his or her case files – Hopkins included, of course. The last time I interviewed him, he was investigating a case that apparently involves a mass abduction of hundreds of people in New York City in the summer of 1993. The story first emerged during one of Hopkins' support group meetings for abductees. One person, Mary, was telling the group about a very vivid dream she had had, though she wasn't sure it was a dream. She recalled being in some sort of huge space filled with people-movers and many, many humans, all completely naked. The aliens were directing them like the physical exam at selective service. And there was a kind of escalator, taking people up to another floor. At that point, two other abductees in the group, Bill and Joan, became very agitated and said, 'Oh gee, I've had a dream just like that.' Hopkins immediately cut off the conversation so that he could explore their experiences individually.

Later, when Hopkins probed into Joan's dream under hypnosis, she recalled the same large space, a strange chart on the wall, and seeing both Mary and Bill there as well, totally naked. Typically, both looked 'out of it' to Joan. Hopkins then asked her what Mary looked like naked. Joan said that Mary was very round-shouldered and that she had a big long scar at the bikini line. Mary, as it happens, is extremely round shouldered and always wears shoulder pads. And she does have a big long scar; it comes from a bladder operation she had as a child. Joan did not see Bill closely, but Hopkins asked her if he had chest hair. Joan said no, and, in fact, he doesn't.

Bill's description of the experience under hypnosis was much the same as

Joan's. He also saw a chart on the wall and though his recollections of it is some-what different than hers, Hopkins is convinced they are describing the same object. Under hypnosis, Mary was less clear about the episode than the other two, but, as Hopkins pointed out, she generally doesn't have the recall that other people tend to have.

The case impresses Hopkins because these three people are not friends in any intimate sense. They only know each other from the support group. 'So here we are again stuck with one of two possibilities,' says Hopkins, a phrase he repeats often. 'Either they have cooked this up as a hoax, in which case you have three virtual sociopaths because there is nothing it for them. Or it happened.'

While Hopkins, an artist at heart, is not the type to quantify such experiences, Jacobs, a 20th century historian with a deep interest in UFOs, is. He feels that these mass abductions occur in half – if not most – of the cases. And as he told me this during our 1994 interview, he recalled a hypnosis session he had completed 'just last night'. The abductee had seen about 15 other humans aboard the craft. His wife and two kids had also been abducted. The man remembered being in line with a group of people who all took their clothes off once they reached a waiting area. And the abductee recalled that directly in front of him was a bald, heavy set, older man who had a mole on his left shoulder. To Jacobs, that kind of detail just smacks of a real – rather than an imagined – event.

This case is typical, notes Jacobs. It shows that the abduction scenario is con-tinuous, like an assembly line. 'They come into a room,' he says, 'and they see 50, 75 or a 100 other people laying on tables and there is a constant stream of people coming in and going out. And we figure it's 24-hours-a-day, 7-days-a-week. This is a very, very big-time widespread program that an enormous amount of energy and efficiency and alien power, so to speak, has been put into.' And all this, he notes, is consistent with Roper Survey results.

HYPOTHESIS TESTING

I wondered if Jacob's words could hold water. The numbers from the Roper Survey were mindboggling and just too large to be real. Robert Durant, a com-mercial pilot with a long interest in UFOs, thought so too, but he actually sat down and worked out 'the numbers'. I found his analysis brilliant. He had decid-ed to put his doubts to the test by quantifying what 'the alien workload' would have to be to match the Roper Survey results. Put simply, and without intending to sound like the set-up for a lightbulb joke, what Durant sought to discover was: how many aliens would be required to perform these millions of abductions?

If these are real physical events carried out systematically by a large work force, reasoned Durant, then the shop floor parameters relevant to a shoe factory or medical facility ought to apply equally well to the case of an alien abduction program carried out on a host planet. But to avoid comparisons with other fanci-ful exercises, like counting the number of dancing angels on the head of a pin, Durant searched the literature for actual data points to plug into his equation. How often is the typical experiencer abducted? Though this varies widely, it seems that 10 times is not an unreasonable number. At what age do abductions begin and cease? Typically they begin around age five and end by age 55. How long did abductions take to accomplish? The periods of missing time reported by abductees range from minutes to days, but most are on the order of two hours. How many aliens does it take to perform an abduction? It's rare, he discovered, for there to be more than about six aliens involved in any one abduction.

Based on that data, Durant came up with some hair-raising numbers about 'the alien work force'. Five million abductees experiencing 10 abductions over a 50-year period yields an astonishing one million abductions per year, or 2,740 per day in the United States alone. If a team of six aliens is required to perform each two-hour abduction, Durant calculated that each team could then perform 12 abductions a day. So to do 2,740 abductions a day, you would need 288 teams, or a total of 1,370 aliens.

Even if you double these figures to account for the fact that most abductions take place at night rather than 24 hours a day, the bottom line, Durant discovered, was that 'about 500 crews, totalling about 3,000 aliens could do the job.' While these figure may appear large, if you compare them with the numbers needed to man naval vessels, says Durant – 5,500 for an aircraft carrier and about 350 for a destroyer – the whole thing begins to look, well, plausible. But this plausibility troubled Durant, who believes in UFOs but not in abductions. It was not his intention to validate the abduction scenario in any way.

Durant's analysis almost had me convinced that the Roper Survey numbers could be real after all. But then Dennis Stacy came along with an equally elegant counter-argument. When Stacy took up Durant's ball, so to speak, and ran with it, the numbers quickly grew way beyond the limits of possibility. Remember, said Stacy, the phenomenon is global. And unless the aliens have a predilection for Americans, Stacy is, of course, correct. It's not one million abductions a year you have to account for, but 22 million a year worldwide. That means you need 11,000 alien crafts, or 66,000 aliens in 11,000 UFOs overhead at any given hour, to carry out the task. And if you take into account the need for support crews, reasonable shifts, and so on, Stacy noted, the numbers, 'keep on growing and growing and growing'.

What possible reason would the aliens have to abduct 200 million people aboard their craft during the past decade? 'And think of the logistics such a fantastic undertaking would involve,' Stacy concluded . 'UFOs would be stacked up over the world's major metropolitan areas, awaiting landing and abduction rights, like so many 747s.'

Stacy is right. The numbers are, as I originally suspected, just too large. But what about the anecdotal reports, those that seemed to support the figures that emerged from the Roper Survey?

The mass abduction cases do hold a lot of promise. They offer the investigator a golden opportunity to cross check the details of the abduction experience from different perspectives. If multiple participants are involved in an abduction, the experience cannot be the product of one individual's fantasy or a hallucination. But there is one problem: in nearly all cases the people involved in the same abduction knew each other previously. The researchers are never really able to prove there had been no collaboration, either consciously or unconsciously, between the alleged abductees. The ideal abduction case would involve two or more people who did not know each other but who gave corroborating details of the same abduction incident to independent investigators. There is no such case.

If abductions are taking place at all, mass abduction cases with dozens, maybe hundreds, or thousands of people involved should provide a critical mass of independent testimony to prove the reality of the phenomenon. And if such mass abduction reports were true, of course, then UFO abduction researchers should have dozens, if not hundreds of abduction reports on the same day. But they do not.

Jacobs attempts to explain away this 'hole' in the data by calling the aliens' secret program 'remarkably efficient and extraordinarily effective.' Besides, the way researchers find out about abductions just makes this secrecy doubly hard to break. Remember, the basic tenant of abduction research – first conceived of by Hopkins back in the late 1970s – is that most people who have had abduction experiences don't really know what has happened to them. Jacobs is convinced that researchers only hear about a tiny fraction of the cases, maybe about .001 percent. People might know that an odd thing has happened here or there, but linking it to a UFO abduction is not something most of them ordinarily do – not until Hopkins came along, anyway.

So as promising as the mass abduction cases first appeared to be, the anecdotal case material does not support the secret invasion scenario either. I don't see any concrete evidence that the entire human race is being unwillingly drafted into some hideous alien genetic experiment to produce alien-human hybrids. Hopkins and I are still friends, I think, despite my scepticism, but our contact is now essentially one of journalist and subject.

From my current vantage point, living in a small rural town about an hour's drive north of New York City, I can still see the glow given off by the vast galaxy of lights that is Manhattan. But what I don't see is a fleet of hovering UFOs, each one patiently awaiting their turn to abduct block by city block of citizens. Somewhere along the way, the numbers have outstripped reality – or vice versa. Life goes on.

RICHARD HALL IS CHAIRMAN OF THE FUND FOR UFO RESEARCH IN WASHINGTON, D.C. DURING THE 1960S HE WAS ASSISTANT DIRECTOR AND FINALLY ACTING DIRECTOR OF THE NATIONAL INVESTIGATIONS COMMITTEE ON AERIAL PHENOMENA (NICAP), AS AN AIDE TO THE LATE MAJOR DONALD E. KEYHOE (USMC, RET.). HALL'S 1988 BOOK UNINVITED GUESTS CONTAINS HIS OVER-ALL VIEWS ON THE UFO SUBJECT. HALL IS A MEMBER OF THE U.S. AUTHORS GUILD AND ALSO HAS WRITTEN A BOOK ABOUT WOMEN WHO FOUGHT IN THE AMERICAN CIVIL WAR. HE HERE PRESENTS A PERSONAL PERSPECTIVE ON THE PAST 50 YEARS OF UFO HISTORY, WHICH HAS BEEN INTIMATELY ENTWINED WITH HIS LIFE.

BRIDGING 50 YEARS OF UFO HISTORY

by Richard Hall

When, on 24 June, 1947, Kenneth Arnold reported seeing strange objects that flew 'like a saucer does when you skip it across water' over the Cascade Mountains of Washington State, I was a teenage schoolboy at The Gilbert School in Winsted, Connecticut. (Fellow alumni include consumer advocate Ralph Nader and author David Halberstam.) Enrolled in the college preparatory Scientific Course, I recall discussing the 1947 sightings with classmates and wondering what these strange objects could be.

After graduating in 1948, I worked for a time in various temporary jobs, including stints as a Connecticut State Forest labourer and fire-fighter. When the Korean War broke out and I was threatened with being drafted into the Army, almost certainly the infantry, I opted to enlist in the fledgling U.S. Air Force and served from 1949 to 1951. Little did I know at that time that the Air Force would later become a major adversary in the quest for information about UFOs.

Some time after leaving the service and returning to my home in Pleasant Valley, Connecticut, I was employed as a clerk at the general store (which included groceries of all kinds, dry goods, two gasoline pumps, and also housed the post office in one corner). One day at work, in 1951 or 1952, a friend and I heard a startling radio newscast:

A flying saucer carrying small beings had crashed somewhere in California. One of the beings had survived the crash and was being rushed to a medical facility to try to keep him alive.

We looked at each other in astonishment and discussed the implications, then waited in vain for follow-up news reports. The story totally vanished; not another word was heard about it! Newspapers next day said nothing, but we were certain of what we had heard on the radio. I no longer recall the exact location in California or any other details.

Being relatively young and naïve, I did not do then what I would have done instantly today: contact the radio station and news service in question and trace the news story. But the recollection is clear, as is another similar event about the same time (probably early in 1952).

The sightings between 1947 and 1952 were not widely reported in newspapers or elsewhere, but I had become aware of some of them while on active Air Force duty stationed at Keesler AFB, Mississippi. Occasionally newswire service reports on UFOs would be posted on the Service Club bulletin board, and the base library had copies of the earliest UFO books, including Donald Keyhoe's *Flying Saucers Are Real* (1950). I remember reading it with some excitement, and finding it to be totally convincing. Apparently we had visitors from space!

The idea languished for a while because news media rarely reported UFO sightings at that time, but the seed was planted. Then on a visit to New York City with friends to see a baseball game in 1951 or 1952 the weather turned foul, the game was cancelled, and we roamed the streets of Manhattan looking for something to do. The brightly flashing marquee of a newsreel theatre caught my attention:

ACTUAL FILMS OF FLYING SAUCERS!

Movietone News in those days presented dramatically narrated news-films. On screen we saw photographs of disc-shaped flying saucers. One, as I recall, showed a dark disc hovering and wobbling in the sky somewhere over Pennsylvania. But the most dramatic film purported to show a crashed disc in a desert environment and a body or bodies on a cot or table under a small field tent. That's about all I can remember.

By now the idea that we apparently had space visitors was very much embedded in my mind, but I passively waited for new developments. Surely the full story would emerge in time. I have had a long wait.

GETTING EDUCATED

In 1954, with a little prodding from my father, I enrolled in the College of Arts and Sciences at Tulane University, New Orleans, Louisiana. My tuition was partly paid for by the GI Bill (a Government program for veterans) and partly by scholarship money. During this time period I became aware of UFO research being done by Len Stringfield in Cincinnati and Civilian Saucer Intelligence of New York (Ted Bloecher, Isabel Davis, and Lex Mebane). As I worked my way through college, I corresponded with these UFO research pioneers. (Ted and Isabel later joined me at NICAP as staff members in 1966.)

About the same time, the Aerial Phenomena Research Organization (APRO) was prominent, and I wrote to them inquiring about membership and newsletter information. When the APRO membership application required that I swear that I was not a Communist, I lost all interest. The 1950s was the height of anti-communist hysteria in the U.S., incited by Senator Joe McCarthy and the notorious House Unamerican Activities Committee, during which right-wing ideologues took any disagreement with their narrow views as being akin to treason.

Meanwhile, I decided to major in mathematics with a minor in philosophy, and was required to work part-time in the mathematics department in exchange for a scholarship. One of my duties was to open and distribute the mail to the maths professors. One day in 1956 a letter came that changed my life. It was an invitation to an astronomer-maths professor to join something called the National Investigations Committee on Aerial Phenomena (NICAP) in Washington, D.C. NICAP proposed to mount a scientific investigation of UFOs and was seeking scientific support. It was signed by Donald E. Keyhoe.

Finding this very exciting, I jotted down NICAP's address and wrote to Major Keyhoe. He responded and welcomed my offer of help with UFO sightings and information in Louisiana. Soon I became one of the early members of NICAP, faithfully forwarding all newspaper stories and similar information to headquarters in Washington, D.C.

During my senior year in November 1957 the first major UFO sighting wave since 1952 began, coinciding with the launch of the dog-carrying satellite Sputnik II by the Soviet Union on 2 November. Sightings were reported widely, with a concentration in Texas and New Mexico.

On 5 November, continuing the southern U.S. pattern, the crew of the U.S. Coast Guard Cutter *Sebago* in the Gulf of Mexico off New Orleans reported seeing a brilliant flying object and tracking it on radar at 5.10a.m. About 10 minutes later, an airman at Keesler AFB, Mississippi (where I had been stationed six years previously), reported seeing an elliptical object approaching from south to north (off the Gulf). The UFO accelerated rapidly and disappeared into clouds. The Air Force base was located some 80 miles east of New Orleans along the Gulf Coast.

Near the culmination of my college career I became a novice UFO investigator, making phone calls and writing letters to obtain witness reports and official information, all of which was forwarded to NICAP. Meanwhile, the wave continued through the end of the month, peaking in mid-month, resulting in well over a hundred credible cases from all over the country. Several good reports also came from Argentina and Brazil.

My fascination with UFOs at this time began interfering with my studies, and mathematics now seemed boring. At the last minute I switched my major course of studies to philosophy, retaining a minor in mathematics. My new focus was on logic and scientific method, which I saw as prerequisites for studying UFOs. This delayed my graduation while I attended night school to catch up on required philosophy courses.

Upon graduation from Tulane in June 1958 I quickly moved to Washington, D.C., hoping to find work at NICAP. But they had no money to offer so I bided my time. I applied for a Federal civil service job as well as for various journalism positions, meanwhile volunteering some time at NICAP. Eventually, as a former Air Force enlisted man, I received a job offer to be a writer-reporter for *Air Force Times*. When I told Major Keyhoe, he immediately made a counter offer: come to work for me at half-time salary, and as soon as we can afford it I will hire you full-time. Without much hesitation I made the fateful decision to follow my heart.

The general history of NICAP is well known, and I have reported my experiences there in some detail elsewhere. Up until this point UFOs had manifested themselves by fits and starts. Now, to my chagrin, they decided to go into hiding altogether. The period of 1958-1963 has to rank as the darkest of UFO 'Dark Ages.' Little or nothing about UFOs was reported by the news media, although scattered (but often significant) sightings were being made. NICAP struggled along trying to survive with little financial support and a staff of one (me). I had a few part-time volunteers as helpers.

Finally, Major Keyhoe decided that we had to lay out the best case for UFOs in a systematic and credible way in order to gain the support we needed. He outlined a report that would draw on the information in our files and asked me to compile it. In this pre-computer age we laboured for several years with yellow pads and typewriters, eventually producing *The UFO Evidence*, a 200,000-word documentary report. Though there had been no waves of sightings since 1957, many individual reports were very impressive. Most people were totally unaware of the cumulative evidence, especially of the overall patterns of UFO appearance and performance.

FATE TAKES A HAND

The official publication date of *The UFO Evidence* was May 1964, but in fact it was delayed at the printers and did not actually see the light of day until July. Meanwhile, the aliens (or the 'fates') decided to intervene on our side. On 24 April, 1964, in Socorro, New Mexico, an elliptical UFO was observed on the ground by Officer Lonnie Zamora, with two small beings standing nearby. This landmark case almost singlehandedly helped break through the pervasive scepticism and put UFOs on the cultural map.

By the time we received the printed copies of *The UFO Evidence* and began distributing them to every member of the U.S. Congress and to major news media, the Socorro case had captured world attention and a flurry of other sightings was being reported. As a result, *The UFO Evidence* received extraordinary news media coverage, including not only major U.S. newspapers coverage, but also stories in the London *Times*, German newspapers, and around the world. Here was NICAP, the upstart organisation, challenging the U.S. Government about UFOs, and backing it up with impressive documentation.

The extended UFO sighting wave from early 1964 into 1968 remains to this day the most intensive and widespread in the history of UFOs. The 1966 sightings in the U.S. led to an unprecedented level of news media reporting, hearings in the Congress, and pressure for a thorough review of the Air Force Project Blue Book UFO investigation.

At NICAP we were under siege – both by UFO reports and by major news media clamouring for information. After many years of struggling for attention to UFOs, we were suddenly overwhelmed; from famine to feast with no middle ground. This period of UFO history is well documented.

Rep. Gerald Ford of Michigan, then Republican leader in the House of Representatives, took a personal interest in the 1966 sightings, several of which had occurred in his home state of Michigan, and this almost guaranteed political action. To satisfy the public demand voiced by the Congress the Air Force, through its Office of Scientific Research, let a contract to the University of Colorado in Boulder for an outside appraisal of the UFO mystery. A respected scientist, Dr. Edward Condon, was selected to lead the program.

The study became known as the Colorado UFO Project (or Condon Committee). Major Keyhoe and I were invited to address the assembled Colorado scientists in November 1966, and I was invited back for several days as a consultant the following spring. My assigned task was to recommend cases to include in a case book of extremely puzzling UFO reports that would be circulated as a challenge to scientists. Like many other aspects of the Colorado project at the time, this promising initiative was never completed.

Edward Condon

From the very beginning Dr. Condon's indiscretions in public talks revealed a strong negative bias and undermined the credibility of the project. After nearly three years Condon succeeded only in fuelling the fires of controversy rather than resolving anything through application of scientific methods.

A recent review by Dr. Michael Swords of Colorado Project documents and the files of key participants has resulted in a damning expose of the internal workings of the project and the extreme biases of some of the scientists. The Air Force told project leaders well in advance of any detailed study that they basically desired to be rid of the UFO problem. It was a public relations headache.

Another thread of the story began in the early 1960s when a prominent scientist at the University of Arizona, Tucson, casually began looking into UFO reports. Dr. James E. McDonald found enough intriguing local sightings to pique his curiosity. He decided to devote some time to a more intensive look at UFOs, and inevitably our paths crossed. By the time of the 1964-1968 wave, we had become close friends and were in constant touch, sharing information. His whirlwind investigation led him to conclude that UFOs were 'the greatest scientific mystery of our times.'

McDonald became a gadfly to the Colorado project, and when its badly flawed study, released in 1969, sought to write off UFOs as unworthy of further scientific investigation, he and Dr. J. Allen Hynek led the counter-attack. The Condon Report also gave the Air Force the excuse it had sought to terminate Project Blue Book and to get out of the UFO business.

Hynek, former scientific consultant to the US Air Force on UFOs, began speaking out publicly, though he had long been working quietly to encourage scientific investigation of UFOs. Between 1967 and his death in 1971, McDonald sought to offset the Condon Report by addressing chapters of the American Institute for Aeronautics and Astronautics (AIAA) all over the country (as part of its Distinguished Lecturer series); the National Aeronautics and Space Administration; aerospace companies; various offices of the Department of Defense; military bases all over the country; and other Government and scientific agencies.

In 1969 both Hynek and McDonald participated in a symposium on UFOs held by the prestigious (and sceptical) American Association for the Advancement of Science, both men urging serious attention to UFO reports. A special UFO subcommittee of the AIAA, then an influential trade association for aerospace and aviation engineers, also added its criticism. Their report dissented from the main findings of the Condon Report, arguing that it was 'unacceptable' to simply ignore and fail to study the many impressive unexplained cases 'on the basis of premature conclusions.'

THE POST-CONDON ERA

This 'thin red line' of dissenters, however, failed to make many converts. Sightings and public interest tapered off and a new UFO Dark Age ensued. After McDonald's untimely death in 1971 I dropped out for a while, since the outlook for progress was so poor. Without McDonald's vigorous, knowledgeable approach I felt that we would get nowhere, and I became very pessimistic about the future of ufology.

NICAP, having over-extended itself trying to encourage a scientific study, gradually faded into insignificance, though for a few years Stuart Nixon and Jack

Acuff managed to keep it alive and did some good work. Nevertheless, NICAP no longer had its former clout with news media and Government agencies; its days were numbered.

The Mutual UFO Network (MUFON), formed in May 1969 by Walter H. Andrus, Jr., became the leading American UFO organization. Many former key personnel of NICAP became active in MUFON. One of them, the late Idabel Epperson who headed NICAP's chapter in Los Angeles, California, persuaded me to join MUFON and to resume an active role. For many years I served MUFON in one capacity or another.

After another five-year gap in publicised sightings, the 1973 UFO sighting wave (mostly in the U.S. and southern Europe) strongly revived public and official interest in UFOs, at least for a while. In that year, Dr. Hynek founded the Center for UFO Studies. His book *The UFO Experience* had been published in 1972. About this time another prominent scientist appeared on the scene and offered his rebuttal of the Condon Report: Dr. Peter Sturrock of the Stanford Institute for Plasma Research (SIPR), Stanford University, California.

Sturrock is a British-born and educated astrophysicist who had worked in radar and atomic energy research in England. Also associated with the AIAA, the American Astronomical Society, and the American Physical Society, Sturrock published his rebuttal as an SIPR document. He also advocated further scientific study of UFOs.

In 1977, with interest elsewhere again going underground, the Groupe d'Etude des Phenomenes Aerospatiaux Non-Identifies (GEPAN) was organised under the auspices of the French Government as part of the French National Center for Space Studies. Dr. Claude Poher, who was appointed head of the project, had become interested in UFOs in 1969 after meeting Dr. Hynek and reading the Condon Report. GEPAN has contributed several carefully investigated, unexplained UFO cases to the literature. Also, the unique cooperation between Government scientists and the Gendarmerie in France has set a standard unequalled elsewhere.

Following still another five-year gap after 1973, UFOs once again manifested as an international sighting wave in 1978, with concentrations in Australia-New Zealand and the Arab countries. In Kuwait, a domed disc landed near an oil pumping station, causing an electromagnetic failure and stimulating a high-level investigation. At the end of the year, radar-visual sightings over New Zealand, accompanied by motion picture films, caused a sensation.

Sometime during the 1970s a new and troubling pattern began to emerge. In 1961 Barney and Betty Hill had reported their roadside encounter to NICAP and I had referred them to Walter Webb for investigation. John Fuller, author of *The Interrupted Journey*, later got involved. Eventually the abduction story unfolded. The 1957 Villas Boas on-board encounter case also was circulating through the UFO community. No one knew quite what to make of these seemingly isolated early abduction reports. By the 1980s, however, hundreds of abduction reports had emerged. For better or for worse, the abduction mystery has dominated the subject ever since.

About the same time, the controversy of 'crashed saucers' re-emerged, largely revived by the intrepid reporting of Leonard H. Stringfield. Almost all serious researchers in the US had written off 'crashed saucers' as hoaxes and wild stories, mainly due to the hoax perpetrated on author Frank Scully about an alleged crash in New Mexico. Now, serious witnesses began to come forth to lend new credence to the stories.

In addition to these startling developments (what might be termed the 'weirding' of ufology), sighting waves seem to have all but ceased in the 1980s. Late in 1989 outbreaks of sightings were reported in Russia, Belgium, and Canada, some of which received international publicity. Nothing else since 1978 would qualify as a well-defined UFO sighting wave, though many countries have had flurries of sightings.

During the 1980s another staple of the modern UFO mystery suddenly became very scarce: the Daylight Disc. For many years, the large majority of UFO sightings have been lights observed at night. The entire character of the UFO phenomenon, therefore, was transformed during the decades of the 1970s and 1980s. What originally seemed to be a rather straightforward mystery involving unorthodox craft flying through the skies, very likely visitors from another planet, became exceedingly complex and far more baffling.

It is tempting to speculate that a correlation exists between the emergence of abductions and the decrease of clear-cut sightings, perhaps signalling a new phase of alien activities. This may be true, but there is no compelling evidence to support such a notion. Besides, we don't know for sure that we really are dealing with aliens.

STATE OF UFOLOGY

In the 50 years I have observed the phenomenon and participated in study of it, we have made great strides in data gathering. In the words of the late J. Allen Hynek, we truly have 'an embarrassment of riches.' Now we need to do a much better job of sifting through it, developing and testing meaningful hypotheses.

For the first 30 years or so, the extraterrestrial (E-T) hypothesis dominated. Since then it has gone in and out of favour. When no absolute proof was forthcoming, some people looked elsewhere for answers. Two broad alternative explanations have been propounded: a socio-psychological origin for the reports or manipulation of humans by (unspecified) external forces. These notions are vague, and do not adequately account for the strongly consistent testimony describing craft and beings. Nor are they falsifiable (testable by scientific methods). Application of scientific instruments could, in principle, test the E-T visitation hypothesis.

The most confounding factor has been the increasing 'strangeness' (even 'weirdness') of UFO report content. Abduction reports contain many seemingly absurd features, but we have no way of knowing whether the 'absurdity' factor signals a problem in the data or merely our lack of a framework for understanding. Our science may be incomplete in some fundamental ways. Surely our scientific understanding of the physical universe and of cosmological questions is in great turmoil.

UFOs remain an intriguing mystery fraught with great significance for the human race. In my estimation, the E-T hypothesis still has the best potential. As I have previously stated, by E-T I mean 'beings from elsewhere.' Instead of coming from another planet in space, they may originate in some realm of existence presently unknown to us (a parallel universe or another dimension), but for all practical purposes they are not from 'here' as we now understand that term. The seemingly magical behaviour they display may simply be due to our lack of understanding of a highly advanced technology. Scientists of previous centuries would have considered a transistor radio to be magic.

We have obtained lots of interesting data pointing to an unexplained phenomenon. Meanwhile, recent scientific findings about planetary systems within reasonable distances of the earth, and apparent past microbiological life on Mars, have rekindled interest in the question of intelligent life elsewhere. As we press on with our inquiries, we need to concentrate on both empirical and theoretical studies. We need to gather and analyse better evidence of all kinds. Although we may currently lack the theoretical framework to fully explain what is going on, advances in physics (the nature of matter), astrophysics, and cosmology may well close the gap.

At the same time, it is imperative that we weed out crackpots, opportunists, and New Age airheads who muddy the UFO waters. Their antics frighten off rational people whose support and skills are vitally needed for pursuing the truth. We need to practice more science, and less imagination; more critical thinking, and less wild speculation. In respect to shoddy reasoning and wishful thinking, little has changed in 50 years.

Despite all the roadblocks we are making great strides in ufological inquiry and we are, I think, winning the battle for human minds. The younger generations and the majority of the population at large, increasingly accept UFOs as a reality. UFOs have persisted for 50 years; now science needs to adjust and to address the problem forthrightly.

It may be, as Thomas Kuhn suggested in his discerning book analysing scientific revolutions, that the present scientific paradigm (tending to exclude UFOs) may only be replaced when the older, closed-minded scientists who embrace it begin dying off and younger scientists adjust to new realities. That process has begun.

A ufological 'harmonic convergence' may be impending in the late 20th Century; perhaps continued UFO events, empirical study, the passage of time, new scientific theories and new technologies will combine to give us the answers we all seek. Since 1904, after all, our aerial technology has advanced from the crude biplane of the Wright Brothers to supersonic aircraft and sophisticated spacecraft.

So far in my lifetime I have witnessed the advent of jet aircraft, transistors, television, personal computers, telecommunication and remote observation satellites, and the first tentative explorations of space outside the earth. At the rate science and technology progress, the day may not be too far off when we discover and possibly communicate with intelligent extraterrestrial life.

The human ego insists that we must be the discoverers. The truth may well be that others have discovered us first. That is the fundamental implication of the E-T hypothesis. If I read the situation correctly, we may have an answer soon.

SOVIET UFOLOGY
IN ITS HUMAN DIMENSIONS

by Vladimir V. Rubtsov, PhD

A MEMORY

On 29 February 1968 I read, as always, the leading daily of the Communist Party of the Soviet Union – *Pravda*. To my surprise, in this issue there appeared an article on the UFO problem, entitled '"Flying Saucers" Again?' signed by three scientists. Indignantly condemning 'absurd, long-buried gossip about secret excursions of Martians or Venusians to our planet', the article concluded, 'All objects flying over the territory of our country are identified either by scientists, or by the people responsible for security of our Motherland. If "unidentified flying objects" really existed, scientists would be first to obtain all information on them and investigate their nature.'

This was bad news, though not unexpected. A few months earlier, in October 1967, there had been formed in Moscow the first Soviet public organization designed to collect and analyse UFO reports: the UFO Department of the All-Union Space-Exploration Committee of the USSR Voluntary Society of Support to the Army, Aviation & Navy. It embraced more than two hundred scientists, engineers, military, journalists, etc. Its elected head was Major-General P. A. Stolyarov, his Deputy for Science was Dr. F. Y. Zigel. On 10 November they spoke on Central TV about the new organization and invited UFO observers to send in reports.

Such reports did arrive and were used by Zigel to prepare the first volume of the typewritten collection *UFO Observations in the USSR*. But in the meantime backstairs forces were at work, and in November the short-lived UFO Department was disbanded. Sometime later the Branch of General & Applied Physics of the USSR Academy of Sciences passed a resolution against UFO

Trail left by a Soviet rocket launch. Compare with descriptions of the glowing 'jellyfish' seen over Petrozavodsk in 1977

research in the Soviet Union.

Until the Party authorities stated their opinion on this subject, those who believed that UFOs were a legitimate subject for study could feel the game was not wholly lost. Surely, we argued, the matter could be thrashed out in open debate? It was not to be. The article I read in *Pravda* that morning crushed our naive hopes.

Two of its authors were really prominent astronomers, even if complete ignoramuses so far as the UFO problem was concerned. But it wasn't their names or their qualifications which carried weight: it was the voice of Authority, informing every Soviet citizen that the so-called 'flying saucers' would from now on be considered as nonexistent.

Replying to the letter I wrote him immediately I read the article, Dr Zigel wrote: 'This article expresses the *official* point of view that closes the UFO problem for many years to come. If you wish, you can continue some microactivities in this field. As for me, I shall move on to different works.'

Well, Zigel was not being wholly truthful. True, he did busy himself with other activities – lecturing, popularising astronomy, studying the Tunguska problem and so forth. But UFOs remained his favourite topic until his death in 1988. That first volume of *UFO Observations in the USSR* was followed by six more, all in Samizdat (that is, clandestine) publication. On a copy of the second volume that he kindly gave me there is a touching inscription: 'Please read with care: the number of copies of this work is four!' Since these typewritten Samizdat publications were officially considered as manuscripts, they were – if not too 'anti-Soviet' – generally tolerated by the authorities.

It so happened that I witnessed and participated in the whole process of the rise, existence, and collapse of that unique phenomenon: Soviet ufology. My 1966 paper was the first Soviet publication to treat the UFO problem as a serious one, and my 1991 book was to prove the first and only Soviet academic monograph taking this approach.

UFOS BEFORE UFOLOGY

But of course, in Russia as everywhere else, there were UFOs before there was such a thing as ufology. Even from before 1900 there were reports many of which are of interest. Between 1900 and the Revolution of 1917, many witnesses observed strange lights in the sky, as well as the classic 'mystery planes' and 'phantom airships'. During the following period, from 1917 to the death of Stalin in 1953, our knowledge is very poor. Such UFO reports as exist are so dispersed in official or academic archives that only by accident are they retrieved. Such reports were generally made by officials; the man in the street thought it prudent to keep silent even when seeing an extraordinary phenomenon.

The reports we possess include some very interesting descriptions of strange crescent-shaped objects which had been observed long before the era of rocket launching.

Thus, in July 1923 a 'flying moon' was seen during two or three minutes by a steamboat mechanic on the Vyatka river, not far from the village of Sosnovka: 'It resembled the moon in shape and brightness... when it vanished behind a forest, we decided it was a devil'. Interestingly, 25 years later, the *kolkhozniks* (collective farmers) living in the villages near Suzdal interpreted in similar fashion the nature of a strange object that periodically appeared in their locality, described by more than one witness as resembling a motor-car headlamp. To these people, steeped in old Russian superstition, it was a 'Fiery Serpent' embodying the soul of a person who had recently passed away.

UFOs were observed from time to time during World War II. On 26 August 1943, platoon commander Shalaginov was at the Kursk Bulge, scene of one of the greatest battles of the war. At about 9.30a.m. he left his observation post and saw 'a crescent-shaped object' which he compared to a dolphin, and which gave the impression it was breathing. 'The sight was very impressive against the background of deafening artillery and shell-bursts'.

Naturally enough, at the time such sightings were interpreted as secret fighting craft of the belligerents. A. I. Klimenko, who observed a low-altitude UFO in August 1942 near Krasnodar, did not doubt that he was seeing a secret Soviet aircraft. As he recalled some 25 years later, 'Thanks to this sighting, I became fully convinced of our final victory!'

When the UFO phenomenon burst in the west, first with the Swedish rockets of 1946, then with the American sightings of 1947 and later, the Soviet attitude was one of mockery. At a solemn meeting celebrating the 35th anniversary of the Revolution, in November 1952, M G Pervukhin caused great amusement with his references to American 'flying saucers' and 'green fire balls'. Taking their cue from this semi-official pronouncement, Russians seemed to take little interest in the UFO phenomenon in the 1950s. Yet even then there were enthusiasts, notably Dr. Y. A. Fomin, who started to collect UFO information on UFOs and gave lectures on the topic.

The witness reports from that time are especially valuable. The position of the Soviet officials was unequivocal: Soviet people never see any mysterious objects in the sky, but even when they sometimes do, specialists can always convincingly account for the events. The 'saucers' were persistently ridiculed in the popular media though in stereotyped formulae and without any attempt to analyse and explain the reports.

Not surprisingly, many UFO observations were never reported by their witnesses. On the other hand, those reports that did reach researchers were uncontaminated: since Soviet witnesses, unlike those in other countries, had no idea how UFOs were 'supposed' to behave, they did not adapt their reports to match accepted models.

Not that everyone in the USSR was ignorant about UFOs; but information was still confined to official agencies. Thus, the chief navigator of Polar Aviation of the USSR, V. I. Akkuratov, mentions a correspondence with the Chief Administration of the North Sea Route concerning observations, in August of 1950, of a disk-like object, which appeared over the settlement of Nizhnie Kresty for three days running. Six years later this same man, piloting a TU-4, was carrying out ice reconnaissance near Greenland. He recalls: 'We came out of some cloud, and unexpectedly noticed a strange flying vehicle moving to the left of us, parallel to our course: it looked like a large lens, pearl-coloured, its edges waving. Knowing of the American air bases in northern Greenland, at first we thought it must be an American aircraft of unknown design. With the intention of avoiding it, we went back into cloud. Forty minutes later, we unexpectedly came out into clear sky and saw on the left the same vehicle. We decided to examine it closely and swiftly swerved to approach it. The strange vehicle also turned and moved in a course parallel to ours at the same speed. After 15 or 18 minutes of flight it left us behind and climbed, eventually disappearing into the blue. We saw no aerials, superstructures, wings or windows on the disc. Neither did we observe exhaust gas or a condensation trail, and its speed, when it went away, was so high that it seemed supernatural.'

RISES AND FALLS OF THE UFO TIDE

Despite such observations, the official view remained unshakeable. Official response to witnesses, too, was far from encouraging. The Moscow Planetarium had a standard reply letter, signed by V. A. Bronshten, a scientific consultant:

DEAR COMRADE,
THE PHENOMENON YOU OBSERVED WAS, IN ALL PROBABILITY, DUE TO AN EXPERIMENT THAT WAS CONDUCTED TO MEASURE THE DENSITY OF THE ATMOSPHERE AT HIGH ALTITUDES WITH THE AID OF A SODIUM CLOUD (LIKE THOSE FORMED IN THE FLIGHT OF SPACE ROCKETS).

This blanket explanation outdoes even the optical UFO theory proposed by

Donald Menzel!

In January 1961, *Pravda* published an interview with Academician L. A. Artsimovich, who denied the existence of the 'so-called flying saucers' 'All talk on this issue. . . stems from the same source, namely unscrupulous and antiscientific information contained in lectures made in Moscow by some irresponsible persons. These reports tell fantastic tales borrowed mainly from the American press, dating from a time when flying tableware was the main sensation in the United States... Are there any new facts to make us admit the existence of all this crockery hovering over our heads? No, there are none. The saucers and other material objects which are said to appear in the sky exist only as reflections on water or rainbows exist, as the play of light in the atmosphere. All the rest is either self-deception or falsification'.

To what extent the establishment itself believed in the universal application of this Menzel-like theory is another matter, but it suited their purpose to believe. The 'irresponsible' Dr Fomin was expelled from the Society for Propagation of Political and Scientific Knowledge, and the Foreign Literature Publishers promptly issued a Russian translation of Menzel's book, with a new introduction by the author who was enthusiastic about the Soviet attitude to the UFO problem.

So, for the space of some five years, amateur ufology disappeared from the Soviet scene. Then in April 1967 the tide turned, with an article 'UFOs – What are they?' by the irrepressible Dr Zigel, published in the popular magazine *Smena*. It was followed during the next five to six months by articles in various journals and newspapers, including an important paper by Jacques Vallee and Alexander Kazantsev; their overall sales swiftly reached several millions.

The Soviet people were little by little freeing themselves from the old fear of the totalitarian state; a new generation was rising for which Stalin and his mass repressions were a remote past, Khrushchev with his 'thaw' a recent past, and Brezhnev with his socialism with a human-like face the not very terrible (and rather dull) present. Articles about UFOs made a sharp contrast with the tedium of everyday publications in official popular media, and evoked great interest. Whether or not readers were asked to send their own UFO observations, they usually did so, though these reports were rarely published.

On 17 May 1967, at 10.08 p.m., I myself happened to witness of a UFO sighting over Kharkov. The object was a small round body (a disk, or a ball), some four angular minutes in diameter, shining with bright white light and having a long orange tail. It rose in the western sky, traversed its southern part and disappeared approximately to the east.

The flight duration did not exceed 20 seconds. It is quite conceivable that I and other witnesses in Kharkov saw a satellite or a missile warhead reentering the atmosphere, but there was one strange feature: the outer appearance of the object (with its tail) remained the same throughout the observation. It seemed to me not so much like a real phenomenon, but as a moving picture in a planetarium.

In the late 1970s, ten years after Zigel made his collection of reports, it was subjected to analysis by three Soviet scientists – L. M. Gindilis, D. A. Men'kov, and I. G. Petrovskaya. They concluded that for one third of these reports there was no conventional explanation such as optical atmospheric phenomena or aerospace testings. Nonetheless, some two thirds of the UFO reports in the work (mainly dated from 1967) seemed to display the latter. It is important to realise that the Soviet ban on public UFO study, though in part attributable to the self-importance of the scientific establishment, was chiefly inspired by political/military considerations. In the race for strategic parity with the USA, flying saucers may not have been not the biggest thing to be sacrificed, but they were certainly one of them.

The censorship (Glavlit) was ordered to prevent any publications on the UFO problem, except those which said there was no problem. Even the term 'unidentified flying objects' was prohibited. Organised research ceased.

UNDERGROUND

The publication of the Condon Report in America was greeted by rapturous articles in the Soviet press. In the late 1960s/early 1970s the government took a leaf out of the Americans' book by instructing official bodies responsible for exploring the atmosphere and space to record and investigate UFO events in order to identify these objects, but in practice these instructions were not very effective.

As for the independent ufologists, they virtually went underground. True, as far as I know, nobody was ever imprisoned for his or her ufological activities. It was permissible to study the UFO problem, individually or even in informal groups. One could, using personal contacts in newspapers, popular-science journals, astronomical observatories, etc., acquaint himself with current UFO reports that were being sent to these bodies by chance observers. The streamlet of such reports did not dry up completely, although it swiftly became fairly thin. From time to time some especially dumbfounded UFO witnesses tried to contact amateur ufologists directly and reported valuable information. Under these conditions the reports received cannot be regarded as representative, though it remained true that they were 'clean' of distorting influences by contrast with countries where there was more reported activity. The numbers were small – in the late 1960s throughout the entire Soviet Union there were no more than 25-30 people actively engaged in UFO studies. In general, they knew each other quite well, exchanging letters and meeting from time to time personally. They collected UFO reports, studied the most interesting cases and typed their reports for circulation within the same small community. Their families were hardly especially happy about these time- and money-consuming activities conducted for the sake of posterity, but on a local scale at least the disinterested enthusiasm of the ufologists was infectious.

Since the immediate prospects for any wider ufological studies looked dim, some brave researchers turned their eyes to the west. Our view of worldwide ufology was sadly incomplete. There were some books in the Lenin Library and the Library of Foreign Literature (both in Moscow), but no ufological journals and therefore no way of keeping abreast of current news. Y. A. Fomin and A. A. Tikhonov were the first Soviet UFO enthusiasts who ventured to communicate with western ufologists – first, with the *Flying Saucer Review* team and the French group GEPAN. After them, some other researchers took the same risks, and lo! this proved permissible! Western ufologists rendered their Soviet colleagues very substantial help in obtaining the literature they needed, though there remained the problem that, for a Soviet citizen, anything which appeared in print was regarded as true, with the result that some rather strange material was accepted as gospel.

One thing which hampered Soviet ufologists was something they shared with their western colleagues: the lack of access to confidential data about space and military tests. Like their British and American opposite numbers, they were liable to mistake rocket launchings and re-entries for genuine UFOs. Nevertheless to scrutinise Dr Zigel's seven-volume collection of UFO reports is to recognise that this ore is rich in gold. Despite the unfavourable climate in which they worked, the underground ufologists maintained remarkably high intellectual and professional standards.

In 1975, Dr Zigel came close to securing the setting up of an official body to study the UFO phenomenon, but his plans came to nothing when controversy once again broke out as to whether they were a legitimate area for scientific study. Soviet ufologists had to return again to their customary low-profile activities. However, the fact that officialdom had come so close to recognising the existence of the problem meant that, unlike in 1968, there was no withdrawal of researchers from this field. On the contrary, the informal UFO study group, led by Zigel, was more active than ever. Dr. L. M. Gindilis and his colleagues published their statistical analysis of a set of Soviet UFO reports. Although, contrary to James Oberg's opinion, this work was neither sponsored, nor inspired by any official agency, it represented a leap forward in scientific UFO studies. An informal study group was created in Leningrad, and in Gorky (now once again Nizhniy Novgorod) some scientists evinced their interest in the problem. Enthusiasts in the provinces did valuable work in the field: though lacking in training and experience, these 'grass-root ufologists' made a valuable contribution to the progress of Soviet ufology.

From time to time important UFO cases came to light by pure chance. For instance, staying with friends in Kislovodsk, I met a Mrs E. Loznaya, who told me, not without hesitation, about her observation of a flying 'Man In Black'. The event took place in the winter of 1936 in the Oktyabriskiy sovkhoz in Kazakhstan, when the witness was 15. Needless to say, her knowledge of ufology was precisely zero; she did not even read popular-science journals. Indeed, at that time I myself was equally unaware of similar observations here or abroad.

Since the term UFO did not appear in the text, and 'flying men in black' were not banned by the authorities, the censors weren't concerned with this anomaly and I was able to arrange for her story to be published. Consequently, a few million Soviet people were able to read the following account:

Early in the morning I went to school by a lonely country road. It was already light, although the sun had not risen. The weather was fine and it was freezing. Suddenly I caught sight of a dark point moving rapidly in the sky to my left. It came closer, grew larger, and in a matter of seconds I saw a man-like figure dressed in black and seen in profile.

This 'man' was, to my mind, of medium height; his black clothes covered him completely, like overalls. His head (more exactly, something like a helmet) and massive ('square') arms tightly fixed to his body were perfectly visible. I saw no hands and feet. I could see behind his back an oval thing like a rucksack.

Looking with fright at the 'flying man' I noticed suddenly that he had changed his course and was now flying towards me. When he turned I saw his right arm was slightly bent at the elbow. Now I saw him full face, but I could not discern his features for in place of a face there was just an entirely black surface.

At that instant I heard an increasing rumble as if it was a flying mechanism and not a living man. By now the distance between us had shortened to about 40 metres. My numb terror had passed and I to look for somewhere to hide, but there was none on the snow-covered steppe. I then turned again towards the 'flying man' and... saw nobody. Maybe he had made an abrupt change in his course, or maybe he had dived in a snowdrift... but the next moment I was running towards my home. This sighting lasted only a minute, but I have remembered it all these years.'

Readers were invited to submit their own remarkable experiences. I read and answered these letters, amazed at their number and quality. Even if the public attitude to the UFO problem was currently negative, following the official line, this was certainly not true of those who had experiences of their own: the individual who had an extraordinary encounter would never again accept the official dogma that the UFO phenomenon was a myth created by the sensation-seeking western mass media.

The letters included descriptions of conventional UFOs, as well as flying humanoids and other anomalies. One example from many: a student from Perm wrote on 26 October 1976 that the previous day, taking a path through a forest meadow, he had met a giant 'man', some three metres tall. The figure was dressed in something like a diving suit, although there was no river or lake within 5 km. Smiling and repeating '*drugo, drugo*' (meaning friend), he held out a thick bundle of banknotes! The student grabbed one: it was a 50-rouble note (not a small amount twenty years ago). After that the figure suddenly rushed to the forest, and the astonished student fled to the village. His letter was probably written in the heat of the moment, for he never responded to my subsequent letters. (Perhaps he was put off by the fact that I asked him to preserve the note for laboratory studies!)

Such local cases are valuable to the researcher, but of course they made no impact on public opinion, less still on official opinion. To change that situation, a large-scale UFO event was needed. And finally such an event did in fact occur!

A TURNING POINT

In the early morning of 20 September 1977, the residents of the comparatively big city of Petrozavodsk (capital of the Karelian Autonomous Republic) saw a luminescent jellyfish appearing in the dark sky and throwing 'a multitude of thinnest ray spurts' over the city. Thanks to careless censorship, the incident was reported by *Pravda* and other newspapers. It raised a lot of questions within the Soviet Union and beyond. Today we know that the 'Petrozavodsk phenomenon' occurred almost (but only *almost*) simultaneously with the launching of the 'Cosmos-955' satellite from Plesetsk launching site. Though it had its anomalous features, what was important about the incident was that it was the stone which triggered an avalanche.

Following the event, a special project was initiated at the Institute of Terrestrial Magnetism, Ionosphere & Radio Wave Propagation of the USSR Academy of Sciences (IZMIRAN) to investigate the physical nature of anomalous atmospheric phenomena. Despite its methodological limitations, this was the first UFO-related project to be carried out by the Academy. It marked the beginning of open professional studies into the UFO problem in our country. An Expert Group on Anomalous Atmospheric Phenomena followed: the military became more attentive to 'anomalous phenomena'. In particular, a MoD research institute, located in Mytishchi (near Moscow) began to collect UFO reports and foreign ufological literature. The latter task was solved quite simply: UFOs were included in the lists of forbidden subjects issued by Glavlit, consequently ufological books and periodicals sent from the West were confiscated. At a later date, I found more than a hundred English-language UFO titles listed by the Russian State Library (formerly Lenin Library): alas, I did not find there my copy of Story's *The Encyclopedia of UFOs* that had been kindly sent to me from England by the late W. Raymond Drake. Probably, it is still in Mytishchi.

Like their colleagues in France and elsewhere, amateur ufologists tried to cooperate with the Mytishchi institute, but it was a one-way co-operation. The institute officials accepted readily any UFO reports, photographs, etc., but never returned them, nor gave any data in exchange.

By the early 1980s, the number of amateurs' was increasing sharply. In Moscow, Leningrad, Kiev, Kharkov and elsewhere, scientific and technical societies and journals organised public clubs for investigation of 'anomalous phenomena in the environment' (the term 'UFO' was still half-taboo). When the first Ukrainian meeting on anomalous phenomena was held in Kiev in 1981, there were twelve doctors of sciences and forty-five candidates of sciences participating: they concluded that the anomalies merited investigation. In succeeding years other conferences and seminars followed. The scientific level of the reports presented was variable, admittedly, but they represented a serious desire to come to terms with the problem.

Now that the Academy of Sciences had in all but name accepted the reality of the UFO problem, its publishing policy underwent some changes. The official scientific publishing house commissioned myself and the Vice-Chairman of the Academic Expert Group on Anomalous Atmospheric Phenomena, Dr Y. V. Platov, to write a book which would provide an introduction to the UFO problem for the Soviet academic community. Naturally, we agreed to write the book, our manuscript obtained the approval of several high-ranking academic readers, and in 1991 it was published under the title *UFOs and Modern Science*.

Whereupon the Soviet Union collapsed. I cannot assert with confidence that there was any cause-and-effect connection between these two events beyond – maybe – a quasi-Jungian synchronicity. But anyway this work of ours was and will for ever remain the first and the last Soviet academic monograph on the UFO problem. *Sic transit…*

FROM ALLEGED 'PSEUDOSCIENCE' TO REAL PSEUDOUFOLOGY

When *perestroyka* began, the new climate greatly facilitated the work of amateur societies: membership grew rapidly. By mid-1988, censorial prohibitions of UFO observation reports were largely relieved: by 1989 they no longer existed.

Yet there was no real breakthrough in the development of ufological studies. In fact, rather the reverse: official science felt itself, for the first time, insecure in its funding, and was consequently disinclined to risk taking a softer line towards the UFO. As for ufology, formerly united against the totalitarian state, it now disintegrated into three camps:

- tabloid ufology, comprising ufologically-oriented journalists and the like, attracted by the now-permitted chance to write sensational articles: they were rarely experienced researchers.

- 'amateur' ufology, largely composed of local study groups and regional associations. The plan was to co-ordinate them all beneath an umbrella, the so-called UFO Center, led by Dr V. G. Azhazha. As a rule, these people sincerely believed that when the efforts of UFO amateurs were united, the

UFO problem would be solved sooner rather than later. In so doing, too many of them displayed a regrettable tendency not only to accept contactees and abductees at their face value, but also to accept their dubious 'messages'.

• scientific ufology, incorporating those rather rarer individuals or groups who aimed to transform ufology into a truly scientific field of investigation.

This polarisation cannot be said to have left ufology in the Former Soviet Union in a healthy state. Nonetheless, I would not sink into pessimism. There are in the CIS countries some researchers, UFO study groups, and organisations that aim at really scientific studies of the phenomenon. We have such serious specialists, engaged in ufological studies, as Dr L. M. Gindilis, Dr Y. V. Platov, Dr A. F. Pugach, Dr M. Y. Shevchenko, and many others. We also have (and this is extremely important) a considerable number of scientists, scholars and engineers who are not prejudiced against the UFO subject matter (as distinct from the majority of their western colleagues) and are therefore ready to study it seriously and professionally.

SOME CONCLUSIONS

It must be admitted that Soviet Man lived in a rather comfortable world. The State took care of him, guaranteed him employment, gave him a home, free medical help, a pension after 60. His income was low by western standards, but so were his expenses. Intellectually, too, it was a secure world: he was brought up to regard the printed word as something sacred. What he read in *Pravda* was truth.

And now this stagnant world has been invaded by something strange, alien and possibly dangerous (though Soviet science-fiction has always depicted extraterrestrials as humane, highly advanced, and of course sharing communist ideals). How should the man or woman in the street react? There are no guidelines. UFOs were not foreseen by Marx, Engels or Lenin, neither were they mentioned in the recent decrees of the Party and State.

It is interesting to note that almost every Soviet UFO witness, encountering a phenomenon completely foreign to him, accepted its objective reality. At the same time, most scholars and scientists rejected the phenomenon's objective reality in favour of their socially-induced picture of the world. Sometimes these patterns intermixed: a professor who saw a UFO at his *dacha* not far from Moscow and in the heat of the moment informed a ufologist about this, was a few days later begging the latter to forget this information.

Perhaps similar patterns obtain in the west: there, too, the climate of 'educated' opinion is generally against anomalous phenomena. But there is a difference between opposing a climate and defying a totalitarian state, particularly when it is the only employer existent. The Soviet UFO debunkers knew well which side their bread was buttered.

In the end, the differences between West and East are of only secondary importance. However he may be conditioned to react subsequently, when his feelings have had time to cool, at the time of the event a Russian, a Frenchman and an American will react alike, in a simple, instinctual way – simple-mindedly perhaps, yet more wisely than some academies of sciences. That's why I would like to describe here, in closing, an incident that happened to a Soviet driver in 1969, whose letter is in my archives.

This driver, Nikolay Zinov, aged 36 at 1969, was on a prospecting expedition in Kazakhstan, at the Dzhambul settlement. On September 11 he was returning by lorry from another settlement together with an engineer, a geologist, and a laboratory assistant. They left Karazhal after dark, by an unfamiliar road: they lost their way and about 5 am Zinov stopped his lorry, deciding to wait for dawn. The motor was still idling. Suddenly he noticed a moving luminous point in the sky. When the point approached the lorry, all saw a flying 'man' of normal height dressed in a silvery scaly 'space suit'. He flew silently, in an almost horizontal position, his arms extended horizontally, over the lorry at an altitude of some two metres, landing about 25 metres away.

'...I swiftly turned my lorry in his direction and switched on my headlights. The man stood still on the ground and was clearly visible. The geologist told me to go and ask him the right way. I jumped out of my cab and ran towards the man. When I was about 3 or 4 metres from him, he rose smoothly to an altitude of about 2.5 metres. I took one or two steps more and addressed him, forgetting even to say a word of greeting: "Comrade, we're lost, show us the right way!" There was no reply, but the man started flying off to the left, gaining altitude as he went.'

Zinov quickly returned to his lorry and followed the man at a distance of some 20 metres. Soon it grew light, and they found themselves on a good dirt road. Taking a glance around, the travellers understood that they had missed their settlement by a hundred kilometres. And the 'man' in the silvery space suit went on ascending until he (or it?) disappeared in the morning sky.

REGARDLESS OF THEIR PHYSICAL REALITY, THE ARGUMENT CAN BE MADE THAT UFOS ARE ONE OF THE MOST WIDELY REPORTED 'PARANORMAL' PHENOMENA IN MODERN MEMORY, IF NOT IN THE ENTIRE HISTORY OF HUMANKIND. WHY THIS SHOULD BE SO, IN THE FACE OF ALMOST CONSTANT NEGLECT AND ACTIVE DENIGRATION BY THOSE WHO SHAPE SOCIETY — POLITICIANS, MILITARY AUTHORITIES, JOURNALISTS, SCIENTISTS AND SO ON — SHOULD PIQUE THE INTEREST OF PSYCHOLOGISTS AND SOCIOLOGISTS, IF NO ONE ELSE. YET SAVE FOR A RELATIVE HANDFUL OF ACADEMIC STUDIES, WE CAN THINK OF NO OTHER 'GRASS ROOTS MOVEMENT' ON SUCH A MASSIVE SCALE THAT REMAINS SO STUDIOUSLY IGNORED BY ORTHODOX AND MAINSTREAM SCIENCE. EVEN AMONG SUCH 'SOFT' DISCIPLINES AS FOLKLORE AND THE STUDY OF URBAN LEGENDS, UFOS ARE VIEWED AS ON A PAR WITH REPORTS OF ELVIS PRESLEY SIGHTINGS, SATANIC CULT ABUSE, AND SPURIOUS SOCIAL WORKERS, ALL OF WHICH PALE IN COMPARISON IN TERMS OF THE RELATIVE NUMBER OF CASES INVOLVED.

AS A TEENAGER IN 1954, ROBERT DURANT, AUTHOR OF THE FOLLOWING SURVEY OF PUBLIC OPINION POLLS, HAD WHAT IS NOW CALLED A 'CLOSE ENCOUNTER' WITH A UFO, AND THUS BEGAN AN INTENSE, LONG-TERM INTEREST IN THE TOPIC. HE IS AN AIRLINE PILOT, AND HAS HELD VARIOUS POSTS IN AIRLINE MANAGEMENT AND WITH THE AIR LINE PILOTS ASSOCIATION. HE CAN BE REACHED IN WRITING AT 106 HESSIAN HILL DRIVE, PENNINGTON, NJ 08534.

PUBLIC OPINION POLLS AND UFOS

by Robert Durant

W ho cares what the public thinks about UFOs? It appears that politicians, bureaucrats, journalists and scientists don't. They have relegated the topic to the 'fringe' since the first public discussion of 'flying saucers' in 1947. But a careful look at the evolution of public opinion on UFOs over the last five decades reveals a surprising disparity between what the Establishment thinks and what Mr. and Mrs. America tell the pollsters.

I found data on public opinion polls related to the UFO issue in the archives of the Gallup Organization and at the Roper Center for Public Opinion Research at the University of Connecticut. A careful search through these sources revealed seven Gallup surveys, six by the Roper Organization, and two by Audits & Surveys, during the period 1947 through 1990.

Most of the polls were keyed to flurries of discussion of UFOs in the press, though the 1990 Gallup poll was done simply because Gallup wanted something for the Halloween week. Like the other polling companies, Gallup routinely uses this type of poll for publicity via news releases.

Unfortunately, the questions asked were superficial, poorly worded, and inconsistent from one poll to another, and there are large time gaps between polls.

1947

The first survey was released by George Gallup on 14 August, 1947. The entire text of the report is worth quoting because it reflects the puzzlement of both the public and a seasoned observer of public reaction to events given wide coverage in the media:

PRINCETON, N.J., AUGUST 14 – Now that the uproar over the 'flying saucers' has subsided it is a good time to take a look at what the general public thought about them.

In the first place the results of publicity received by the discs would have been the answer to a press agent's prayer. Nine out of ten Americans have heard about the phenomena, which were first reported June 25.

As a test of the public's knowledge about current events, this looms very large indeed and places the saucers on a par with Orson Welles's 'Invasion from Mars,' and the Loch Ness Monster and Tom Thumb golf. As an indication of how the saucer story spread, it need only be pointed out that at the same time only about half the people had heard about the Marshall Plan, and only 61 per cent had heard or read about the Taft-Hartley labour bill.

Among college graduates only 2 per cent said they had not heard of the saucers, while 17 per cent of those with grammar school education or less were ignorant of the subject.

When it comes to having an idea what the 'celestial crockery' really was, answers that people give are divided among (1) no idea at all; (2) imagination or hoax; (3) something real.

What Do You Think These Saucers Are?

No answer, don't know	33%
Imagination, optical illusion, mirage, etc.	29%
Hoax	10%
U.S. secret weapon, part of atomic bomb, etc	15%
Weather forecasting devices	3%
Russian secret weapon	1%
Other explanations	9%

Guesses ranged all the way from the practical to the miraculous. Among the latter was a woman, citing biblical text, who said it was a sign of the world's end. A man in the west thought the discs were radio waves from the Bikini atomic bomb explosion, while another man saw in them a new product being put out by the 'DuPont people'.

A few smelled a publicity or advertising stunt, while others felt sure that the saucers were after all only some kind of meteor or comet.

Further study of earlier 'information' polls shows that the 90 per cent who know about the saucers compare with the eight out of ten voters who last January did not know what the Wagner Act contained, and the 51 per cent who couldn't tell what 'balancing the budget' means. A recent event which approached the saucers in penetration of public consciousness was the Georgia governor's battle last winter of which 84 per cent of the people had heard.

Gallup was plainly astonished by the high percentage of Americans who recognised the subject. This theme, repeated in later surveys, undoubtedly reflects the intensity of news coverage devoted to saucer sightings in the summer of 1947.

1950

In May 1950, a Gallup news release summed up the second survey with this head-

HAVE YOU SEEN A UFO?

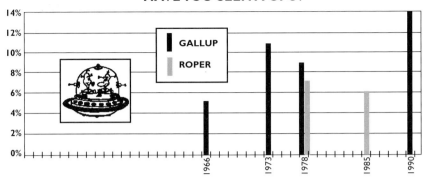

ARE UFOs REAL? ARE UFOs ALIEN SPACECRAFT?

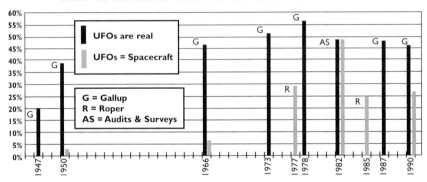

DOES INTELLIGENT LIFE EXIST IN OUTER SPACE?

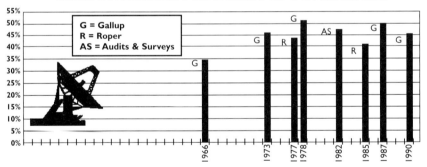

NO OPINION OF UFOs

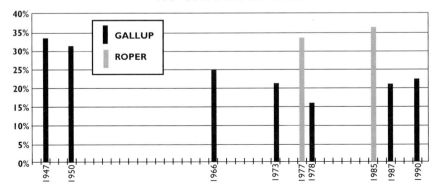

line: 'Just what are those flying saucers – a secret weapon? Public inclined to view mystery discs as military experiments; fewer regard them as illusions.'

Something had happened in the intervening three years to cause a major shift in public opinion about saucers. In the 1947 survey, most opted for optical illusions or hoaxes. Now the favourite explanation was the secret military weapon.

And the influence of government pronouncements was noted by Gallup:

Although President Truman and other government officials have denied knowing anything about flying saucer experiments, there has been persistent talk that something is back of the odd aerial sights which so many people claim to have seen.

What Do You Think These Flying Saucers Are?

Army or Navy experiments, new weapons, military secrets	23%
Optical illusion, pipe-dream, hoax, etc.	16%
Some kind of new airplane	6%
Comets, shooting stars, something from another planet	5%
Russian weapon, something from Russia	3%
Weather devices	1%
Miscellaneous	3%
No such thing	6%
Don't know	32%
Haven't heard of them	6%

The concept of extraterrestrial devices sneaks in under the heading of 'Comets, shooting stars, something from another planet.' This confused category probably reflects the absence of any public discussion of space exploration or exobiology, but it gives us a clue that the idea was being considered by at least a few respondents. In retrospect, it seems nearly impossible that the ET hypothesis was virtually absent in the public mind as of May 1950, but that is what the poll shows.

1966

Flying saucers continued to receive regular media coverage, and authors such as Donald Keyhoe wrote widely read books and articles promoting the ET hypothesis and calling for Congressional investigations. Despite this intense public interest and constant media coverage of the controversy, Gallup waited 16 years before his next flying saucer survey. He explained the reason for the poll this way: 'Since the late 1940s, scientists and military officials have been investigating hundreds of reported sightings of unidentified flying objects. A recent rash of sightings prompted a Congressional hearing last month and also this special survey.'

The gap between the 1947 and 1950 surveys and the one published in May 1966 is unfortunate, because several vital conceptual shifts took place during that period. These are revealed by the questions posed, which clearly imply the emergence of the extraterrestrial nature of saucers as a popular hypothesis, and also accept the fact that very large numbers of Americans had had their own UFO sightings. The earlier surveys virtually ignored the idea of visitors from outer space and acted as if saucer sightings were something that happened to someone other than the person answering the poll. By 1966, saucers obviously appeared much more immediate and personal to the general public.

Have you ever heard or read about 'flying saucers'?
Yes – 96%, No – 4%

In your opinion, are they something real, or just people's imagination?
Real – 46%, Imagination – 29%

Have you, yourself, ever seen anything you thought was a 'flying saucer'?
Yes – 5%, No – 95%

Do you think there are people somewhat like ourselves living on other planets in the universe?
Yes – 34%, No – 46%

The number of Americans who reported a flying saucer sighting translated to about five million when the Gallup findings were projected to the entire population. But the definition of 'real' was ambiguous at best. Gallup reported that six per cent of the respondents thought flying saucers originated in outer space.

Apparently the concept of 'real' was used by the interviewers and the respondents to distinguish between physical phenomena on the one hand and hoax or fantasy on the other. Under the heading of 'real', the respondents listed (1) experimental projects, Air Force tests; (2) actual vehicles from outer space; (3) burning gases or 'swamp gas'; (4) meteors, shooting stars; (5) weather balloons; (6) supernatural revelations.

Here we see a dramatic difference in the perception of the issue by ufologists, for whom 'real' almost universally meant extraterrestrial spaceships, and the public at large, who adopted more prosaic definitions.

Gallup also found a strongly positive correlation between educational levels and the acceptance of the reality of flying saucers and/or life elsewhere in the universe, with better educated respondents having a higher acceptance. Other studies of UFO percipients have confirmed this correlation.

1973

The November 1973 Gallup survey revealed that the number of persons claiming a UFO sighting had more than doubled in the intervening seven years.

An astonishing 11 per cent of the adult population, or more than 15 million Americans, have seen a UFO (unidentified flying object) – double the percentage recorded in the previous survey on the subject in 1966. The figure was five per cent.

In addition, the latest survey shows approximately half of the persons interviewed (51 per cent) believing that these flying objects – sometimes called 'flying saucers' – are real and not just a figment of the imagination or cases of hallucination.

The same survey shows nearly half of all persons interviewed (46 per cent) believed that there is intelligent life on other planets. This represents a sharp increase in the percentage with this belief since the 1966 survey when the figure was 34 per cent.

Once again, Gallup notes the very large number of people who have heard of unidentified flying objects, the term with which the subject had been dignified by the 1970s. (Gallup has to explain to its readers that UFOs were once called flying saucers!) 'Almost everyone (95 per cent) has at least heard or read about UFOs. For something so highly publicised, this finding may, at first, not seem unusual.

However, in terms of the history of the public's awareness of other incidents or events, this figure is extraordinarily high. In fact, this awareness score is one of the highest in the 37-year history of the Gallup Poll.'

Unfortunately, few detailed questions were asked in the 1973 survey. In response to the question, 'In your opinion, are they something real, or just people's imagination?', 51 per cent opted for real, compared with 46 per cent in the 1966 survey. In response to the question, 'Do you think there are people somewhat like ourselves living on other planets in the universe, or not?', 46 per cent said yes, compared with 34 per cent who answered affirmatively in 1966.

This survey established another fact of great significance for our culture, if not for ufology, in that it clearly demonstrated for the first time that nearly half of all adult Americans believed that intelligent life exists beyond our planet. In common with previous surveys, college-educated respondents were most enthusiastic about sentient life in space, with 57 per cent responding positively.

Unlike the 1966 survey, in which a small but substantial belief in the extraterrestrial nature of UFOs was documented, the 1973 survey made no attempt to discern what the respondents meant by 'real' UFOs.

It should be noted that the 1973 survey was conducted four years after the closing of Project Blue Book, with its widely disseminated negative conclusions on UFOs, and publication of the equally negative conclusions of the congressionally mandated University of Colorado (Condon) Committee. (An excellent review of the anti-UFO climate in intellectual, scientific, government and journalistic circles during this time frame can be found in historian David M. Jacob's *The UFO Controversy in America*, 1975.) Yet the percentage of persons believing that UFOs are 'real,' and the number reporting personal sightings, increased.

A provocative aside in the report tells us of a 1971 Gallup survey which disclosed that 'Top leaders in 72 nations found 53 per cent expressing a belief in the existence of human life on other planets while 47 per cent ruled out the possibility. The survey was of leaders in science, medicine, education, politics, business and other fields, selected by careful sampling methods from the *International Who's Who*.'

1977

The Roper Organization asked two questions about UFOs in January 1977.

Now here is a list of some different things. Would you tell me for each one whether it is something you believe in, or something you're not sure about, or something you don't believe in?

The existence of life somewhere else in the universe

Believe in	44%
Not sure about	29%
Don't believe in	26%

UFOs (unidentified flying objects) from somewhere else in the universe

Believe in	29%
Not sure about	33%
Don't believe in	37%

1978

Gallup's 1978 survey found 57 per cent thought UFOs were real, nine per cent reported a sighting, and 51 per cent thought there are people somewhat like us on other planets. The term 'flying saucer' does not appear, nor is there any discussion of the meaning of 'real.'

This represents the high-water mark for public belief in the 'reality' of UFOs.

The Roper Organization also did a survey in 1978, asking only if the respondent had seen a UFO, and seven per cent answered 'yes.'

1982

Audits & Surveys, in a report sponsored by Merit Report, asked:

Do you believe that some form of intelligent life does or does not exist in outer space?'

Does exist	47%
Does not exist	37%
No opinion	16%

They also asked:

Which one statement best describes your belief about unidentified flying objects from outer space visiting here on earth?

They definitely have been here	11%
They probably have been	38%
They probably have not been	25%
They definitely have not been	15%
No opinion	11%

1985

In January 1985 the Roper Organization asked:

Do you believe in UFOs (unidentified flying objects from somewhere else in the universe)?

Believe in	25%
Don't believe in	39%
Not sure about	36%

And in the same survey:

Do you believe in the existence of life somewhere else in the universe?

Believe in	41%
Don't believe in	21%
Not sure about	38%

In July 1985 Roper asked:

Have you seen a UFO (unidentified flying object)?

Yes	6%
No	93%
Don't know	1%

1987

In March 1987 Gallup released a report with a headline that accentuated the positive, trumpeting the statistic that 'Only one third of the public deny existence of UFOs, extraterrestrial life.' The 'not sure' or 'undecided' members of the population have been substantial in all the flying saucer surveys, and in this headline Gallup correctly emphasised that the nay-sayers actually amount to only 34 per cent of the population.

With only one out of three citizens saying 'nonsense' and the rest either believers or fence-sitters, one wonders about the reason for the contempt with which the subject is treated by those who are presumably sensitive to public opinion, such as politicians and media executives.

1990

The most recent Gallup survey was published in 1990. It is a departure from previous surveys in many ways, mainly in that it is a lengthy review of 'belief in psychic and paranormal phenomena' in America, with UFOs considered only as one not particularly significant paranormal event or belief. Questions concerning UFOs and belief in extraterrestrial life comprise only four out of a total of 40 questions in the survey.

The report discusses belief in extraterrestrial life in this thoughtful commentary: 'To about one-half of all Americans, the question is when we come into contact with extraterrestrial beings, not if. Forty-six per cent of Americans believe that there are 'people somewhat like ourselves living on other planets in the universe.' This number is essentially the same as measured by Gallup in 1973, and thus has apparently not been affected by our increasingly sophisticated exploration of our solar system and the universe.'

The belief that UFOs are 'real' declined in the 1990 survey to 47 per cent from a peak of 57 per cent in 1978 and 54 per cent in 1973.

For the first time in the 43-year span of its existence, the Gallup UFO survey inquired directly into the question that is of paramount interest to ufologists, namely, is there a firm connection in the public mind between belief that UFOs are real and belief in extraterrestrial life? This issue would seem self-evident to most of us in the field of UFO research, and was implicit in the questions asked by Gallup from 1966 on, but apparently John Q. Public thought otherwise. Only 27 per cent reported belief that UFOs have actually touched down and visited earth.

The 27 per cent figure vividly illustrates the distinction in the public mind between 'real' and the ET hypothesis. To 'believers' this is probably a disappointing statistic, but it must be at least equally disconcerting to the sceptics.

The 1990 Gallup survey showed 14 per cent reporting that they had seen a UFO. The trend is as follows: 1973 – 11 per cent, 1978 – nine per cent (Gallup), 1985 – seven per cent (Roper). The puzzling variations in these statistics is probably the result of the three per cent to six per cent margin of error in the results. But the most serious problem they pose to ufologists concerns the validity of our database of sightings, which apparently comprises only a minute fraction of the total number of UFO sightings in America. The polls translate into roughly 2,000 sightings per day, assuming two witnesses per sighting.

Respondents were asked if they believed that UFOs were 'real,' but, unfortunately, without the rigorous definitions used by Roper, and the response is down in 1990 to 47 per cent, compared with a peak in 1978 of 57 per cent. Those who believe that the answer to UFOs can be found in 'imagination' are essentially stable throughout the period from 1973 through 1990 at around 30 per cent. The swing vote seems to be those with no opinion either way, whose numbers increased from 16 per cent in 1973 and 1978 to 22 per cent in 1990.

1991

A special poll commissioned by ufologists was conducted in 1991 by the Roper Organization as part of an effort to answer one of the most vexing questions in abduction research, namely, how many persons are 'abductees'? The poll is unique in that it was designed by UFO researchers, was funded as an independent project, and had a population sample about three times as large as the other polls reported in this summary, resulting in a very small (1.4 per cent) margin of error. Of interest to us is only one of the many questions asked in the survey, 'Have you ever seen a UFO?'

How often has occurrence happened to you?

Has happened	7%
More than twice	1%
Once or twice	6%
Has not happened	92%
Don't know	1%

The poll singled out a group of 595 respondents who were identified as socially 'influential' and politically active trendsetters. Ten per cent of the 'influential' group reported seeing a UFO.

1995 – 1996

Several polls were taken in this time frame, and they confirm the 51 per cent acceptance level of the proposition that 'UFOs are real.' A survey taken in Germany asked if the respondent thought alien spacecraft had landed, and 25 per cent answered affirmatively.

INTERPRETING THE NUMBERS

To me the steady increase of belief in the 'reality' of UFOs and the ET hypothesis during the first 30 years of the controversy is difficult to explain. The very high awareness level of the public doubtless results from massive media coverage of the topic. But we must distinguish between awareness of the controversy and the public's interpretation of its meaning.

My admittedly subjective recollection is that the UFOs were bashed by the media, bashed by establishment science, and bashed by the full authority and prestige of various branches of the federal government. I can't think of a topic other than drug abuse that has had such a uniformly bad press as UFOs. How is it that in the face of this avalanche of denial of the reality of UFOs, the public steadily gained a belief in that disputed reality?

Even more puzzling is the sudden and substantial reversal of opinion after 1978-80. What opinion-forming force was at work from 1947 through 1978? The figures clearly show a steady trend in all five polled areas. But what occurred subsequent to 1978 that shifted belief in the opposite direction?

Belief in the existence of extraterrestrial life also declined, in spite of a pro-

ET propaganda blitz that began in the late 1970s and continues to this day. Presidents Reagan, Bush, and Clinton, as well as NASA and the nearly ubiquitous Carl Sagan, have all made mighty efforts to sell space exploration and the associated ET concept to the general public.

Ironically, the selling of SETI [Search for Extraterrestrial Intelligence] has often served as a platform to denounce belief in UFOs. SETI's most articulate spokesmen are quick to dismiss UFOs from serious consideration. (NASA spent $70,000 on one brochure promoting SETI, while the Fund for UFO Research has disbursed an average of $27,000 annually since its inception.)

Why has the man in the street persistently refused to follow the establishment line on UFOs? This issue can and should be pursued without reference to the nature of UFOs – that is, whether unidentified flying objects are event-level reality or psychological aberrations. From a totally sceptical vantage, social science has a unique opportunity to study a new religion in the making. Questions of this sort should be of major importance to sociologists, political scientists and historians.

The UFO poll data cry out for interpretation. I shared the data gathered from the polls with a group of prominent ufologists who were kind enough to comment. Several made the point that there is likely to be under-reporting when the public is asked about belief in a topic generally demeaned by the establishment, whether it be ghosts or UFOs or even racist beliefs. For example, in 1988, 50 per cent of the voting age public cast Presidential ballots, while 57 per cent claimed they did. In this interpretation, the poll data is actually very conservative, in that more people believe UFOs are real than the polls show.

Professor David Jacobs remarked: 'Debunkers are fond of saying that the public was 'primed' to believe in little green men from outer space when the UFO phenomenon began. Countless 'scientists' and others have made this argument. (e.g. William Hartmann in *UFOs: A Scientific Debate*). However, what your data show is just the opposite. In the beginning, the vast majority of the public did not believe in little green men, and most significantly, the first poll shows that the extraterrestrial hypothesis was so minor that it did not even warrant a category by itself.'

My favourite explanation for the slow but ultimately overwhelming public acceptance of the reality of UFOs is found in the statistics that ask if the respondent has ever seen a UFO. Those who say 'yes' don't go running to the press with their story. Instead, they confide in their closest friends. The climate of mockery and ridicule surrounding the UFO issue forces discretion on all but the very brave or silly. In this way the belief system has propagated within our society by intimate personal contact, bypassing all the standard means of communication.

Whatever the reason may be, UFO proponents have won the war for public opinion. For every Fundamentalist Christian there are five UFO believers. Roman Catholics comprise by far the largest Christian denomination in the United States, and UFO believers outnumber them by a ratio of better than two to one. UFO believers outnumber the voters who placed Reagan and Bush and Clinton in office.

These statistics ought to be brought forcefully to the attention of journalists and politicians, who seem locked into the view that belief in UFOs is an aberrant opinion held by a small portion of the population. The fact is that when a pundit makes a joke about UFOs, only one out of three listeners or readers laughs. The rest are either offended or uneasy. That 'UFOs are real' is now a solidly mainstream belief.

WHATEVER OR NOT UFOS EXIST AS PHYSICAL OBJECTS, THERE IS NO QUESTION THAT UFO MYTHS EXIST. 'EVEN WHEN THE PHENOMENON HAS BEEN IDENTIFIED, THE ACTORS OF THE UFO MYTH – THE WITNESSES WHO HAVE THE ORIGINAL EXPERIENCE, THE UFOLOGISTS WHO INVESTIGATE IT AND THE MEDIA WHO REPORT IT EACH MAKE THEIR OWN CONTRIBUTION TO PROPAGATE AND FEED THE MYTH'. MARCEL DELAVAL, A BELGIAN SCIENTIST WHO LIVES AND WORKS IN ITALY, HAS FOR MANY YEARS BEEN A PERCEPTIVE OBSERVER OF THE ITALIAN SCENE, AND HAS MADE A NOTABLE ANALYSIS OF IFOS – IDENTIFIED FLYING OBJECTS. IN THIS PAPER HE ILLUSTRATES THE PROCESS WHEREBY MYTHS ARE CREATED AND FOSTERED, WITH EXAMPLES DRAWN FROM HIS OWN INVESTIGATIVE EXPERIENCE.

HE MAY BE CONTACTED AT MARCEL.DELAVAL@JRC.IT

THE FORCE OF A MYTH

by Marcel Delaval

I. THE ROLE OF THE WITNESS

This story takes place in July 1987, in a pleasant hilly region in the north of Italy, in the vicinity of the small city of Varese, also known as 'The Garden City'. It is the summer, and the warmth incites people to stay outside. The house of the witnesses concerned is far enough from the city to allow a good view of the sky. Over a period of several weeks, J. B., his wife, their daughter and some neighbours have observed a brilliant light from their balcony, to the east or south-east, not only during the evening but also early in the morning. They have also seen moving lights manifesting strange trajectories.

J. B. is an engineer with three diplomas. We may consider him the main witness, in the sense that it is he who has taken the lead throughout the affair. Very intrigued by his observations, in August 1985 he decided to get in touch with the local newspaper *La Prealpina*. He told them: 'Every evening, for almost three weeks, I have seen through the window a luminous object exhibiting strange behaviour. I am an engineer, I know the laws of physics and mathematics, I rule out the possibility that it could be a satellite. I would like somebody to explain to me what it is… As a scientist, I don't believe in the existence of other worlds, in fact I have not once mentioned the word UFO in telling my story. On the basis of my knowledge, I cannot explain the nature of the object and I would like some competent person to give me an explanation'.

After reading his story in the newspaper, I made an appointment with the family and went to their house on the same evening. J. B. seemed proud to display astronomical books opened on the table, as if to demonstrate that he knew something about astronomy. As the observations had taken place over several weeks, it was quite difficult to reconstruct precisely what had happened. Fortunately, during my visit the daughter called out, saying that the object in question was visible, just as it had been during the previous evenings. And indeed a brilliant object was visible towards the south-east, which was I was quickly able to identify as the planet Jupiter, as we could confirm with binoculars. Disappointed by this rational explanation, J. B. argued that this could not explain their early morning observations.

Back home, a brief check on the planet's position at that period of the year showed that Venus was visible early in the morning in approximately the same direction. Since the witnesses saw only one object at a time, and with their description of the luminous phenomenon, the identification was relatively easy. When he was told of this, J. B. gave the impression of trying to save the situation, appealing to the movement of the lights that they had also seen during the previous weeks.

Even if we could not positively explain them, we had previous experience of reports of lights displaying strange trajectories in this geographical area. We had established that they were the lights of aircraft landing at the nearby Malpensa airport. At that point of their flight path, the airplanes are flying towards the witnesses, at one moment giving the impression of hovering in the air, moving rapidly a moment later. It seemed likely that the reports of strange behaviour came about when these varied flight characteristics were fused into a single and seemingly anomalous phenomenon.

That J. B. finally accepted the explanation of Jupiter and Venus seemed to be confirmed by his refusal to receive a visit from RAI National Television. 'It was not worth their while to come,' he told them, 'there was nothing to see for the moment (even though apparently the same phenomenon was still there) and it would be a waste of money'. However, interrogated the following day for the second time by the newspaper *La Prealpina*, he repeated his claim that 'the moving lights were something else': consequently the mystery continued to be propagated through the media. Even if there was no explicit reference to the extraterrestrial explanation, the UFO context was still implied by the media if one read between the lines.

The behaviour of J. B. can be understood if we judge it in a psychological context. He was probably embarrassed by the bustle generated by the media, the ufologists, the astronomers… and above all with regard to the importance given to his titles and diplomas not only by the media, but also by himself. His all too human response to the situation was to try to save face.

2. THE ROLE OF THE UFOLOGISTS

A myth can also be propagated by irresponsible ufologists. That they are perfectly capable of inventing stories is demonstrated by the story of 'the two blue dwarfs' of Viggiù, a small village not far from the scene of the previous case. The events took place in the early hours of 4 October 1979 at the periphery of the village, in the garden of the house of A. N., a 38-year-old workman employed by a refuse collection company.

The night was dark and starlit. As usual, A. N. was leaving home early to go to work. At 3.15a.m. he went to the garage, took out his Vespa scooter, started the motor, switched the lights on and wheeled the vehicle to the path in the garden. Unexpectedly he saw two small blue dwarfs, not higher than 70 to 90cm, at a distance of about ten metres. They were walking in his direction, gesticulating and floating 20cm above the ground. Their appearance was human, with two arms and two legs, but they were extremely thin. He did not notice any hair but was impressed by their luminous eyes, just like those of a cat in the night. He did not notice their clothes. They seemed to be discussing together but he did not hear any word.

A. N. left his scooter for a moment with its motor running and the headlight directed to the strange beings. He was walking in their direction when the motor stopped running and the light switched off. Not at all frightened by his vision, he went on walking forward with the intention of capturing the dwarfs. He was about to seize the first one on his left when it disappeared horizontally through a grille. When he turned to his right to grab the second one, it too had vanished. He returned to his Vespa, and was surprised to hear the motor start to run and to see the light illuminating the path again without any intervention by him. The entire experience had lasted only a few minutes.

This strange case has never been explained, not necessarily because it is unexplainable but because no psychological study of the witness has been done. It seems likely that it is in that direction that we should look for an explanation. However, it is not for that reason that I am citing the case here. For there is a second and no less interesting aspect of this story: the generation of a parallel myth in the form of 'Men In Black'.

MIBs are those mysterious characters who make their appearance in a number of UFO stories: characteristically, they will menace and intimidate the witnesses and/or the ufologists with the apparent intention of forcing them to conceal the truth. Typically, they wear black clothes and travel in sinister black cars. Well, in 1985 my colleague and myself had the honour to be identified as MIBs by a ufologist writing in the publication *Sky Sentinel*.

We had been informed about the 'blue dwarfs' story through the newspaper *La Prealpina*. We made initial contact by telephone with the family of A. N., agreed to meet them and came to Viggiù on 6 October 1979, to make an investigation on-site. We began by recording the testimony, inside the house. Then we went out into the garden to make some measurements of distances and angles, using a compass and a Geiger counter; we did not notice any anomaly. At this point I should record that my colleague was French and I am Belgian, thus we both come from French-speaking countries. We both work for the Nuclear Research Centre of the CEE and have a leisure-time interest in ufology. All this information is important for what follows.

Six years after the events of the blue dwarfs of Viggiù, C. N., a ufologist with religious leanings, published an article from which I reproduce the following extracts. The words in italic represent my comments:

'One day (December 14th) [In reality it was December 6th], two men came to Viggiù and, without hesitation, entered the garden. They were dressed in dark clothes [I don't like the colour black and do not possess any black clothes!] and one of them had a strange apparatus in his hands, pointing it in specific directions and showing a moving needle. The man orientated the apparatus, turned round and, without hesitation, went to the exact place where the dwarfs appeared, during the night of October 4th [Well, of course: A. N. had previously shown us the place]. All of this lasted only a few minutes. A. N. saw all this from behind the curtain of the window. Seeing that the two men did not intend to go away, he went out of the house and faced them. Immediately, one of them extracted a pass from his pocket and said he was an engineer from the Nuclear Research Centre. Then, speaking in an incomprehensible language [Obviously, if you don't understand French!], the men inspected in detail the path and the garden where the two 'visitors' were seen. A. N. was attentively observing their behaviour and, not understanding the function of the apparatus, asked what it was. It is a Geiger detector, said the man who presented himself as an engineer [I don't like the titles!], in perfect Italian but with an evident foreign accent. The other man never talked in Italian [I never realised the handicap of my colleague!] After another five minutes, without greeting [It seems we have no manncrs, cither!] both went away. They got into the car hidden outside [Our car was not parked in the garden for the very good reason that we did not wish to disturb the site] and A. N. saw them going away, from behind the bushes. Only at that time he noticed that the auto, a big black car [Actually, it's a white Citroen GS!] did not have any plates [Really? It carries red/white Belgian plates]. The A. N. case put on record quite a rare event in Italy, the visit of the Man In Black. In fact, the Research Centre having been interrogated [I never heard anything about it], denied absolutely the fact [Of course we made the enquiry in our private capacity, unconnected with our work]. 'Whoever they may be', the intruders [This sounds as though the writer has his own ideas on the matter] were surely not employed by the Research Centre [I am sorry to contradict, but we surely are!], which is not interested in UFOs.'

Observe the atmosphere of mystery generated by this description! The black clothes, the strange apparatus, the official aspect of the visit, the military behaviour of their movements, the strange language they spoke, the silence of the colleague, the big black car hidden outside. It is easy to imagine how easily this story or others like it could be propagated by others, who do not bother to check the information: and so legends are born.

3. THE ROLE OF THE MEDIA

It may also happen that some reporters, more concerned to entertain their audience than to establish the truth or otherwise of the facts, will distort the story by altering or omitting information, or by refusing to correct a mistake even when confronted with contrary evidence.

On 16 December 1991, G. M., the presenter of the TV program *Mixer* on one of the leading Italian channels, showing a photo of a supposed alien, said 'News from the same source was leaked: a photograph in fact, that is already the subject in a way of an international detective story. The first version is that which you see. The three-dimensional reconstruction, in colour, of the original shows an extra-terrestrial being. But what validity can we attribute to this case?' Then followed a general discussion about UFOs, but not on the photograph he had displayed.

Scandalised by this misleading presentation of the facts, the Italian UFO group CISU published a press denial, on 17 December, explaining that the photo was that of a model which had been made in Canada for the specific purpose of a movie reconstruction of the Roswell case. The model was exhibited in the 'Pavillion du monde insolite' at the Universal Exhibition of Montreal (1981-1984). The model appears to be clothed in a diver's suit, and lies inside a cylinder of plex-iglass. The photo had nothing to do with a 3-D reconstruction and had been cut in such a way that the zip of the diver's suit was not visible. It seems that G. M.'s reply to the complaint was: 'We showed the photo but we did not say 'this is an extraterrestrial'.

About one month later, on 30 November 1992, G. M. transmitted yet again the same film sequence, despite CISU's denial in the press. Once again, the consequence was to propagate misleading information and to feed the myth.

4. A CONVERGENCE OF ROLES

Sometimes a resonance effect can be produced when the events and the role of the different actors – the witnesses, the ufologists and the media – converge.

On 30 May 1987, a hundred people are gathered at Crosia, in the province of Cosenza in Italy, in honour of the statue of the virgin who has been seen crying a few days before in a church of the region. Unexpectedly – though the event is predicted by a spirit medium among the assembly – a light appears in the sky at 10p.m. It executes strange movements in the sky and is immortalised for six minutes by the video camera of a witness. The light is even called 'the star of the virgin' by those who witness it.

To begin with, the event was interpreted in a religious context: then the ufologists intervened and it was re-interpreted as a UFO event. In fact the sighting took place just 40 years after the legendary first 'official' UFO case, the 24 June 1947 sighting by Kenneth Arnold. Looking for similar cases is a characteristic process whereby a witness seeks to give added credibility to his/her own testimony, as the French writer Pierre Lagrange has observed. In this case, on the one hand those looking for a religious event drew an analogy with the 1917 visions of Fatima, 70 years earlier; on the other hand, the ufologists identified it with the Arnold case, 40 years earlier.

On 17 October 1988 an analysis of the video and a reconstruction of the trajectory of the light (from a hand-held, moving camera!) were presented by the members of the Italian UFO group CUN on the Italian Television RAI 2. At one moment a clear disc shape appears with a hole in the middle and notches at the periphery. The impression that comes immediately to mind is that it is due to a zooming effect, as indeed the female interviewer sensibly suggests: but C. M., the Chemical Engineer appointed to the CUN group, denies that this could be the case. By a strange coincidence, the shape of the disc on the video is similar to that of one of the objects observed by Arnold in 1947 and represented on the cover page of the magazine *Fate* in 1948: needless to say, the representatives of CUN make the most of this resemblance. A former civil pilot, a member of the same group, even adds in an interview for the *Corriere 7 Giorni*, 'I am sure that it is not a terrestrial object'.

Years later, similar photographs continued to be published by the press. In November 1990 the Belgian ufo group SOBEPS published their interpretation of the famous disc shape. According to them, it was due to the internal structure of the video camera, seen when the autozoom is trying to focus on a point of light This phenomenon can easily be reproduced by anyone using a video camera.

In spite of this evidence, in December 1990, M. C., a member of the CUN group, rejected the explanation, arguing that in the Crosia video a central hole was visible, by contrast with the SOBEPS photograph. The hypothesis was even ignored by R.P. (also of CUN) in the videotape *UFO-Dossier Europa*. Then in July 1993 the Italian review *FOCUS* published a photo of the video of a lamp filmed with the zoom opened to its maximum position: the central hole is clearly visible and the analogy with the Crosia case is obvious. Eventually, after six years, CUN accepted the SOBEPS explanation; but their acceptance was immediately overturned in November when, during the TV program *Studio Aperto*, another member of the same group once again showed similar pictures, entirely ignoring the mechanics of the video camera.

Even if we grant the possibility, however improbable, that what the video camera recorded was a genuine luminous phenomenon in the sky, it is also true that the observation of what seemed to be a simple point of light took on a special significance due to the religious context of the observation. This significance was compounded by the analogy with the 60-year old Fatima visions and the coincidence with the 30-year old Arnold case. Add to that the lack of criticism and objectivity of certain ufologists committed to a belief system, add too the unwillingness of the media to check the information they receive, and the chain of 'misinformation' is complete. A myth has been created.

5. CONCLUSIONS

Whether the UFO phenomenon is real or unreal, we can see that the actors who take part in the UFO story – the witnesses, the ufologists and the media – create, feed and propagate the mystery. An archetypal scenario is frequently observed. In the first instance the witnesses, convinced that they have experienced an exceptional event and acting in good faith, want to communicate their wonder to other people, to the ufologists or to the media. From this moment, the UFO cases acquire some sort of official recognition that may act as a catalyst, attracting other witnesses, ufologists and the media.

By the time the case has been identified as a banal event like an astronomical phenomenon or something else, a threshold may have been reached beyond which it can become difficult for the actors of the myth to retract their claims without losing face. At this stage the temptation to ignore or distort the facts can be very strong. Other motivations such as profit, bad faith, ignorance or intellectual dishonesty can also motivate the actors. Some ufological magazines, like other commercial publications, are subjected to market constraints: they must collect enough material, they must publish on time – and they must sell. This too may lead to a manipulation of reality. UFO cases identified as explainable events do not interest many people and are not profitable, in the true sense of the word. This is why denials are rarely published.

Serious researchers can spend much energy seeking the truth, correcting mistakes and trying to get their denials published. Meanwhile the myths continue to spread because that is what some of the actors want, and because they meet a basic need of human nature.

UFOLOGY STARTS WITH THE SIGHTING, AND TAKES SUBSTANCE WHEN THAT SIGHTING IS INVESTIGAT-
ED. EVERYTHING ELSE – ANALYSING THE DATA IN SEARCH OF PATTERNS, JUGGLING THE PATTERNS TO
ELABORATE A FEASIBLE THEORY – THESE ARE SECONDARY TO THE PRIMARY TASK OF THE UFOLOGIST:
FIELD INVESTIGATION.

NO ONE KNOWS THIS BETTER THAN JENNY RANDLES, WHO FOR TWENTY FIVE YEARS HAS
BEEN THE DRIVING FORCE OF UFOLOGY IN BRITAIN – ITS MOST EXPERIENCED INVESTIGATOR, ITS
MOST PROLIFIC AUTHOR, ONE OF ITS MOST PERCEPTIVE ANALYSTS. HARD-HEADED, YET OPEN TO POS-
SIBLE EXPLANATIONS ACROSS THE SPECTRUM FROM NUT-AND-BOLTS TO PARALLEL REALITIES, SHE HAS
BEEN SEEN BY SOME AS TOO CREDULOUS, BY OTHERS AS TOO SCEPTICAL. WHAT NO ONE HAS EVER
QUESTIONED IS THE HONESTY WITH WHICH SHE HAS PURSUED THE TRUTH. MOST UFOLOGISTS WILL
SUBSCRIBE TO THE PRINCIPLES SHE SETS OUT IN THIS RETROSPECTIVE PAPER: BUT HOW MANY OF US
ADHERE TO THEM WITH SUCH DEDICATION?

JENNY RANDLES MAY BE CONTACTED AT 1 HALLSTEADS CLOSE, DOVE HOLES, BUXTON
SK17 8BS: PHONE/FAX +44 (0)1298 814 473.

A FEW HOME TRUTHS

by Jenny Randles

This celebration of the 50th anniversary of the modern UFO enigma brings the reminder that I have now been a UFO investigator in Britain for some 25 years. Whilst age brings with it wisdom, they say, I wonder if that can be true of my time within ufology?

Once I looked up to the 'oldies' in the field for my inspiration – people like Hynek and Vallee guided me through the minefield that this subject can present to the newcomer. Now I get letters from a new generation of UFO enthusiasts who hope I may provide them with some inspiration in what is a very different UFO reality from the one I entered in 1972.

Today's new band of starchasers seem every bit as besotted as earlier genera-tions were with the Extraterrestrial Hypothesis, despite its obvious shortcomings. Indeed, with the mass of conspiracy theory rammed down their throats by TV every day and the huge financial rewards enjoyed by those who promote greys, cover-ups and crashed spaceships (which contrast with the public apathy and pal-try sums offered to anyone who talks soberly about UFO research) there has never been a bigger incentive not to think objectively about UFOs. It has become almost a disadvantage to do so.

Because of this, our subject is in crisis. I do not think that too wild a state-ment. As I write, a TV producer has just called to ask me to argue 'on behalf of ufologists' that the moon landings – one of the greatest technical achievements in the history of mankind – never really happened. But they did, I protested, and I do not know any bona fide ufologist who seriously believes otherwise, I added rapidly. Oh, well any old nutter will do instead, seemed the gist of the reply. I wondered how many might be tempted to take the cheque waved in front of them, waffle incoherently before the camera and grab those few minutes of fame without questioning the repercussions. After all who loses out in that sort of game?

The answer, of course is: integrity – the biggest casualty of today's UFO age. For this kind of thing happens all the time in the 1990's. Ufology is such a useful weapon in the TV ratings war, it has become many a producer's personal addiction. Result: we ufologists have lost control of our own phenomenon. With money-making schemes (some more scam than scheme) grabbing the headlines, ufology has been handed over to the public relations agencies, showbiz promoters, TV hucksters and insurance companies, none of which favours serious research. UFO stories regularly appear in which the press never bother to interview a real ufologist to provide any sort of balance. Papers have been known to invent bogus ufologists for the sake of their story, when they cannot get some genuine mug to talk claptrap to order!

On the occasions when the media do try to provide objectivity, they are liable to be threatened with legal action by those who promote the more extreme aspects of the UFO phenomenon. (This I know from first-hand experience.) Even the most serious researcher must ask, wouldn't it be better to run with the crowd (and take the money) rather than write for a pittance, abused by one's peers, dragged through the courts, dismissed by media and public alike as 'another of those loonies'.

Serious UFO researchers have become an endangered species. Nevertheless, even among the younger generation there are those who believe that serious UFO research is a worthwhile activity, and to them I offer a few golden rules I have learnt from my hundreds of case investigations, illustrating them with examples which also give some idea of the climate of opinion in which those investigations were carried out.

RULE 1: IF YOU DON'T SOLVE AT LEAST NINE OUT OF TEN CASES YOU ARE DOING SOMETHING WRONG.

It is a truth generally acknowledged, and rarely questioned, that 90-95 per cent of all UFO sightings have rational explanations. They become IFOs (Identified Flying Objects) after responsible investigation. But though the majority of ufologists accept this as a rule-of-thumb guide, few investigators behave as if they believe it.

In 1989 I was lecturing in Dallas, Texas, to a largely stunned audience, weaned on 'greys' and MJ-12 and hardly expecting what I had to offer, which probably seemed to them like hostile scepticism. Leaving my hotel and walking into the city centre that night I saw an extraordinary phenomenon in the sky – three, swirling cloud-like ovals of light that seemed to pulse and dance in mid air. I gazed with fascination, but realised that none of my companions was batting an eyelid. Obviously this was something they knew all about.

It was, of course, a novelty at the time – a computer-controlled searchlight projecting laser beams onto the underside of clouds to create these dancing ovals. I could well see how the uninitiated might imagine it to be the tripod landing gear on an Adamski scout craft or the lights at each apex of one of today's glut of triangular UFOs.

Two years later calls flooded in to our UFO group in Manchester. People on the Pennine roads near Huddersfield in West Yorkshire were seeing strange things to their west. They described a dancing triangle of lights. They thought they were seeing UFOs and the police, equally puzzled, were giving them no reason to think otherwise.

Needless to say, their story rang a clear bell with me. Next night, same time, I went and stood in the garden of my Stockport home. There, to my north, were the swooping dancing lights. They were far off – not right on top of me as at Dallas – but my suspicion was proven correct. The UFO was a laser light show. I realised that these beams are so powerful, they can be seen up to 60 kilometres away. From an oblique angle, in a town far from that where the searchlights are being used (in this case Manchester, to promote a new nightclub), chances are that nobody local to the UFO sightings would have a clue what was happening.

The moral is that UFO investigators must familiarise themselves with the latest technology, by reading scientific journals and aviation magazines. The latter are important, because more and more UFOs are resolved as misperceptions of unfamiliar craft such as airships, pilotless drones and novel aircraft using sophisticated technology. To eliminate them, the ufologist must first identify them.

RULE 2: THE MORE WITNESSES THERE ARE, THE LESS LIKELY IT'S REALLY A UFO.

At first glance this idea seems ridiculous. Surely the more eyewitness testimony we get for a sighting, the stronger the evidence? Unfortunately, experience dictates otherwise. Real UFOs – and yes, I do believe there are genuinely new phenomena behind some sightings – tend to be very isolated events. I found this out during one of my very first cases.

The scene was Oldham, now recognised as being at the heart of one of Britain's biggest window areas. It was October 1972 and the location was Cairo Mill. A strange object like a blue dome with struts across it was seen to hover at a peculiar vertical angle alongside the building. One of the security guards saw it clearly. So did the factory cat – which fled and was in hiding for some days afterwards. Yet the other security guard, only metres away and in a position where he ought to have seen the object, apparently witnessed nothing at all.

Was he simply unobservant? I don't think so. I believe that many other cases such as this also demonstrate that UFOs appear within a very definite 'sphere of influence'. Whether this is a physical space determined by the phenomenon or a psychic space somehow determined by the witness is not yet clear. What is clear is that the second guard saw nothing because there was nothing to see – that is, for him to see. Even if half Oldham had seen this (still unresolved) close encounter, I would remain unimpressed. Instead it would convince me that there was an IFO explanation. That might seem paradoxical, but experience shows that, when mass sightings occur, in seeming defiance of the 'sphere of influence' process, they are likely to prove IFOs rather than UFOs.

On 31 December 1978 we had literally thousands of witnesses to sightings around northern Europe. They saw a trail of lights – often described as being windows on the side of a cigar-shaped craft. Fire brigades were called out in response to reports of crashing aircraft. I personally collected 100 report forms from witnesses who ranged from air traffic controllers and police officers to housewives and drunken party revellers.

This mass sighting covered such a wide area at more or less the same time (around 7.05 pm) that one thing was instantly clear: whatever the object was, it had to be at a very high altitude to be seen so widely. Eyewitness descriptions of a 'craft' the size of an airliner at a height of maybe 3,000 metres had to be wrong. The object was spread over several kilometres of sky and was at least twenty times higher than estimated.

In this case, we know with certainty that what people were seeing was the spectacular re-entry into our upper atmosphere of the blazing booster rocket from a Cosmos satellite launched in Russia a few days before. The metal fragments were being consumed by the heat of friction, forming a chain of debris many kilometres long. The 'windows' in the side of a 'cigar-like craft' were optical illusions caused by witnesses – in effect – 'joining the dots' and making the understandable, but in this case entirely erroneous assumption that they were seeing a single object close to the ground.

Every UFO sighting is filtered through our human perception, with all the opportunities for misperception this entails. And that's only the start: it then must run the gauntlet of our beliefs, our expectations and our fears. By the time the witness tells his story to an investigator it may unconsciously have been considerably transformed from what was really visible.

On 6 January 1995, an unidentified object was seen (for under five seconds) by the two air crew of a British Airways Boeing heading into Manchester Airport. The case became highly celebrated, and media worldwide featured it as 'one of the big ones'. Even the Civil Aviation Authority in their January 1996 'Air Miss' report claimed they could not identify the 'craft' (which – unlike the Boeing – was not visible on radar) and made the bizarre comment that they would leave the possibility that it was an alien spacecraft to those better qualified to judge. Such an ill-considered remark was almost guaranteed to make the media hail this case a classic: my suggestion that it might have been a fireball meteor was not well received. Yet in fact the encounter becomes much less dramatic once you accept that these pilots only 'thought' they saw a solid, structured craft rush past their cockpit. Many of those who witnessed the 31 December 1978 re-entry thought exactly the same thing. Pilots are human too, and just as likely as anyone to read alien structure behind what is really no more than a mass of lights.

The phenomenon above the Peak District that winter's night was undoubtedly physically real and without question puzzling to the men who saw it. But it does not follow that the object was a structured craft: only that they perceived it as one. Many space vessels are constructed in the shipyards of the human mind.

RULE 3: NEVER SAY NEVER.

Not every incident can be explained within a matter of days. A solution can take years, even decades, to come about. It is important to remember that, while every UFO is a potential IFO, there is no such thing as a proven UFO. It is simply a category to which a puzzling sighting is assigned pending further developments.

A recent dramatic example is the remarkable photograph taken by a scientist at Williamette Pass, Oregon, in 1966. What appears to be a triple image of a flattened disc is seen rising from a snow-covered forest. There even seems to be a plume of snow being sucked from the woods from its underside. For 30 years this was highly regarded – a credible witness, a daylight photograph that defied solution and what looked like an example of 'novel physics' with the object pulsing in and out of reality to create three distinct images during the fraction of a second that the camera shutter was open.

Only it was no such thing. Brilliant investigation by Irwin Wieder was followed by on-site reconstruction and led to an explanation nobody could have predicted. The UFO was nothing more than a roadside signpost photographed from a moving car: the blurring created by the motion caused it to be distorted beyond recognition. This remarkably down-to-earth conclusion might have eluded attention forever but for Wieder's perseverance.

I saw this process in operation myself with the 23 seconds of colour movie film taken in January 1973 by Peter Day at Cuddington on the Oxfordshire/Buckinghamshire border. The footage depicts a pulsing orange ball of light moving low behind the tree line and has often been used in TV documentaries as a prime example of a UFO.

When I first discovered the case around 1977, I spent some personal time investigating it. Peter Warrington and I took the original film to Kodak, who established the veracity of the film and certain key features of the object. The suggestion was made that it might be ball lightning. With Kodak's help we staged a private seminar at which the film was studied by some of the country's leading atmospheric physicists. Ball lightning was eliminated for various cogent reasons. A MoD munitions expert wondered if it might be orange searchlights atop helicopters. It was an intelligent suggestion, but we found that that particular project was not operational at the time.

When I took on the job of BUFORA director of investigations in 1981, I ordered a full appraisal of this now eight-year-old case. There had always been concern over the link with the crash of an F-111 jet some 50km away later that same morning. Peter Day felt the UFO he had filmed might have led to its accident. Indeed, as of 1996, he still prefers this possibility.

Some of those re-investigating the case for BUFORA suggested that Day had filmed the crashing jet itself. However, the film was taken at just after 9a.m. (according to Day) and the jet crashed 40 minutes later. There is no way it could have been flying around on fire for so long. A split developed amongst investigators as a result. I agreed with the view that there must have been a connection between these two extremely unusual events, but my investigations confirmed that Peter Day was correct in his timings. Moreover, they were confirmed by other witnesses – school children at the village of Long Crendon. I tracked down many of these (now adults) and from their stories there was no doubt that 9.05a.m. was the latest possible time they could have seen the UFO. I also established that a faint engine noise may have been heard.

I traced the history of the F-111 crash, as far as I could. The plane first developed a fault at around 9a.m. and flew in circles until it caught fire and crashed. In other words the plane first had problems at the time when the UFO appeared. Surely this was no coincidence. I developed a 'best guess' that the F-111 dumped fuel on first developing its fault. Using afterburners to ignite this outflow, a ball of blazing aviation fuel emerged from the plane. This became trapped in a thermal layer at a cloud boundary level around 2,000 feet and literally rolled along in the wake of the jet for several minutes. It was this fireball which was seen by witnesses and filmed by Peter Day. The jet may well by then have been some distance ahead and so was not clearly audible. It was also not visible being above the cloud.

When in 1992 Scottish researcher Steuart Campbell finally secured a copy of the official report through the US Freedom of Information Act, we learnt that the F-111 had developed an electrical fault. It did indeed dump fuel more or less on top of Long Crendon at just after 9a.m. The process was very quickly abandoned, perhaps because the crew saw the consequence in the form of the fireball. They then flew on for 40 minutes trying to use up fuel hoping to make an emergency landing back at USAF Upper Heyford. When the fault developed into a fire, however, they had to bail out.

So as it turned out our guess came pretty close to what had happened. The case also provides a perfect illustration of why, speaking of finding explanations, one should never say never.

RULE 4: FIRST HAND IS THE ONLY HAND

Most of us have favourite cases. We have read about them in books, perhaps for years, and consider them to be of the sort of quality that convinces us of UFO reality.

One often cited is the Lakenheath/Bentwaters affair of August 1956. We knew nothing about it until it was revealed by chance during the University of Colorado government funded UFO investigation in 1968. One of the participants from the USAF told the investigating scientists of his role, assuming they knew about the case anyway because they were supposed to have been provided with all of the US government data on UFOs. But this case was being hidden away somewhere. The same is even more true in the UK, where the sighting happened. Despite attempts to squeeze data out of the MoD and a search of the Public Record Office files, all we turned up was a passing reference in a 1957 briefing memo about radar cases.

According to the generally accepted version, what occurred was that strange targets were picked up on radar around East Anglia that August night. They milled about in unusual ways and were visually witnessed near the USAF base at Bentwaters in a famous incident where a ground-based witness at the control tower saw a light looking upwards and a passing USAF transport aircraft saw the yellow smudge flying beneath its path. The radar target was tracked heading slowly westwards towards Lakenheath where it was also detected. Shortly afterwards two Venom night fighters were scrambled from Waterbeach and sent in pursuit. According to the American version, these were single-seater jets. One had to return to base with some fault, but the other made a lock-on with airborne radar, reported seeing the clearest target ever witnessed by the pilot and then described how the glow jumped from the front to the back of the jet as it tried to close in on the UFO. After a game of cat and mouse the pilot ran out of fuel and returned to base.

In 1978 the only British confirmation of this matter occurred during publicity for the movie *Close Encounters of the Third Kind*. A version of the events was serialised by a national newspaper. and retired squadron leader Freddie Wimbledon came forward, confirmed he had scrambled the Venoms, and broadly supported the above story.

Things might have stayed like that forever, but during early 1996 I was making a TV documentary on the British government's UFO files. By good fortune, and helped by the resources of the BBC, I traced the air crews of both Venoms. The airmen were willing to talk openly and without any reservation. The first surprise was that the US version of events was wrong in several respects.

First, both Venoms had a pilot and a navigator. I talked to three of the four crew (the fourth emigrated some years ago). Both crews had retained their log books so that we could put together an accurate portrait of the events of that night. None of the witnesses had any idea that the case was a major incident in UFO lore because, contrary to popular belief, they did not see any UFO that night at all! Nor had any of them heard of Freddie Wimbledon, though they agreed he might have scrambled them without their being aware of his identity. Their communications that night were mostly with the Americans who were directing them to radar targets previously detected.

The airmen admit that the incident stands out in their memory as strange. It was the only time they were scrambled over land and at such a low height (under 1,500m). On all other occasions the radar had detected a possible intruder out over

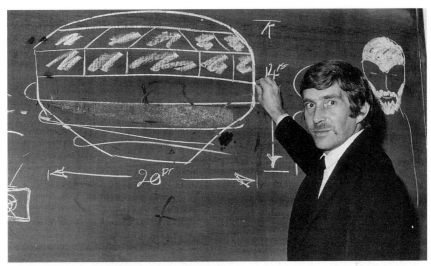

Alan Godfrey, possible British UFO abductee

the North Sea and their job was to intercept it before it even got as far as Britain. They were not accustomed to be asked to fly between Lakenheath and Ely over sleeping fields to look for something unidentified quite low down.

Though they did detect the UFO on radar, it was never 'the clearest target they had ever had'. There was no game of cat and mouse. Nor did the object suddenly move from front to rear of their aircraft. Instead they told me they were pursuing a stationary target that did not seem to move at all during their investigation. This was the problem. They kept flying past it in the black sky as they were closing at such speed, with only the radar echo to guide them. I asked if it could have been a weather balloon invisible in the darkness. They agreed that it could have been ; their assumption that it wasn't was based at least partly on the excitement of the USAF personnel they were talking with.

I still do not know the answer to the August 1956 case, of course. We may never know. But it is obvious that the high status afforded to this sighting is at least partly due to the supposed aerial ballet between RAF Venom and the UFO. The story appears to have been seriously over-rated. Maybe the men did encounter a UFO, but on the basis of what they told me, we cannot rule out the idea that they chanced upon a weather balloon.

It could be argued that the case remains important because of what had happened before the RAF became involved. But even this seems questionable, seeing how the American version over-played the role of the RAF airmen and incorporated such fundamental errors.

RULE 5: IT IS THE WITNESS'S STORY, NOT YOURS.

The Alan Godfrey case from November 1980 is one of Britain's best-known examples of an apparent alien abduction. Whilst serving as a West Yorkshire police officer at 5a.m. one cold night he went to look for some straying cattle and instead confronted a large object straddling the road ahead. This was like a spinning top, rotating violently and causing the trees and bushes to shake. The wet road surface underneath the object was swirled dry by the hovering UFO.

I have little doubt that Godfrey really did see something quite remarkable that night – although I have an open mind as to whether it was a constructed craft that would have gone clang if you threw a rock at it, or some sort of unusual atmospheric energy rotating like a tornado.

The idea that it was a spaceship was, I think, raised not so much by the witness as by the media and even by his contact with ufology. Indeed, if you check through close encounter cases carefully you will find how often that same worrying scenario may be true. We ufologists serve as architects of UFO reality.

Certainly, Alan Godfrey suffered a 'memory blink'. One moment he was looking at the object and the next it was gone, the sky was dark and he seemed to be some distance further down the road. But was there a time lapse during which he was possibly abducted by aliens? This, of course, is the belief shared by many of the ufologists most closely involved with the case, and it stemmed from a site reconstruction carried out by investigators.

In no way am I seeking to suggest that any individual invented a time lapse or forced Godfrey into the acceptance of one. It does not work like that. The investigation process is more subtle, working as a subconscious interaction. But I do have reservations that there is missing time to be accounted for here. At the best estimate in any case it was only 15 minutes in duration, and I suspect that when you are seeing a UFO at five o'clock in the morning 15 minutes can go astray fairly easily without needing to be explained as abduction by aliens.

However, once it had been accepted by Godfrey that there was a time gap, the possibility of an on-board alien abduction soon offered itself. He told me later that during the six months between his sighting and his regression hypnosis sessions he read books about UFOs and aliens, and he could never be certain that his 'memory' under hypnosis had not been stimulated in this way. He remains adamant that he saw a real UFO above the road, but has always seemed to me less positive about the status of his abduction recall.

Possibly Alan Godfrey was abducted. I know that 'real abductions' (however we ultimately explain them) do occur and it would be folly to reject this case as a possible candidate. But we have a duty to consider alternative possibilities. Suppose, for a moment, that there was no missing time; that Godfrey blinked and the UFO disappeared – or he doesn't recall driving the hundred metres or so towards it. If so, then what do we make of his apparent 'memory' of being kidnapped inside a strange room by a large bearded alien called Yosef, a big black dog and some little robots that uttered beeping sounds?

It is difficult to express this sort of comment without seeming to imply criticism of the witness or of the investigators. But we need to face the fact that the process of evaluating a witness's story and the protocols of investigating it can lead everyone involved toward an outcome which may have already been predetermined, unconsciously, by the UFO community. I have come upon cases in which I am satisfied that what investigators (and soon afterward the witness) firmly believe to be an alien abduction was simply an accident created in rather dubious circumstances.

In another incident a local group met a witness who had taken some camcorder footage of a light moving across the sky. Investigation revealed to my personal satisfaction that the UFO was a weather balloon. However, the witness was not persuaded by this idea and soon afterwards met another investigator with more liberal views. The conclusion was soon mutually reached that there had been a period of missing time, though the witness had never mentioned it to the previous investigators: hypnosis then began to search for a hidden abduction.

Someone was clearly right and the other wrong. If the UFO was a balloon,

Jim Templeton's 1964 photo of his daughter on Burgh Marsh with a mysterious 'alien'

there was no time lapse, no abduction. The case illustrates the danger of passing witness testimony through a filter of belief, especially when the physical facts have yet to be established. Unfortunately, too many ufologists cherish vested interests which drive them to jump to premature conclusions.

RULE 6: DIG DEEP

If the last piece of advice is followed closely, it does not follow that witness testimony should be accepted at face value. But what should be the course of action when the witness does not claim to have suffered a time lapse and has no desire to search for a missing abduction memory, yet where you feel there has to be more to it than meets the eye?

Take the case of Carlisle fireman Jim Templeton, who in May 1964 took a puzzling photograph which I had seen many times in books and magazines. But I knew almost nothing about the background to the case because ufologists had not

255

investigated – they had simply fallen in love with the quirky photo and papered their walls with it.

Templeton had been out on Burgh Marsh with his wife and two daughters on a Sunday picnic, during which he had taken colour photos of his younger daughter holding a bunch of flowers. Upon development one picture had been 'spoiled' by what appeared to be a man in a white spacesuit floating behind Elizabeth's head.

I started to hunt for Templeton. I was lucky, and even though it was now almost 30 years since his sighting I found him. We had several phone conversations, and eventually I visited him and his wife and heard their recollections. Soon I had information on the case I could never have dreamed of.

For a start I learned about the visitation by the Men in Black. Neither Jim nor his wife ever called them this, of course. Their knowledge of UFOs was minimal. The two men in dark suits claimed to be from the government and treated Jim in typically ridiculous MIB fashion – using numbers instead of names and trying to browbeat him into accepting a mundane explanation. They also asked obscure questions which in today's UFO terms were rather sophisticated, probing about his case and ultimately getting so irate at his replies that they drove off in their big black Jaguar car and left him dumped on the marsh facing a long walk home.

More emerged. I found that Templeton had suffered a run-in with the MoD who confiscated subsequent slides he took at the site. I found that he was at a place where British space rockets were being built and that within days of his sighting at the launch site of one of these rockets (Woomera in Australia) a UFO had been recorded on cameras filming the launch.

What had begun as the investigation of a single puzzling photo led me down pathways of exploration which I am still investigating today. The moral is, never assume there is no more to a case than what appears on the surface. Be prepared to dig deep.

BY WAY OF CONCLUSION

I do not pretend that simply by adhering to these principles, all the problems that beset UFO research will suddenly disappear. I can only say that I personally have found them to be valuable guidelines to follow. They have helped me see that behind the illusion of ufology as it is popularly perceived there is a phenomenon very worthy of study. But to get to that point we must first unlearn a good deal that we have been conditioned to believe in during our formative years.

Thankfully, there is no better way to do this than to go out into the field and investigate some actual UFO sightings. This is the best dose of realism than anyone can get. In today's media-saturated world, finding UFO sightings is one thing nobody should have much difficulty in doing. The tough part comes when you start to investigate those sightings and try to figure out what they mean.

A TWENTIETH-CENTURY MYTH

by Hilary Evans

ooking back to that day, 50 years ago, when the flying saucers arrived, we can see that they were unquestionably an idea whose time had come. We sense an air of inevitability, both in the way the UFO was originally formulated, and in the way it subsequently developed. The simple, original myth gave birth to a rich family of sub-myths, some springing from popular culture, some from within the dedicated UFO research community, each interacting with the other.

Any anomalous phenomenon is likely to attract a cluster of more-or-less related phenomena which broaden its appeal and underpin its acceptability. The original Loch Ness Monster attracted a proliferation of seemingly similar creatures so that 'lake monsters' are now an accepted anomaly category. Developing from a one-of-a-kind event to stereotype, and from stereotype to variations-on-a-theme, is how myths come into being.

It is safe to say that no anomalous phenomenon has generated so rich an anomaly-cluster as the flying saucer. Kenneth Arnold's straightforward, uncomplicated sighting is now so embedded in a sprawling aggregate of associated happenings that the core phenomenon has been well-nigh lost sight of. The naïve observers who witnessed strange things in the 1947 skies would be astonished to see their simple sightings associated with mutilated cattle and circles in cornfields, unmarked black helicopters and unidentified Men in Black, saucer crashes in the desert and saucer bases in the Antarctic, malevolent djinns and benevolent Control Systems, contactees taken on interplanetary tours, abductees subjected to inter-species breeding. Yet one by one, over the past fifty years, these and many more have been attached to the original phenomenon, constituting a wonderfully rich and elaborate mythology unmatched in the world's folklore.

THE INNOCENT MYTH

For the starry-eyed innocents of the 1940s, the flying saucers were wonder enough in themselves. Yet no one had been really surprised by *The Coming of the Saucers* – the title of the 1952 book Kenneth Arnold wrote with Ray Palmer. Astonished, amazed, excited – yes; but not surprised. As though people had been expecting the saucers to show up, sooner or later; as though they were waiting for Arnold – or if not him, someone else – to proclaim his sighting. The news, when it came, flashed around the planet in hours – clear indication that humankind, whether or not it formulated the idea clearly, had been anticipating just such an announcement.

The first response had to be that the saucers were artifacts created by a foreign power, and presumably a hostile one. For the United States, this meant Soviet Russia; and the notion that the Russians might be responsible was one that persisted for a long time. As late as the 1960s, Dr Don Boys of Indianapolis could publish a book with the title *Flying Saucers – Myths, Madness or made in Moscow?*

An alternative to the Russian bogey was the Nazi bogey. Only two years had passed since the end of the war in Europe; it was entirely plausible that during its final days the Nazis had established bases in Antarctica, a region they were known to have explored before the war. They were known, too, to have experimented with disc-shaped aircraft, and to have developed rocket propulsion. Combining secret bases with secret technology offered a plausible scenario, persuasively detailed by Italian investigator Renato Vesco in *Intercettateli Senza Sparare* ('Intercept but don't shoot'). Were Nazi survivors cherishing dreams of re-establishing the Master Race with the help of the UFO? For a generation still scarred by the trauma of a global war, it was not difficult to believe. The Nazi roots of the flying discs provided the saucer myth with one of its earliest but most durable sub-myths: Vesco's book would be republished and his ideas seriously re-evaluated in the 1990s.

But as witness after witness reported their observations, it became evident that the saucers displayed a capability which exceeded anything terrestrial technology could match. They flew too fast, they turned too sharply, they changed their configuration, they split and reunited, they came out of nowhere and vanished into nowhere. What's more, they came in a bewildering variety of shapes and sizes, from spheres the diameter of a football to giant rectangles the length of a football field. Faced with this challenge, it was simple logic to reason that if they didn't come from anywhere on our planet, they must come from somewhere beyond it.

It was a logical step, and it was taken confidently. Considering the implications of the step, it is astonishing how easily the man and woman in the street found a place for the extraterrestrial explanation in their belief-systems. But of course it wasn't as abrupt as it seemed: there had been a century of conditioning to prepare them for it. Just as religious conversions may be triggered by a vision of the Virgin Mary, but are the result of prolonged subconscious gestation, so the flying saucer myth, sprung by Arnold's sighting, sprouted in ground which had been long prepared.

THE MYTH OF OTHERWORLDLY VISITATION

The idea that there may be other inhabited worlds is an archetypal concept which we humans have toyed with throughout history: Baron Münchhausen was just one of the many space voyagers celebrated in popular literature. But what had hitherto been a diverting fantasy became less improbable when, toward the close of the 18th century, the Montgolfier brothers built a balloon and enabled man to escape his planet. Those first tentative flights lifted their adventurous travellers only a few hundred metres off the ground, yet they opened the way for far-reaching speculation, rooted now in fact rather than fantasy. The fictions of Jules Verne and H. G. Wells were explicit formulations of the idea in terms of the science of their day, and their precedent was followed and expanded in the 1920s and 1930s. It is no exaggeration to say that virtually every feature of the flying saucer myth – paralysing rays and levitating beams, telepathic communication and alien abduction – was anticipated by the ingenious authors who contributed to *Amazing Stories*, *Air Wonder Stories* and their contemporaries.

So plausibly did these writers detail their scenarios – Hugo Gernsback, the pioneering publisher of the sci-fi pulps, insisted his authors' fictions be firmly rooted in scientific fact – that by the outbreak of war interaction with beings from other planets was an accepted possibility. On 30 October 1938 the hysteria unleashed by the radio adaptation of *The War of the Worlds* demonstrated how firmly that possibility had been accepted by ordinary people. For thousands, the myth had become a terrifying reality. So it followed that, when the saucers came, they found the world ready to receive them. With wonder, certainly, but not with surprise.

That is not to say, however, that everyone was ready to go along with the idea that – to quote the title of Jimmy Guieu's 1954 book, *Les Soucoupes Volantes Viennent d'un Autre Monde* – the flying saucers come from another world. While many were prepared to agree, many others retreated to a more sceptical position. Yes, they conceded, the otherworldly origin of flying saucers was a logical inference – but only on the premise that there were any flying saucers to be explained. But suppose there weren't? Suppose the claimed sightings were less substantial than they seemed? Suppose the entire corpus of witness testimony was nothing but delusion or misinterpretation?

There was historical precedent. Claims to have seen and met the Virgin Mary and other religious figures had been made throughout history: could so many thousands of visionaries all have been hallucinating? Yes, there was good reason to suppose so. Closer still was the parallel with the witchcraft mania which raged from the 15th to the 18th century. It took centuries for the world to accept the possibility of collective delusion on so large a scale, but eventually witchcraft was reclassified as social myth. So, the sceptics argued, might it not be the same with the flying saucers?

Those reluctant to accept the extraterrestrial hypothesis welcomed the idea that all UFOs could be attributed to illusion or delusion. But in denying that anything out of the way was being seen, the sceptics defied an enormous weight of testimony, much of it provided by patently sincere and honest people who were neither drunk, drugged or otherwise out of their minds. To assert that none of these claims had any foundation in physical reality was unacceptable to investigators like Donald Keyhoe, whose conclusion that 'Flying Saucers are Real' – the title of his landmark article in *True* magazine – was considered persuasive by those who could not bring themselves to set so much testimony aside. Clearly, objects were being seen flying, which people were unable to identify; ergo, UFOs existed.

What's more, they existed as physical fact. At this stage it seemed possible, and indeed sensible, to think of the UFOs as physical spacecraft from civilisations like our own, albeit manifestly more advanced. Tens of thousands of sightings were being reported, and they lent themselves to methodical cataloguing, classified systematically as 'daylight discs', 'nocturnal lights' and so on. Charts were made showing the various shapes, much like the spotters' guides to WW2 aircraft. The 'nuts-and-bolts' approach seemed the scientific approach. It was still legitimate to conceive of the saucer myth as a science in the making.

Certainly, if true, the claims being made were awesome in their significance. They implied nothing less than the most momentous happening in human history. The death of Captain Mantell was a sobering reminder of the sinister realities underlying the myth. Already, books with such titles as *Flying Saucers on the Attack* were warning of a possible threat, not simply to individual witnesses but to humankind.

THE COSMIC MYTH

It was recognised that, before such extraordinary claims could be accepted, extraordinary proof would be needed. However, with reports pouring in from round the globe, it seemed only a matter of time before the proof would be there for all to see.

But the good intentions of the scientific investigators had been shadowed, from the start, by the equally well-intentioned but deplorably unscientific activities of people who were impatient of this approach – who felt, intuitively, that flying saucers represented something far more profound than other people's spacecraft. Rejecting the idea that they might be hostile, they hailed the craft as visitations from higher realms well-disposed to the human race, bearing messages from Inter-Planetary Parliaments, Galactic Commands, Cosmic Brotherhoods.

The proliferation of ingenious theories which enriched the myth during the golden age of the flying saucer is a tribute to the human imagination. Did the saucers come from the past, the future or a parallel space-time continuum? Kurt Glemser, unable to make up his mind, authored both *Flying Saucers and Inner Earth* and *Flying Saucers from the Fourth Dimension*. One author proposed that *God Drives a Flying Saucer*, another pointed a finger at the djinns of Islamic theology. That flying saucers were satanic was an axiom of fundamentalist believers: yet evangelist Billy Graham was not alone in likening them to angels. Still others saw them as heralding Armageddon – *Flying Saucers: Portents of the 'Last Days'* was one apocalyptic interpretation. Perceptive commentators pointed out that UFO manifestations always seemed to be one step ahead of Earth technology: could it be that advanced civilisations were subtly guiding us towards a new understanding of our place in the cosmos?

While the True Believers prepared landing pads and laid out light arrays where the visitors could land their spacecraft (an aspect of the myth superbly documented in Douglas Curran's *In Advance of the Landing*), others offered more down-to-earth though equally innovative explanations. A veteran researcher into the paranormal, the Austrian countess Wassilo-Serecki, proposed that UFOs might be living creatures inhabiting Earth's atmosphere. In his *They Live in the Sky*, New Zealander Trevor James Constable told how infra-red photography, combined with 'elementary principles of spiritual science' enabled him to take photos in the California desert which showed just such 'invisible' creatures. Those who shrank from the extra-terrestrial hypothesis welcomed this more mundane alternative: Kenneth Arnold himself ultimately came to take the view that UFOs are space animals.

THE ENCOUNTER MYTH

If the flying saucers could visit our planet, they could land on it. And while the smaller spheres might be unmanned probes, the larger UFOs surely contained crews: it was the next logical step in the development of the myth. Just as few had been surprised by the flying saucers in the first place, few were surprised when the first witnesses came forward to tell of meetings with their occupants.

Surprised, once again, no; but the contact claims encountered scepticism not only from those who questioned flying saucers as such, but also from those who accepted them as scientific fact. The first story which laid the foundations for the new development of the myth was that told by George Adamski. He told it well, and persuasively, and seemed to provide confirmation; but doubters were able to find flaws in his story, which grew progressively less plausible as he elaborated it with fairy-tales travelogues of flights to distant planets.

This did not, of course, prevent him being taken as role-model by a shoal of imitators. The great age of the contactees represents the UFO myth at its most colourful, as Howard Menger and Truman Bethurum told of their romantic encounters with glamorous spacewomen and Cecil Michael told of his *Round Trip to Hell in a Flying Saucer*. Another traveller was Colorado farmer Buck Nelson, who was flown to Mars, the Moon and Venus, accompanied by his dog Teddy. Alabama citizen John Womack was given an 'anti-demon pill' which protected him against the malevolent spirits who inflict such suffering on humanity. Many otherworldly beings were found to be living on Earth: author Brad Steiger's second wife was one of these 'starpeople', and checklists of tell-tale signs were drawn up whereby people could discover whether they, too, were of extraterrestrial origin. Perhaps the most fortunate of all was Elizabeth Klarer from South Africa whose out-of-this-world romance with Akon from Meton led to her bearing him a child.

Such tales entertained the public, who flocked to lecture-halls and convention arenas where the contactees enjoyed celebrity status. But they infuriated serious researchers like Keyhoe, whose painstaking efforts to obtain support from the government and the scientific establishment were undermined by these stories which seemed to make flying saucers a laughing-stock. What was especially aggravating was that, while these stories were hard to believe, they were equally hard to disprove. The hard-headed compilers of sighting catalogues were reluctant to include Adamski's or Menger's encounters alongside their sober factual reports: but on what grounds could they justify their discrimination?

'A MODERN MYTH'

But while some applauded and some discounted the contactees, there were others who, without going so far as to accept them, yet saw in them a deeper significance. The experience of Orfeo Angelucci, a contactee from California, inspired the book which first proclaimed the mythic quality of the UFO. Carl Jung's *Flying Saucers: a Modern Myth of Things Seen in the Skies* placed the flying saucer myth, and the contactee legends in particular, in the historical tradition of archetypal folklore. For the first time since they had appeared, Jung sanctioned a view of the saucers which neither accepted them at face value, nor dismissed them wholesale as did the sceptics, but saw them as a genuine phenomenon occurring on a different level of reality.

Other researchers carried the idea into farther reaches of the unknown. John Keel's anarchic *Operation Trojan Horse* (1970) invited his readers into a 'Disneyland of the Gods' in which the saucer people interacted with mothmen, ghost-fliers, Men In Black and Cosmic Jokers. Jerome Clark and Loren Coleman pushed speculation deeper still, proposing a 'paraufology' which linked UFOs to fairy lore, angelic visitations and New Age channelling. Whatever the soundness or otherwise of these concepts, they served to open minds to possibilities beyond the nuts-and-bolts realities of mainstream ufologists while avoiding the mysticism of the saucer cults.

But though such suggestions offered an alternative to taking the flying saucers at face value, they were even less likely than the hard-line extra-terrestrial hypothesis to appeal to the scientific establishment. They too lacked any kind of support in observed fact; by linking the UFO to fairies and religious visions, they took the phenomenon yet deeper into the unprovable and improbable. So while paraufology enriched the myth with stimulating new perspectives, it did nothing to establish the phenomenon as a legitimate subject for scientific study.

A SCIENTIFIC MYTH

If the scientific establishment felt any misgivings about dismissing the UFO, it was the contactees who provided them with moral justification. Tale after tall tale, often told in privately printed brochures published at the author's expense, testified to the cult character of much UFO activity. At popular conventions such as George Van Tassel's at Giant Rock, California, or homespun get-togethers such as Buck Nelson's at Mountain View, Missouri, a colourful melange of marginal people gathered and swapped stories. A scientist had to be very sure or very careless of his tenure to risk his reputation by associating himself with so unstable a phenomenon.

Nevertheless, a few did: such respectability as ufology attained was almost entirely due to the efforts of the astronomer Allen Hynek. Others were generally from the behavioural sciences. When in 1949 Mrs Dorothy Martin of Chicago claimed that guardian aliens would help her group to evacuate a catastrophe-doomed Earth, the tense build-up to the scheduled event, and the devastating anti-climax when it failed to occur, were closely followed by Leon Festinger and his sociologist colleagues who infiltrated the group. Their findings, published in the classic study *When Prophecy Fails*, not only seemed to confirm that the saucers and their occupants were a delusion but also threw a revealing light on the strategies whereby True Believers sidestep logic to accommodate myth.

If the scientists found the contactees a sufficient reason to entirely dissociate themselves from the UFO phenomenon, those who remained convinced that it presented a genuine challenge tried to pursue their activities as though the contactees were a regrettable complication but irrelevant to the true UFO problem. By now, serious UFO research was global. Dedicated investigators in Sweden and Spain, Australia and Italy were pursuing the enigma with astonishing diligence. Journals such as France's *Lumières dans la Nuit* and Belgium's *Inforespace*, Denmark's *UFO-Nyt* and Spain's *Stendek*, stand as monuments to countless man-hours of patient, methodical work, listening to puzzled peasants and questioning bewildered housewives. Though procedures were primitive, improvised and arbitrary, the sheer volume of reports generated an impressive build-up of data, however crude and uneven their value. First as card-indexes, later as computerised data-bases, the catalogues built up into compelling evidence that the myth had a basis in reality.

Any research is only as good as those doing the researching, and though the larger organisations published manuals and guides, and even held investigator training sessions, groups varied widely in their attitude to the phenomenon. Some were virtually religious congregations, others were local clubs providing an excuse for socialising and friendly skywatching; in between, every shade of commitment or open-mindness was represented. Nevertheless, despite inevitable quarrels and rivalries, researchers felt themselves members of a worldwide community, working towards a common goal. They knew one another by name if not in person, and at public conferences and private colloquiums they met to exchange views and share findings.

THE ABDUCTION MYTH

For all their extravagance, the effect that the contactees had on serious UFO research was not entirely negative. True, mainstream ufologists distanced themselves from individuals such as George King, with his claims to be the selected representative of Earth in the Intergalactic Parliament and to have participated in the massive aerial battle which saved our planet from destruction by hostile aliens. ('On July 8th, 1964, the greatest event in the history of the world took place.') But the mere existence of a maverick fringe was evidence that there was something to be on the fringe of. Like the hoaxers who almost from the start had been a regrettable but inevitable feature of the UFO scene, they provided a kind of confirmation that the phenomenon was real. For a parasite to exist, there must be a host.

For the serious ufologist, to distance oneself from the cultists and contactees was not too difficult. It was less easy when the contactees gave place to the abductees. Essentially, there was no major discontinuity between the contactees and the abductees – the life-enhancing experience of Betty Andreasson, for example, who believed her abductors were messengers from God, could be assigned to either category. Contactees and abductees alike had personal stories to tell of encounters with aliens; neither was able to back up the stories with any evidence. The difference between them was one of plausibility.

A characteristic of the contactees which had always provoked scepticism was the claim, made by Adamski, King, Siragusa and many more, to have been individually chosen for their special qualities: even the kindest observer could not but question why, from all humanity, these unremarkable people had been picked out. With the abductees it was different: they were chosen at random, for no discernible individual qualities. Where the contactees had been treated like honoured guests and taken on guided tours of the spacecraft, even a sightseeing flight round the galaxy, the abductees found themselves anonymous guinea-pigs in a laboratory-like setting where they were subjected to impersonal physical examination; sometimes the females would be impregnated, sometimes the men would have sperm samples taken. Some were able to take a positive view of their experience, and even had their lives and lifestyles enhanced as a result – becoming vegetarian, giving up smoking, taking up sculpture, discovering healing powers, receiving valuable spiritual insights. But for most of the abductees, being abducted was a negative experience – unpleasant, upsetting and ultimately unrewarding.

Those who championed the abductees solicited belief by showing how the experiences fitted into a scenario whereby the aliens were seeking biological and especially genetic information about our species. But it was this very mundane character of the abduction claims which made them, if anything, less plausible than the claims of the contactees. The more 'real' the stories were made to sound, the more clearly the discrepancies and contradictions emerged. The nature of the abduction experience, the conduct of the abductors, raised questions which received no convincing answers.

Above all, it was the sheer numbers of alleged abductees which was the strongest argument against their physical reality. Their numbers ran into thousands; furthermore, a well-conducted public opinion poll seemed to show that several million people had been abducted in the United States alone. But how could this be reconciled with the total lack of independent confirmation? Abduction was a physical happening; the victim had to be physically transferred from the Earth to the spacecraft. It was hard to accept that on not one single occasion was this transfer independently witnessed in convincing circumstances. On the contrary, in more than one instance the claimed abductee was known to have been comfortably on Earth when s/he was supposedly being abducted onto a distant spaceship.

Despite its implausibility, this new development of the UFO myth commanded a degree of acceptance never attained by the contactees. Where the contactees had rarely secured substantial support – though one of Dorothy Martin's group was a college professor – the abductees found friends in high places. Barney and Betty Hill, the first to achieve worldwide notice, were the subject of a book by John Fuller, a writer of some repute. University professors of recognised standing committed themselves to the view that whereas the contactees' stories had been fantasies, those of the abductees were grounded in fact. An author of fantasy fiction told in what purported to be 'a true story' how he himself had been abducted by aliens. Later came a claim, put forward in all seriousness by a respected researcher, that the Secretary-General of the United Nations was an abduction victim.

This readiness to accept abduction stories at face value was revealing not only about the mentality of the public from whom the abductees recruited themselves, but also of the mind-set of those who championed them. The reliability of testimony obtained via hypnosis, the infallibility of lie detectors as an objective guarantee of truth, were affirmed by the believers and challenged by the sceptics. When Alvin Lawson and his colleagues demonstrated that 'imaginary abductees' could tell tales every bit as convincing as the 'true abductees', his findings were shrugged off by the believers who stigmatised his methodology as flawed and his conclusions unjustified. Yet the psychologist Kenneth Ring produced scientific documentation for his assertion that there was a segment of the population who were by their psychological make-up 'encounter-prone'.

THE WHITE HOUSE LAWN MYTH

If the contactees showed the myth at its most colourful, the abductees showed it at its most profound. On whatever level of reality the experiences were taking place, deep-lying facets of human behaviour were being revealed. And because so much more was at stake, no facet of the UFO myth so polarised the UFO research community. The question of why no abduction was ever convincingly witnessed while it was happening posed more pointedly than ever what had always been the fundamental problem with UFOs: their elusiveness.

From the start of the era of flying saucers, their now-you-see-me-now-you-don't behaviour contributed to their myth-like character. Like ghosts, fairies and the Virgin Mary, they left witnesses in doubt whether they meant to be seen or not. With UFO sightings running into hundreds of thousands, it was evident that the UFOs were not overly concerned to be inconspicuous. On the other hand, if they wanted to be seen, why didn't they hover over Trafalgar Square, circle the Eiffel Tower, land on the White House lawn? Why were the contactees and abductees ordinary men and women rather than leading scientists or eminent politicians?

Researchers could only speculate: and explanations offered by the aliens themselves were not much help. The flying saucer myth was at its wooliest and wordiest when the aliens sought to explain their purposes. In 1967 Stefan Denaerde spent two days in an alien spacecraft on the seabed of Holland's Oosterscheldt, while beings from the planet Iarga crammed him with information 'which will set the present generation to thinking': but no useful consequences resulted. It was no different with *Why We Are Here*, a book actually written by 'J. W.' from Jupiter, channelled by Gloria Lee: her death in 1962, after fasting for 66 days following his instructions, did not inspire confidence in alien wisdom. *Flying Saucer Intelligences Speak*, Laura Mundo's telepathic messages from outer space VIPs and many more long-winded texts were provided for our enlightenment, rivalling the spiritualists' messages from the dead in their richness and diversity. Alas, they resemble them also in their lack of checkable fact or testable information.

THE SAUCER CRASH MYTH

Despite their reluctance to reveal practical guidance on curing cancer or achieving free-energy space travel, it was a natural assumption that the beings from whom these channelled messages emanated hailed from civilisations boasting far greater wisdom than ourselves. On the whole, like the Mahatmas of theosophy, the Great White Brotherhood, or the mysterious sages of other mythologies, they were presented as infallible. But perhaps even they, like us earthlings, could be let down by the extraterrestrial equivalent of pilot error or metal fatigue. For another colourful strand, woven into the fabric of the UFO myth almost from the start, has been the legend that one or more saucers had crashed, leaving them – and sometimes their occupants – available for inspection.

On 8 July 1947, shortly after Arnold's landmark sighting, a USAF airbase in New Mexico released the news that the debris of a crashed saucer had been retrieved from an isolated ranch near Roswell. The fact that the authorities would rush to the media with such an announcement is in itself a significant indication how rapidly the UFO myth had taken hold.

The story was retracted as swiftly as it had been released, but other crashed-saucer reports came in – from Spitzbergen in 1952; from Heligoland in 1955; from Chitpec, Mexico in 1964. In May 1978 thousands saw a UFO which crashed in a remote mountain area of Bolivia. None of these stories was substantiated, but they inspired investigators to keep probing. Leonard Stringfield unearthed a remarkable number of witnesses who, either anonymous or cloaking their identity, felt the time had come to reveal how they had been among the experts secretly flown to a remote desert location to examine a saucer which had crashed with its occupants.

The one thing a crashed saucer should have been able to provide was physical evidence that scientists could touch and analyse. The failure to produce any such evidence killed interest in the stories, and the legend of the crashed saucer vanished from sight for many years. But the growth of the conspiracy myth provided a possible way to retain belief in the crashes: suppose there was indeed physical evidence, but it was being kept from public knowledge? In 1980 the Roswell story was dusted off and re-examined, leading to a controversy which filled books and television debates with conflicting testimony, false witness, spurious documents and mutual recrimination between the contradictory protagonists. Other crash stories, like that at Aztec in 1948, fuelled the debate; film footage was found which ostensibly showed post-mortem examination of the saucer occupants.

THE CONSPIRACY MYTH

The same year that the Roswell legend was revived, 1980, ended with a strange story from a more accessible source, Rendlesham in England. Rumours picked up by local investigators led to a story of a landed UFO, which was subsequently found to be backed by impressive supporting evidence – an official memo from the American Commanding Officer to the British Ministry of Defence, and a tape recording allegedly made by the same officer while scouring the nearby woods for the object. Unfortunately, the contingent circumstances were so ambiguous, the tape so unconvincing, that even such official evidence could not be accepted at face value. Clearly, something occurred at Rendlesham; but what that something was, remained open to conjecture. And yet somebody, somewhere, knew the truth.

Such incidents gave rise to yet another sub-myth: the claim that governments have been deliberately concealing the truth about UFOs from the public. As with many facets of the UFO myth, this was not without substance, for of course no government reveals its every action at every step, particularly in a matter so lacking in proven fact. Confronted by this widespread but elusive phenomenon, authorities were often at a loss how best to proceed; this indecision fuelled the myth that they had something to conceal, and over the years a series of conspiracy stories – 'Flying Saucers at Edwards Air Force Base', 'The Riddle of Hangar 18', 'Guidebook to Area 51' – were added to the UFO lore.

Yet the evidence for a planned programme to withhold information about UFOs was weak and ambiguous, and counter-versions of the myth were offered as an alternative. These held that the governments knew perfectly well that there were no UFOs, but were exploiting the UFO myth for their own sinister purposes. Sometimes this was to conceal their own clandestine operations – this was advanced as an explanation for the 1980 Rendlesham affair and the 1989 Belgian wave, for example. An alternative explanation was that the government was taking advantage of a UFO event – or in some versions, deliberately fabricating such an event – by way of testing public response; this was alleged of the 1979 Cergy-Pontoise case in France, among others.

THE REALITY AT THE HEART OF THE MYTH

From time to time, ufologists have resorted to the 'best case' approach, highlighting cases which continued to defy explanation and which, therefore, constituted a valid reason for belief in UFOs as a phenomenon. Unfortunately the history of UFO investigations shows that, whenever a seemingly strong case is given a thorough counter-investigation, cracks start to appear in the fabric, and only too often the case collapses entirely. The 1954 Premanon case in France, the 1959 Domsten encounter in Sweden, the 1975 Zwischbergen photos investigated by Wim van Utrecht – here were three ostensibly impressive cases which were shown by further analysis to be explicable in conventional terms. In the light of such disillusionment, sceptics could be forgiven for suggesting that every case, if sufficient information were available and if sufficient investigation were carried out, would eventually emerge as capable of a natural or mundane explanation.

Nevertheless, some cases continued to defy investigation. Of these, the most impressive were those where, instead of the usual spontaneous observation by an individual unprepared for the experience, the sightings were recurrent, and consequently able to be investigated, even witnessed, by experienced investigators ready for what they might see. At Yakima in Washington State, Piedmont in Missouri, Hessdalen in Norway, anomalous luminous phenomena were observed and repeatedly recorded with monitoring equipment. However, if these cases established the substantial character of the phenomenon, they also showed what it was not.

At Hessdalen, UFO myth came face to face with UFO reality. Many of the local residents had reported structured artifacts with flashing lights – sightings which conformed to the UFO myth. But the hundreds of photos obtained by the investigators revealed nothing but luminous blobs and streaks. It was the confrontation of subjective impression with objective fact. There was no doubt that the phenomenon physically existed, for there was instrumental confirmation to support the sightings: but there was nothing to suggest the presence of extraterrestrial visitors. On the contrary, everything pointed to some natural phenomenon, though perhaps one unknown to science, and certainly one which behaved in very curious ways.

There were other genuinely challenging UFO phenomena. The foo fighters of WW2, the sightings of USAF pilots in the Korean War documented by Richard Haines, continue to defy explanation. Though theories abound, we still don't know for sure what Kenneth Arnold saw in June 1947, or what Paul Trent photographed at McMinnville on 11 May 1950, or what the 1946 Scandinavian ghost rockets were, or what caused Frederick Valentich and his aircraft to vanish over Australia in 1978. Embedded as they are in the UFO myth, these puzzles are perhaps destined to remain unanswered: perhaps the UFO myth itself is destined to remain ambiguously poised between fact and fantasy.

Most of you who read this book will never have known a time when there was no such thing as a UFO. Yet there was such a time. UFOs are a creation of our time, and when their time came, they were born. With the perspective of fifty years' hindsight, we can see that the flying saucer mystery reaches deep into ourselves and far out into the cosmos we inhabit. We are lucky to be living at the time of so rich and revealing a myth.

THE BEST UFO BOOKS IN ENGLISH

Every book about UFOs, however good or however bad, has something to tell us about the phenomenon. This personal selection by the editors is mostly of good books, but also includes some thought-provoking personal approaches, and some which, though they may be wrong-headed or even downright crazy, nevertheless help to give us a rounded picture of this many-faceted phenomenon.

We regret that it was not practicable to include foreign-language books. Many excellent books have never been translated: one of us (HE) owes a special debt to two French writers, Michel Carrouges and Pierre Vieroudy, who first made me start to take the UFO phenomenon seriously. It is deplorable that such important books as those of Ballester Olmos, probably the finest investigation studies in the UFO literature, should not be available in English.

I. GENERAL SURVEYS, HISTORIES, REFERENCE
Peter Brookesmith *UFO: the Complete Sightings Catalogue* 1995
Jerome Clark *The UFO Encyclopedia* (3 vols) 1990-1996
Condon & Gillmor (ed) *The Scientific Study of Unidentified Flying Objects* 1969
Hilary Evans & John Spencer (ed) *UFOs 1947-1987* 1987
Lawrence Fawcett & Barry J Greenwood *Clear Intent: the Government Coverup of the UFO Experience* 1984
Paris Flammonde *The Age of Flying Saucers* 1971
Curtis G Fuller (ed) *Proceedings of the First International UFO Congress* 1980
Loren Gross *UFOs, a history* 1974 and on-going
Richard Hall (ed) *The UFO Evidence* 1964
Allan Hendry *The UFO Handbook* 1979
J Allen Hynek *The UFO Experience* 1972
David Michael Jacobs *The UFO Controversy in America* 1975
Gordon I R Lore Jr & Harold H Deneault Jr *Mysteries of the Skies* 1968
Donald H Menzel & Lyle G Boyd *The World of Flying Saucers* 1963
Jenny Randles & Peter Warrington *UFOs, a British Viewpoint* 1979
Edward J Ruppelt *The Report on Unidentified Flying Objects* 1956
Margaret Sachs *The UFO Encyclopedia* 1980
Carl Sagan & Thornton Page *UFOs, a Scientific Debate* 1972
Ronald D Story *The Encyclopedia of UFOs* 1980; *UFOs and the Limits of Science* 1981
Jacques Vallee *Challenge to Science: the UFO Enigma* 1966; (with Janine Vallee) *Anatomy of a phenomenon* 1965

2. SPECIFIC CASES OR GROUPS OF CASES
Bill Chalker *The OZ files* 1996
Isabel Davis & Ted Bloecher *Close Encounter at Kelly and Others of 1955* 1978
Ann Druffel & D Scott Rogo *The Tujunga Canyon Contacts* 1980
Festinger, Riecken & Schachter *When Prophecy Fails* 1956
John G Fuller *Incident at Exeter* 1966
Richard F Haines *Advanced Aerial Devices Reported During the Korean War* 1990; *Project Delta: a Study of Multiple UFOs* 1994
Ion Hobana & Julien Weverbergh *UFOs from Behind the Iron Curtain* 1972
Greg Long *Examining the Earthlight Theory* 1990
Harley D Rutledge *Project Identification* 1981
Frank F Salisbury *The Utah UFO Display* 1974
Wim van Utrecht & Fritz van der Veldt *Unidentified Aerial Object Photographed Near Zwischbergen, Switzerland, on July 26 1975* 1994
Walter N Webb *Encounter at Buff Ledge* 1994

3. INDIVIDUAL VIEWPOINTS
Steuart Campbell *The UFO Mystery Solved* 1994

Jerome Clark & Loren Coleman *The Unidentified* 1975
C G Jung *Flying Saucers* 1959
John A Keel UFOs: *Operation Trojan Horse* 1970
Donald Keyhoe *The Flying Saucers are Real* 1950
Philip J Klass *UFOs Identified 1968*; *UFOs Explained* 1974; *UFOs: the Public Deceived* 1983
James M McCampbell *Ufology* 1973
Keith Thompson *Aliens and Angels: UFOs and the Mythic Imagination* 1991
Jacques Vallee *Passport to Magonia* 1969; *Forbidden Science* 1992

4. ASPECTS

Janet & Colin Bord *Life Beyond Planet Earth?* 1991
Charles Bowen (ed) *The Humanoids* 1969; *Encounter Cases from Flying Saucer Review* 1977
David Clarke & Andy Roberts *Phantoms of the Sky* 1990
Paul Devereux *Earthlights* 1982
Timothy Good *Above Top Secret* 1987
Richard F Haines (ed) *UFO Phenomena and the Behavioural Scientist* 1979; *Observing UFOs* 1980
Mark Moravec *PSIUFO Phenomena* 1981
Michael A Persinger & Gyslaine F Lafrenière *Space-time Transients and Unusual Events* 1977
Jenny Randles & Peter Warrington *Science and the UFOs* 1985
Brad Steiger (ed) *Project Blue Book* 1976
Dennis Stillings (ed) *Cyberbiological Studies of the Imaginal Component in the UFO Contact Experience* 1989
Renato Vesco *Intercept – But Don't Shoot* 1971

5. THE ABDUCTION PHENOMENON

C D B Bryan *Close Encounters of the Fourth Kind* 1995
Thomas E Bullard *UFO Abductions: the Measure of a Mystery* (2 vols) 1987
Raymond E Fowler *The Andreasson Affair 1979*; *The Andreasson Affair Phase Two* 1982
John G Fuller *The Interrupted Journey* 1966
Charles Hickson & William Mendez *UFO Contact at Pascagoula* 1983
Betty Hill *A Common Sense Approach to UFOs* 1995
Budd Hopkins *Missing Time* 1981; *Intruders* 1987; *Witnessed* 1996
David M Jacobs *Secret Life* 1992
Philip J Klass *UFO Abductions, a Dangerous Dame* 1988
Coral & Jim Lorenzen *Abducted! Confrontations with Beings from Outer Space* 1977
David Pritchard & John Mack (eds) *Alien Discussions: Proceedings of the Abduction Study Conference* 1994
John Rimmer *The Evidence for Alien Abductions* 1984
D Scott Rogo (ed) *UFO Abductions* 1980
Jim Schnabel *Dark White: Aliens, Abductions and the UFO Obsession* 1994

6. ON THE MARGIN

Bill Adler (ed) *Letters to the Air Force on UFOs* 1967
Roy Craig *UFOs: an Insider's View of the Official Quest for Evidence* 1995
Douglas Curran *In Advance of the Landing: Folk Concepts of Outer Space* 1985
Desmond Leslie & George Adamski *Flying Saucers Have Landed* 1953

INDEX

Fairfield, 111
Fatima, visions at, 244
Faulkner, Gordon, 105, 108
Festinger, Leon, 261
fiery serpent, 221
Figuet, Michel, 157-159
Flickinger Report, 146
Flitcroft, 62-63, 64, 65
flying moon, 221
Foltz, Charlie, 131-138
foo-fighters, 5, 26, 266
Friedman, Stanton T., 6, 7
Friend, Colonel Robert, 109, 111, 116
Fuhr, Edwin, 120-130
Gallup, 72, 230-237
GEPAN *see Groupe d'Etude des Phenomenes Aerospatiaux Non-Identifies*
ghosts, 194-195
ghost rockets, 5, 35, 38-40
Glemser, Kurt, 259-260
Godfrey, Alan, 253-255
Graham, Billy, 260
Graves, Sheriff 'Tex', 142-143
Green, Dr David, 144
Groupe d'Etude des Phenomenes Aerospatiaux Non-Identifies, 151-159, 183, 216, 224
GRUDGE, 29, 58, 73, 88
Guieu, Jimmy, 258
Haines, Richard F., 160-164
Hansen, Myrna, 146
Heard, Gerald, 75-76
Hellier, Charles, 78
Hessdalen, 266
Hill, Betty and Barney, 10, 204, 216, 263
Hillsdale College, Michigan, 11
Hind, Cynthia, 194
Holloman Air Force Base, 115-116
Honey, Carol, 67
Hopkins, Budd, 203-208
Hunrath, Karl, 55-56
Hynek, Dr J. Allen, 11, 83-84, 95-102, 116-118, 121, 146, 215-216, 217, 261
Institute of Terrestrial Magnetism, Ionosphere & Radio Wave Propogation, 226
International Flying Saucer Bureau, 81
IZMIRAN see Institute of Terrestrial Magnetism, Ionosphere & Radio Wave Propogation
Jacobs, David, 205-206, 208, 209, 235, 239
Jacobsson, Colonel Bengt, 38
Jarrold, Edgar, 79, 81-82
jellyfish, 226
Jung, Carl, 261

Jupille-sur-Meuse, 168
Jutland, 189, 193
Karambakuwa, Lloyd, 197
Kazantsev, Alexander, 223
Keel, John, 261
Keesler Air Force Base, 213
Kempff, Colonel, 38, 39-41
Keyhoe, Major Donald E., 74-75, 82, 85-92, 213, 233, 259, 261
Kharkov, 223
Kirtland Air Force Base, 113-114, 147
Klimenko, A. I., 221
King, George, 262
Krasnodar, 221
Kuwait, 216
Lagrange, Pierre, 244
Lakenheath, 252-253
Langenburg, Saskatchewan, 121-130
Lauber, Corporal Lyn, 139, 144
Lawson, Alvin, 263
Lear, John, 147
Lee, Gloria, 264
Lemuria, 70
Leslie, Desmond, 62, 78
Liddel, Dr Urner, 89
Lipp, James E., 73
Long Crendon, 251
McChesney, Dr Albert, 144-145
McCoy, Colonel H. M., 7-8
McDonald. James E., 95, 96-98, 100, 215
MacNamara, Dr Allen, 124-125
Maarup, car-stop case, 188-189
Mack, Dr John E., 196, 207
Mannor, Frank, 117-118
Manchester airport case, 250
Mantell, Captain Thomas, 13, 76, 87-88, 89, 259
Manuel Soto, 180
Marcel, Major Jesse A., 6
Martin, Domokos, 186-187
Martin, Dorothy, 261, 263
mass hysteria, 197
men in black, 48, 81, 82, 225, 242, 256
Menzel, Donald H., 73-74, 223
MIB *see men in black*
Miller, R. Dewitt, 71
MOA *see Aerial Operative Command (Spain)*
Monnerie, Michel, 155-156
Monticello, 95
Moody, Sergeant David, 114, 117
moon landing revisionism, 247-248
Moscow Planetarium, 222
Muchena, Clifford, 196
MUFON *see Mutual UFO Network*
Münchausen, Baron, 258

270